Activist Documentary Film in Pakistan

This book, the first academic book on Pakistani documentary cinema, traces the development of activist filmmaking practices in Pakistan which have emerged as a response to the consequences of religious fundamentalism, extremism, and violation of human rights. Beginning with the period of General Zia-ul-Haq's Islamization process (1977–88), it discusses a selection of representative documentary films that have critically addressed and documented the various key transformations, events, and developments that have shaped Pakistan's socio-political, socio-economic, and cultural history. Such activist filmmaking practice in Pakistan is today an influential factor in addressing the politics, and negative and oppressive effects of the Islamization era, discriminatory laws, particularly gender-discriminatory *Sharia* laws, violation of human and citizen rights, authoritarianism, internal strife, the spread of religious fundamentalism and the threat of Talibanization, and oppressive tribal customs and traditions. The contribution of Pakistani documentary filmmakers stands as a significant body of work that has served the cause of human rights, promoting awareness and social change in Pakistan, particularly regarding gender rights.

Rahat Imran holds a PhD in Cinema Studies from the Simon Fraser University, British Columbia, Canada. She has held a Post-doctoral Research Fellowship in the Department of Film Studies, Media Studies, and Media Education at the University of Bremen, Germany. Currently, Dr. Imran is affiliated with the Institute of Social and Cultural Studies, University of the Punjab, Lahore, Pakistan. She is completing her second book on Comparative Cinemas.

Routledge Contemporary South Asia Series

1 Pakistan
Social and cultural transformations in a Muslim nation
Mohammad A. Qadeer

2 Labor, Democratization and Development in India and Pakistan
Christopher Candland

3 China–India Relations
Contemporary dynamics
Amardeep Athwal

4 Madrasas in South Asia
Teaching terror?
Jamal Malik

5 Labor, Globalization and the State
Workers, women and migrants confront neoliberalism
Edited by Debdas Banerjee and Michael Goldfield

6 Indian Literature and Popular Cinema
Recasting classics
Edited by Heidi R.M. Pauwels

7 Islamist Militancy in Bangladesh
A complex web
Ali Riaz

8 Regionalism in South Asia
Negotiating cooperation, institutional structures
Kishore C. Dash

9 Federalism, Nationalism and Development
India and the Punjab economy
Pritam Singh

10 Human Development and Social Power
Perspectives from South Asia
Ananya Mukherjee Reed

11 The South Asian Diaspora
Transnational networks and changing identities
Edited by Rajesh Rai and Peter Reeves

12 Pakistan–Japan Relations
Continuity and change in economic relations and security interests
Ahmad Rashid Malik

13 Himalayan Frontiers of India
Historical, geo-political and strategic perspectives
K. Warikoo

14 India's Open-Economy Policy
Globalism, rivalry, continuity
Jalal Alamgir

15 The Separatist Conflict in Sri Lanka
Terrorism, ethnicity, political economy
Asoka Bandarage

16 India's Energy Security
Edited by Ligia Noronha and Anant Sudarshan

17 Globalization and the Middle Classes in India
The social and cultural impact of neoliberal reforms
Ruchira Ganguly-Scrase and Timothy J. Scrase

18 Water Policy Processes in India
Discourses of power and resistance
Vandana Asthana

19 Minority Governments in India
The puzzle of elusive majorities
Csaba Nikolenyi

20 The Maoist Insurgency in Nepal
Revolution in the twenty-first century
Edited by Mahendra Lawoti and Anup K. Pahari

21 Global Capital and Peripheral Labour
The history and political economy of plantation workers in India
K. Ravi Raman

22 Maoism in India
Reincarnation of ultra-left wing extremism in the twenty-first century
Bidyut Chakrabarty and Rajat Kujur

23 Economic and Human Development in Contemporary India
Cronyism and fragility
Debdas Banerjee

24 Culture and the Environment in the Himalaya
Arjun Guneratne

25 The Rise of Ethnic Politics in Nepal
Democracy in the margins
Susan I. Hangen

26 The Multiplex in India
A cultural economy of urban leisure
Adrian Athique and Douglas Hill

27 Tsunami Recovery in Sri Lanka
Ethnic and regional dimensions
Dennis B. McGilvray and Michele R. Gamburd

28 Development, Democracy and the State
Critiquing the Kerala model of development
K. Ravi Raman

29 Mohajir Militancy in Pakistan
Violence and transformation in the Karachi conflict
Nichola Khan

30 Nationbuilding, Gender and War Crimes in South Asia
Bina D'Costa

31 The State in India after Liberalization
Interdisciplinary perspectives
Edited by Akhil Gupta and K. Sivaramakrishnan

32 National Identities in Pakistan
The 1971 war in contemporary Pakistani fiction
Cara Cilano

33 Political Islam and Governance in Bangladesh
Edited by Ali Riaz and C. Christine Fair

34 Bengali Cinema
'An other nation'
Sharmistha Gooptu

35 NGOs in India
The challenges of women's empowerment and accountability
Patrick Kilby

36 The Labour Movement in the Global South
Trade unions in Sri Lanka
S. Janaka Biyanwila

37 Building Bangalore
Architecture and urban transformation in India's Silicon Valley
John C. Stallmeyer

38 Conflict and Peacebuilding in Sri Lanka
Caught in the peace trap?
Edited by Jonathan Goodhand, Jonathan Spencer and Benedict Korf

39 Microcredit and Women's Empowerment
A case study of Bangladesh
Amunui Faraizi, Jim McAllister and Taskinur Rahman

40 South Asia in the New World Order
The role of regional cooperation
Shahid Javed Burki

41 Explaining Pakistan's Foreign Policy
Escaping India
Aparna Pande

42 Development-induced Displacement, Rehabilitation and Resettlement in India
Current issues and challenges
Edited by Sakarama Somayaji and Smrithi Talwar

43 The Politics of Belonging in India
Becoming Adivasi
Edited by Daniel J. Rycroft and Sangeeta Dasgupta

44 Re-Orientalism and South Asian Identity Politics
The oriental Other within
Edited by Lisa Lau and Ana Cristina Mendes

45 Islamic Revival in Nepal
Religion and a new nation
Megan Adamson Sijapati

46 Education and Inequality in India
A classroom view
Manabi Majumdar and Jos Mooij

47 The Culturalization of Caste in India
Identity and inequality in a multicultural age
Balmurli Natrajan

48 Corporate Social Responsibility in India
Bidyut Chakrabarty

49 Pakistan's Stability Paradox
Domestic, regional and
international dimensions
*Edited by Ashutosh Misra and
Michael E. Clarke*

**50 Transforming Urban Water
Supplies in India**
The role of reform and partnerships
in globalization
Govind Gopakumar

51 South Asian Security
Twenty-first century discourse
Sagarika Dutt and Alok Bansal

**52 Non-discrimination and Equality
in India**
Contesting boundaries of social justice
Vidhu Verma

53 Being Middle-class in India
A way of life
Henrike Donner

54 Kashmir's Right to Secede
A critical examination of
contemporary theories of secession
Matthew J. Webb

55 Bollywood Travels
Culture, diaspora and border
crossings in popular Hindi cinema
Rajinder Dudrah

**56 Nation, Territory, and
Globalization in Pakistan**
Traversing the margins
Chad Haines

**57 The Politics of Ethnicity
in Pakistan**
The Baloch, Sindhi and Mohajir
ethnic movements
Farhan Hanif Siddiqi

**58 Nationalism and
Ethnic Conflict**
Identities and mobilization after 1990
*Edited by Mahendra Lawoti and
Susan Hangen*

59 Islam and Higher Education
Concepts, challenges
and opportunities
Marodsilton Muborakshoeva

60 Religious Freedom in India
Sovereignty and (anti) conversion
Goldie Osuri

**61 Everyday Ethnicity in
Sri Lanka**
Up-country Tamil identity politics
Daniel Bass

**62 Ritual and Recovery in
Post-Conflict Sri Lanka**
Eloquent bodies
Jane Derges

63 Bollywood and Globalisation
The global power of popular
Hindi cinema
*Edited by David J. Schaefer and
Kavita Karan*

**64 Regional Economic
Integration in South Asia**
Trapped in conflict?
Amita Batra

**65 Architecture and Nationalism in
Sri Lanka**
The trouser under the cloth
Anoma Pieris

**66 Civil Society and
Democratization in India**
Institutions, ideologies and interests
Sarbeswar Sahoo

67 Contemporary Pakistani Fiction in English
Idea, nation, state
Cara N. Cilano

68 Transitional Justice in South Asia
A study of Afghanistan and Nepal
Tazreena Sajjad

69 Displacement and Resettlement in India
The human cost of development
Hari Mohan Mathur

70 Water, Democracy and Neoliberalism in India
The power to reform
Vicky Walters

71 Capitalist Development in India's Informal Economy
Elisabetta Basile

72 Nation, Constitutionalism and Buddhism in Sri Lanka
Roshan de Silva Wijeyeratne

73 Counterinsurgency, Democracy, and the Politics of Identity in India
From warfare to welfare?
Mona Bhan

74 Enterprise Culture in Neoliberal India
Studies in youth, class, work and media
Edited by Nandini Gooptu

75 The Politics of Economic Restructuring in India
Economic governance and state spatial rescaling
Loraine Kennedy

76 The Other in South Asian Religion, Literature and Film
Perspectives on Otherism and Otherness
Edited by Diana Dimitrova

77 Being Bengali
At home and in the world
Edited by Mridula Nath Chakraborty

78 The Political Economy of Ethnic Conflict in Sri Lanka
Nikolaos Biziouras

79 Indian Arranged Marriages
A social psychological perspective
Tulika Jaiswal

80 Writing the City in British Asian Diasporas
Edited by Seán McLoughlin, William Gould, Ananya Jahanara Kabir and Emma Tomalin

81 Post-9/11 Espionage Fiction in the US and Pakistan
Spies and 'terrorists'
Cara Cilano

82 Left Radicalism in India
Bidyut Chakrabarty

83 "Nation-State" and Minority Rights in India
Comparative perspectives on Muslim and Sikh identities
Tanweer Fazal

84 Pakistan's Nuclear Policy
A minimum credible deterrence
Zafar Khan

85 Imagining Muslims in South Asia and the Diaspora
Secularism, religion, representations
Claire Chambers and Caroline Herbert

86 Indian Foreign Policy in Transition
Relations with South Asia
Arijit Mazumdar

87 Corporate Social Responsibility and Development in Pakistan
Nadeem Malik

88 Indian Capitalism in Development
Barbara Harriss-White and Judith Heyer

89 Bangladesh Cinema and National Identity
In search of the modern?
Zakir Hossain Raju

90 Suicide in Sri Lanka
The anthropology of an epidemic
Tom Widger

91 Epigraphy and Islamic Culture
Inscriptions of the Early Muslim Rulers of Bengal (1205–1494)
Mohammad Yusuf Siddiq

92 Reshaping City Governance
London, Mumbai, Kolkata, Hyderabad
Nirmala Rao

93 The Indian Partition in Literature and Films
History, politics, and aesthetics
Rini Bhattacharya Mehta and Debali Mookerjea-Leonard

94 Development, Poverty and Power in Pakistan
The impact of state and donor interventions on farmers
Syed Mohammad Ali

95 Ethnic Subnationalist Insurgencies in South Asia
Identities, interests and challenges to state Authority
Edited by Jugdep S. Chima

96 International Migration and Development in South Asia
Edited by Md Mizanur Rahman and Tan Tai Yong

97 Twenty-First Century Bollywood
Ajay Gehlawat

98 Political Economy of Development in India
Indigeneity in ransition in the state of Kerala
Darley Kjosavik and Nadarajah Shanmugaratnam

99 State and Nation-Building in Pakistan
Beyond Islam and security
Edited by Roger D. Long, Gurharpal Singh, Yunas Samad and Ian Talbot

100 Subaltern Movements in India
Gendered geographies of struggle against neoliberal development
Manisha Desai

101 Islamic Banking in Pakistan
Shariah-compliant finance and the quest to make Pakistan more Islamic
Feisal Khan

102 The Bengal Diaspora
Rethinking Muslim migration
Claire Alexander, Joya Chatterji and Annu Jalais

103 Mobilizing Religion and Gender in India
The role of activism
Nandini Deo

104 Social Movements and the Indian Diaspora
Movindri Reddy

105 Religion and Modernity in the Himalaya
Edited by Megan Adamson Sijapati and Jesscia Vantine Birkenholtz

106 Devotional Islam in Contemporary South Asia
Shrines, Journeys and Wanderers
Edited by Michel Boivin and Rémy Delage

107 Women and Resistance in Contemporary Bengali Cinema
A freedom incomplete
Srimati Mukherjeez

108 Islamic NGOs in Bangladesh
Development, piety and neoliberal governmentality
Mohammad Musfequs Salehin

109 Ethnics in Governance in India
Bidyut Chakrabarty

110 Popular Hindi Cinema
Aesthetic formations of the seen and unseen
Ronie Parciack

111 Activist Documentary Film in Pakistan
The emergence of a cinema of accountability
Rahat Imran

Activist Documentary Film in Pakistan
The emergence of a cinema of accountability

Rahat Imran

LONDON AND NEW YORK

First published 2016
by Routledge

2 Park Square, Milton Park, Abingdon, Oxfordshire OX14 4RN
711 Third Avenue, New York, NY 10017

Routledge is an imprint of the Taylor & Francis Group, an informa business

First issued in paperback 2017

Copyright © 2016 Rahat Imran

The right of Rahat Imran to be identified as author of this work has been asserted by him/her in accordance with sections 77 and 78 of the Copyright, Designs and Patents Act 1988.

All rights reserved. No part of this book may be reprinted or reproduced or utilised in any form or by any electronic, mechanical, or other means, now known or hereafter invented, including photocopying and recording, or in any information storage or retrieval system, without permission in writing from the publishers.

Notice:
Product or corporate names may be trademarks or registered trademarks, and are used only for identification and explanation without intent to infringe.

British Library Cataloguing in Publication Data
A catalogue record for this book is available from the British Library

Library of Congress Cataloging in Publication Data
Names: Imran, Rahat, author.
Title: Activist documentary film in Pakistan : the emergence of a cinema of accountability / Rahat Imran.
Other titles: Routledge contemporary South Asia series ; 111. Description: New York : Routledge, 2016. | "2016 | Series: Routledge contemporary South Asia series ; 111 | Includes bibliographical references and index.
Identifiers: LCCN 2015042336| ISBN 9781138885769 (hardback) | ISBN 9781315715230 (ebook)
Subjects: LCSH: Documentary films–Production and direction–Pakistan. | Documentary films–Pakistan–History and criticism. | Documentary films–Political aspects–Pakistan. | Feminism and motion pictures. | Pakistan–Social conditions. | Pakistan–Politics and government.
Classification: LCC PN1995.9.D6 I47 2016 | DDC 070.1/8–dc23
LC record available at http://lccn.loc.gov/2015042336

ISBN: 978-1-138-88576-9 (hbk)
ISBN: 978-1-138-47771-1 (pbk)

Typeset in Times New Roman
by Taylor & Francis Books

To Imran, Momin, Louis Baba, and Bibi Jan.
You complete my little world.
An ever enduring thanks to Syed Asad Ali: You taught me how to read and write, and cherish books. Your prayers keep my little world going.

Contents

List of illustrations		xiv
Preface		xvi
Acknowledgement		xviii
Special thanks		xx
Abbreviations		xxi
	Introduction	1
1	Towards a theory of 'Cinema of Accountability': Critical perspectives on activist film practices	14
2	Injustices on film: A reading of activist documentaries against the legacy of Islamization	40
3	Cinema on Terror: Charting the militant mix of politics, religion, and Talibanization	84
4	Victims of a vicious system: Women, violence, and human rights	129
	Conclusion	186
	Appendix 1: The Hudood Ordinances	204
	Appendix 2: The Law of Evidence	206
	Appendix 3: The Blasphemy Law	208
	Appendix 4: Background to the radicalization of madrasas in Pakistan	211
	Appendix 5: Laws of Qisas and Diyat	214
	Glossary	217
	Index	221

List of illustrations

	Map of Pakistan.	xxvi
2.1	Archival photo still from *Jaloos* of police action against women demonstrators during Zia-ul-Haq's regime on 12 February, 1983.	44
2.2	Image from *Jaloos* of the women's commemorative procession in February, 1988.	45
2.3	Ghulam Sakina narrating her ordeal in *Who Will Cast the First Stone?*	47
2.4	Anousheh dressing up as a boy in *Don't Ask Why*.	51
2.5	Anousheh dressed up as a boy in *Don't Ask Why*.	52
2.6	Anousheh attending a *Jamaat-e-Islami* Women's Wing study session in *Don't Ask Why*.	53
2.7	Image from *For A Place Under the Heavens* of a women-only religious sermon at a five star hotel.	55
2.8	Image from *For A Place Under the Heavens* of a doll being used for tutorial on bathing a Muslim woman's body for burial.	56
2.9	Justice (Retd) Majida Rizvi of the Sindh High Court elaborates on the *Hudood* laws in *Hudood Ordinance 1979: Divine Law, or Law of One Man?*	61
2.10	Justice (Retd) Nasira Javed Iqbal of the Lahore High Court elaborates on the Law of Evidence in *Hudood Ordinance 1979: Divine Law, or Law of One Man?*	62
2.11	Archival still image from *A Sun Sets In* of Bishop Dr. John Joseph after he committed suicide outside the gates of the Sahiwal Sessions Court.	66
2.12	Archival image of Bishop Dr. John Joseph from *A Sun Sets In*.	67
3.1	Image of carpet-weavers from *Terror's Children*.	87
3.2	Image of Khal from *Terror's Children*.	88
3.3	Image of musicians from *Reinventing the Taliban?*	91
3.4	Sharmeen Obaid-Chinoy interviews Maulana Sami-ul-Haq in *Pakistan: On a Razor's Edge*.	96
3.5	Sharmeen Obaid-Chinoy with tribal elders and residents of the village of Wazirthand in the Khyber Agency in *Pakistan's Double Game*.	103

3.6	Sharmeen Obaid-Chinoy speaking with protestors at a *Jamaat-e-Islami* rally in Islamabad in *Pakistan's Double Game*.	104
3.7	Image of earthquake destruction from *Cold Comfort*.	106
3.8	Image from *Cold Comfort* of children receiving *madrasa* education.	107
3.9	Image from *Cold Comfort* of a girl cooking on makeshift arrangements at the refugee camp.	108
3.10	Sharmeen Obaid-Chinoy speaks with a patient at a paraplegic and rehabilitation centre in Peshawar in *Pakistan's Taliban Generation*.	110
4.1	Image of burn victim from *Stove Burning: Neither Coal Nor Ashes*.	131
4.2	Image of burn victim from *Stove Burning: Neither Coal Nor Ashes*.	132
4.3	Image of burn victim from *Stove Burning: Neither Coal Nor Ashes*.	133
4.4	Image of burn victim from *Burnt Victims: Scars on the Society*.	137
4.5	Image of filmmaker Sharmeen Obaid-Chinoy during the filming of *Saving Face*.	140
4.6	Image of unmarked graveyard for *karo kari* victims from *Shame: A Tale of Karo Kari*.	144
4.7	Image of female victim of *karo kari* from *Shame: A Tale of Karo Kari*.	145
4.8	Image of female victim of *karo kari* from *Shame: A Tale of Karo Kari*.	149
4.9	Image of filmmaker Mohammad Ali Naqvi (first left in back row) with Mukhtaran Mai (third from left in back row) during the filming of *Shame*.	151
4.10	Image of Mukhtaran Mai from *Shame*.	155
4.11	Image of filmmaker Mohammad Ali Naqvi (centre), Mukhtaran Mai (left), and Mai's friend Naseem Akhtar (right) during the filming of *Shame*.	157
4.12	Image of filmmaker Samar Minallah during the filming of *Swara: A Bridge Over Troubled Waters*.	162
4.13	Image of *swara* girl from *Swara: A Bridge Over Troubled Waters*.	163
4.14	Image of *swara* girl from *Swara: A Bridge Over Troubled Waters*.	164
4.15	Image of *swara* girl from *Swara: A Bridge Over Troubled Waters*.	165
4.16	Image of *swara* girls from *Swara: A Bridge Over Troubled Waters*.	166

Preface

This interdisciplinary research and investigation is inspired by developments in the ever-expanding realm of Cinema and Film Studies that has been gaining substantial popularity and attention as a pedagogical tool in academia worldwide, and among cross-disciplinary students alike. Correspondingly, although there is considerable academic literature available on cinemas from the Arab world and the Third World, a theoretical study on the contribution of Pakistani filmmakers, particularly women filmmakers and documentary films, is conspicuous by its absence as it relates to both the Muslim world and the Third World. It is the intent of this introductory study to fill this void through a close, and detailed, contextual reading of selected Pakistani documentary films that use a religion, gender, and culture-sensitive and specific approaches from within a Muslim society to take up issues of human rights, religious fundamentalism, and gender-discrimination, among others, and to place discussions within activist documentary cinema frameworks to add new dimensions to existing Film Studies scholarship. In addition, this study introduces representative filmmakers, organizations, and collaborative ventures that have contributed to the emergence of a specifically activist and human rights-oriented film movement in contemporary Pakistan. In doing so, it places these cinematic productions and their producers as pedagogical, intellectual, and political interventions through cinema in the issues and the historical times and events they examine and critique rather than any kind of over-simplified fear-inducing 'native informants'.

The intent here is to see the role and contribution of these documentary productions and their makers in constituting the emergence of a new activist theoretical framework and filmic category of a 'Cinema of Accountability' – a framework from within the Muslim world that is rooted in *resistance* to religious fundamentalism and violations of human rights, and takes up crucial, sensitive, and neglected issues to press for social change and reforms, and foster cross-cultural communication for solidarity. Likewise, this study also identifies an emergent 'Cinema on Terror' framework that specifically traces and portrays the historical and political roots of religious fundamentalism in contemporary Pakistan, and fostering of militant activities and ideologies promoted through religious seminaries that espouse a violent global *jihadist* agenda.

The selection of films and their contextual readings in this introductory study are supported by detailed background information in order to present as complete a picture of the developments and events the filmmakers aim to portray and document. Thematic chapters on films offer an interdisciplinary study of intersections of religion, politics, and law through cinematic depictions, highlighting the emergence of an activist documentary film movement in Pakistan that has its roots in religious fundamentalism, and the pedagogical utility of documentary cinema as a tool for consciousness-raising. Further, appendices aid in understanding and contextualizing various topics and laws discussed in the selected films.

This study has entailed vast archival research for collection of films, and relevant historical data for contextual background of topics and various socio-political developments. Whereas every effort was made to acquire good quality photographs and film stills, due to various limitations, copyright issues, and poor prints of some ill-preserved films, the results have been limited at times.

In discussing a host of human rights topics, intersections of political motivations and legal aspects, and gender and socio-cultural issues through Pakistani documentary cinema, that may also resonate with conditions in other Muslim societies, it is hoped that this study will be of use and interest for a variety of academic purposes, and cross-disciplinary scholars such as those working in the fields of Film and Cinema Studies, Media Studies, Women's/Feminist Studies and gender issues, Cultural Studies, Comparative Studies, human rights, history, politics, Islamic *Sharia* laws, South Asia, Muslim societies, and the Third World, as well as journalists and media researchers.

Beginning to write a first introductory study on any subject is certainly challenging, and can be replete with self-doubts. But I assured myself constantly that someone has to do this. I hope this study will open the way for more critical work on related subjects and topics from Pakistan, and beyond.

For myself, I can say that watching some of these films was the most difficult part – especially watching images from my home country unfold that told a story of such dreadful deterioration. I also realized that images and stories of pain, even if not directly one's own, and however unfamiliar or far removed from one's immediate environments, can leave haunting emotional impressions that refuse to go away – I learnt that agonies and helplessness suffered in silence can be the most resounding when given a voice. I learnt that as viewers, we must all become accountable to our conscience and sense of justice.

Acknowledgement

Submitting the manuscript from my hometown of Lahore, Pakistan, brings this journey full circle, and is my humble tribute to all the voices of resistance and courage documented by the equally committed and brave filmmakers in this study.

It is with great respect and gratitude that I thank the following for their encouragement, guidance, and support in the completion of this book:

First, and foremost, a very special thanks to my father, Dr Manzur-ul-Haq Hashmi. You taught me life's finest lesson: 'It isn't life that matters, it's the courage you bring to it.'

I shall remain indebted to you for your untiring help in acquiring films, locating filmmakers and reports and literature during my doctoral studies in Canada, not to mention your continued hospitality and support in Pakistan during the completion and submission of this manuscript.

My heartfelt gratitude to Mr Farrukh Hussain for his patience and support in collecting research material, and tracing documents and films. Your time, help, and consideration have been invaluable.

Organizations and individuals in Pakistan and Canada:

My Ph.D. supervisory committee at Simon Fraser University (SFU), Canada: Dr Martin Laba and Dr Gary McCarron; Dr Ishtiaq Ahmed, Stockholm University, Sweden. It has been an honour and privilege to be in such good hands, and learn from you all. I shall forever be indebted to you.

My 'unofficial' advisor during my doctoral studies, dearly loved professor and invaluable friend at SFU, the late Dr Roman Onufrijchuk. The news of your passing as I submit this manuscript has been truly devastating. The completion of this project owes so very much to your advice at every stage. You will always be loved and cherished beyond measure. Memories of your immense kindness, humour, and wisdom will always stay with us.

The staff at *Simorgh* Women's Resource and Publication Centre, Lahore; *Aurat* Foundation Publication and Information Service, Lahore; *ASR* Women's Resource Centre, Lahore; *Shirkatgah* Women's Resource Centre, Lahore; Ethnomedia & Development, Islamabad; National Commission for Peace and Justice (NCJP), Lahore; Ali Institute of Education, Lahore; AGHS Legal Aid Cell, Lahore;

National Commission on the Status of Women (NCSW), Islamabad; Interactive Resource Centre (IRC), Lahore; *Ajoka* Theatre for Social Change, Lahore; Lahore International Children's Film Festival (LICFF), Lahore; Human Rights Commission of Pakistan (HRCP), Lahore; Society for Protection of Rights of Children (SPARC); Lawyers for Human Rights and Legal Aid (LHRLA), Karachi; Pakistan Women Lawyers Association and Legal Aid (PAWLA), Karachi; Actionaid Pakistan, Islamabad; National College of Art (NCA), Lahore; Pakistan Central Board of Film Censors (Ministry of Culture and Tourism), Islamabad; Mr Farrukh Hussain, Scientific Officer, Pakistan Council of Scientific and Industrial Research (PCSIR), Lahore; Ms Neelam Hussain, Director, *Simorgh* Women's Resource and Publication Centre, Lahore; Mr Cecil Shane Chaudhry, Executive Director, and Mr Peter Jacob, Executive Secretary, NCJP, Lahore; Ms Benish Patress, Administrative Officer, NCJP, Lahore; Mr Shoaib Iqbal, Director LICCF Lahore; Ms Marvi Sirmed, UNDP, Islamabad; Mr Asha'ar Rehman, Resident Editor, *The Daily Dawn*, Lahore; Ms Huma Patrick, AGHS Legal Aid Cell, Lahore; Mr Saleem Khilji, Sustainable Development Policy Institute (SDPI), Islamabad; Mr Shehram Mokhtar, Head of Media Sciences, Shaheed Zulfikar Ali Bhutto Institute of Science and Technology (SZABIST), Karachi; Ms Mirfat Hishmat Habib, Media Resources, SFU Library, Burnaby, BC, Canada.

Pakistani filmmakers: Samar Minallah (Ethnomedia & Development, Islamabad, Pakistan); Sharmeen Obaid-Chinoy (Sharmeen Obaid Films, Karachi, Pakistan); Sabiha Sumar and Dr S. Sathananthan (Vidhi Films, Karachi, Pakistan); Ahmar Rehman (Visionaries Division, Lahore, Pakistan); Sharjil Baloch (BBC, Karachi, Pakistan); Mohammad Ali Naqvi (Sixty 4th Street Media, New York, USA).

I would like to thank the following departments at SFU for their generous financial help during my doctoral research that has culminated in this publication: Dossa Endowment Fund Graduate Student Travel Award, Centre for the Comparative Study of Muslim Societies and Cultures (CCSMSC), Department of History; Graduate Support Award, Faculty of Communication, Art, and Technology (FCAT); John Juliani Award for Film and Theatre, School for the Contemporary Arts; SFU Graduate Fellowships and Scholarships, Department of Dean of Graduate Studies; Travel and Research Grant, from a Ph.D. supervisor's Social Sciences and Humanities Research Council (SSHRC) of Canada grant.

A very special thanks and acknowledgement to the European Commission-funded 7th Framework Programme for awarding me the Marie Curie Bremen–TRAC COFUND Post-doctoral Fellowship position (2013–15) at the Department of Film Studies, Media Studies, and Media Education, Excellence Initiative, at the German Elite University of Bremen, Germany, that enabled the completion of this manuscript. I shall remain indebted to you for the opportunity to spend a most cherished and memorable time in Germany, particularly the ever-vibrant city of Berlin where this book publication commenced.

Special thanks

Imran's immeasurable love, encouragement, and delightful cooking, and our son Momin's eventful visit during the memorable summer of 2014, spent in the wonderfully lively environment living at the Maybachufer Strasse in Berlin were indeed anyone's dream to complete a project close to their heart. It was here in a fifth floor apartment overlooking the lush tree-lined Landwehr Canal on a very pleasant afternoon that I signed this my very first book contract, nervous and excited, but amazingly determined. I owe this special day to you all, and the great city of Berlin!

Abbreviations

Introduction:

DFP	Directorate General of Films and Publications (Government of Pakistan)
FCO	Foreign and Commonwealth Office (Britain)
KP	Khyber Pakhtunkhwa province (Pakistan)
NGO	Non-Government Organization
NWFP	North West Frontier Province of Pakistan
PEMRA	Pakistan Electronic Media Regulatory Authority
PTV	Pakistan Television Corporation
UNESCO	United Nations Educational, Scientific and Cultural Organization
USAID	United States Agency for International Development

Chapter 1: Towards a Theory of 'Cinema of Accountability': critical perspectives on activist film practices

KP	Khyber Pakhtunkhwa province (Pakistan)

Chapter 2: Injustices on film: a reading of activist documentaries against the legacy of Islamization

AHRC	Asian Human Rights Commission
APWA	All Pakistan Women's Association
ASR	Applied Socio-economic Research Foundation and Resource Centre (Pakistan)
CBC	Canadian Broadcasting Corporation
CBO	Community Based Organization
CII	Council of Islamic Ideology (Pakistan)
CPS	Christian Punjabi Sweepers
CRSS	Center for Research for Security Studies (Pakistan)
FSC	Federal *Shariat* Court (Pakistan)
HRCP	Human Rights Commission of Pakistan

xxii *Abbreviations*

IRC	Interactive Resource Centre (Pakistan)
JIWS	Journal of International Women's Studies (USA)
JKLF	Jammu and Kashmir Liberation Front
LHC	Lahore High Court (Pakistan)
LHRLA	Lawyers for Human Rights and Legal Aid (Pakistan)
MMA	*Muttahida Majlis-e-Amal* (United Action Front, Pakistan)
MNA	Member National Assembly
NCJP	National Commission for Justice and Peace (Pakistan)
NCSW	National Commission on the Status of Women (Government of Pakistan)
NGO	Non-Government Organization
NOC	No Objection Certificate
PAF	Pakistan Air Force
PAWLA	Pakistan Women Lawyer's Association
PCO	Provisional Constitutional Order
PML	Pakistan Muslim League (Pakistan)
PPC	Pakistan Penal Code
PPP	Pakistan People's Party
PPPP	Pakistan People's Party Patriots
PTV	Pakistan Television
PWA	Progressive Women's Association (Pakistan)
PWLA	Punjab Women Lawyer's Association (Pakistan)
SCBA	Supreme Court Bar Association (Pakistan)
SDPI	Sustainable Development Policy Institute (Pakistan)
TTP	*Tehreek-e-Taliban* Pakistan
UNDP	United Nations Development Programme
UNIFEM	United Nations Development Fund for Women
USAID	United States Agency for International Development
USCIRF	United States Commission on International Religious Freedom
WAF	Women's Action Forum (Pakistan)
WMM	Women Make Movies

Chapter 3: Cinema on Terror: charting the militant mix of politics, religion, and Talibanization

AHRC	Asian Human Rights Commission
AIB	Association for International Broadcasting
ANP	Awami National Party (Pakistan)
AP	Associated Press
BBC	British Broadcasting Corporation
CBC	Canadian Broadcasting Corporation
CDI	Centre for Defense Information
CFR	Council on Foreign Relations
CIA	Central Intelligence Agency (USA)

Abbreviations xxiii

CNN	Cable News Network (USA)
CPJ	Committee to Protect Journalists
GHQ	General Headquarters (Pakistan Army)
HBO	Home Box Office (American Satellite Television Network)
HRCP	Human Rights Commission of Pakistan
HRW	Human Rights Watch
IAK	Indian Administered Kashmir
IDPs	Internally Displaced Persons
IHC	Islamabad High Court (Pakistan)
IHK	Indian Held Kashmir (Indian part of Kashmiri territory ruled by India)
IMDb	Internet Movie Database
ISI	Inter-Services Intelligence (Pakistani intelligence agency)
ISIS	Islamic State of Iraq and Syria
ISPR	Inter-Services Public Relations (Pakistan)
JuD	*Jamaat-ud-Dawa* (Pakistan)
JUI	*Jamiat-e-Ulema* Islam (Pakistan)
KP	Khyber Pakhtunkhwa province (Pakistan)
LeJ	*Lashkar-e-Jhangvi* (Pakistan)
LeT	*Lashakar-e-Tayyaba* (Pakistan)
MDI	Centre for Religious Learning and Propagation
MDI	*Markaz al-Daw'a wal Irshad* (Pakistan)
MI	Military Intelligence (Pakistan)
MMA	*Muttahida Majlis-e-Amal* (United Action Front, Pakistan)
NATO	North Atlantic Treaty Organization
NDTV	New Delhi Television (India)
NUS	National University of Singapore
NWFP	North West Frontier Province of Pakistan
NYTT	New York Times Television
PATA	Provincially Administered Tribal Areas (Pakistan)
PBS	Public Broadcasting Service (American Television Network)
PIPS	Pakistan Institute of Peace Studies
PTSD	Post-Traumatic Stress Disorder
RAW	Research and Analysis Wing (Indian foreign intelligence agency)
SAARC	South Asian Association for Regional Cooperation
SBS	Special Broadcasting Service (Australian Public Broadcasting Radio and Television Network)
SDGT	Specially Designated Global Terrorist Designation
SSP	*Sipah-e-Sahaba* Pakistan
TTP	*Tehreek-e-Taliban* Pakistan
UNHCR	The United Nations Refugee Agency
WMM	Women Make Movies
WSJ	Wall Street Journal (USA)
WSWS	World Socialist Web Site

Chapter 4: Victims of a vicious system: women, violence, and human rights

AI	Amnesty International
AIDS	Acquired Immune Deficiency Syndrome
ANAA	Asian-American Network Against Abuse
ASF	Acid Survivor's Foundation of Pakistan
ASTI	Acid Survivors Trust International
BBC	British Broadcasting Corporation
CEDAW	UN Convention on the Elimination of all Forms of Discrimination Against Women
CII	Council of Islamic Ideology (Pakistan)
CNN	Cable News Network (USA)
DSP	Deputy Superintendent Police
FIA	Federal Investigation Agency of Pakistan
HBO	Home Box Office (American Satellite Television Network)
HIV	Human Immunodeficiency Virus
HRCP	Human Rights Commission of Pakistan
ILO	International Labour Organization
KP	Khyber Pakhtunkhwa province (Pakistan)
LHRLA	Lawyers for Human Rights and Legal Aid (Pakistan)
MMWWO	Mukhtar Mai Women's Welfare Organization (Pakistan)
MoWD	Ministry of Women Development (Pakistan)
NGO	Non-Government Organization
NWFP	North West Frontier Province of Pakistan
PPC	Pakistan Penal Code
Project SAAVE	Stand Against Acid Violence
PWA	Progressive Women's Association (Pakistan)
PWHRO	Pakistani Women's Human Rights Organization
UN	United Nations

Conclusion

AHRC	Asian Human Rights Commission
AIE	Ali Institute of Education (Lahore, Pakistan)
ALRC	Asian Legal Resource Centre
BBC	British Broadcasting Corporation
BFI	British Film Institute
BNU	Beaconhouse National University (Pakistan)
CIDA	Canadian International Development Agency
FCC	Forman Christian College University (Lahore, Pakistan)
GB	Gilgit-Baltistan province (Pakistan)
IICFF	Islamabad International Children's Film Festival (Pakistan)
IRC	Interactive Resource Centre (Lahore, Pakistan)
IVSAA	Indus Valley School of Art and Architecture (Karachi, Pakistan)

Abbreviations xxv

KICFF	Karachi International Children's Film Festival (Pakistan)
KP	Khyber Pakhtunkhwa province (Pakistan)
KU	Karachi University (Pakistan)
LCWU	Lahore College for Women University (Pakistan)
LICFF	Lahore International Children's Film Festival (Pakistan)
LIDF	London International Documentary Festival (UK)
LUMS	Lahore University of Management Sciences (Pakistan)
NCA	National College of Arts University (Pakistan)
NFB	National Film Board (Canada)
NGO	Non-Government Organisation
PEMRA	Pakistan Electronic Media Regulatory Authority Ordinance
Project SAAVE	Stand Against Acid Violence
PTV	Pakistan Television Corporation
PU	Punjab University (Pakistan)
SZABIST	Shaheed Zulfikar Ali Bhutto Institute of Science and Technology (Pakistan)
UNDP	United Nations Development Programme
UNIFEM	United Nations Development Fund for Women
VAW	Violence Against Women
WISE	Women's International Shared Experience
WLUML	Women Living Under Muslim Laws
WRRC	Women Reclaiming and Redefining Culture
ZAB	Zulfikar Ali Bhutto

Appendix 2

CII	Council of Islamic Ideology (Pakistan)

Appendix 4

KP	Khyber Pakhtunkhwa province (Pakistan)
MISARC	Madanjeet Singh Institute for South Asia Regional Co-operation
NWFP	North West Frontier Province of Pakistan
PMEB	Pakistan Madrasa Education Board
SDPI	Sustainable Development Policy Institute (Pakistan)

Appendix 5

AI	Amnesty International
HRCP	Human Rights Commission of Pakistan
NCSW	National Commission on the Status of Women (Government of Pakistan)
PPC	Pakistan Penal Code

Map of Pakistan.
Source: http://www.infoplease.com/atlas/country/pakistan.html.

Introduction

> We realized that the important thing was not the film itself but that which the film provoked.
> Solanas, Fernando. 1969 'Cinema as a Gun.' *Cineaste*. Vol 3, No. 2: pp. 20.

Pakistan came into existence as a homeland for Muslims after the partition of India in August 1947, which marked the end of British colonial rule in the Indian sub-continent. Since independence, Pakistan's complex history has been dotted with various political upheavals that have included long and oppressive periods of dictatorships, religious fundamentalism, and some periods of relative democracies.

As part of a former colony, Pakistan also inherited its former rulers' governmental institutions, policies, and laws, a most significant one of these legacies being the educational system (still in force to a large extent), which included the production of educational documentary films through government organs. From the very beginning a filmmaking institution, the Directorate General of Films and Publications (DFP), was already in place in 1947, with a mandate to produce and disseminate documentaries on important aspects of Pakistan's national life, land and people, promotion of arts, cultural heritage, and socio-economic development and uplift programmes with a distinct emphasis on the promotion of a 'national' identity.[1] Other state institutions involved in the production and dissemination of documentary films include federal ministries, the armed forces, state-sponsored educational institutions and cultural organizations, and the state-owned media organ, the Pakistan Television Corporation (PTV) that came into existence in 1964.[2]

The subject of this book – the emergence of activist documentary filmmaking practices in contemporary Pakistan – is inspired by a crucial and decisive historical period in the country's development, one that has come to be known as the Islamization period.[3] The Islamization process, initiated during the period of General Zia-ul-Haq's long dictatorship (1977–1988), stands as the most formative era in Pakistan's history as it transformed the country from a rather secular society to one governed by *Sharia* laws. This period witnessed a *Sharia*-led *Wahhabist*[4] 'Islamization' process, spurred on by a brazen *politicization* of religion, which Zia declared he had been ordained by 'divine' powers to institute in Pakistan.[5] In an interview to the foreign media Zia emphatically announced: 'I have a mission, given by God, to bring Islamic order in Pakistan.'[6] The main tool used by Zia to this end was the politicized *Islamizing* of the Pakistani criminal justice system through the imposition of rigid *Sharia* laws.[7]

The Islamization period saw the rise of dramatic curbs on media and the arts, and a host of other regulatory and state directives that curtailed human rights, women's rights, and other freedoms on the pretext of an Islamic *religious* identity.[8] As the Zia regime used politicization of Islam as its vehicle for control, suppression, and governance, consequently Pakistan experienced a gradual descent into Islamic fundamentalism, and ultimately, the rise of a threat of Talibanization in the country.

However, at the same time that Zia was using state machinery to curb freedoms and citizen rights through the promulgation of *Sharia* laws, there was also a significant emergence of various resistance movements in Pakistan in the early 1980s with a focus on invigorating and activating the values and practices of a free and tolerant civil society.

Led primarily by educated segments in Pakistan's urban cities, sectors of civil society began to mobilize against the various state-imposed fundamentalist laws, practices, and curbs on freedom of speech and expression during the Zia regime. Consequently, these struggles produced a significant era of resistance, which consolidated in various forms including: the emergence of an organized women's resistance movement; non-governmental women's organizations and legal aid cells that stood up against gender-discriminatory practices and laws; print media journalists and publications that sought to mobilize public opinion against Islamization; writers and poets who used literary media to voice their concerns and write and disseminate critiques of the government's repressive policies; theatre groups that took to street performances to create public awareness, not only in major cities, but also in remote villages; students and other activists that supported human rights, religious tolerance, and a return to a progressive, and democratic system.

Rooted in the Islamization era, these various forms of resistance that have continued to spread, strengthen, and oppose religious extremism, and advocate a return to the freedoms assured by a secular and moderate political system, were to eventually also include the emergence of activist documentary filmmaking practices in Pakistan.

The prevailing repressive political conditions in Pakistan prompted numerous and varied alliances and collaborations over decades, and today these partnerships between various human-rights and women's-rights organizations, legal fraternities, broadcast media outlets, as well as independent filmmakers, individual activists, performing artists, writers, and journalists, play a significant role in supporting the production of activist documentary filmmaking in contemporary Pakistan.[9] This emerging filmmaking practice has also grown to include awareness and advocacy projects, and campaigns around social and public issues such as legal literacy, women's empowerment, education, and health issues, among others. Today, the contribution of Pakistani documentarists stands as a significant body of activist filmic work that has served the cause of human rights, consciousness-raising, and promoting awareness and social change in Pakistan, particularly regarding gender rights, through a culture and religion-sensitive critique, and exposé.

This study is inspired by the need to evaluate the merit and contribution of contemporary Pakistani documentarists and their work, during and since the Islamization period, in the light of what I argue is an emergent activist documentary film category of 'Cinema of Accountability' from within the Muslim world – an activist cinema that probes and critiques religious fundamentalism, discriminatory laws, and various forms of violation of human and citizen rights, and holds policy makers, and perpetrators accountable. This evaluation regards the activist films under consideration as deeply embedded in the daunting project of human rights and social change in Pakistan, and the analyses offered in this work 'read' the content of the films precisely in terms of the social and political conditions against which these films were meant to intervene.

Focus: 'Cinema of Accountability'

This study identifies the various representative filmmakers, organizations, collaborations, topics, and themes that can be seen to constitute a definitive activist documentary film movement in contemporary Pakistan – one that seeks to investigate and expose crucial, yet neglected, socio-political and cultural issues and limitations that impact and violate human and citizen rights. Hence, in doing so, these producers and productions question and seek answers, promote awareness and consciousness-raising, and advocate social, legislative, and political change through what I argue can be collectively defined as an emergent theoretical framework and documentary film category of a 'Cinema of Accountability' from within a Muslim country.

I examine the emergence and significance of activist documentary film and video practices in contemporary Pakistan, from the perspective of independent filmmakers, NGOs, and a governmental organization. For the scope of this project, I focus on representative documentary films that share the activist aim of addressing and exposing the effects of politicization of religion, religious fundamentalism and militancy, and the marginalization of minorities on the pretext of promoting an 'Islamic' identity, and suppression and violation of human rights, including women's rights, and violence against women.

As its main timeframe, discussions of films primarily focus on the period beginning with the Islamization process initiated in 1977 under President General Zia-ul-Haq's eleven-year martial law regime (1977–1988), and the transformations experienced by Pakistani civil society under another military dictator, President General Pervaiz Musharraf (1999–2008), and his post 9/11/2001 alliance with the US in the so-called 'War on Terror'.

Beginning with the period of General Zia-ul-Haq's Islamization process, this study reads and discusses a selection of representative documentary films that have critically addressed and documented the various key transformations, events, and developments that have shaped Pakistan's socio-political, socio-economic, and cultural history through the lingering intersections of politics, religion, and law. The focus is on the emergence of an activist filmmaking practice in Pakistan that can be seen as an influential factor in addressing the politics and negative and oppressive effects of the Islamization era; discriminatory laws; violation of human and citizen rights; authoritarianism; internal strife; spread of religious fundamentalism and threat of Talibanization; influence of *madrasas* (religious seminaries) in promoting extremism and pro-*Al Qaida* ideologies; and oppressive tribal customs and traditions. This examination seeks to distinguish and identify the collective activist efforts of this emergent filmmaking practice as a documentary 'Cinema of Accountability', both in retrospect as a filmic revisionist-history, and one that can serve as a counter-history in contemporary terms.

I use a contextual-reading approach (i.e. embedded in Pakistan's specific history, politics, religion, laws, and culture) to examine a selection of issue-oriented documentaries to illustrate the connection between these films, and the historical and political events and developments (including religious fundamentalism and imposition of various *Sharia* laws), and socio-cultural practices and factors that inspired their production. As the focus of this study is to investigate the activist and socio-political role of these films and filmmakers in the emergence of activist documentary filmmaking and video practices in Pakistan, a contextual-reading approach highlights not only the history, environments, constraints, problems, and topics they address, but also the socio-political and socio-cultural conditions under which they were made, and which the films aspire to expose.

Since many of the films discussed in this study may not be readily accessible to readers, another aim of the detailed 'reading' approach here is to try to *show* the films on paper as completely as possible, and let the filmmakers, their subjects, and the productions speak for themselves.

Where relevant, reference to formal and stylistic approaches in documentary cinema elaborate on their relevance to the politics and address of individual films and their topics.[10]

For the scope and length of this book, a maximum of six representative documentary films are discussed in detail in Chapters Two, Three, and Four. These chapters group productions and filmmakers/organizations according to their common topics and interrelated themes, rather than a strictly chronological order of production. The choice and placement of films is ordered according to the theme of each chapter title to establish an historical, contextual, and narrative pattern in keeping with the overall topic, timeframe, and intent of this study.

Objectives for analyses

This study examines how films reflect societies, and how they can have an impact on garnering public support for social change. Using a contextual-reading approach for film analyses, it is the aim of this book to investigate the following:

1   How do these Pakistani filmic documentations of historical events, legislative reforms, human rights violations, socio-political injustices, violence against women, and effects of religious fundamentalism contribute to creating an

activist, and anti-religious fundamentalism documentary film category from within an Islamic state? In seeking accountability for a variety of issues and abuses, what role have these documentary films and filmmakers played in their social and political resistance against powerful political institutions, controversial laws, religious extremism, and human rights abuses? These questions and aspects will ascertain the value, and effectiveness of these films as advocacy and consciousness-raising tools towards an exposé of various governmental policies, excesses, and neglect, as well as the cruelty meted out by tribal customs and traditions in Pakistani society.

2   What is the significance of these documentary films as activist tools for advocating change and reform by recording and disseminating the socio-political and historical memory and remembrances of otherwise powerless, marginalized, and minority individuals and groups whose voices would otherwise be erased from political and social discourse, and consideration? As allies in doing so, how do these Pakistani films, and the critical topics they have broached, benefit and contribute to the larger global cause for human rights and religious tolerance by shaping a new documentary cinema category of 'Cinema of Accountability'?

3   As they have revisited their history as insiders/participants to record and report on critical issues that have influenced their nation, what is the significance and contribution of these Pakistani documentary films and their makers in documenting and preserving a religion, gender, and culture-sensitive filmic revisionist/counter-history of their country's troubled socio-political landscape themselves, and communicating their content cross-culturally to build broader alliances and solidarity for reform and social change?

4   What potential activist role can such filmmaking practices continue to play in the future for spreading awareness and consciousness-raising about crucial issues, and promoting social change in Pakistan? (e.g. through the emergence of film studies institutes and a steady crop of trained filmmakers familiar with the socio-political and cultural history and problems of their region; exhibition possibilities through film clubs, film festivals, TV channels, and availability on the Internet). What are the constraints and limitations that need to be addressed for utilizing a greater activist potential of documentary cinema in Pakistan?

Methodology

This study focuses on a contextual 'reading' of a selection of issue-oriented documentary films collected from Pakistan through field research, personal requests to independent filmmakers, non-governmental as well as government organizations and their archives, human rights organizations, and film media outlets.

An inter-disciplinary approach (Documentary Film and Cinema Studies, history, politics, human rights, Islam/religion and *Sharia* laws, Cultural Studies, and Women's/Feminist Studies) is applied to situate topics and themes for textual analyses, and discussion of the selected documentary films that address issues of religious fundamentalism and extremism, politicization of religion, *Sharia* laws, human rights and social justice, tribal traditions and customs, and violence against women. Since there is no prior academic study on Pakistani activist documentary film practices, studies and theoretical perspectives from the afore-mentioned fields help to combine and develop a strong critical base from which to examine these documentary films, evaluate their activist intent in the Pakistani context, and support conclusions.

The above-mentioned approach and areas are supported by field research findings in Pakistan that include reports and data collected from government ministries and archives, non-governmental organizations and their archives, film studies institutes, news media outlets and archives, cultural organizations, and film festival archives; personal communication with filmmakers and civil society activists; as well as from the Internet.[11]

Secondary sources (academic texts and journals) aid in investigating the historical, cultural, and religious factors that contribute to the topic of this book. To situate the chosen film productions historically and politically, analyses are supported by texts that provide a background to the topics addressed in the films. These include literature on the regional socio-political developments pertaining to the Islamization period and after. Historical perspectives provide a background to Pakistan's Islamization period under General Zia-ul-Haq; studies on regional politics contextualize and situate Pakistan's descent into religious fundamentalism, tilt towards extremism and Talibanization, and the spread of a *madrasa* (religious seminaries) culture across the country; studies on Islam, *Sharia*, and Islamic jurisprudence help to explain and discuss various Islamic laws promulgated during the Islamization period, and their particularly marginalizing effect on the status of women and religious minorities. Perspectives on various forms of violence against women and tribal notions of 'honour' facilitate in contextualizing the subjugation and victimization of women through violent acts such as acid-attacks, stove-blasts, 'honour-killings', and 'honour-rape'. Media sources and reports are used to contextualize and elaborate on specific developments and events related to film discussions and topics.

Chapter summaries

Given the scarcity of academic research available on the emergence and practice of contemporary documentary cinema, activist or otherwise, from Pakistan, it is the intent of this book to fill this gap.[12] To this end, it is imperative to formulate a structure of theoretical frameworks that can be extended to conduct a contextual reading of the Pakistani documentaries discussed in this book; aid film scholars and interdisciplinary students in understanding a new activist body of cinematic representations inspired by historical events, religious fundamentalism, legal transformations, regional developments, and the various human rights topics addressed through these issue-oriented productions; and to establish the emergence of a 'Cinema of Accountability' as a new activist film genre and framework from within the Muslim world that specifically addresses a distinct set of issues and problems as explored and critiqued by Muslim filmmakers from their perspectives as partakers of the historical, socio-political, and cultural environments they portray in their works.

Chapter One, entitled 'Towards a Theory of "Cinema of Accountability": Critical Perspectives on Activist Film Practices', discusses relevant activist documentary Film Studies themes and perspectives, including feminist documentary frameworks, which can be borrowed from to expound the topic of this study. These perspectives include: 1) Perspectives on the Contextual and Historical Approach to Documentary Filmmaking; 2) Perspectives on the Activist and Political Intent of Documentary Film; 3) Feminist Perspectives on Documentary Film and Activism; 4) Parallels with Other Activist Film Currents (i.e. perspectives on Third Cinema, Cinema Novo, and a post-Third-Worldist approach).

Additionally, in the section entitled '"Spatial Boundaries" and Pakistani Women Filmmakers' Moroccan Islamic scholar, Fatima Mernissi, offers perspectives on the gender-specific 'spatial boundary' as a means of allocation of power and appearance of women in the public sphere in Islamic societies. This discussion aids in examining the role and contribution of Pakistani women filmmakers in their quest to probe and document critical junctures in their country's socio-political and cultural histories particularly regarding critiques of religious fundamentalism, gender-discriminatory *Sharia* laws, and patriarchal tribal customs in orthodox and conservative regions where women's active participation and appearance in the public arena is rare, and their defiance of norms can entail serious consequences to personal safety.

As well, the section entitled 'Pakistani Cinema under Islamization' offers a brief synopsis of the developments that were shaping and impacting the Pakistani film industry during the Islamization period. This contextualization illustrates the roots of the emergence of activist documentary filmmaking practice in Pakistan as a consequence of resistance to religious fundamentalism and oppressive state directives.

Supported by the thematic and critical perspectives discussed in Chapter One, the following chapters offer an interdisciplinary contextual reading and analyses of a selection of representative issue-oriented films.

Chapter Two, entitled 'Injustices on Film: A Reading of Activist Documentaries Against the Legacy of Islamization', discusses films that deal with the legislative reforms and socio-political transformations wreaked under the Islamization period (*Jaloos (Procession); Who Will Cast the First Stone?; Don't Ask Why; For a Place Under the Heavens; Hudood Ordinance 1979: Divine Law, or Law of One Man?; A Sun Sets In*). The Islamization period (1977–1988) stands out in Pakistan's history primarily because it was dominated by the promulgation of several rigid *Sharia* laws and state directives introduced under the dictatorship of General Zia-ul-Haq on the pretext of establishing an Islamic order that would transform the country's identity into an 'Islamic state'.[13] Hence, beginning with President General Zia-ul-Haq's dictatorial regime, this chapter offers a contextual reading of activist documentary films that trace the legacy of the Islamization period, and are rooted in issues and events that represent the intersection of politics, religion and law, and their transformative impact on the legislature and socio-political environment of Pakistan.

8 *Introduction*

Beginning with a background to the women's resistance movement and organizations that emerged in response to the promulgation of gender-discriminatory laws, this chapter focuses on representative films, filmmakers, organizations, and collaborative productions that question and critique the implications, and consequences of the imposition of *Sharia* laws during the Islamization period. These laws include the *Zina Hudood* Ordinance, the Law of Evidence, and the Blasphemy Law, and their impact on the Pakistani socio-political landscape, women's legal status, religious minority groups, and the violation and curtailment of individual and human rights on the pretext of establishing an 'Islamic identity'.[14]

Chapter Three, entitled 'Cinema on Terror: Charting the Militant Mix of Politics, Religion, and Talibanization', reads films that address the complex, long-term consequences of religious extremism and militancy, and the subsequent spread of Talibanization and a radical *madrasa* (religious seminaries) culture in Pakistan as a consequence of the post 9/11/2001 Pak–US collaboration in the so-called 'War on Terror'.[15]

A selection of six films made by Pakistani independent documentary filmmaker Sharmeen Obaid-Chinoy in this chapter constitute what I argue stands as a distinct documentary category of 'Cinema on Terror' – one that traces the roots and ideologies of *jihadist* organizations, religion-based militancy, terrorism, and *jihadist* violence. These films (*Terror's Children; Reinventing the Taliban?; Pakistan: On A Razor's Edge; Pakistan's Double Game; Cold Comfort; Pakistan's Taliban Generation*) address, and seek accountability for, the militant mix of politics and religion that have emerged as a worldwide threat in the form of growing religious extremism, and particularly the emergence of Talibanization in Pakistan and its tribal regions that gained momentum during military dictator President General Pervaiz Musharraf's rule (1999–2008), as he clung to power as a frontline US ally. Contextual readings of Obaid-Chinoy's films highlight the continuum of Pakistan's involvement in the US 'War on Terror' in the region, the consequent growing internal political and ideological strife, and the influence of *madrasas* that became instrumental in fostering pro-Taliban and *Al Qaida* influence and ideologies.

Selection of thematically related films in this chapter form a connective link with the far-reaching impact of General Zia's Islamization process discussed earlier in Chapter Two. Leading from issues of politicization of religion, religious fundamentalism, and discriminatory judicial transformations that pushed Pakistan towards a continuing descent into religious extremism on the pretext of an Islamic identity in the previous chapter, a focus on Obaid-Chinoy's films in this chapter illustrates the emergence of a 'Cinema on Terror' in response to an era of terrorism driven by religion-based militancy with a global *jihadist* agenda that finds its hub in a nuclear-armed Pakistan.

Readings of Obaid-Chinoy's investigative and reflective films contribute to understanding the growth and role of Pakistani activist documentary film practices, and the filmmakers as critical insiders reviewing their history, religious identity, and the transformative regional developments impacting their homeland.

Chapter Four, entitled 'Victims of a Vicious System: Women, Violence, and Human Rights', focuses on issues of extreme forms of victimization and violence against women and violation of their rights that have been an ongoing factor in Pakistan. Continuing from themes of intolerance and religious extremism from the previous chapters, selection of issue-oriented documentary films in this chapter add to the activist category of 'Cinema of Accountability' as Pakistani filmmakers investigate the socio-cultural and socio-economic factors underlying various forms of violence against women and gender rights violations. These films specifically address issues of horrific acts of stove-blasts and acid attacks (*Stove Burning: Neither Coal Nor Ashes* (*Na koella bhye na raakh*); *Burnt Victims: Scars on the Society; Saving Face*), and so-called 'honour' related crimes such as 'honour-killing' (*Shame: A Tale of Karo Kari*) and 'honour-rape' (*Shame*), and gender-biased tribal practices such as *Swara* (*Swara: A Bridge Over Troubled Waters*) that are instigated by patriarchal mindsets and inflicted on women to either subjugate them, or to victimize or use them to serve vested interests.[16]

A contextual reading of representative activist documentary films in this chapter highlight the failure of the state to ensure women protection and justice, and emphasizes the activist role of Pakistani filmmakers and their respective productions in seeking accountability for state-apathy and gender biases in the law-enforcement system.

In addition to a discussion of individual films, this chapter provides an overview of Pakistani independent filmmaker Samar Minallah's various other collaborative productions made under the auspices of her non-governmental organization, *Ethnomedia & Development* – an organization that has been at the forefront of producing documentaries, investigative and advocacy films for legislative and social change, dissemination of activist music-videos, and specializes in community outreach initiatives and campaigns in some of the most conservative and backward regions of Pakistan such as the Khyber Pakhtunkhwa province (KP).[17] This discussion illustrates the emergence of an activist filmmaking organization that is focused on various women's issues and their empowerment, among others, highlighting the pedagogical utility of documentary cinema as a visual medium, particularly in low-literacy regions, for seeking social change and justice through consciousness-raising.

The 'Conclusion' synthesizes previous contextual discussions on the chosen documentary films, and their topics, placing the activist intent of these productions within the thematic and theoretical documentary film perspectives and approaches used in their readings.

The concluding chapter offers a critical overview, and assesses the direction Pakistani activist documentary film practices have taken in establishing a contemporary documentary 'Cinema of Accountability' and 'Cinema on Terror' that particularly questions the effects of politicization of religion, fundamentalism, extremist ideologies, and issues of human rights. It discusses the activist role and contribution of Pakistani films and filmmakers, organizations and collaborations in drawing attention to critical phases, developments, and events in Pakistan's history and socio-cultural life. In doing so, the concluding chapter reviews their input towards documenting a committed, revisionist counter-history, and creating an activist Pakistani documentary film category that can be defined as a 'Cinema of Accountability' – one that has emerged and developed from within, and despite, the country's own context of religious, socio-political, and cultural constraints.

Further, the 'Conclusion' takes into account issues pertaining to the exhibition of Pakistani activist documentary films, both locally and internationally, through film festivals and other distribution outlets to examine their activist significance in the public sphere, and in cross-cultural communication.[18]

As well, based on the representative films discussed in the book, the 'Conclusion' identifies the gaps and limitations that still exist for the promotion of documentary cinema in terms of access to funding, exhibition, and production facilities within Pakistan. This discussion takes into account the role of foreign collaborations and exhibition outlets in strengthening and furthering the activist intent of Pakistani filmmakers such as in screening films that have critiqued religious fundamentalism, controversial *Sharia* laws, and various other sensitive socio-political and gender issues that local channels would find it difficult to exhibit in an environment of authoritarian regimes, religious fundamentalism, and restrictive censorship policies.

The 'Conclusion' ends with a critical discussion of the potential activist role documentary filmmaking practices can continue to play as an audio-visual medium in the future for consciousness-raising and advocacy for social change in Pakistan, particularly given the dismally low literacy rate in the country.[19]

This chapter addresses new developments such as the emergent trend of Film Studies institutes and departments in Pakistan's academia, and expanding exhibition sites offered by the growth of television and media organizations and emerging film festivals and film clubs in the country, as well as the expanding cross-cultural exhibition opportunities offered by new technologies. It stresses the potential pedagogical, investigative, and expository role new graduating filmmakers can play in taking the Pakistani documentary 'Cinema of Accountability' further for consciousness-raising, and to build pressure for political, social, and legislative reforms.

In the light of the afore-mentioned discussions, the 'Conclusion' points towards the activist potential of documentary cinema in promoting social and political reforms in contemporary Pakistan, and the advantage new filmmakers can exercise through their knowledge and familiarity with the delicate balance needed to deal with particularly sensitive issues and nuances concerning religion, gender, and cultural traditions in what is by turns, a complex, conservative, and volatile society and region such as theirs, hence strengthening the activist, issue-oriented 'Cinema of Accountability' paradigm.

Notes

1 The first film produced by the Directorate General of Films and Publications (DFP) in 1948 commemorated Pakistan's independence from India. Films made by the directorate are also sent to foreign diplomatic missions, and embassies, both Pakistani and others in host countries. *DFP Brief*, the Government of Pakistan, August 11, 2010.

2 As part of a former British colony, India, Pakistan also retained Commonwealth status, thus enjoying continued support in educational endeavours through various channels such as the British Council. Similarly, other post-partition avenues have included UNESCO, and USAID, and various other international NGOs such as ActionAid, Oxfam, the Norwegian Agency for Development Cooperation, and the German Heinrich Böll Stiftung Foundation, among others, which have been involved in collaborative film production ventures in Pakistan.
3 General Zia-ul-Haq's Islamization period (1977–1988) is also referred to as the Islamization process by various critics and writers.
4 *Wahhabism*, a Saudi Arabian variant of Islam that follows a literal interpretation of Islam, was introduced by the Saudi cleric Muhammad ibn Abd al-Wahhab in the eighteenth century who sought to remove the multifarious readings of the Quran that evolved in the centuries after Prophet Muhammad. Backed by the House of Saud, the *Wahhabist* views were adopted as Saudi national policy, under which 'infidels' were to be dealt with harshly, while local customs, laws, saints, or rituals – anything not found in a literal reading of the Quran – were to be abandoned as idolatry. Robert Marquand, 'The Tenets of Terror', *The Christian Science Monitor.* October 18, 2001. Accessed at: http://www.csmonitor.com/2001/1018/p1s2-wogi.html on April 3, 2015.
5 Hence, in the context of Pakistan, I choose to use the term and connotation of 'politicization of Islam', as this was done through an organized and systemic process during General Zia-ul-Haq's dictatorship to legitimize his rule and powers, and serve political motives and objectives. The Western construct of 'political Islam' tends to negate or/ and undermine the spiritual aspects of the Islamic religion and faith, which in fact have been marginalized, and 'politicized' to serve vested interests by ruling regimes and leaders in Pakistan. For further discussion see Mubarak Ali, 'Politicization and Commercialization of Religion: The Case of Pakistan', in idem, Pakistan in Search of Identity, Pakistan Study Centre, University of Karachi, Karachi, Pakistan, 2009, p. 125.
6 Interview given to the British Broadcasting Corporation (BBC) on April 15, 1978. Jebran Chamieh, 'Contemporary Fundamentalist Regimes and Movements', in idem, *Traditionalists, Militants and Liberals in Present Islam*, Research and Publishing House, Montreal, Canada. 1995, p. 170.
7 *Sharia* Laws: Islamic socio-religious laws. These laws are based upon the *Quran*, the holy text of the Muslims dating back more than 1400 years and believed by Muslims to be the Divine word as revealed by God through the Angel Gabriel to Prophet Mohammad, and the *Sunnah* (The Islamic Traditions based on Prophet Mohammad's life). The principles of *Sharia* laws serve as the foundation for Islamic jurisprudence, and are based on the interpretation of rules of guidance as contained in the *Quran*. For detailed definition and functions of *Sharia* see H. A. R. Gibb, *'The Shari'a'.* Accessed at: http://answering-islam.org/Books/Gibb/sharia.htm on April 3, 2015.
8 In Pakistan, 1977 marked the suspension of civilian rule and the constitution as General Zia's politicization of religion and self-proclaimed 'divine' mandate to steer the country towards a religious identity, ruled by Islamic laws as the supreme order, took hold. Zia's Islamization also extended to strict curbs on the Pakistani media, including, at the time, Pakistan's only television channel, the state-run Pakistan Television Corporation. For further details on curbs on Pakistani media under various regimes, see Shahid Nadeem, 'Silencing the Nation: Censorship Acts Since 1947', in Neelam Hussain, Samiya Mumtaz, and Samina Choonara (eds), *Politics of Language*, Simorgh Women's Resource and Publication Centre, Lahore, Pakistan, 2005, pp. 159–86 (p. 159).
9 Although today many NGOs, groups, and individuals are involved in social welfare and advocacy work in Pakistan, for the scope of this book only a selection of those organizations, individuals, groups, and fraternities are included in chapters on films whose alliances and collaborative and/or independent productions have made a

significant contribution to the emergence of an activist documentary film practice defined in this study as a 'Cinema of Accountability' in contemporary Pakistan.
10 As the focus is on the contextual-reading of the selected films as per their topics and the historical events and other factors that inspired their production, it is not the aim, nor within the scope, of this study to discuss formal aspects in greater detail.
11 These sources include reports and data from relevant government ministries and departments in Pakistan (e.g. Ministry of Culture; Ministry for Women's Affairs; National Commission on the Status of Women; Censorship Board of Pakistan; Pakistan Electronic Media Regulatory Authority (PEMRA); Ministry of Law; Ministry of Religious Affairs); and Non-Governmental Organizations (NGOs) (e.g. human rights, women's rights, and legal aid organizations).
12 So far, only one comprehensive history of Pakistani cinema has been attempted, by the (late) Pakistani filmmaker Mushtaq Gazdar, whose volume, written in English, covers the topic of Pakistani mainstream commercial cinema from 1947 up to 1997, but does not address documentary or activist film practice in Pakistan. See Mushtaq Gazdar, *Pakistan Cinema 1947–1997*, Oxford University Press, Karachi, Pakistan, 1998.

However, I have discussed Pakistani women documentary filmmakers in a separate version of an earlier article in the *Encyclopedia of Women & Islamic Cultures*: Rahat Imran, 'Cinema: Films Made by Women Screen Writers, Directors, Producers: Women Documentary Filmmakers: Pakistan', *Encyclopedia of Women & Islamic Cultures*. Brill, 2010. Brill Online: http://referenceworks.brillonline.com/search?s.q=rahat+imran&s.f.s2_parent=s.f.book.encyclopedia-of-women-and-islamic-cultures&search-go=Search.
13 For a chronological list of important events during General Zia-ul-Haq's eleven-year martial law reign, see Shahid Javed Burki and Craig Baxter (eds), *Pakistan Under the Military: Eleven Years of Zia-ul-Haq*. Westview Press, Boulder, San Francisco, and Oxford, 1991, pp. 155–82.
14 See Appendices 1, 2, and 3 for explanation of the *Zina Hudood* Ordinance, the Law of Evidence, and the Blasphemy Law.
15 The plural of *madrasa* is *madaris* in Urdu. However, the commonly used plural term of '*madrasas*' in English is used in this text.
16 *Swara*: tribal custom and practice of giving away of minor girls in forced marriages as compensation to settle disputes or avenge murders.
17 The Khyber Pakhtunkhwa (KP) province was formerly known as the North West Frontier Province (NWFP). Following intense lobbying and demand by political leaders for a regionally and ethnically representative name for their province, the North West Frontier Province was renamed as the Khyber Pakhtunkhwa Province (KP) in April 2010. 'NWFP Officially Renamed as Khyber-Pakhtunkhwa', *OnePakistan News*, April 15, 2010. Accessed at: http://www.onepakistan.com/news/top-stories/40700-NWFP-officially-renamed-Khyber-Pakhtunkhwa.html on December 4, 2010.
18 For example, in 2001, despite the religio-political constraints influencing Pakistan's cultural life and the arts, it became host to an international film festival, the *Kara*Film Festival. Since its inception, this non-political and non-profit-making film festival, held annually in the country's port city of Karachi, had been exhibiting and promoting independent filmmakers and their films from within Pakistan and abroad. For details of the *Kara*Film Festival, visit: http://www.karafilmfest.com/about.htm Accessed on April 4, 2015.
19 According to figures released by the British Foreign and Commonwealth Office (FCO) in April 2011, Pakistan's literacy rate in 2011 stood at: Male: 63%, Female: 35.2%, Total: 49.9%. Accessed at: http://www.factba.se/fco-page.php?bc=PK on January 13, 2016.

According to a UNESCO report, Pakistan's literacy rate is projected to reach 60 percent by 2015. 'Global Literacy Rate: Pakistan Ranks 113th Among 120 Nations', *Business Recorder*, October 24, 2012. Accessed at http://www.brecorder.com/top-news/

1-front-top-news/87662-global-literacy-rate-pakistan-ranks-113th-among-120-nations-.html on April 4, 2015. However, it is reported that Pakistan missed the projected UN literacy target in 2015. For details see Riazul Haq, 'Education Woes: Pakistan Misses UN Target With 58% Literacy Rate', *The Express Tribune*, June 5, 2015. Accessed at: http://tribune.com.pk/story/897995/education-woes-pakistan-misses-un-target-with-58-literacy-rate/ on January 13, 2016.

1 Towards a theory of 'Cinema of Accountability'

Critical perspectives on activist film practices

Introduction

Cinema Studies perspectives relevant to the understanding of the emergence of Pakistani documentary film practices as activist interventions are discussed in this chapter. In the absence of a theoretical framework or pre-existing study from which *specifically* contemporary Pakistani documentary films, activist or otherwise, can be evaluated, it examines key perspectives on documentary filmmaking from outside Pakistan that serve as building blocks for a theory relevant to documentary productions discussed in this book. Hence, broader existing critical perspectives from film scholars and theorists on documentary film serve as an informing framework for these Pakistani productions, and the foundational activist context for their analyses. Subsequently, these frameworks facilitate in defining an emergent activist film category of a 'Cinema of Accountability' from within a Muslim state in which the achievement of activist film faces daunting challenges. Additionally, a discussion on the concept of 'Spatial Boundaries' as allocation of gender power in Islamic societies helps to evaluate the role of Pakistani women filmmakers operating in the public domain, particularly in conservative regions dominated by orthodox norms and patriarchal mindsets, such as the tribal areas in the Khyber Pakhtunkhawa Province (KP) where women's public presence is discouraged. The last section in this chapter, entitled 'Pakistani Cinema under Islamization' offers a brief context for the developments that were impacting Pakistani cinema in an environment of religious fundamentalism, state censorship, and restrictive policies during General Zia-ul-Haq's dictatorship.

As discussions on films will later illustrate, drawing parallels, and translating the following perspectives in contemporary political terms will explore their applicability to activist documentary filmmaking practices in contemporary Pakistan.[1]

There are four overarching themes by which a theoretical framework for this book is structured. Film-studies themes and perspectives, including feminist documentary frameworks, which can be borrowed from to expound the topic of this book include: 1) Perspectives on the Contextual and Historical Approach to Documentary Filmmaking; 2) Perspectives on the Activist and Political Intent of Documentary Film; 3) Feminist Perspectives on Documentary Film and Activism;

4) Parallels with Other Activist Film Currents (i.e. perspectives on Third Cinema, Cinema Novo, and a post-Third-Worldist approach).

1. Perspectives on the contextual and historical approach to documentary filmmaking

Documentary film perspectives discussed in this section will aid in reading the historical contexts and background to the productions discussed in this study.

The beginnings of contemporary Pakistani activist documentary filmmaking practices, as analysed in this study, are inspired by and rooted in the critical historical period of President General Zia-ul-Haq's eleven-year dictatorship (1977–1988), and the socio-political and judicial transformations that began to take shape during his Islamization drive. Consequently, it is crucial to begin by contextualizing films in this historical period in order to understand the productions it motivated, and the continuing influence of the transformations during this phase on Pakistani society and the emergence of activist filmmaking in the country.

A consideration of contextual and historical perspectives is important in evaluating the activist involvement, intent, and success of Pakistani documentarists in relation to the issue-oriented films discussed here. These issues include: the effects of politicization of religion; religious fundamentalism; discriminatory judicial reforms that particularly affect women and religious minorities; human rights violations; gender rights; gender-specific tribal customs and practices; and issues of violence against women.

Perspectives on the contextual and historical approaches to documentary filmmaking facilitate in addressing the position of Pakistani documentary filmmakers in their particular historical and political contexts. Secondly, these perspectives assist in situating and understanding the chosen films as socio-cultural and socio-political productions, and the ideological currents that are the basis and key determinants for their creation.

Arab film historian and scholar Viola Shafik points out that it is vital to make connections between the prevailing socio-political conditions and the historical period and events that motivated such filmic works for an in-depth analysis.[2] From this perspective, it is important to take into account the position of Pakistani documentary filmmakers as themselves part of the culture, religion, and history they seek to depict and critique in their films, and to contextualize the issues they raise accordingly in their productions. As Pakistani documentarists have represented a history, memory, and environment of which they themselves have been participants, their subjects, topics, and environs, and the historical time frames of their films, need to be considered in totality to facilitate a contextual-reading of their productions for content analyses. This approach will illustrate the connection between the historical timeframe and the consequential and connective links of their activist intent that saw the emergence of an activist documentary 'Cinema of Accountability' in the country.

Likewise, film scholar Chuck Kleinhans stresses the significance of a film/video work's context – the historical moment in which a work was produced, distributed, and exhibited, and the audience it reaches. Similarly, he emphasizes contextualizing the filmmaker's own position regarding his/her productions: that is, the relationship of the filmmaker to political, personal, historical, social, and institutional conditions.[3] As Kleinhans argues, documentary filmmakers must be deeply engaged in the political and social issues they represent in their work:

> Makers have to think like political organizers – with both intensity and distance, attention to the immediate and the long range, to the tactical and the strategic, and to the individual and the group – in other words to the complexity and richness of the immediate historical moment and its potentials and possibilities.[4]

Similarly, in her post-colonial critique, Vietnamese-American film scholar and filmmaker Trinh T. Minh-ha calls for a re-evaluation of representations of history with an emphasis on 'lived history' that would defy stereotypes and counter dominant discourses and representations.[5] Her focus is on the necessity to deconstruct and re-examine history through the eyes and narratives of those who have been the victims of violent histories, as opposed to the frequent distortions of dominant and 'authoritative' media.[6] Trinh's perspective on claiming the right to revisit one's own history as insiders can be applied to Pakistani documentarists who have returned to their past to counter official discourses and seek answers for the present and the future, particularly regarding issues of religious fundamentalism and human rights.

In his essay entitled *For an Imperfect Cinema*, Cuban film theorist and filmmaker Julio Garcia Espinosa stresses the need to revolutionize the very concepts of art and cinema, and to understand them as progressive forces towards social change. Espinosa advocates a democratization of art and urges artistic accessibility, arguing for what he calls an 'imperfect cinema' that would break class and artistic hierarchies and speak to all as a solution.[7] This 'imperfect cinema', he contends, would render art as an activity available to all in the service of social, political, and cultural responsibilities, instead of art as an elitist practice in the hands of a few who can dictate its terms, directions, and significance. Espinosa stresses the importance for science and art to merge, and the participation of sociologists, scientists, and others from various disciplines to participate in artistic activities in order to break down the class and disciplinary barriers that hinder artistic progress that could translate into a better and more just society. He is critical of art as an elitist activity, and suggests that art should be everyone's domain against traditional views that separate artistic/cultural producers and consumers.

According to Espinosa, such a collective revolution can be facilitated by an 'imperfect cinema' that would be created by the 'masses' regardless of technological finesse. This 'imperfect cinema', which he likens to the process of impartial media reporting and coverage, would expose relations of dominance and power instead of merely criticizing them, and enable a more popular engagement with art and politics:

> We should endeavor to see that our future students, and therefore our future filmmakers, will themselves be scientists, sociologists, physicians, economists,

agricultural engineers, etc., without of course ceasing to be filmmakers ... we cannot develop the taste of the masses as long as the division between the two cultures continues to exist, nor as long as the masses are not the real masters of the means of production ... A new poetics of cinema will, above all, be a 'partisan' and 'committed' poetics, a 'committed' art, a consciously and resolutely 'committed' cinema – that is to say, an 'imperfect' cinema.[8]

The emergence of Pakistani 'activist documentary' (as defined in this research) does not have its roots in filmmaking per se, but is rather embedded in ongoing resistance movements supported by a host of cross-disciplinary actors. This activist documentary then merges science and art (creativity) to break down disciplinary barriers that can hinder 'committed' art, as stressed by Espinosa in his call for an 'imperfect cinema'. It would be important to assess the extent to which Pakistani documentarists have achieved their effort of creating a socio-political version of an 'imperfect cinema'; that is, one that not only deviates from the country's mainstream commercial cinema industry, and the state-owned media that are regulated by government policies, but one that can also be seen as carving out its own niche as an activist documentary 'Cinema of Accountability' that questions and challenges state policies, laws, and official versions of history, and engages with crucial social and political developments.[9]

It can be argued that just as alliances and struggles in Pakistan gave birth to new channels of activism such as women's organizations, legal aid cells, human and gender rights watch groups, and theatre-for-social-change groups, all with a shared agenda for resistance and consciousness-raising, they also led to the emergence of an 'activist documentary' filmmaking practice in the country. In the absence of professional filmmaking training and academies at the time, this development was facilitated by the arrival of cost-effective and accessible video technology in the 1980s. Since then, these practices have been supported by old and new collaborations and participations that have included a wide cross-section of professionals and civil actors: women's rights activists; human rights and legal fraternities; educationists; sociologists; psychologists; journalists; writers; academics; poets; performing artists such as singers and theatre artists; local and international non-government organizations; and later, even government organizations. Additionally, ordinary people and individuals have been involved in the exercise by offering first-hand testimonies and accounts of their specific experiences and struggles. In this context Espinosa's concept of an 'imperfect cinema' is most relevant to activist collaborations between Pakistani documentary filmmakers, and their subjects and participants that range from a vast cross-section of society and disciplines.

It is important to examine the contribution of Pakistani documentarists who have opposed religious fundamentalism and authoritarian suppression as participants of their specific culture, history, religion, and politics. In particular, Pakistani women filmmakers and their female subjects (both of whom have broken the socio-cultural and religious spatial barriers that could set limits on their very appearances in public spaces in a Muslim society, particularly in the ultra-conservative tribal regions of the country) have bravely seized the opportunity to document and present their personal experiences and testimonies. Towards this end, both Trinh and Espinosa's perspectives assist in evaluating Pakistani documentarists' role as agents of social change and political resistance who have challenged dominant official, patriarchal, and fundamentalist forces in Pakistan through their respective productions.

Correspondingly, film scholar Bill Nichols calls attention to the situation of the filmmaker in the making of the film, and his/her own position regarding their depictions. He points to what can be termed as 'auto-ethnography', that is, 'when the filmmaker and subject are of the same stock.'[10] In the case of Pakistanis who have been part of the history, culture, and transformations that they depict in their films, Nichols' view helps to reflect on the significance of Pakistani filmmakers' familiarity and identification with their own religious, socio-cultural, historical, and socio-political issues and constraints, including the nuances of sensitive religion and gender-specific issues in an Islamic society.

Hence, relevant to their activist intent, Pakistani filmmakers' own situation also needs to be considered as this factor can affect their representations. For example, the socio-political and censorship constraints under which Pakistani documentarists may have to operate can be decisive and influential factors in their productions. In Pakistan's case, this examination provides an insight into the limitations, constraints, and challenges documentarists may have to contend with in their investigation, and depictions. For example, the risks and constraints Muslim Pakistani filmmakers, especially women filmmakers, may face in depicting and critiquing issues of religious fundamentalism and questioning the impact of discriminatory *Sharia* laws and tribal customs in Pakistan, particularly in the county's hostile, and ultra- orthodox tribal environments and belts. An assessment of these factors is important to contextualize the socio-political positioning of Pakistani filmmakers, particularly Muslim women filmmakers, and their attempt to appropriate their, and their subjects', right to deconstruct and question the impact of religious fundamentalism on their society and citizen rights.

Other perspectives that contribute to the contextual and historical approach to documentary filmmaking and the role of the filmmaker in this study include film scholars Paula Rabinowitz on the pedagogical aspects and 'instructional use' of documentary film;[11] Keith Beattie on the use of archival footage from the past, and its use in documentaries in the present as a means of contestation and re-investigation of history;[12] and Jack C. Ellis and Betsy A. McLane on the impact of video technology on documentary filmmaking in the 1980s, and the subsequent arrival of cable and satellite transmissions that began to transform global broadcasts by reaching wider audiences.[13]

2. Perspectives on the activist and political intent of documentary film

Perspectives on the activist and political intent of documentary film assist in understanding the chosen Pakistani films as socio-cultural and socio-political productions, and the ideological currents that are the bases and key determinants for their production, and their makers' political and activist intent.

Film scholar Thomas Waugh puts forth the concept of the 'committed documentary', one that consciously pursues the particular 'activist' stance of instigating socio-political change in the events and issues it addresses. He elaborates on his definition of the 'committed documentary', and documentarists:

> By 'commitment' I mean, firstly, a specific ideological undertaking, a declaration of solidarity with the goal of radical socio-political transformation. Secondly, I mean a specific socio-political positioning: activism, or intervention in the process of change itself.[14]

Waugh's perspective helps to identify and evaluate the contribution of an emergent 'committed documentary' category in the Pakistani context, and its contribution to filmic pedagogical activism with a specific focus on social change.

Similarly, film scholar Erik Barnouw identifies the various roles a documentary filmmaker can play simultaneously. These, he argues, can include a complex combination of the reporter, travel lecturer, chronicler, observer, guerrilla, ethnographic filmmaker, war reporter, and prosecutor, among others. He stresses that:

> None of these fields can be neatly separated. They never occur separately. The documentarist is always more than one of these. Yet different occasions, different moments in history, tend to bring different functions to the fore. This was true in the first decade of documentary, and it remained true in later decades.[15]

Barnouw's perspectives on a documentarist's multiple functions is useful in identifying the various roles played by Pakistani documentarists in their respective films, and how their stylistic, activist, and political intent complement each other in their filmic approaches and representations.

Other studies on the activist and political intent of documentary film facilitate discussions on issues of activism, consciousness-raising, awareness, advocacy, and the deliberative, persuasive, judicial, and historical intent and role of documentary film. These include film scholars Michael Renov on the significance of the documentary filmmaker as a historiographer who brings oral histories and the submerged accounts of people and social movements to public notice,[16] and the significance of offering an alternative picture and voices, particularly regarding issues that pertain to women's experiences that challenge the patriarchal, official, and institutionalized standpoint;[17] and Bill Nichols whose work identifies the 'legislative and deliberative',[18] and 'judicial and historical'[19] intent and role of documentary film in promoting social change.

Documentary scholarship in this section and category addresses the articulation of human rights and their violation through documentary media, and hence supports in evaluating the activist and political intent of Pakistani documentarists in recording and disseminating the voices, oral histories, and testimonies of communities and individuals seeking accountability for rights violations, and injustices. In particular, these film perspectives help raise the question of how do the filmic efforts of Pakistani documentarists contribute to empowering marginalized segments to have their say about human rights violations and oppression? How does their filmic intervention highlight the effects of politicization of religion, its consequences for the transformation of the Pakistani society, and the struggle against discriminatory and rigid state laws and directives imposed on the pretext of religion and a national 'Islamic' identity? In terms of 'committed documentary', how do Pakistani activist filmic productions serve as a body of historical testimony – one that situates its makers as revisionist counter-historians aligning themselves with their fellow native subjects in the process of seeking accountability?

The aforementioned approaches and questions assist in evaluating the significance of Pakistani documentary films as a filmic counter-historical record that challenges official versions by exposing historical facts and events that would otherwise be obscured from public scrutiny and memory. For example, in the context of Pakistani documentarists, Renov's perspectives on the role of documentary film as revisionist history and historiography can be stretched to include a broader human rights angle and issues as opposed to women's issues alone.

3. Feminist perspectives on documentary film and activism

Perspectives in this section include feminist scholarship on documentary film, its political and activist intent, and the importance of this scholarship in consciousness-raising, and fostering women's empowerment and social change.[20] Extending these feminist perspectives to include a wider human rights stance as well, this scholarship supports the activist intent of Pakistani documentaries on gender issues that focus on the marginalized status of women in a gender-discriminatory socio-legal environment, and tribal customs and traditions that can brutally affect women's lives.

It is important to mention here that despite the gender-specific oppression perpetrated through the Islamization process, since the country's birth as a 'Muslim' state in 1947 women have continued to be part of the Pakistani film industry, theatre, news media, and the television industry as writers, journalists, producers, directors, actresses, musicians, singers, performing artists on stage, and classical dancers.[21] However, their participation in the emergence of activist documentary filmmaking has its roots in the Islamization period. Four prominent Pakistani women documentarists whose films have centred around the effects of religious fundamentalism, women's issues, human rights, and social issues, and who have also won acclaim and awards at international film festivals are Sabiha Sumar, Sharmeen Obaid-Chinoy, Samar Minallah, and Maheen Zia.[22] Their participation in documentary filmmaking has been spurred by gender discriminatory Islamic *Sharia* laws such as the *Zina Hudood* Ordinance and the Law of Evidence promulgated during the Islamization period (Sabiha Sumar); religious fundamentalism; terrorism; Talibanization; and gender oppressions (Sharmeen Obaid-Chinoy); socio-cultural tribal traditions and customs such as *Swara*, and related gender oppressions (Samar Minallah); and socio-political issues such as the role of law enforcement agencies; political corruption; environmental and development issues (Maheen Zia).

It is also significant to note that women filmmakers and women's non-governmental organizations were amongst the first to choose documentary film as their activist medium to investigate and document the implications of Islamization, religious extremism, and other human rights issues despite the religious, social, and cultural restrictions and limitations that could hinder their creative progress as Muslim women and activists in an Islamic society, as well as the authoritarian and highly restrictive political environment at the time. Their contribution through the documentary medium emphasizes the need to examine the significance and effectiveness of women's, and feminist, documentary practice as an activist tool of resistance and consciousness-raising in a Muslim state, particularly in an environment of religious fundamentalism and other marginalizing practices that subjugate human rights as subsequent discussions on films will illustrate.

Feminist perspectives on documentary film, and its utility as a tool for activism, and consciousness-raising, extend the theoretical application of feminist frameworks to be inclusive of other essentially non-feminist issues as well, such as the broader realm of human rights. The following scholarship assists in identifying the development of Pakistani filmmakers' own distinct 'standpoints' in the production of their films; for example, the representation of their specific patriarchal, social, and religious contexts, and their depictions of marginalized and victimized groups and individuals.

According to feminist scholar Nancy C. M. Hartsock, feminism is 'a mode of analysis, a method of approaching life and politics, rather than a set of political conclusions about the oppression of women'.[23] She asserts that women who develop a feminist standpoint because of their marginalized status will have a more critical view of the world than their oppressors as they devise strategies to resist oppression and gain empowerment as the underprivileged group.[24] Correspondingly, it can be argued that the espousal of a similar mode of analysis and culture and history-specific standpoint by Pakistani women documentary filmmakers serves as a practical strategy for advocacy and social change through their chosen medium.

Efforts of Pakistani women documentarists lend credence to feminist scholar Susan Moller Okin's focus on the logic and need for rethinking women's rights as essentially an issue of human rights, and hence equal rights. Okin stresses that activists and policy makers should endeavour to make international and national human rights agendas responsive to the predicaments of women.[25]

In their broader application to Pakistani women documentarists, Hartsock and Okin's perspectives help to define the work of these filmmakers as a documentary film category driven by a distinctly *Muslim* feminist standpoint with a focus on women's rights as *human* rights in a Muslim society threatened by religious fundamentalism, extremism, and gender biases. They are telling their stories themselves as opposed to being represented or stereotyped by foreign filmmakers, and media, or being restricted by human rights organizations and researchers as statistical case studies confined to annual reports, or journal articles. This can be seen as an encouraging development as these filmmakers use documentary media as an activist tool to represent and analyse their female subjects' specific problems as human rights issues in a Muslim society.

Speaking from a 'Post-Third World' perspective, film and cultural studies scholar Ella Shohat suggests that Third-World feminisms have very different and diverse problems and areas in which to struggle and reclaim their rights.[26] This is perhaps all the more true when seen in the light of the complex mix of religion and religious fundamentalism, gender biases, politics, and socio-cultural practices, taboos, and constraints in a Muslim society like Pakistan. Shohat calls for a revision of feminist film theory, saying that 'in cinema studies, what has been called "feminist film theory" since the 1970s has often suppressed the historical, economic, and cultural contradictions among women.'[27] Shohat stresses the need to examine issues of nation, race, and gender regarding Third World women because they are negotiating and conducting their resistance against oppression on several, and very different, levels as compared to Western feminists. She argues for new models to view post-Third Wordlist feminist work as opposed to using the old paradigms of Eurocentrism:

> Examining recent Third-World feminist cultural practices only in relation to theories developed by what has been known as 'feminist film theory' reproduces a Eurocentric logic whose narrative beginnings for feminism will inevitably always reside with 'Western' cultural practices and theories seen as straightforwardly pure 'feminism', unlike Third World feminism, seen as 'burdened' by national and ethnic hyphenated identities.[28]

Shohat's critique offers analytical directions for evaluating how Pakistani women filmmakers and their female subjects are uniquely positioned in opposing and critiquing *Sharia* laws, and religious fundamentalism from *within* a Muslim society, without disowning or undermining their *own* Muslim identity. At the same time, Shohat's analytical direction raises the question of how does this ownership and positioning in terms of their own religious and national identity, and gender, also complicate, or restrict, the path of these women documentarists' and their female subjects' activist intent and resistance in a patriarchal society and conservative environments? This enquiry assists in ascertaining the struggle, defiance, and success of Pakistani women filmmakers in achieving their activist intent, and their contribution to a 'Cinema of Accountability'. Shohat's perspectives can of course be inclusive of all activist productions discussed in this study that address issues of marginalization and human rights in Pakistan as a Third World country, not only women filmmakers per se.

Shohat argues for a separate post-Third World feminist category that needs to be applied to identify and recognize such film practices as a diverse and distinct entity in order to appreciate and evaluate it. She stresses that any discussion of Third World must also address the question of the 'national'. Shohat elaborates:

> Rather than merely 'extending' a preexisting First-World feminism, as a certain Euro-'diffusionism' would have it, post-Third-Worldist cultural theories and practices create a more complex space for feminisms open to the specificity of community culture and history. To counter some of the patronizing attitudes toward (post-) Third-World feminist filmmakers – the dark women who now also do the 'feminist' thing – it is necessary to contextualize feminist work in national/racial discourses locally and globally inscribed within multiple oppressions and resistances. Third-World feminist histories can be understood as feminist if seen in conjunction with the resistance work these women have performed within their communities and nations. Any serious discussion of feminist cinema must therefore engage the complex question of the 'national'.[29]

This view on the 'national' question provides an important perspective on Pakistani documentarists' work (not just feminist) in relation to their constraints, limitations, and socio-cultural aspects, particularly the religious and spatial bind so very specific to Muslim women in conservative settings. Further, this view sheds light on their efforts to expose the effects of Islamic fundamentalism, while operating from within the delicate balance of their, and their subjects' national and religious identities. Shohat's perspective gives guidance to the various diversities (historical, cultural, ethnic, religious, socio-political differences, taboos, identities, obligations and loyalties, and various cultural and religious limitations) that Pakistani documentary filmmakers (not just women) have worked with, or around, to represent their cases and critiques. These perspectives can aid further to highlight the country-specific complex political, historical, and cultural differences and problems that distinguish, and beset, the Pakistani society (South Asia) in particular, as opposed to generalizing/essentializing issues (e.g. issues pertaining to the politically manipulated Islamization process, rise of religious extremism and Talibanization, and gender-specific tribal customs) under the broad umbrella of the 'Muslim world' that is usually taken to mean the Middle East/ Arab regions.

Correspondingly, feminist film scholar Julia Lesage points out the political dimensions of feminist documentary film, stating that its particular objective is politically motivated for consciousness-raising and opposing and challenging patriarchal domination of women. Lesage elaborates:

> [T]he women's very redefining of experience is intended to challenge all the previously accepted indices of 'male superiority' and of women's supposedly 'natural' roles. Women's personal explorations establish a structure for social and psychological change and are filmed specifically to combat patriarchy. The filmmaker and her subjects' intent is political.[30]

Lesage's assertion stresses the 'political' scope and utility of feminist documentary through a collective voice – the subjects' as well as the filmmakers' – a factor that is well-understood and illustrated by Pakistani filmmakers' productions in their quest for socio-political and judicial reforms, and protection of human rights.

On the other hand, Lesage also points out that the very strength of such documentaries that record women's *individual* experiences as representations of realism can also be their limitation politically, as they can exclude women's *collective* experiences that can be instrumental in building pressure for social change.[31] However, in the case of Pakistani women documentarists, it can also be argued that with limited resources and opportunities to produce and exhibit their work, and as members and potential victims of the same socio-political environments, oppressive gender-discriminatory laws, and marginalizing practices as their subjects, under the circumstances these filmmakers make use of their privilege and filmmaking ability to at once speak for a collective political intent aimed at social change and reforms.

In her discussion of feminist realism in documentary film, Lesage points to the suitability and usefulness of *cinéma vérité* as a tool and documentary style that favours the feminist agenda. She asserts that 'the major political tool of the contemporary women's movement has been the consciousness-raising group', for which *cinéma vérité* has the potential to prove a most useful feminist tool.[32] Lesage elaborates on the distinct characteristics that can distinguish feminist *cinéma vérité* documentaries as vehicles for change:

> The feminist documentaries represent a use of, yet shift in, the aesthetics of *cinéma vérité* due to the filmmaker's close identification with their subjects, participation in the women's movement, and sense of the film's intended effect ... If one looks closely at the relation of this politicized genre to the movement it is most intimately related to, we can see how both the exigencies and forms of organization of an ongoing political movement can affect the aesthetics of documentary film.[33]

Equally, defending the merits of 'the visual dullness of talking heads' as a narrative style in feminist documentary, Lesage points to its practical utility in encompassing a political and activist intent. She argues that the use of 'talking heads' gives the subjects of the film a chance to speak for themselves, thereby giving voice to 'that which had in the past been spoken for women by patriarchy'.[34]

Similarly, film scholar Barbara Halpern Martineau notes the implications of different documentary techniques used by feminist filmmakers to get their message across. Making a distinction between the use of talking heads to represent some official or authoritative position, and the use of 'talking heads' of people who are telling their own stories, Martineau stresses that women speaking directly to an audience communicate an instant speaker–viewer relationship, thereby creating a feminist bonding for change and resistance.[35] Correspondingly, the same activist intent can be extended to include others also (not only women) who find a voice and platform in Pakistani documentary films to press for justice and accountability, regardless of gender or a purely 'feminist' perspective.

Lesage and Martineau's perspectives aid in evaluating the impact of using talking heads as a strategy to highlight human rights issues by Pakistani documentarists, and how such a strategy adds to their filmic activism by letting their subjects tell their own stories. These perspectives facilitate in examining how Pakistani filmmakers have sought to foster their human rights/feminist, political, and activist agendas, and to study the mergence of theoretical and formal documentary frameworks that provide their subjects a crucial space to speak for themselves, and be their own witnesses and advocates, for example, as in the case of those victimized by biased and discriminatory laws, specific forms of violence and tribal customs (particularly women), or marginalized as religious minorities. Hence, it is significant to note the formal use of talking heads as an activist strategy to empower subjects and victims to have their say in documentaries discussed in this study, be they reportorial, participatory, observational, biographical, or a combination of styles.

Correspondingly, feminist film scholars Diane Waldman and Janet Walker discuss the value and relevance of autobiographical representations and the 'historiographical agency' to tell others' stories in feminist documentary. They believe that since women's history runs as counter-history against patriarchy, they have been 'particularly attuned to the necessarily partial and subjective nature of history writing', and urge 'the potential use of feminist work on autobiography, identity and memory for a documentary theory charged to explain the operations of documentary film as historiography.'[36] In particular, they emphasize the need to fill the vacuum that surrounds women's own accounts in documentary film, stressing the value and relevance of autobiographical representations and the 'historiographical agency' to tell others' stories in feminist theories of autobiography.[37]

Another characteristic of feminist theories of autobiography the authors point to is the emphasis on the lasting significance of the past not only for the present but also for the future. They emphasize the need to fill the void that surrounds women's own accounts in documentary film, suggesting that 'feminist theory-informed' literature can guide the way for filmic depictions that call attention to the lives of 'everyday women'.[38]

Likewise, while the authors stress the need to question the power of the anthropologist and the ethnographic filmmaker, they also point out their value in empowering the filmmaker/subject by providing them the opportunity to speak out:

> Documentaries initiated by people who take up a camera to film their own lives or by people and filmmakers coming together to tell common stories must be appreciated as at least potentially radical, and these documentaries must be instated in the archives of documentary history. Many documentary films and videos spring from deep convictions held jointly by filmmakers and by subjects *as* filmmakers.[39]

On the issue of representing reality and 'realism' in feminist documentary, they point to the formal complications this may entail in addressing a political intent:

While often accused of falling into the realist illusion that documentary films present real women, feminist documentary practices and studies have in fact looked for ways to avoid the illusionist pitfall while at the same time acknowledging the political stakes in representing the images and voices of women who are not professional actors and whose documentary representation seeks to build consensus with actual women for audiences of these films.[40]

Waldman and Walker's perspectives on filmic historiography and autobiography support the significance of Pakistani documentaries in terms of their potential to create consciousness-raising and awareness that could impact future reforms by mobilizing public opinion for social change. Further, it is significant to examine the various differing documentary stylistic approaches and modes Pakistani documentarists have used as a method to depict their subjects and activist intent. For example, as filmmakers how have their combinations of participatory, observational, expository, reportorial, archival compilation, oral histories, voice-overs, and off-screen commentaries and interviews, contributed to their activist agenda to highlight socio-political and human rights issues and problems requiring reforms and justice? What lasting documentary significance do these films achieve by contrasting the voices of powerful elites, officialdom, and groups that hold power over decision-making, including religious scholars and extremist groups, and those that bear the brunt of their politics, ideologies, and decision-making powers? How are the realities and concerns of subservient and marginalized groups (the poor, the illiterate, minorities, women, and children) represented and promoted through the documentary medium as an activist intervention? Waldman and Walker's perspectives offer analytical direction in seeking potential answers to such questions and the critical examination of the activist intent of Pakistani documentaries discussed in this study.

The above perspectives offer a context for the evaluation of Pakistani documentarists' contribution as archival documentation of a socio-cultural and political history and events that is shared between them and their subjects, empowering both to speak through issue-oriented activist investigation, and exposé of a variety of issues that impact and subjugate human rights and individual freedoms – in turn, creating a valuable revisionist filmic history that is based on first hand accounts, and multi-faceted discussions of crucial issues facing contemporary Pakistani society that require reforms.

'Spatial boundaries' and Pakistani women filmmakers

Generally speaking, Pakistani society, largely conservative as it may be, is not rigid or restrictive regarding women's appearance and participation in the public sphere per se, particularly in the urban areas and large cities. However, public critical debates on Islam or critique of religion by *either* gender (leave alone women), particularly the validity of *Sharia* laws in contemporary times, is strongly discouraged both by society and the state, and can prove to be highly risky. Hence, it is significant to consider the role of Pakistani women filmmakers as *Muslim* women stepping out in the public arena to document and question various issues such as those relating to state policies and apathy, religious fundamentalism, discriminatory and controversial laws, and patriarchal practices and tribal customs, including the treatment and status of women with regard to their citizen and individual rights and standing in the ultra-conservative and orthodox regions of the country.

Moroccan Islamic scholar Fatima Mernissi points out the significance of 'spatial boundaries' that can tend to restrict women's public participation in rigid and fundamentalist Islamic societies. Mernissi explains that this 'spatial' restriction is based on the norms of allocation of power in Muslim societies that is a determinant of the participation and visibility of women in the public sphere:

> Muslim sexuality is territorial: its regulatory mechanisms consist primarily in a strict allocation of space to each sex and an elaborate ritual for resolving the contradictions arising from the inevitable intersections of spaces. Apart from the ritualized trespasses of women into public spaces (which are, by definition, male spaces), there are no accepted patterns for interactions between unrelated men and women. Such interactions violate the spatial rules that are the pillars of the Muslim sexual order. Only that which is licit is formally regulated. Since the interaction of men and women is illicit, there are no rules governing it ... Any transgression of the boundaries is a danger to the social order because it is an attack on the acknowledged allocation of power. The link between boundaries and power is particularly salient in a society's sexual patterns.[41]

Although Mernissi's perspective is largely centred around gender in terms of allocation of space regarding sexuality and power, this gender-specific perspective on ' boundaries' in the Islamic context in Muslim societies can be borrowed to highlight the activist role of Pakistani women documentarists, as well as their female subjects, in defying boundaries and navigating their way as Muslim women in rigidly patriarchal, and orthodox regions in Pakistan, particularly the tribal belts in the Khyber Pakhtunkhawa Province bordering Afghanistan.

In particular, by investigating and documenting critical and controversial developments, events, and issues across the breadth of the country, Pakistani women documentarists have cut through the 'social order', 'spatial boundaries', and the religious and socio-cultural constraints detailed by Mernissi. In the process of crossing such specified boundaries that carry the potential to restrict the appearance of Muslim women in the public domain, it can be argued that Pakistani women filmmakers have also defiantly re-appropriated their own and their women subjects' share and visibility in the public sphere to question critical issues, particularly related to religion, through the filmic medium as subsequent discussions on films will illustrate. And in doing so, they have challenged gender-specific marginalization and victimization, particularly on the pretext of religion, as a citizen and human rights issue without disclaiming their own Muslim identities, or rejecting their faith and religious beliefs.

Ironically, for their activist intent, these women filmmakers have also selected the film medium considered by Islamic religious extremists as an instrument of 'Western' culture that corrupts and secularizes.[42] Hence, it is significant to examine how filmmaking intervenes in politics of space, both in its content and as a practice, particularly in the case of Pakistani women filmmakers documenting and critiquing the effects of religious fundamentalism as Muslims themselves from *within* the environment of a Muslim society.

Where relevant, the above arguments and perspectives facilitate an evaluation of their filmic contributions as per an emergent *Muslim* women's cinematic resistance film category that not only defies socio-religious taboos, but also exposes and critiques discriminating religious doctrines, laws, and gender-specific practices through the perspective and voices of Muslim women, both as documentarists, and their female subjects.[43] As they boldly step out in the public sphere to investigate sensitive issues such as *Sharia* laws and gender-discrimination in conservative and orthodox regions, among others, these filmmakers and their productions defy patriarchal constraints in their quest to seek accountability, and to realize their activist intent.

4. Parallels with other activist film currents

Parallels and perspectives from activist film currents such as the Third Cinema and Cinema Novo manifestos and movements of the 1960s and 1970s, and post-Third-Worldist approaches serve to draw a comparison with the activist intent and function of documentary filmmaking practices in contemporary Pakistan. To a large extent, as discussions on films will later depict, the political and theoretical contexts of these cinema frameworks are re-appropriated (if unavowedly), translated, and applied in contemporary terms to Pakistani documentarists and their work.

Emphasizing the utility and impact of 'documentary' film as a means by which a 'cinema of subversion' can be advanced, and the status quo of the 'System' challenged, Third Cinema exponents, Fernando Solanas and Octavio Getino, elaborate:

> The cinema known as documentary, with all the vastness that the concept has today, from educational films to the reconstruction of a fact or a historical event, is perhaps the main basis of revolutionary filmmaking. Every image that documents, bears witness to, refutes or deepens the truth of a situation is something more than a film image or purely artistic fact; it becomes something which the System finds indigestible ... Pamphlet films, didactic films, report films, witness-bearing films–any militant form of expression is valid, and it would be absurd to lay down a set of aesthetic work norms.[44]

In Pakistan's context, the 'system' can be stretched to be inclusive of officialdom,[45] and state versions of particular historical events and transformations in society.[46] The objective in the Pakistani context has not been to subvert the dominant commercial film culture, but to introduce a new one – in this case an activist documentary category that translates into a 'Cinema of Accountability' – and hence to inform and train a new audience through consciousness-raising. In Pakistan's case, this 'system' can be interchanged to stand as a reference to the political and official versions of history and events, and socio-cultural oppressions and dominance, instead of the dominant mainstream Pakistani commercial cinema industry and its monopoly over filmmaking and distribution, such as Hollywood in the West.[47]

Similarly, it can be argued that contemporary Pakistani documentarists are not only providing an alternative counter-history, informed by investigation and supported by testimonies, but also a record that challenges the status quo, and demands accountability.

Ethiopian-American Third World film scholar Gabriel H. Teshome elaborates on the utility and significance of Third Cinema as a tool in the service of retaining and preserving popular memory as opposed to an official and political account of the past.[48] He stresses the significance of Third Cinema as a valuable ongoing vehicle for preserving and promoting shared memories and histories of 'the wretched of the earth', in addition to its application as a political tool to further Third World activisms and struggles:

> Third Cinema, as guardian of popular memory, is an account and record of their visual poetics, their contemporary folklore and mythology, and above all their testimony of existence and struggle. Third Cinema, therefore, serves not only to rescue memories, but rather, and more significantly, to give history a push and popular memory a future.[49]

Similarly, Brazilian film theorist Glauber Rocha's definition of Cinema Novo as a global non-commercial cinematic movement for liberation from oppression and exploitation finds a new resonance and application for the Pakistani experience decades later:

> Wherever there is a film-maker prepared to film the truth and to oppose the hypocrisy and repression of intellectual censorship, there will be the living spirit of Cinema Novo … Wherever there is a film-maker of any age or background, ready to place his cinema in the service of the great cause of his time, there will be the living spirit of Cinema Novo.[50]

In his discussion of Third Cinema,[51] as defined by Argentinian filmmaker Fernando Solanas, and Spanish filmmaker Octavio Getino, film scholar and documentary filmmaker Michael Chanan points to the enrichment and evolution this concept achieved across Latin American countries by various filmmakers as they adopted the essence of its non-commercial, activist, and political effectiveness in addressing their particular national socio-political issues. Chanan points to the shifting and expanding geographies of Third Cinema aesthetics, and its political appeal which have been aided in no small measure by advancements in new cost-effective and accessible film production technologies.[52] As well, he points out, these influences were not limited to Latin America, but extended to other continents too. Third Cinema aesthetics began to serve a transnational function when it attracted international attention, and influenced filmmakers in regions as far as Egypt, and Morocco. Similarly, a General Assembly of Third-World filmmakers was held in Algeria in 1973 to consider the role of film in the struggle against imperialism and neo-colonialism, and the problems of international cooperation.[53]

It can be argued that the new geographical shifts in the activist essence and spirit of Third Cinema and Third Aesthetics have also extended to Pakistani documentary films. This spirit can be traced in the activist intent of Pakistani filmmakers who are working in another culture, and investigating its historical and political realities. Today, this contemporary geographical shift, that includes foreign/Western-funded collaborative film productions in Pakistan, is focusing on critiquing militancy wrought on the pretext of religious identity through Islamic fundamentalism, violence, terrorism, and violation of human rights in another part of the world. Hence, the activist spirit and intent of Third Cinema and Third Aesthetics remains intact as discussed by many prominent Latin American filmmakers in Michael Chanan's documentary, *The Roots of Third Cinema: New Cinema of Latin America* (2010).[54] Further, the cross-cultural communication of this activist intent is strengthened as technological developments such as cable networks, satellite transmissions, and growing number of TV channels, and other Internet and online outlets such as the YouTube and web portals expand global viewing platforms for circulation and exhibition of documentaries from all over the world (overriding political, temporal, and spatial constraints) both those made in democracies and under dictatorships.[55] These technological advancements are enhancing and fostering the production and international reach of 'third cinema, third video, and even third television' that Chanan pointed out in his article in 1997, stressing the need to identify their expanding and changing geographies.[56] As this study illustrates more than a decade and a half later, the new and 'expanding' geography for Third Cinema can be seen to be inclusive of discussion on Pakistani activist documentaries as well.

In light of the criteria set out by the above scholars, it can be argued that the Third Cinema and Cinema Novo perspectives and manifestos have been re-appropriated (if unavowedly) by Pakistani documentarists to forge their own distinct 'activist documentary' category at another time, in other contexts, and on another continent.

Correspondingly, film scholar Ella Shohat draws attention to a post-Third-Worldist view of Third Cinema perspectives to shed light on their broad contextual scope, both formal as well as political.[57] Pointing to an 'eclipse of the revolutionary paradigm', Shohat asks: 'what, then, are some of the new modes of a multicultural feminist aesthetics of resistance? And in what ways do they simultaneously continue and rupture previous Third-Worldist film culture?'[58] Shohat goes on to elaborate on the cinemas of resistance of the past, and how their interpretation and application can vary in different contexts:

But the resistant practices of the films advocated by Glauber Rocha, Julio Garcia Espinosa, Fernando Solanas and Octavio Getino are neither homogenous nor static; they vary over time, from region to region, and, in genre, from epic costume drama to personal small-budget documentary ... As with Third-Worldist cinema and with First-World independent production, post-Third-Worldist feminist films and videos conduct a struggle on two fronts, at once aesthetic and political, synthesizing revisionist historiography with formal innovation.[59]

Shohat's perspectives on Third Cinema and post-Third-Worldist feminist films can be extended to include the broader realm of activist documentary film practices that have emerged in contemporary Pakistan. Just as these Latin American manifestos and film movements sought to challenge and subvert the status quo of official and state versions of history by advocating an independent, alternative, and counter-history approach, Pakistani documentarists have sought to do likewise in their historical contexts.

However, although the above-mentioned frameworks can facilitate discussion and evaluation, a significant basic difference and distinction that needs to be remembered in the development and emergence of Pakistani activist documentary is that it was not primarily inspired by poverty, social and class discrimination, or purely political oppression alone. Rather, it is rooted in the oppressive effects of politicization of religion that included imposition of rigid Islamic *Sharia* laws, and their consequent impact on the violation of citizen and human rights, particularly women. It can be argued then, that the spirit of 'Cinema Novo' in the Pakistani context has evolved into an activist documentary film category that can be defined as a documentary 'Cinema of Accountability'. Today, this emergent activist film category not only seeks to depict realities, social ills, and problems in contemporary Pakistani society, but in doing so has keenly begun to provoke debate and demand answers and reforms (e.g. from Islamic scholars and legal experts, government and law enforcement bodies, and patriarchal and tribal institutions as depicted in the films discussed) for violations and excesses wrought on the pretext of religion (Islamic/Muslim national identity), culture, and so-called 'honour'.

The above-mentioned frameworks, film perspectives, and parallels with other cinema currents facilitate discussion of Pakistani documentary films that deal with a host of issues: politicization of religion; women's marginalization; minority and human rights abuse; *Sharia* laws; politics, Islamic fundamentalism, and religious extremism; terrorism; and consciousness-raising about gender-specific tribal and cultural practices, including violence against women, that are the subject of films in the following chapters. Together, the themes and perspectives discussed in this chapter facilitate an inter-disciplinary contextual-reading and analysis of the selected issue-oriented films, and aid in establishing a theoretical foundation and definition of the emergent activist film category from within the Muslim state of Pakistan – one that can be distinguished as a 'Cinema of Accountability'.

5. Pakistani cinema under Islamization: a brief synopsis

A lengthy discussion on this topic during the eleven-year dictatorship of General Zia-ul-Haq is not within the scope of this book. However, a concise synopsis of the developments in Pakistani film industry during the Islamization period highlights the transformations that were being enforced by the state and fundamentalist Islamic ideologies, and contextualizes the emergence of activist documentary filmmaking practice in Pakistan that is rooted in issues of religious fundamentalism.

During, and since, the late 1980s in Pakistan, the activist and creative intent began to shift to documentaries made by independent filmmakers and non-governmental organizations since the advent of video technology (home-VCRs), easy availability of pirated versions of Indian Bollywood feature films, and government neglect and strict censorship policies discouraged the production and exhibition of meaningful mainstream films that could focus on socio-political issues. During the regime of General Zia-ul-Haq's martial law, there was a tremendous decline in quality film production, while a culture of mediocre, violent films emerged in an environment of widespread human rights violations, corruption, and violence. Pakistani filmmaker, and historian Mushtaq Gazdar explains the overall deterioration of the Pakistani society during General Zia-ul-Haq's martial law years, and its impact on Pakistani cinema:

> In consequence, the country went through a period of crimes, killings, and violation of human rights and this gave rise to a most appallingly unstable law and order situation. Likewise, the cinema culture was adversely affected by the happenings in the country. The coming years saw the development of a new genre of cinema, glamourizing violence, and advocating brutality as a normal form of vengeance.[60]

For example, most notable of this emergent cinema was *Maula Jat*[61] (1979), a lengthy (180 mins) Punjabi feature film filled with intense depictions of violence and vengeance, which won unprecedented popularity with Pakistani audiences, and its portrayal of the soft-spoken but merciless villain – Nuri Nath, 'a man obsessed with vanquishing anyone who claims to be more powerful than him' – closely echoed Zia-ul-Haq's own soft-spoken but ruthless character.[62] However, two months into its running, the Zia government moved to have it banned, as Gazdar explains:

> Later Zia's government decided to ban the film by cancelling its censor certificate for reasons other than the political insinuations in the movie. It was ridiculous that an administration which, at public floggings, fixed microphones near the mouths of the victims to amplify their agonized screams for the edification of the huge crowd, and which made elaborate arrangements to stage public hangings of condemned convicts of military courts, considered the film too violent for viewing by the general public.[63]

However, as the producer managed to obtain a stay order from the High Court against the Censor Board, the film continued to run continuously for two and a half years while the litigation proceeded. But on expiration of the stay order, the film was forcibly taken down from cinema houses by the police.[64]

Against such a political backdrop, it becomes obvious why Pakistani filmmakers and non-governmental organizations that intended to serve an activist purpose, began to turn to documentary film as their tool for resistance and consciousness-raising. This emergent activity also saw the rise of foreign donor collaborations as with foreign channels and rights organizations for the production and exhibition of their films.

During the Zia era, the Pakistani commercial film industry continued to experience an all-time decline, as many cinema houses were demolished to make way for shopping malls and commercial plazas, while film production itself remained at a miserably low level due to lack of funding and modern equipment, low turnout of audiences, government neglect, and competition from Indian Bollywood films (allowed exhibition in Pakistani theatres after a ban was lifted after nearly four decades in 2008), all taking precedence in the few good cinemas that remain in provincial capitals.[65] Pakistani journalist and cultural critic Nadeem F. Paracha points out: 'By the early 2000's, an industry that once produced an average of 80 films annually was now struggling to even churn out more than two films a year.'[66]

Over the years, the number of cinemas in Pakistan declined from 750 in the 1970s, to 300 in 2008.[67] Additionally, the rising cost of land and the advent of cable networks further reduced their numbers. In Lahore alone, the provincial capital of Punjab and hub of the Pakistani film industry after partition from India, only 23 cinemas remained of the 63 cinemas that existed in 1973.[68]

However, it is promising to note that since 2007 Pakistani mainstream cinema has been on its way to a modest recovery and revival despite the many hurdles that remain such as access to funding, high import taxes on equipment, an environment of religious extremism and threat of attacks on cinema houses by pro-Taliban militants, and government apathy towards the promotion of domestic cinema.[69]

Nevertheless, a new crop of independent Pakistani filmmakers are beginning to lure audiences, both at home and abroad, with slick and entertaining mainstream cinema productions, and modern multiplexes are beginning to make an entry at least in the major cities of the country.[70] Once again, new digital technologies are enabling a fresh generation of Pakistani filmmakers to inject life in the hitherto crippled film industry, and produce works for their home audiences.[71]

Conclusion

In the absence of a theoretical framework from which contemporary Pakistani activist documentary filmmaking practices can be evaluated, it has been the intent of this chapter to survey, analyse, and synthesize key works on activist documentary filmmaking from outside Pakistan as building blocks for a theory relevant to Pakistan. The themes considered in this chapter include:

1. Perspectives on the contextual and historical approach to documentary filmmaking and the role of the filmmaker (Viola Shafik; Chuck Kleinhans; Trinh T. Minh-ha; Julio Garcia Espinosa; Bill Nichols; Paula Rabinowitz; Keith Beattie; Jack C. Ellis and Betsy A. Lane).
2. Perspectives on the activist and political intent of documentary film (Thomas Waugh; Erik Barnouw; Michael Renov; Bill Nichols).
3. Feminist perspectives on documentary film and activism (Nancy C. M. Hartsock; Susan Moller Okin; Ella Shohat; Julia Lesage; Barbara Halpern Martineau; Diane Waldman and Janet Walker), and the concept of 'Spatial Boundaries' with regard to gender in Muslim societies (Fatima Mernissi).
4. Parallels with other activist film currents such as the Third Cinema, Cinema Novo, and post-Third-Worldist approaches (Fernando Solanas and Octavio Getino; Gabriel H. Teshome; Glauber Rocha; Michael Chanan; Ella Shohat).

Additionally, perspectives on gender-specific 'spatial boundaries' (Fatima Mernissi) in the Islamic context in Muslim societies helps to elaborate on the role of Pakistani women documentarists in navigating their way as Muslim women in rigidly patriarchal and orthodox regions in Pakistan, particularly the tribal belts bordering Afghanistan.

Similarly, a brief synopsis of the developments in the Pakistani film industry under the Islamization period (Mushtaq Gazdar) highlights transformative fundamentalist Islamic ideologies and strict censorship policies that were being enforced by the state at the time, hence contextualizing the emergence of an activist documentary filmmaking practice in Pakistan that is rooted in issues of religious fundamentalism as its starting point. This synopsis also briefly elaborates on the present revival of the cinema industry in Pakistan, spurred on by a new generation of filmmakers, digital technologies, and the advent of multiplexes in the country.

Together, the themes and perspectives discussed in this chapter facilitate an interdisciplinary contextual reading and analyses of the selected issue-oriented films, and aid in establishing a theoretical foundation that leads to the definition of the emergent activist film category from within the Muslim state of Pakistan – one that can be distinguished as a 'Cinema of Accountability' in the following chapters on films.

Notes

1. The categories of perspectives and frameworks, although listed separately in this chapter, combine to assist analyses in all the chapters on films, given the overlaps that occur in terms of their prevailing themes, subjects, and content. (For example, law and gender, politics and human rights, and gender and human rights).
2. Viola Shafik, 'Introduction', *Arab Cinema: History and Cultural Identity* (revised edition), The American University in Cairo Press, Cairo, Egypt, New York, 2007, p. 4.

3. Chuck Kleinhans, 'Forms, Politics, Makers and Contexts: Basic Issues for a Theory of Radical Political Documentary', in Thomas Waugh (ed.), *"Show Us Life": Toward a History and Aesthetics of the Committed Documentary*, The Scarecrow Press, Inc. Metuchen, NJ, and London, 1984, p. 320.
4. Ibid., p. 318.
5. Trinh T. Minh-ha, 'An All-Owning Spectatorship', *When the Moon Waxes Red: Representation, Gender, and Cultural Politics.* Routledge, New York, USA, 1991, p. 81.
6. Ibid., pp. 100–1.
7. Julio Garcia Espinosa, 'For An Imperfect Cinema', in Michael Chanan (ed.), *Twenty-Five Years of the New Latin American Cinema,*. BFI Books, UK, 1983, p. 28. The original essay was published in *Cine Cubano*, No. 66/67, in 1970.
8. Ibid., p. 31.
9. The Pakistani commercial cinema industry, also nick-named Lollywood, (after the Punjab provincial capital city, Lahore, where the industry is concentrated) can be seen as a smaller version of the Indian film industry, Bollywood, that has been producing very similar romantic musicals and action films.
10. Bill Nichols, 'Why Are Ethical Issues Central to Documentary Filmmaking?', *Introduction to Documentary*, Indiana University Press, Bloomington, IN and Indianapolis, IN, 2001, p. 18.
11. Paula Rabinowitz, 'Wreckage Upon Wreckage: History, Documentary, and the Ruins of Memory', *They Must Be Represented: The Politics of Documentary*, Verso, London, New York, 1994, p. 17.
12. Keith Beattie, 'Finding and Keeping; Compilation Documentary', *Documentary Screens: Non-fiction Film and Television*, Houndsmills, Palgrave, 2004, pp. 125–9.
    Keith Beattie gives the examples of *The Atomic Café*, a film made in 1984, which created a new anti-war message using old archival footage from WWII (ibid., p. 137), and the contestation of history and long-held beliefs in films like *JFK*, which reinvestigates and re-evaluates history through archival footage (ibid., p. 143).
13. Jack C. Ellis and Betsy A. McLane, *A New History of Documentary*, Continuum, New York, London, 2005, pp. 258–64.
14. Thomas Waugh, 'Why Documentary Filmmakers Keep Trying to Change the World, Or Why People Changing the World Keep Making Documentaries', in Thomas Waugh (ed.), *"Show Us Life": Towards a History and Aesthetics of the Committed Documentary*, The Scarecrow Press, Inc. Metuchen, N.J. and London, 1984, p. xiv.
15. Erik Barnouw, *Documentary: A History of the Non-Fiction Film.* Oxford University Press, Oxford, 1974, p. 29.
16. Michael Renov, 'Towards a Poetics of Documentary', in Michael Renov (ed.), *Theorizing Documentary*, Routledge, New York, London, 1993, p. 27.
17. Michael Renov, 'The Subject in History: The New Autobiography in Film and Video', *The Subject of Documentary*, University of Minnesota Press, Minneapolis, MN and London, 2004, pp. 109–10.
18. Bill Nichols, 'What Are Documentaries About?', *Introduction to Documentary*, Indiana University Press, Bloomington, IN and Indianapolis, IN, 2001, p. 70.
19. Ibid., p. 70.
20. Although the word 'feminist' as per its Western connotation has been appropriated by Western-educated Pakistani women's rights activists and academics, I use 'feminist' perspectives on documentary film in the broader terms of gender rights as human rights issues, rather than strictly women's rights alone. Subsequent discussions of films, and issues pertaining to women, will highlight the limitations of this term in the Pakistani socio-historical and political context that is further complicated by issues of religion, tribal traditions and customs, and *Sharia*-based gender-specific legislations in a Muslim state.
21. For further details on Pakistani women's participation in films visit *Pakistan Film Magazine.* Accessed at: http://mazhar.dk/film/history/ on March 14, 2015.

36 *A Theory of 'Cinema of Accountability'*

22 For further details on these filmmakers and their productions see Rahat Imran, 'Cinema: Films Made by Women Screen Writers, Directors, Producers: Women Documentary Filmmakers: Pakistan', *Encyclopedia of Women & Islamic Cultures*, Brill, 2010, Brill Online. Access at Brill Online: http://referenceworks.brillonline.com/search?s.q=rahat+imran&s.f.s2_parent=s.f.book.encyclopedia-of-women-and-islamic-cultures&search-go=Search.
23 Nancy C. M. Hartsock, 'Fundamental Feminism: Process and Perspective', *The Feminist Standpoint Revisited and Other Essays*, Westview Press, CO, 1998, p. 35.
24 'The Nature of a Standpoint', ibid., p. 107.
25 Susan Moller Okin, 'Feminism, Women's Rights, and Cultural Differences', in Uma Narayan and Sandra Harding (eds), *Decentering the Centre: Philosophy for a Multicultural, Postcolonial, and Feminist World*, Indiana University Press, Bloomington, IN and Indianapolis, IN, 2000, p. 28.
26 Ella Shohat elaborates on 'post-Third-Worldist' formulation: 'Whereas the term "postcolonial" implies a movement beyond anticolonial nationalist ideology and a movement beyond a specific point of colonial history, post-Third-Worldism conveys a movement "beyond" a specific ideology – Third-Worldist nationalism. A post-Third-Worldist perspective assumes the fundamental validity of the anticolonial movement, but also interrogates the divisions that rend the Third-World nation.' Ella Shohat, 'Framing Post-Third-Worldist Culture: Gender and Nation in Middle Eastern/North African Film and Video'. Accessed at: http://english.chass.ncsu.edu/jouvert/v1i1/SHOHAT.HTM on March 15, 2015.
27 Ella Shohat, 'Post-Third-Worldist Culture: Gender, Nation and the Cinema', in Anthony R. Guneratne and Wimal Dissanayake (eds), *Rethinking Third Cinema*, Routledge, New York and London, 2003, p. 52.
28 Ibid., p. 53.
29 Ibid., p. 54.
30 Julia Lesage, 'The Political Aesthetics of the Feminist Documentary Film', in Patricia Erens (ed.), *Issues in Feminist Film Criticism*, Indiana University Press, Bloomington, IN and Indianapolis, IN, 1990, p. 224.
31 Ibid., p. 224.
32 Ibid., pp. 229–30.
33 Ibid., pp. 235–6.
34 Ibid., pp. 233–4.
35 Barbara Halpern Martineau stresses the use of talking heads as a style particularly effective for conveying a feminist message: 'It seems useful at this point to make a general distinction between the use of talking heads to represent some official or authoritative position, and the use of talking heads of people who are telling their own stories. Another, more formal three-part distinction can be made among: 1) Interviews where the subject addresses someone who is either off-screen or on; 2) candid or informal discussions filmed in close-up; and 3) direct address to the camera, where the subject appears to be talking to the audience.' Barbara Halpern Martineau, 'Talking About Our Lives and Experiences: Some Thoughts About Feminism, Documentary and "Talking Heads"', in Thomas Waugh (ed.), *"Show Us Life": Toward a History and Aesthetics of the Committed Documentary*, The Scarecrow Press, Inc., Metuchen, NJ and London, 1984, p. 259.
36 Diane Waldman and Janet Walker, 'Introduction', in Diane Waldman and Janet Walker (eds), *Feminism and Documentary,* University of Minnesota Press, Minneapolis, MN, 1999, pp. 1–2.
37 Ibid., p. 22.
38 Ibid., pp. 22–3.
39 Ibid., p. 17.
40 Ibid., pp. 11–12.

41 Fatima Mernissi, 'The Meaning of Spatial Boundaries', in Reina Lewis and Sara Mills (eds), *Feminist Postcolonial Theory: A Reader*, Routledge, New York, 2003, p. 489.

42 Hamid Naficy, 'Islamizing Film Culture in Iran', in Richard Tapper (ed.), *The New Iranian Cinema: Politics, Representation and Identity*, I. B. Tauris Publishers, London, New York, 2002, p. 27.

43 Today, one can find a substantial body of literature, research, critiques, and scholarly work on films made in the Muslim world, and by Muslims filmmakers, both men and women. This is a clear indication that the film tradition has also been successfully and defiantly used by Muslim women, both for artistic and consciousness-raising purposes, despite claims by orthodox Islamic scholars and clerics regarding women's participation in the public arena as 'un-Islamic'. Discussions and critiques of films and filmmakers from other Muslim countries that have seen their share of religious fundamentalism, unjust and discriminatory socio-cultural practices, and political/colonial upheavals range from volumes on Post-colonial, Maghrebian, North African, Iranian, Turkish, and Arab cinema, and also include Diaspora cinemas pertaining to these regions. For example, see following volumes: Shohini Chaudhuri, *Contemporary World Cinema: Europe, the Middle East, East Asia and South Asia*, Edinburgh University Press, 2005; Gönül Colin-Dönmez, *Women, Islam and Cinema*, Reaktion Books Ltd, UK, 2004; Kenneth W. Harrow (ed.), *African Cinema: Postcolonial and Feminist Readings*, Africa World Press, Inc, Asmara, Eritrea, 1999; Gonul Colin-Donmez, *Cinemas of the Other: A Personal Journey with Filmmakers from the Middle East and Central Asia*, Intellect Books, Bristol, UK, Portland, OR, 2006; Oliver Leaman (ed.), *Companion Encyclopedia of Middle Eastern and North African Film*, Routledge, London and New York, 2001; Roy Armes, *Postcolonial Images: Studies in North African Film*, Indiana University Press, Bloomington, IN and Indianapolis, IN, 2005; Hamid Naficy, *An Accented Cinema: Exilic and Diasporic Filmmaking*, Princeton University Press, Princeton, NJ, 2001; Roy Armes and Lizbeth Malkmus, *Arab and African Film Making*, Zed Books Ltd, London and New Jersey, 1991; Richard Tapper (ed.), *The New Iranian Cinema: Politics, Representation and Identity*, I. B. Tauris Publishers, London, New York, 2002; Hamid Dabashi, *Close Up: Iranian Cinema, Past Present and Future*, Verso Press, UK, USA, 2001; Rebecca Hillauer, *Encyclopedia of Arab Women Filmmakers*. (translated from German into English by Allison Brown, Deborah Cohen, and Nancy Joyce), The American University in Cairo Press, Cairo, New York, 2005.

44 Fernando Solanas and Octavio Getino, *'Towards a Third Cinema'* (1969) in Bill Nichols (ed.), *Movies and Methods*, University of California Press, Berkley, CA, 1994, pp. 55–6.

45 Pakistani journalist and media historian, Zamir Niazi, notes on state censorship policies during General Zia-ul-Haq's Islamization period: 'Blanket censorship of all printed and audio-visual matter was imposed in October 1979 (along with an "indefinite postponement" of general elections and a ban on all political parties). It covered all dailies, periodicals, books, pamphlets, posters, handbills, photographs, motion pictures, dramatic and stage productions, phonographic records, radio and television programmes ... All entry points in the country were heavily guarded – land, sea and air. Specialities of the Customs officials dealing with printed matter were to blacken the "objectionable" portions with thick markers, tear off pages and photographs or seize offending publications and confiscate them.' Zamir Niazi, 'Darkness at Noon', *The Web of Censorship*, Oxford University Press, Karachi, Pakistan, 1994, p. 3.

46 For example, for critical discussions on state-enforced manipulation of historical facts in Pakistani school curricula and history and social studies textbooks by respective authoritarian regimes see: K. K. Aziz, *The Murder of History: A Critique of History Textbooks Used in Pakistan*, Vanguard Books, Lahore, Pakistan, 1993; and A. H. Nayyar and Ahmad Salim (eds), *The Subtle Subversion: The State of Curricula and*

38 A Theory of 'Cinema of Accountability'

Textbooks in Pakistan: Urdu, English, Social Studies and Civics, Sustainable Development Policy Institute, (SDPI), Islamabad, Pakistan, 2002.

47 In their manifesto, entitled 'Towards a Third Cinema,' Fernando Solanas and Octavio Getino described First Cinema primarily as the Hollywood production model of big monopoly, capital finances, and big spectacle cinema, Second Cinema primarily as European authorial and art cinema, and Third Cinema as an alternative to dominant mainstream commercial cinemas. According to film theorist Paul Willemen: 'Solanas aligns First, Second and Third Cinemas with three social strata: the bourgeoisie, the petit bourgeoisie, and the people, the latter included industrial workers, small and landless peasants, the unemployed, the lumpenproletariat, and students, etc.' Paul Willemen, 'The Third Cinema Question: Notes and Reflections', in Jim Pines and Paul Willemen (eds), *Questions of Third Cinema,* 1989, London, BFI, 1989, p. 9.

48 H. Gabriel Teshome, 'Third Cinema as Guardian of Popular Memory: Towards a Third Aesthetics', in Jim Pines and Paul Willemen (eds), *Questions of Third Cinema*, London, BFI, UK, 1989, pp. 53–4.

49 Ibid., pp. 63–4.

50 Glauber Rocha, 'The Aesthetics of Hunger' (1965), in Michael Chanan (ed.), *Twenty-Five Years of the New Latin American Cinema*, BFI Books, UK, 1983, p. 13.

51 Solanas and Getino, 'Towards a Third Cinema'.

52 Michael Chanan, 'The Changing Geography of Third Cinema', *Screen*, 38.4, Winter 1997, pp. 372–88.

53 Ibid., p. 336.

For further details of the General Assembly of Third-World Filmmakers see: 'Resolutions of the Third World Filmmakers Meeting, Algiers, December 5–14, 1973', *Black Camera*, 2.1, Winter 2010, pp. 155–65.

54 *The Roots of Third Cinema: New Cinema of Latin America,* Michael Chanan, (28 min 40 secs). English sub-titles. Channel 4, UK, 1983. Accessed at: http://vimeo.com/12888864 on March 18, 2015.

55 Chanan 'The Changing Geography of Third Cinema', p. 381.

56 Ibid., pp. 383–4.

57 Shohat '*Framing Post-Third-Worldist Culture: Gender and Nation in Middle Eastern/ North African Film and Video*' Accessed at: http://english.chass.ncsu.edu/jouvert/v1i1/SHOHAT.HTM on March 18, 2015.

58 Ella Shohat, 'Post-Third-Worldist Culture: Gender, Nation and the Cinema', in Anthony R. Guneratne and Wimal Dissanayake (eds), *Rethinking Third Cinema*, Routledge, New York and London, 2003, p. 54.

59 Ibid., p. 55.

60 Mushtaq Gazdar, '1977–86: A Decade of Decadence', *Pakistan Cinema 1947–1997*, Oxford University Press, Karachi, Pakistan, 1998, p. 154.

61 *Maula Jat*, Yunus Malik, 1979 (180 min.), Punjabi, Pakistan.

For detailed discussion on *Maula Jat* and the cinema environment in Pakistan during the Zia regime see Nadeem F. Paracha, 'Maula Jatt: The Secret History', *The Daily Dawn*. October 19, 2014. Accessed at: http://www.dawn.com/news/1138375/maula-jatt-the-secret-history on March 18, 2015.

62 Gazdar '1977–86: A Decade of Decadence', p. 164.

63 Ibid., p. 166.

64 Ibid., p. 166.

65 Jam Sajjad, 'Indian Movies Dominate Lahore Cinemas', *The Daily Nation*, August 3, 2009. Accessed at: http://www.nation.com.pk/pakistan-news-newspaper-daily-english-online/Politics/03-Aug-2009/Indian-movies-dominate-Lahore-cinemas on March 18, 2015.

66 Nadeem F. Paracha, 'New-wave of Pakistani Cinema: Zinda and Kicking', *Dawn.com*. September 26, 3013. Accessed at: http://www.dawn.com/news/1045365/new-wave-of-pakistani-cinema-zinda-and-kicking on March 18, 2015.

67 Aftab Bokra, 'Indian Films Breathe Life into Pakistani Cinemas', April 25, 2008. Accessed at: http://www.reuters.com/article/idUSISL17078720080425 on March 18, 2015.
68 According to a survey conducted by film experts in 1973, there were 63 cinemas in Lahore, 18 in Rawalpindi, 19 in Multan, 19 in Faisalabad, 11 in Gujranwala, 12 in Sialkot, 12 in Peshawar, 86 in Karachi, 20 in Hyderabad, six in Sukkur, and eight in Quetta. The number had reduced to 23 in Lahore, 12 in Rawalpindi, 14 in Multan, 13 in Faisalabad, 10 in Gujranwala, eight in Sialkot, 36 in Karachi, four in Hyderabad, one in Sukkur, and five in Quetta. Shoaib Ahmed, 'Advent of Cable Industry Brings Doom to Cinema', *The Daily Times*, September 22, 2005. Accessed at: http://archives.dailytimes.com.pk/national/22-Sep-2005/advent-of-cable-industry-brings-doom-to-cinema on January 11, 2016.
69 However, given the recent surge in local productions, and the steady releases of Bollywood films, a trend towards multiplexes is developing. For further discussion see Mazhar Zaidi, 'Cinema in Pakistan: The Way Ahead', *The Daily Dawn*, June 4, 2014. Accessed at: http://www.dawn.com/news/1109137/cinema-in-pakistan-the-way-ahead on April 11, 2015.

For a discussion on the rise of multiplexes in Pakistan also see Annabel Symington, 'Movies Begin to Take Root in Pakistan.' *The Wall Street Journal*, March 20, 2014. Accessed at: http://www.wsj.com/articles/SB10001424052702303546204579439371307729670 on June 25, 2015.

Novelist and writer Bina Shah points out: 'In 2006, Pervez Musharraf, as president, began to ease restrictions on the importation of Indian films, which had been banned in Pakistan since the war between the countries in 1965. The newly available Bollywood productions drew so many viewers that multiplexes were built to meet the demand. The new capacity, in turn, gave a new generation of Pakistanis, either trained abroad or already working in television and advertising, an incentive to start making movies of their own. With advances in digital filmmaking permitting lower budgets and an audience already exposed to high-quality international cinema, Pakistanis began to produce bold works.' Bina Shah, 'Pakistani Cinema's New Wave', January 14, 2014. *The New York Times*. Accessed at: http://www.nytimes.com/2014/01/15/opinion/shah-pakistani-cinemas-new-wave.html?hp&rref=opinion&_r=1 on March 18, 2015.
70 Jon Boone, 'Pakistan's Movie-makers Dig Deep to Revive Film Industry', *The Guardian*, May 31, 2013. Accessed at: http://www.theguardian.com/world/2013/may/31/pakistan-film-competition-bollywood on March 18, 2015.
71 For discussion on the role of digital technologies in the revival of film production in Pakistan see: Wajahat Ali, 'Hollywood. Bollywood. Karachi? The Life, Death, and Rebirth of Pakistani Cinema', *Digital Trends*, June 21, 2015. Accessed at: http://www.digitaltrends.com/movies/pakistani-film-cinema/ on June 25, 2015.

2 Injustices on film

A reading of activist documentaries against the legacy of Islamization

Introduction

As General Zia-ul-Haq sought to legitimize his dictatorial rule by Islamizing the country's criminal justice system through the imposition of the *Hudood* Ordinances, the Law of Evidence, and the Blasphemy Law, socio-legal issues came to dominate the emergence of activist documentary film practice in Pakistan. (See Appendices 1, 2, and 3 for explanation of these laws.)

Taking Zia's Islamization period that transformed the socio-political landscape of Pakistan as the starting point, this chapter will discuss the role of six chosen representative documentary films, independent documentary filmmakers, organizations, and collaborations in depicting the oppressive effects of politicization of religion on the Pakistani civil society, particularly on women, and religious minorities.[1] In tracing the legacy of the Islamization era, these contextual readings of films highlight the *politicization* of religion through the intersection of religion, politics, and law that played a critical role in the promulgation of rigid *Sharia* laws, mentioned above, that served in curtailing individual rights and freedoms, marginalization of women's rights and their legal status, and victimization of religious minorities, such as the Christian community. These filmic readings shed light on the serious repercussions the Islamization period had on the transformation of the Pakistani society from a fairly secular and progressive one to one suffocated and held hostage by fear and punishment through Zia's cunning manipulation of religion to legitimize and entrench his dictatorship on the pretext of bringing an 'Islamic' order and identity to Pakistan. At the same time, the depictions and critiques offered by these documentaries and their makers highlight the activist voices and filmic practices that have contributed to the roots and emergence of an investigative and oppositional Pakistani documentary category that this book defines as a 'Cinema of Accountability' – one that is committed to consciousness-raising, advocacy, social change, and a struggle for upholding human rights by questioning and rejecting the negative and suffocating impact of Islamic fundamentalism and extremism by filmmakers from within a Muslim state.

In conclusion, this chapter will evaluate the activist role and contribution of these representative films, filmmakers, organizations, and collaborations in investigating, highlighting, and preserving a critical counter-history of Pakistan's descent into religious fundamentalism and its far-reaching effects on society, and their significance in the development of an emergent filmic channel of struggle and resistance.

To facilitate a contextual discussion of filmmakers and organizations that have specifically focused on the legacy of the Islamization period, the chapter will begin with a brief background to the organized women's resistance movement that emerged as a significant consequence of this era, and has continued to be an oppositional force in its struggle against religious fundamentalism, violation of human rights, and curtailment and marginalization of women's rights and equal status.[2]

Background to the women's resistance movement and organizations in Pakistan

It is important to note that until the introduction of the *Zina Hudood* Ordinance in 1979, the women's organizations that existed in Pakistan were non-political entities, mainly involved with social welfare work for women, children, and the poor.[3] However, the beginning of the 1980s saw an unprecedented mass mobilization of politically inclined women in Pakistan to take on and challenge gender-discriminatory laws, thereby initiating an organized women's movement in the country that had a political as well as a 'feminist' and social agenda. Realizing that women were the first targets of Zia's politically motivated Islamization and *Sharia* laws, educated urban women were amongst those who began to form alliances to protest against the new laws. Among the various women's organizations that have come into existence over the years, the *Shirkat Gah* (Participation Forum), *Simorgh*, the *Aurat* Foundation (Woman Foundation), Progressive Women's Association (PWA), and *ASR* (Impact – Applied Socio-economic Research Foundation and Resource Centre) emerged as major multidisciplinary resource centres that fostered activism and research on women's issues. Similarly, the legal fraternity also sprang into action, and free legal aid cells came into existence such as the AGHS Legal Aid Cell, the Pakistan Women Lawyers Association (PAWLA), and Lawyers for Human Rights and Legal Aid (LHRLA). Catering mostly to poor women implicated in *Zina Hudood* Ordinance cases, they also arranged shelter for them. The majority of these non-government organizations (NGOs) are free of any direct political affiliation, and largely depend upon international donor agencies for funding.

These organizations and fraternities have also worked collaboratively on various activist and advocacy projects (including documentary films) to push for the amendment or repeal of existing discriminatory laws, and formulation of new ones. Other significant areas of intervention have included domestic violence against women, education, development, discriminatory laws and customs, healthcare, and spreading family planning awareness and choices for women.[4]

The women's organizations mentioned above have evolved into research and resource centres for human rights scholars and activists. These organizations introduced a new wave of women's activism and pedagogical experiments in Pakistan as part of their resistance. These include education and media awareness campaigns, international networking, writing and publishing, and participation in international women's conferences to forge cross-cultural alliances. They also regularly organize seminars and workshops to highlight women's rights issues in Pakistan, while conducting awareness programmes in rural areas through their research teams.[5]

It was also against the changing scenario brought on by Islamization that a vast number of urban Pakistani women started to travel to the West to study women's issues and gender development. They returned with the aim of generating an activism-oriented women's movement for emancipation and equal rights, as a result of which numerous NGOs began to emerge to fill the need.[6] These organizations are run and staffed by trained professionals that include educators, sociologists, artists, lawyers, and human rights activists, with a shared and collaborative focus on education, research, publishing, advocacy, and activism in the areas of human and gender rights. It is significant to note that most of these NGOs also offer internships in various disciplines and areas of research on human rights and women's issues as part of their advocacy and training programmes, thereby extending their activist agendas and base.

The countrywide resistance by women's organizations and the legal fraternity, as well as the international community, placed substantial and sustained pressure on successive Pakistani governments to review Zia-ul-Haq's Islamization measures (and particularly the *Zina Hudood* Ordinance) for amendments and repeal. Responding to this pressure, another military dictator, President Pervaiz Musharraf, established the National Commission on the Status of Women (NCSW) in July 2000 as a permanent and autonomous statutory body that would make recommendations on laws and policies relating to women, without the influence of the government.[7] The twenty-member commission set up to review the *Zina Hudood* laws was headed by a retired High Court Judge, Majida Rizvi, the first woman judge to have been appointed to a High Court in Pakistan.

Other significant organizations that, among a host of other issues, also focus on women's rights through collaborative campaigns, and documentary filmmaking are the Human Rights Commission of Pakistan (HRCP), and the Interactive Resource Centre (IRC), respectively.

Jaloos (*Procession*) (*Simorgh* Productions 1988)

Following from the above discussion that elaborated on women's organized resistance to General Zia-ul-Haq's Islamization of the criminal justice system, *Jaloos* (Procession) (1988),[8] a documentary made by *Simorgh* Productions, is an appropriate film to begin this chapter, and indeed the focus of this chapter, as well as the overall intent of the book.[9] Although the focus of this film is the women's movement and resistance against state-enforced legislation, *Jaloos* symbolically also sets the activist tone for the countrywide, and continuing, atmosphere of resistance and opposition to military dictatorships, politicization of religion, religious fundamentalism, and consequent curtailment of individual, minority, and women's rights and freedoms in Pakistan.[10]

Made as a commemorative film, *Jaloos* documents the procession organized by women's rights organizations in the Punjab provincial capital, Lahore, on February 12, 1988, while Zia was still in power.[11] This procession honoured the historic first demonstration on February 12, 1983 against the proposed legislation of the Law of Evidence prepared by the Council of Islamic Ideology (CII) in April 1982.[12] Through continued resistance by women's groups and organizations, the actual promulgation of the draft was delayed again and again. Finally, it became law in October 1984, and since then the subject and focus of continuing resistance and opposition.[13]

The commemorative focus in *Jaloos* is on the 1983 peaceful rally, led by the Women's Action Forum (WAF), which had launched a countrywide public protest against the new laws.[14] February 12 now marks National Women's Day in Pakistan, observed each year with rallies and other events by WAF and women's organizations across the country. Through off-screen narration throughout the film, *Jaloos* uses a straightforward educational approach to list the judicial reforms imposed by Zia, including the *Zina Hudood* Ordinance and the Law of Evidence, that eroded and seriously impacted women's legal rights and equal status as citizens. (See Appendices 1 and 2 for details on these laws).

Jaloos offers women's perspectives on the emergence of the Pakistani women's movement against the Islamization process and gender-discriminatory *Sharia* laws, and serves as a filmic historical record told through a symbolic representation that intertwines with the memory of an earlier, key, procession, reflected through archival still images. The off-screen narrator, Mehnaz Rafi, a long-time women's rights activist and politician, traces the origins and inception of a united and organized anti-Islamization movement in Pakistan in which various women's organizations and other segments of civil society came together to oppose and reject these judicial measures. The film's narration highlights the fact that it was the women's organizations under the umbrella of WAF and the Punjab Women Lawyers Association (PWLA) who were the first to mobilize public participation and support, and take to the streets to oppose Zia's martial law regime and policies. The film reveals that since 1983, each year a similar procession had marked the anniversary of the first rally, taking the same route on the Mall Road, Lahore, and was invariably roughed up by the waiting combat police contingents during Zia's tenure.

Jaloos pays tribute to the new generation of educated urban women who were the first to mobilize a historic public dissent against Zia's discriminatory laws of Evidence, *Qisas*, and *Diyat* in 1983. Over 300 women had assembled on the Mall Road to take part in the protest march to the Lahore High Court, but the peaceful rally turned violent when around 500 policemen stopped the participants, and baton-charged and tear-gassed the women's procession.[15] The protesters braved the street fight with the police, and despite being beaten and arrested, several women managed to reach the Lahore High Court to join male lawyers who garlanded them as a token of mutual victory.[16] This single incident of militancy and resolve served to unite and foster new male–female collective alliances in the country, and led to a committed activism against dictatorship, Islamization, and religious fundamentalism.[17] Archival still photographs interspersed in the film stand as powerful testimony to the 1983 protest rally. Today, these grainy images of women being brutalized by police capture and preserve not only the dark episodes of state-sanctioned violence of the past, but equally underscore the spirit and defiance by members of Pakistan's civil society that subsequent dictatorial and authoritarian regimes and policies have failed to discourage and contain.

Footage from the 1988 commemorative rally shows women and men from all classes and walks of life congregating on Lahore's main thoroughfare, the Mall Road, in the presence of an ominous and heavily armed combat police presence, to participate in the procession. Through off-screen commentary we learn these marchers included civil society activists, poor people from rural areas, labourers, lawyers, human rights activists, trade union activists, journalists, housewives, and social workers from all parts of Pakistan.

Jaloos does not exhibit high production values with grainy footage, and shot with an unsteady, handheld video camera operating cautiously, given the heavy police presence.[18] Depicting people carrying placards and women delivering fiery speeches as the crowds cheer and chant slogans, and interspersed with gripping still photographs of the 1983 crackdown and police brutality, the film captures the energy, and resolve of a unified public dissent against Zia's Islamization designs. In doing so, it also establishes a link with the sustained and unwavering opposition to authoritarianism, religious extremism, and gender- and minority-discrimination on the pretext of Islam. Perhaps, the most striking feature that comes across in the film is that the small urban demonstration of a few hundred in 1983 has become a major procession of thousands by 1988, with participants from all walks of life and regions of the country and with a significant male presence as well. Furthermore, the documentary presents an early account through images of those lawyers and activists who were to emerge as the influential voices for social change in Pakistan.[19]

Figure 2.1 Archival photo still from *Jaloos* of police action against women demonstrators during Zia-ul-Haq's regime on 12 February, 1983.
Source: *Simorgh* Productions, Lahore, Pakistan.

Figure 2.2 Image from *Jaloos* of the women's commemorative procession in February, 1988.
Source: *Simorgh* Productions, Lahore, Pakistan.

Today, as many more processions and public rallies by the Pakistani civil society strive to press for the review and repeal of laws introduced during the Islamization period, and continue to speak out against growing religious fundamentalism and oppressive governments, this simple 22-minute documentary film has acquired its own archival utility and significance as an historical record that contests the past.[20] The film serves as a valuable counter-history record that holds the past accountable for the subsequent state of affairs.[21] In doing so, the film reinforces the utility of documentary cinema as a pedagogical tool to record events as historical evidence that would also hold instructional value for the future.[22] As well, in drawing attention to transformations that were unfolding early in the Islamization period, *Jaloos* also conveys a symbolic beginning for subsequent Pakistani documentarists such as Sabiha Sumar, whose emergence as a filmmaker is rooted in the same period of state-oppression and civil society's resistance. Sumar's work can be seen as the beginning of a documentary 'Cinema of Accountability' in Pakistan.

Who Will Cast the First Stone? (Sabiha Sumar 1988)

In a prevailing climate of oppressive laws introduced during the Islamization process, Sabiha Sumar launched her filmmaking career with her first documentary film, *Who Will Cast the First Stone?* [23] Made in 1988, the year General Zia-ul-Haq dismissed a civilian government and dissolved the National Assembly on the grounds that the process of Islamization was not being conducted adequately, this film would be the first of a series of films made by Sumar that chart the course and effects of Islamization and dictatorships in Pakistan. Working as an independent filmmaker, Sumar has continued to take up issues of women's oppression, religious fundamentalism, patriarchal domination, and socio-political biases as topics for her documentaries.[24] Sumar's films have been collaborative ventures with foreign media, and aired largely on foreign television channels such as ZDF/Arte, a German-French cultural channel, Channel 4 UK, and the Canadian Broadcasting Corporation (CBC).

Sumar undertook a study of women convicted under the *Zina Hudood* Ordinance and initiated a signature campaign as chair for the Committee for the Repeal of the *Hudood* Ordinances in 1987/88.[25] Taking her protest further, she embarked on the production of *Who Will Cast the First Stone?* on the topic of the *Zina Hudood* Ordinance and its impact on women.[26]

The title of Sumar's documentary film *Who Will Cast the First Stone?* (1988) refers to the punishment of 'stoning to death' prescribed for adultery and extra-marital sex in Islamic countries ruled by *Sharia* laws, newly imposed in Pakistan by the *Zina Hudood* Ordinance.[27] Sumar's research revealed that at the Karachi Central Jail, women had been jailed primarily for having had extra-marital sex or marrying somebody of their own choice, while many ended up in prison simply because they reported their rape cases to the police, which was then used against them as an admission of having had sex outside of marriage. They languished in jail until the complaint of rape was taken up. As Sumar noted, 'There were 69 women in jail at that time – this is the late '80s – and of these, 68 were booked for *Zina.*'[28] The film documents individual case studies of women and men who had been implicated, convicted, or imprisoned under the *Zina Hudood* Ordinance. These are complemented by interviews with lawyers and judges, religious scholars and leaders, members of women's rights organizations and activists, as well as ordinary citizens such as factory workers.

Focusing on case studies, *Who Will Cast the First Stone?* records the ordeal of Roshan Jan, Ghulam Sakina, and Shahida Parveen, three of the many women imprisoned in the Karachi Central Jail who had been charged under the *Zina Hudood* Ordinance. The three imprisoned women narrate their experiences at the hands of a gender-biased and discriminatory socio-legal system, and air their views on *Sharia* laws and religion. The stories that emerge shed light from women's perspectives on the fundamentalist approach to religion as each woman recounts how her own family or husband used the provisions in the *Zina Hudood* Ordinance to have her put away on concocted charges of adultery, fornication, or extra-marital sex. The women were deprived of their rights in property cases, child custody, or marrying out of choice, and they were abandoned for allegedly bringing shame and dishonour to their families.[29]

Roshan Jan, a prisoner who had been awaiting trial for eighteen months at the time of the interview, recounts how her husband threw her out and remarried.

When she filed for divorce, he falsely accused her of *Zina* (adultery), and had her jailed under the *Zina Hudood* Ordinance. As per law, only her husband or father could have had her bailed out, both of whom refused – the husband on the pretext that she is a morally corrupt woman and deserves her punishment, and the father on grounds that she had brought dishonour to the family and should either return to her husband or stay in prison rather than return to his house. Providing the background to her predicament, Roshan Jan reveals that both her husband and father had wanted to sell her into prostitution after she was married off to her husband at nine years of age, and when she resisted, her husband and father conspired to have her put away on adultery charges.

Shahida Parveen, the second prisoner interviewed, reveals she was implicated by her first husband for adultery and rape under the *Zina Hudood* Ordinance after she obtained a divorce from him and remarried out of choice. The Shahida Parveen case received immense attention in the national press in 1987 following a trial court's verdict that both she and her second husband, Mohammad Sarwar, be stoned to death. What led to this conviction was her first husband's failure to register their divorce.[30] Her first husband's brazen response in the film is that even if she was released, she would most likely become a victim of an honour-killing, a view that is passionately shared and endorsed by various men Sumar interviews on the street for their response to the case.[31]

The third woman, Ghulam Sakina, notes that she was implicated and charged under the *Zina Hudood* Ordinance in the abduction case of a girl, and for allegedly being an accomplice to adultery and rape. Explaining her case, Sakina recounts that on repeatedly asking back for some money she had lent a neighbour, who refused to return it, Sakina slapped her. As retaliation, the neighbour's

Figure 2.3 Ghulam Sakina narrating her ordeal in *Who Will Cast the First Stone?*
Source: *Vidhi* Films, Karachi, Pakistan.

policeman husband had her implicated as an accomplice in an abduction case that was reported in his jurisdiction. As a result of her conviction, she had to spend four years in prison, taking her one-and-a-half-year-old daughter with her, while her husband remarried in her absence, and refused to get her out on bail.

Against a backdrop of the above cases that illustrate the wide net and loopholes that strengthened the *Zina Hudood* Ordinance against women, Sumar interviews various activists, lawyers, and judges who offer their opposing views on the subject. What emerges are the many tensions and contradictions that had taken root in Pakistan in the wake of the Islamization process and religious fundamentalism. Approached by Sumar for his views on the *Zina Hudood* Ordinance and its negative implications for women, a former judge of the Federal *Shariat* Court (FSC), Justice Zahoor-ul-Haq, vehemently defends the *Sharia* laws as 'divine' and 'supreme', arguing that they cannot be meddled with or amended by human beings, as he emphasizes the Law of Evidence as necessary to promote a pious society. Turning around the issue of the Law of Evidence as unjust and discriminatory, Haq argues, 'If women could testify on their own behalf and accuse men as perpetrators in rape cases, it would become an impossible society for men to live in.' As a retort to the judge's assertions, through voice-over, Sumar includes the narration of the Safia Bibi case (1983), in which a sixteen-year-old blind rape victim was asked to identify her rapists.[32]

The women activists Sumar speaks to criticize Islamization and *Sharia* laws as nothing more than patriarchal ploys to subjugate and terrorize women, particularly the already marginalized segments that are most likely to be economically dependent on men, illiterate, and who are without recourse to legal aid, or even an understanding of the laws under which they can be implicated or convicted. Nasreen Azhar, an activist and founding member of WAF interviewed in the film, points out that the *Zina Hudood* Ordinance presents an easy option for men to use if they want to put a woman away. All they have to do is implicate her under this law if they want property or to get married again. Given the slow and gender-biased legal system, it would be years before an accused woman's case comes up for a hearing, while she languishes in jail. Azhar categorically states that our 'main fight is against the Mullah (Muslim clergy)', connecting inextricably gender-discrimination and biases in society and law directly to Islamist manipulation of religion. Similarly, human rights lawyer Asma Jahangir points out that even if a woman does manage to prove her innocence and is freed from jail, she will 'forever be stigmatized, and face an unsympathetic attitude from the police, society, and the system'.

Talking to Sumar in the film, former Acting Chief Justice of the Pakistan Supreme Court, (the late) Justice Dorab Patel, stresses the need for the reinterpretation of *Sharia* laws according to the times, and goes on the record with his own incisive criticism of the *Zina Hudood* Ordinance. He states that the new laws have created two types of citizens – Muslims on the one hand, and non-Muslims and women on the other. While Muslims cannot be convicted on the evidence of non-Muslims, non-Muslims can be convicted on the evidence of Muslims: 'For example, if there is a theft in my house, and I am the only witness, I cannot give evidence as I am a non-Muslim, although I may be the Chief Justice of the Supreme Court of Pakistan'.[33]

Sumar caps her documentary debate on religion and the *Zina Hudood* Ordinance with an interview with (the late) Begum Raa'na Liaquat Ali, the wife of the first prime minister of Pakistan following the partition of India in 1947, and the founding member of the All Pakistan Women's Association (APWA). Ali, who was a leading figure in the struggle for Pakistan's independence, categorically opposes any official interference in religion by the state:

> 'State has no business to meddle with religion. Jinnah, the founder of Pakistan, made it very clear in his speech after independence that this will be a country where religion will remain a personal and private matter for all majority and minority citizens alike.'[34]

Juxtaposing conflicting debates and giving voice to an educated and progressive segment of the society, religious fundamentalists, women prisoners, and on-the-street observers, *Who Will Cast the First Stone?* documented for the first time on film the grim situation for Pakistani women affected by the *Zina Hudood* Ordinance. Through their own narrations and testimonies, the film gives abundant evidence of police brutalities, the patriarchal and socio-cultural subjugation of their voices and rights, and the biases that oppose women's status in the male-dominated judicial system itself.[35] It is significant to note that the victimized women who speak out are mostly uneducated and belong to the most economically marginalized sections of the society. Yet, in this film, these women demonstrate the courage in their opposition to Zia's dictatorial regime and to fundamentalist Islamic doctrines that inhibit the emergence of equality and justice in Islam. Speaking out in direct and forceful language, Ghulam Sakina challenges the system and the military dictator to prove the validity of these laws in Islam itself. In a pained and angry outburst, Sakina shares her fears and apprehensions at the time:

> 'Where is the dignity in this brand of Islam for women? Women living within the confines of four walls are prone to being dragged to jails due to these laws. What kind of Islam is this bastard trying to impose on us. He is the proverbial one-eyed monster of the 15th century. May God grant him death. All that remains is to strip women naked in public in the name of religion.'[36]

Given the oppressive circumstances under which *Who Will Cast the First Stone?* was made, it is a significant counter-historical and activist filmic documentation that has preserved rare testimonial evidence from women convicted under the *Zina Hudood* Ordinance. Denied the right to testify on their own behalf in court, Sumar gives her subjects the unique cathartic opportunity to be their own witnesses and to testify without the constraints of the *Sharia* laws, particularly the Law of Evidence that would otherwise silence them.

What comes across forcefully in *Who Will Cast the First Stone?* is, on the one hand, the strong opposition to Zia's dictatorship, Islamization, and curbs on freedoms, regardless of the class barriers and education level of Sumar's subjects as they stress the need for a collective struggle for democracy, judicial reforms, gender equality, and equal citizenship rights. On the other, we see the rigid fundamentalist approach to Islam that had begun to seep in and entrench itself in Pakistan's socio-political fabric. In an interview, Sumar remarked on her experience of filming her female subjects in *Who Will Cast the First Stone?* who had been imprisoned under Islamic laws:

> 'My film argued for their freedom, or rather they argued in the film, for their freedom ... It was sad that these women were asking for their basic rights: to be able to decide whom they shall marry or to have the right to fight for the custody of their children.'[37]

In investigating and drawing international attention to a most oppressive period in Pakistan's political and legislative history, *Who Will Cast the First Stone?* performed its own legislative and deliberative role.[38] Aired on Channel 4 in Britain, Sumar's observational and participatory documentary went on to win the Golden Gate Award in San Francisco in 1998.[39] The film also laid the foundation for Sumar's subsequent productions that continued to focus on issues of religious fundamentalism, women's rights, and the struggle for democracy.

Don't Ask Why (Sabiha Sumar 1999)

Sumar continued her investigation into the lasting impact of the Islamization era reforms through her next television documentary, *Don't Ask Why*, made in 1999, eleven years after the release of *Who Will Cast the First Stone?* [40] Pursuing a biographical journey through the diary and reflections of Anousheh, a seventeen-year-old girl belonging to a middle-class family in Karachi, this participatory and observational film[41] probes the implications of religious fundamentalism on another generation of Pakistani women who find themselves growing up and living under this drift towards rigid Islamic doctrines.[42] To emphasize her focus on her main character's predicament, and the thrust of the film to question the status quo from a teenager's point of view, Sumar confines her own interaction in the film to Anousheh while letting her subject interact and explore her own questions with the other characters in the film, and then confiding in her diary and the filmmaker.

Sumar uses her subject to represent the majority of young women faced with similar dilemmas – conflicting socio-political factors that get confused with religious debate. Anousheh, whose father had embraced ideals of Zia's Islamization, speaks of the confusions and disappointments she faces as a consequence of the socio-religious constraints placed on her freedoms. Through her interactions and discussions with her father, the film tracks the emerging tensions, conflicts, and

Figure 2.4 Anousheh dressing up as a boy in *Don't Ask Why*.
Source: *Vidhi* Films, Karachi, Pakistan.

ensuing questions about gender inequality in Islam for a generation of young women in Pakistan.

Don't Ask Why opens with a bubbly Anousheh painting a moustache and thick eyebrows on her face with an eyebrow pencil, dressing up in jeans and a casual loose shirt as a boy her age would do, with a cap on her head and an unlit cigarette dangling from her lips. While her father laughs at her attempt to be like her brothers, he also chides her and tells her to go and change her clothes as it is time for prayer. The incident not only sets the tone for the rest of the film, but also illustrates Anousheh's understanding of her constraints as a female. She confides to her diary the restrictions imposed on her, wishing she could settle abroad, have a career, and marry out of choice. Anousheh's thoughts in the film on her sister's upcoming marriage reveal her absolute distaste for arranged marriages, finding them 'scary'. However, asked by Sumar if she would marry someone like her father, Anousheh's instant and touchingly honest reply is in the affirmative, saying she adores her father.

Early in the film, Anousheh tells Sumar that 'for the last 17 years my father has ruled my life, and after marriage my husband will rule for the next fifty years'. This realization, combined with a passive submission to what her fate might be, heightens the sadness that permeates her aspirations and dreams throughout the film, serving as a collective reflection on girls her age who, despite privilege and education, could find their freedom curtailed due to the conservative turn Pakistani society had begun to take. For example, in one scene, Anousheh argues with her mother over the length of a *sari* blouse she wants to wear at the upcoming

52 *Legacy of Islamization*

Figure 2.5 Anousheh dressed up as a boy in *Don't Ask Why*.
Source: *Vidhi* Films, Karachi, Pakistan.

wedding of her sister.[43] The mother's nervous statement that it is too short and revealing, and her apprehensions about the father's objections, point to how the impact of Islamization had begun to seep into the most trivial and personal of issues.[44]

Through recordings from her diary, Anousheh shares her questions with the filmmaker and the audience as she struggles to understand and come to terms with the limitations placed on her despite her own strong belief in Islam. Although not an outright rebel in her approach or speech, the main thrust of Anousheh's questions to her father, a man she adores but with whom she privately does not agree, revolve around her critique of Islam and its gender discrimination. While accepting her religion as an integral part of her life, she questions why women have to stand behind men to pray, why Islam allows men to have four wives, why she cannot go out to a restaurant to celebrate the end of her high-school exams with her friends, why she cannot dress the way she wishes to, and why she cannot apply to university as some of her friends were doing? When Anousheh's questioning gets too intense and direct, her father, an educated man who has been shown answering all her questions till now, is quick to tell her to just accept the dictates of the *Quran* and Islam, and 'don't ask why'. He thereby categorically refuses to enter into an open debate on religion or to evaluate Islamic doctrines. Sumar uses the father's response to reflect upon the fundamentalist interpretations of the *Quran* and Islam.

In one scene, Anousheh articulates her belief that the *Quran* needs to be 'reinterpreted by women in order to claim their rights from within their religion'. In a surprisingly mature manner for her age, she is quick to point out:

'Here men are like God. If you question them you can be killed ... Everything is related to fear: fear of God, of the clergy and religious parties, fathers and so on, and piety because they don't want to go to hell.'

On the other hand, Anousheh's periodic attendance at a *madrasa* run by the women's wing of the Islamic political party, the *Jamaat-e-Islami*, in search for answers to her religious confusions only strengthens her resolve and understanding that Islam needs to be modernized. We see a respectful Anousheh, with her head covered by a scarf, sitting very attentive, but visibly confused and rather frightened, in a religious studies class run by young and enthusiastic *Jamaat-e-Islami* women clad in heavy veils and *burqas*, even in the company of women.[45] Preaching with an emotionally charged emphasis on an orthodox and fundamentalist interpretation of the *Quranic* text, the women of the *madrasa* claim Islam to be the only righteous path that can truly liberate women without exploiting them, in contrast to the West. Through this depiction, Sumar provides a disturbing insight into the organized infiltration of religious extremism through *madrasas* within the ranks of women – conditioned by a manipulative religio-political system to believe that in their lack of choices and subservience to a patriarchal order lay their path to piety, salvation, and liberation.

Through Anousheh's confusions depicted in the film, including her fear that if her father finds her diary, he will 'kill me as my whole life is recorded in it', Sumar contrasts the stark difference between her own growing up years before

Figure 2.6 Anousheh attending a *Jamaat-e-Islami* Women's Wing study session in *Don't Ask Why*.
Source: *Vidhi* Films, Karachi, Pakistan.

Islamization when religion was a private matter, and the post-Islamization generation of young women who are being deprived of freedoms and choices. In voice-over, Sumar sums up her understanding of what has happened to her homeland:

> 'The only importance we accord our youth is when they become martyrs. You talk to a boy in a village in India, and he'll tell you that he wants to become Shah Rukh Khan. A girl will tell you she wants to become Rani Mukherjee [both are famous actors].[46] You talk to a boy in the city of Karachi (Pakistan), the little boy who comes to clean your car window, and he'll tell you "I want to become a martyr because that way I'll become famous. I'll be a hero." As for a little girl in Karachi, she doesn't even know how to dream.'[47]

In exploring the conflicts in Anousheh's life as a case study in *Don't Ask Why*, Sumar highlights the vast and visible difference between her own growing up years in a secular society in which religion and state were separate entities, and how the lives of another generation of young women in the same socio-cultural environment is now being shaped by religion. Connecting Sumar's own secular past to Anousheh's oppressive present, we see the stifling impact of Zia's politicization of religion as *Don't Ask Why* depicts the pervasive intersection of Islam and politics in the domestic, personal, and public spheres.

Like a cautionary tale, the film is an early reflection on the influence of religious fundamentalism that continued to influence Pakistani society well after the Zia regime had ended, and despite subsequent democratically elected governments, including that of Benazir Bhutto.[48] This influence becomes evident as Sumar moves from Anousheh's biographical account in *Don't Ask Why* (1999) to journey further into the socio-political transformations shaping Pakistan in her next documentary, *For A Place Under the Heavens* (2003).

For a Place Under the Heavens (Sabiha Sumar 2003)

In her third documentary, *For a Place Under the Heavens* (2003), dedicated to her daughter Dhiya, Sabiha Sumar takes a reflective, autobiographical, and personal journey through her hometown of Karachi to document the history and effects of religious fundamentalism since 1977.[49] This time, when another military dictator, General Pervaiz Musharraf, is in power, Sumar, accompanied by her little daughter, searches for answers through conversations with those among whom she herself grew up. The autobiographical journeys and encounters she records are complemented by interviews with religious and legal scholars and women from a cross-section of society, including religious activists. Sumar inserts discussions with her three friends, Nausheen, Saba, and Aliya, and other women speaking on either side of the fundamentalist debate to present a wider picture of the divisions and tensions within contemporary Pakistan. In particular, Sumar engages with collaborations between the state and clergy, the impacts of religious doctrines, and the constraints these doctrines inflict on women's freedom and rights in particular.[50]

The film opens with Sumar walking through her childhood home in Karachi, narrating her memories of growing up in a home filled with music, her father's recitations of Sufi poetry, and her parents' lively social life, which included entertaining friends with alcoholic drinks.[51] In a scene from an old home movie of her own birthday party, Sumar points out her mother. She recounts her mother's story of moving from Bombay (now Mumbai), India, to Pakistan during the partition of the Indian sub-continent, a time when Muslim women in India wore the veil. In contrast, Sumar recalls that growing up in Karachi she never saw women veiling, including her mother, who chose not veil in her new Muslim homeland. Showing an old clip of a dance performance at a nightclub from her father's personal collection of films, Sumar reminisces about a very different middle-class life her parents knew, one which she barely got a chance to experience as it evaporated in her own youth under the rule of General Zia.[52]

In her dialogue with Sumar, Nausheen talks of the new trend of veiling with a *hijab*, both among sections of upper and middle-class women. Nausheen further points out that their generation had never even heard of the word '*hijab*' till recently as veiling was an import from the Arab world, and alien to the Indian sub-continent.[53] Going through archival newspaper clippings of significant events in Pakistan's history since its independence in 1947, Sumar and Nausheen begin

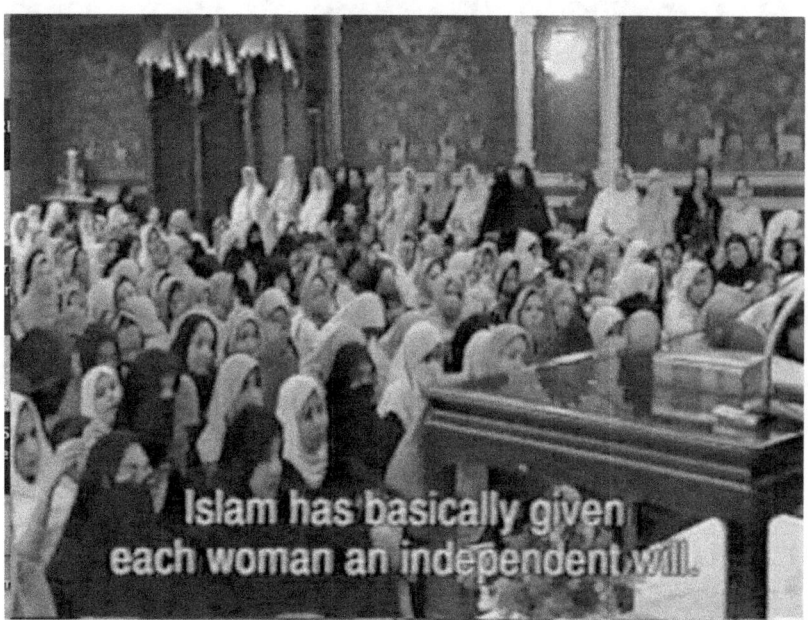

Figure 2.7 Image from *For A Place Under the Heavens* of a women-only religious sermon at a five star hotel.
Source: *Vidhi* Films, Karachi, Pakistan.

56 *Legacy of Islamization*

to piece together a chronology of the socio-political developments that led to the present oppressive environment. Discussing the significant dates, laws, events, elections, military coups, and dictatorships as they emerge from the media clippings and reports, they arrange the pattern of political upheavals that transformed their society.

Another new trend that Sumar records is the emergence of the women's-only religious sermons, led by female preachers, in the new 'piety driven' atmosphere of the country. As an example, a large group of heavily veiled women is shown attending a religious gathering, one which Sumar herself attends and describes as one of the many 'expensive affairs arranged with meticulous detail in five-star hotels all over the country'. Her comment highlights the highly effective role played by social class and money, and how these factors contribute to the organization of such an exclusive and 'pious environment'.

In another instance, Sumar contrasts another women's gathering at a religious sermon, 'in a humble neighbourhood', where a doll is being used in a demonstration by a group of veiled women to educate their congregation on the correct 'Islamic' way to bathe a woman's dead body, and how to drape it in the prescribed white coffin cloth. This eerie 'educational' clip, as well as the discussions at both gatherings about lifestyles that can lead to a place in 'either heaven or hell as there is no escape possible', sharply indicate the extent to which religious

Figure 2.8 Image from *For A Place Under the Heavens* of a doll being used for tutorial on bathing a Muslim woman's body for burial.
Source: *Vidhi* Films, Karachi, Pakistan.

fundamentalism has penetrated across social, and economic divides. Following her attendance at both events, a somewhat shocked and dismayed Sumar ponders:

> 'Did I say I was born in a secular Pakistan? I guess I was wrong. I now realize that I was raised in a schizophrenic society suspended precariously between Islamic ideology and secularism.'

In voice-over, Sumar wonders that given the economic problems in the country, and the curtailment of their rights in the name of religion, shouldn't working-class/ poor women, despite their faith, be far more willing to reject religion? Linking class and piety, Sumar blames the political, secular and liberal parties in the country for having failed to harness such a force at the grassroots level that could oppose religious intolerance, and the growing tilt towards extremism and fundamentalism:

> 'Our ruling elites have always been the feudals, the army and the clergy who all have interests tied together. It would take a power struggle to change the balance, which these political parties and women's organizations have been avoiding so far.'

In another scene, Sumar speaks with Sorraiya, another veiled woman who proudly talks about her son's participation and subsequent 'martyrdom' in what she terms '*jihad*' in Kashmir (India).[54] Asked if she regrets his decision to go on this '*jihad*', Sorraiya replies: 'I feel the loss as a mother, but when I think of the cause, I see his martyrdom as the greatest honour God could bestow on a person. He has been saved from hell and will go straight to heaven.' She thus parrots a justification for Islamic militancy, suicide killings, and bloodshed that have swept across the world, images of which continue to dominate coverage of Pakistan and Islam in the international media.[55]

Addressing Sumar's concerns in the film about the deepening emphasis on fundamentalist Islam, Islamic scholar Mufti Nizamuddin, who spends his time teaching Islamic Studies in *madrasas,* defends the rise of orthodox Islam. He argues that these religious seminaries are useful as 'ideological centres' that are 'paving the way for an Islamic revolution that cannot be achieved through Western-style democracies and parliamentary systems.'[56] Why Pakistan needs an Islamic revolution is not an issue the cleric delves into. As for the status of women in Islam, Nizamuddin blames women for failing to achieve their share of power, saying: 'They have not demanded their rights. Islam does not stop women from moving forward. They can come forward and take charge.' When asked if men in Pakistan would be willing for that to happen, he responds with a sarcastic laugh: 'It would take a revolution. No one relinquishes power easily.'

In contrast, Sumar interviews Hina, an aspiring female model. Young, defiant, and confident, Hina dismisses any notions that the state, Islam, or society has the right to dictate her life. She says, 'You can't totally deny the system, but I do a lot of things and get away with them. You need brains to get past the cracks in the system. I have learned to do that and am enjoying my life immensely.' Next, we see Hina being made up by male make-up artists for the photo-shoot that follows, showing her posing in a red, revealing dress.[57] Such contradictions depict the tensions that have engulfed a society torn between modernity, progress, religion, and the extremist factions that promote intolerance for their own survival.

Adding a legal and theological perspective to the rise of fundamentalist Islam and gender discrimination in Pakistan, Shaheen Sardar Ali, a former Pakistani provincial minister and legal expert whom Sumar interviews at her home in Britain, explains:

> 'It is interesting that out of the 6,666 verses of the *Quran*, only six create gender hierarchies. 6,660 call for gender equality. How come that in 1400 years of jurisprudential evolution, knowledge and analysis 6660 outweighed the 6? Because it was a male elite who were jurists, judges, scholars, legislators, and rulers and they picked just half a dozen verses to override the others. In terms of gender hierarchies, these half a dozen also came with a pre-condition that males provide for women. From a strictly legal perspective, even this precondition disappears if there are no males in a household, and the woman is the provider.'[58]

Sardar Ali rejects confrontational politics when it comes to religion, saying it can be counter-productive as this is a sensitive issue. Sumar, however, rejects this avoidance as taking refuge in the verses of the *Quran* and sidestepping the necessity of a power struggle if patriarchal control and fundamentalism are to be challenged. As Sumar observes, 'Listening to Shaheen I could not help wonder where Christian women would be today if they were still interpreting the Bible?'

The most chilling scene, one that underlines the urgent need to curtail fundamentalist Islam in Pakistan, as elsewhere, is one in which Sorraiya, whose son was martyred in Kashmir, reads from his letter talking about the joy he feels at going on *jihad*. This is followed by her young, widowed, heavily veiled daughter-in-law supporting the logic of *jihad* and martyrdom by preaching their blessings to her orphaned young son. Emphatically she asks the boy if he is ready for martyrdom, to which the child is shown clapping and saying a cheerful 'yes' that he has already been conditioned to affirm, despite his young age and ignorance of the implications.

Against a backdrop of her engaged in a discussion with her friends, Sumar ponders in voice-over:

> 'There is no end to our discussions. Why is there no support, neither financial nor ideological, for secular politics in Pakistan? Clearly people of Pakistan would be willing to buy into an ideology that is relevant to their daily concerns. Why is it that no leader, not even Benazir Bhutto, has been able to reverse the trend of Islamization and put the ghost of General Zia-ul-Haq to rest?'

These are questions that the majority of secular and progressive Pakistanis of her generation continue to ask, both in Pakistan, as well as part of the Diaspora.

Sumar ends her film with another clip from her own birthday home-movie, which merges into a very similar clip of her daughter's birthday party. Concluding her personal journey through the transition from one generation to the next, she reminisces:

> 'It is the same house forty years later, and it is my daughter Dhiya's tenth birthday. I tell Dhiya when people stop asking questions it is a dangerous time. When she grows up I want her to ask, does half the nation benefit from being covered under layers of cloth or does the other half benefit? Or is it a small coterie of rulers that benefits at the expense of both?'

As Sumar's various subjects vie for a 'place under the heavens' on either side of the religious debate, no doubt women emerge as the most vulnerable victims, caught in a web of religious loyalties and political manipulation, deprived of both equal status and freedom.

Together, *Who Will Cast the First Stone?* (1988), *Don't Ask Why* (1999), and *For A Place Under the Heavens* (2003) complete Sabiha Sumar's deliberative and reflective journey into her country's past, and today stand as a significant sequential filmic documentation of Pakistan's grim history of its descent into religious fundamentalism. Her documentaries provide the connective background for the subsequent escalation of extremist ideologies and militancy in Pakistan that are espoused by religious and *jihadist* factions for vested interests.

Hudood Ordinance 1979: Divine Law, or Law of One Man? (National Commission on the Status of Women (NCSW) 2005)

The countrywide resistance by women's organizations and the legal fraternity, as well as the international community, continued to place immense pressure on successive governments to review Zia-ul-Haq's Islamization and the *Zina Hudood* Ordinance for amendments and repeal. Hence, there was a call for the establishment of a permanent, independent, and autonomous statutory body that would make recommendations on laws and policies relating to women, without the influence of the government. This call resulted in the establishment of the National Commission on the Status of Women (NCSW) by, ironically, another military dictator, President Pervaiz Musharraf, in July 2000 as he sought to present a progressive image to the West. The twenty-member commission set up to review the *Zina Hudood* laws was headed by a retired High Court Judge, Ms Majida Rizvi. However, given that the NCSW is a government body, whose chairperson and employees are recruited by the government of Pakistan, it is only understandable that it has to work within the constraints and parameters of state policies and religion, despite its 'autonomous' status and relative freedoms. Over the past decade, the NCSW has also extended its projects to include radio shows, and documentaries for legal literacy and consciousness-raising.[59]

It is a significant addition that NCSW's very first documentary film, *Hudood Ordinance 1979: Divine Law, or Law of One Man?* (2005), revolves around the implications of the Ordinance for women – a law that still took centre stage even after a lapse of 25 years since its promulgation.[60] For the first time we see the country's leading legal experts, policy-makers, lawmakers, rights activists, politicians, religious scholars, as well as women convicted under the *Zina* laws, forcefully debate the gender-discriminatory nature and weaknesses of the *Hudood* Ordinance on film, from a government platform.

Tracing the promulgation of the *Hudood* laws during the Islamization period which replaced the century-old penal code with *Sharia* laws, this counter-historical film revolves around a single question asked by the off-screen narrator: 'What was the need for the imposition of the new law? And what were the political motives for this arbitrary action?' We hear responses and views from over a dozen prominent people, among them legal experts, rights activists, government officials, lawyers, and politicians.

Among those who critique and stress the need for judicial amendments, and repeals are Syed Afzal Haider, lawyer and Member Special Committee on *Hudood* Ordinance who states that the *Hudood* Ordinance was enforced by Zia alone, as no intellectuals, scholars, public, or those who had dissenting views were even consulted. He points out that the Ordinance is less about *Hudood* and more about 'penalties'. Sharing Haider's views, Justice (Retd) Shaiq Usmani, Member Special Committee on *Hudood* Ordinance states categorically that this 'Ordinance should not be called *Hudood* Ordinance. This is Zia's Ordinance.' Terming the Ordinance as 'unimplementable', Hina Jillani, lawyer, rights activist, and Member Special Committee on *Hudood* Ordinance says the primary motive of the military regime was to legitimize itself, and that it just used the name of Islam. She notes that this law was not introduced to promote Islam as even the Islamic scholars are divided on its validity. Mehnaz Rafi, Member National Assembly (MNA), and a Member of the Pakistan Muslim League (PML) political party points out the word *Hudood* has been used to give the impression that it is an 'Islamic' law, while Sherry Rehman, Member National Assembly, and member Pakistan People's Party Patriots (PPPP) political party points out that the *Hudood* Ordinance is against the Constitution of Pakistan as Article 25:1,2,3 of the Constitution states that 'there shall be no discrimination on the basis of sex, gender, race, or class'. Anis Haroon, belonging to the *Aurat* (Woman) Foundation stresses that the *Hudood* Ordinance is full of loopholes, and is being used to simply victimize or trap the minorities and women.

In the film Islamic scholars offer their opinions on the *Hudood* Ordinances. Dr Khalid Masood, Chairman, Council of Islamic Ideology (CII) states that the *Hudood* Ordinance is based on the interpretations of *fiqhas* (Islamic jurisprudence) of Islamic sects according to the situations of that time, therefore it is neither completely un-Islamic, nor totally 'Islamic'. Legal scholar Tufail Hashmi explains that the *Hudood* laws begin with the statement that they are according to the *Quran* and the *Sunnah*. He points out that out of 100 sections, only 18 relate to *Hudood*, while the rest are penal laws. Some are procedural laws, and some are just definitions, and they do not relate to the *Quran* or the *Sunnah*. Majida Rizvi, Justice (Retd) of the Sindh High Court, states that the *Hudood* Ordinance violates

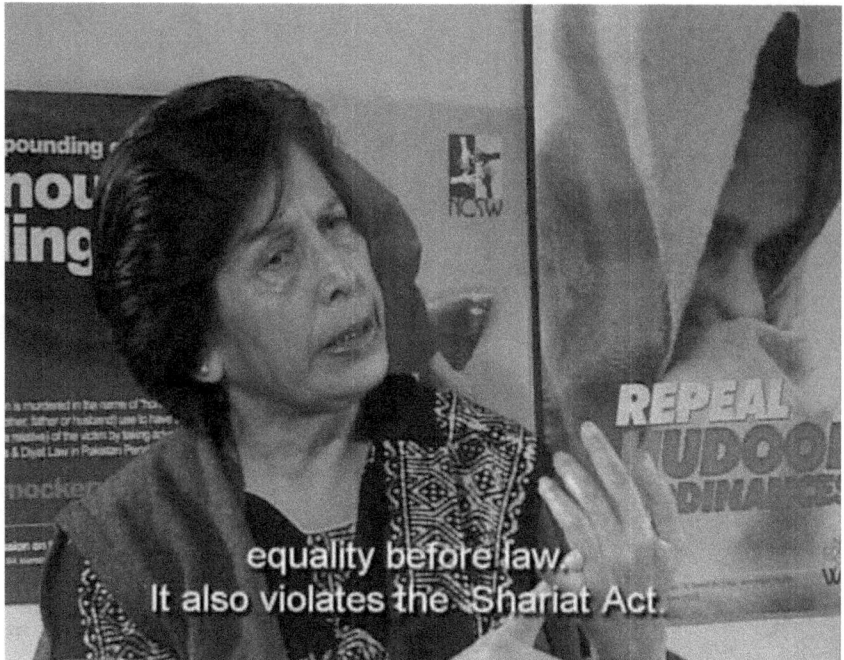

Figure 2.9 Justice (Retd) Majida Rizvi of the Sindh High Court elaborates on the *Hudood* laws in *Hudood Ordinance 1979: Divine Law, or Law of One Man?*
Source: National Commission on the Status of Women, Islamabad, Pakistan.

the constitutional guarantees regarding equality before law, and that it also violates the *Shariat* Act.

As footage reveals women languishing in prison, we learn from Zia Awan, lawyer, rights activist and president of the Lawyers for Human Rights and Legal Aid (LHRLA) organization that due to these laws 'there has been a 50% increase in the number of women prisoners'. This factor is elaborated by former Chief Justice Sindh High Court, Nasir Aslam Zahid (Retd): '122 women's cases are still under trial. Of these 58 women are accused under the *Zina* Ordinance.' Justice (Retd) Nasira Javed Iqbal of the Lahore High Court elaborates further:

'Since 1979, 90% of imprisoned women have been the victims of the *Zina Hudood* Ordinance. When I was a judge, 10 to 15 such cases came to my court daily in which brothers, uncles, even fathers registered cases against their sisters, nieces, or daughters – accusing them and their husbands of adultery only because they married without family consent.'

Regarding the of the Law of Evidence, which seriously impacted recourse to justice, particularly for women, her husband, former Chief Justice Lahore High

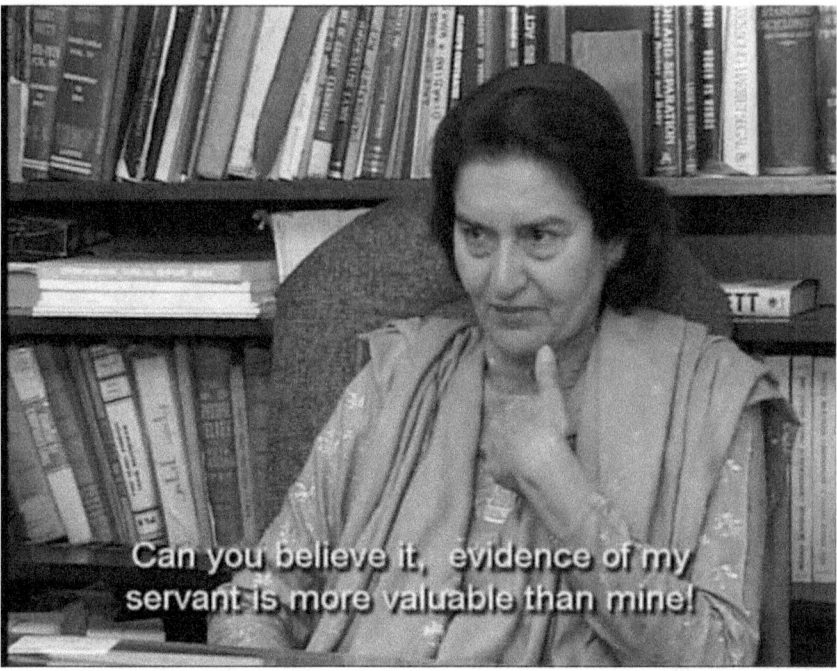

Figure 2.10 Justice (Retd) Nasira Javed Iqbal of the Lahore High Court elaborates on the Law of Evidence in *Hudood Ordinance 1979: Divine Law, or Law of One Man?*
Source: National Commission on the Status of Women, Islamabad, Pakistan.

Court, Javed Iqbal narrates in the film a case of blatant manipulation, and victimization that came to him:

> 'A female student who had gone into a male professors' room for a meeting found herself locked in his room from the outside by male students belonging to a religious party, who then claimed that adultery was being committed inside. One of them brought an imam (leader of mosque prayers) from a nearby mosque to be a witness. When I asked the imam if he had seen the act of adultery, he said "no I did not see it, but when the door opened, both seemed very confused as they came out, and the boys said adultery had been committed."'

Following the testimonial stories of three poor women, Zafran Bibi, Basri, and Zahida, who had been accused falsely under the *Zina Hudood* Ordinance, former Chief Justice of Sindh High Court, Justice (Retd) Nasir Aslam Zahid spells out the Islamic penalty for false accusation in the *Quran*. He explains that if an accuser is unable to bring four eyewitnesses against a woman accused of adultery, he would never be accepted as a witness for any case again, as according to

Surah Noor of the *Quran*, Verse number 4, he would be deemed a 'wicked transgressor'.

Correspondingly, Nasira Javed Iqbal explains the issue from a legal and woman's perspective saying that according to the *Quran*, two male witnesses are required for business matters, but if you cannot find two men, then you should get the witness of one man and two women. So that if one forgets, the other would remind her. That is still one witness only. On the other hand, giving her own example as a woman, she elaborates on the limitations of the law:

> 'A judge and advocate myself, I can debate and adjudicate an agreement, but I can not sign it. When I want to verify a document, I can even ask my male servant to be the witness. Because as a lawyer I know that if I sign it, we will have tremendous problems in proving its authenticity. I will be asked why only one woman has signed it, and not two? It would be very difficult to prove the document. Does it make sense that the evidence of my male servant is more valuable than mine?'

Turning to the punishment of stoning to death as prescribed in the *Zina Hudood* Ordinance, Justice (Retd) Shaiq Usmani informs us in the film that in Islam the penalty for *Zina* is lashes, but for the *Hudood* Ordinance the *ulema* (religious scholars) have prescribed it as *rajam* (stoning to death) of which there is no mention in the *Quran*. Similarly, lawyer, Hina Jillani pinpoints to yet another lacuna in the law that discriminates against women. She explains that if a girl is 16, she is considered an adult, and that even a nine-year-old girl, who has attained puberty, would be treated and punished as an adult. Hence, there is no difference between a minor and an adult female under the *Hudood* Ordinance.

The only voice to defend the *Hudood* laws is that of the heavily veiled Samiya Raheel Qazi, Member National Assembly, and Member of the *Muttahida Majlis-e-Amal* (MMA) (United Action Front) religious party who categorically defends these laws as 'divine', saying: 'This is a Western agenda to oppose the Islamic articles of our constitution.' Qazi's views are a troubling reminder that despite hers being the only voice of defence in the film, it is the long and influential shadow of the Islamization period that has persistently hindered the repeal of the *Hudood* laws.

The film ends with another off-screen question from the narrator: 'Why, despite such flaws and weaknesses, have these laws not been repealed?' Anis Haroon answers that when political parties come to power they compromise, and the issues pertaining to women are not given the priority they had promised. The film concludes with a list of 15 NCSW recommendations for repeal and amendments scrolling down the screen.

Although the debates and recommendations for the repeal of the *Hudood* laws remain inconclusive due to their sensitive religious nature and connotations, the film indicates significant progress on the part of a government body and civil society resistance in Pakistan. Taking into its fold prominent legal experts and scholars, *Hudood Ordinance 1979: Divine Law, or Law of One Man?* serves as the government's own counter-history[61] document that addresses seminal judicial transformations in the country during the Islamization period, hence playing a judicial and historical role.[62] It is not so much the topic and discussion of *Sharia* laws, and subjugation of rights themselves that make the point here – issues already addressed in *Simorgh*'s and Sabiha Sumar's films – but rather the fact that these critiques that hold the Islamization period accountable, and stress on the repeal of the *Hudood* laws, are now being expressed from the platform of a government organization, formed specifically for the purpose of reviewing them.

The NCSW's foray into documentary film production shows that this medium is being used by a government institution as well for consciousness-raising and to push for reforms. Hence, documentary film practice in Pakistan has strengthened new activist collaborations with civil society actors, as the long journey between *Jaloos* (1988) and the NCSW production (2005) indicates.[63] From being beaten and arrested on the streets of Lahore in the '80s for resisting the *Hudood* Ordinances, we see legislators and activists now pursuing those very issues collectively under the patronage of a federal government body, although any major results still remain to be achieved. Made in collaboration with the *Ajoka* Theatre for Social Change, a theatre company founded by theatre activists Shahid Nadeem and his wife Madeeha Gohar during Zia's regime, this NCSW documentary clearly indicates a new government–civil society collaboration and alliance with a shared agenda for reform. This development is a significant achievement for Pakistani women's organizations and activists who have continued to sustain their struggle for legal reforms, and have exerted pressure on all successive governments since Zia-ul-Haq to acknowledge and redress their concerns.

A Sun Sets In (National Commission for Justice and Peace (NCJP) 2000)

Despite the potential for injustices unleashed by the promulgation of the Blasphemy Law during the Zia regime, *A Sun Sets In* (2000) by Shahid Nadeem[64] is the only Pakistani documentary film that addresses this issue. It is a commemorative film following a tragic case of suicide by a Christian clergyman, Dr Bishop John Joseph (1932–1998) who became an icon of struggle against such discriminatory laws that mandated capital punishment, and rendered minorities as social outcasts in their own country.[65] Although the Bishop's struggle indicates that there has always been mounting domestic and international pressure to repeal the Blasphemy Law, public discourse and filmic critique have remained limited and constrained due to religious sensitivities.[66]

A Sun Sets In presents a life sketch of Dr Bishop John Joseph, who committed suicide in 1998 to protest against religious intolerance and the discriminatory treatment meted out to religious minorities as a result of the Blasphemy Law (for details of the Blasphemy Law, see Appendix 3).[67] In documenting the Bishop's life and work, the film also summarizes the politicization of both religion and law that Pakistan's politicians and religious leaders have continued to exploit to their advantage.⁶⁸ The film became a rallying point against religious intolerance, and led to an international outcry for the repeal of the Blasphemy Law.

Produced by the Lahore-based National Commission for Justice and Peace (NCJP), a Catholic organization, the film primarily focuses on the life of Bishop Joseph's contributions, paying tribute to his unwavering commitment to religious equality and his ongoing campaign against state-endorsed laws and directives that affected all religious minorities and their equal citizenship rights.⁶⁹ Through interviews with his family members, friends, and colleagues that include members of the Christian clergy, and supported by off-screen commentary, still photographs, and archival film footage, Nadeem constructs the Bishop's life sketch: his early days as a student, his work among the poor and disadvantaged, his standing as the 'people's Bishop' and an 'activist Bishop' in his community, and the events that instigated his tragic suicide.

The film begins in Bishop Joseph's home village of Khushpur, the oldest and most prominent Christian settlement in the Punjab province near the industrial city of Faisalabad, which has also been the hub for Christian learning in the country. Interspersed with devotional songs, still photographs from his youth, and footage of his participation in Church activities and services, the film also introduces the Bishop as the first Punjabi priest to rise to the position after almost a 30-year gap. Coming from a prominent Christian family known for their commitment and service to the Catholic Church and to education, we learn that the Bishop had been a leading voice in his community, not only in his official capacity but also as a staunch advocate for minority rights and interfaith harmony. As an accomplished intellect, he carried out his advocacy through literary and cultural activities, and international conferences, besides taking a keen interest in the translation of the Bible and psalms into local languages as a way to harmonize the Church with local cultures. The documentary highlights his work and affiliation with centres for the blind and those suffering from leprosy, as well as his community service regardless of religious or class distinctions, such as his support for Muslim widows, and his participation in the construction of a mosque in Khushpur.

Convinced that the Church could not remain a silent spectator to General Zia-ul-Haq's discriminatory laws that affected religious minorities, we learn that Bishop Joseph galvanized the entire Church community in Pakistan to form a movement to oppose them, founding the Muslim–Christian Relations Commission with the intention to study Islam. But it was particular cases under the 295-C of the Blasphemy Law that solidified the Bishop's resolve even further, as he vowed to lay down his life to protest the manipulative law if it was not repealed.⁷⁰

In one significant case, on April 5, 1994, as they left their lawyer's office in Lahore after a court hearing, three Christian defendants in a Blasphemy case were fired upon by people riding by on a motorbike. One of them, Manzur Masih, died on the spot, while the others were seriously injured. A Christian human rights activist escorting them, was also seriously injured. We learn from a long-time supporter and friend of the deceased, the Christian human rights activist, educator, and decorated Pakistan Air Force (PAF) pilot Group Captain (Late) Cecil Chaudhry, that during the funeral service at the Sacred Heart Cathedral, Lahore, 'the Bishop came down from the altar and kissed the feet of the dead man, vowing that he would lay down his life fighting against the Blasphemy laws'.[71]

Following this commitment, it was the subsequent Ayub Masih case that proved to be the fatal stroke for the Bishop. Masih, a Christian man who had been arrested and charged in October 1996, was convicted and sentenced to death under the 295-C of the Blasphemy Law in April 1998 at the Sessions Court in the Sahiwal district of the Punjab province. A month later, on May 6, 1998, while Masih's appeal was still in court, Bishop Joseph drove from Faisalabad to the Sessions Court in Sahiwal, accompanied by his driver Patras Samuel and another priest, Father Yaqub. While he asked the two men to wait in the car, the Bishop walked up to the court entrance and committed suicide with the pistol he had carried with him outside its gate to protest Ayub Masih's death sentence.[72] Perhaps the most glaring inconsistency in this Blasphemy case was that Ayub Masih had been accused of promoting British writer Salman Rushdie's novel, the *Satanic Verses*, a book that itself had earned the author a *fatwa* (religious edict) for a death sentence from no less than the Iranian religious leader Ayatollah Ruhollah Khomeini in 1989. Cultural anthropologist and Islamic scholar Linda Walbridge, also interviewed in the film, points out that grounds for such an allegation could only be baseless, as Ayub Masih was the son of illiterate and poor parents who worked as sweepers, and would most likely have been illiterate and uneducated himself.[73]

Accompanied by the still photograph of his dead body lying in a pool of blood outside the gate of the Sahiwal Sessions Court after he shot himself in the head, colleagues recount the Bishop's last day and their interactions with him, which, in retrospect, they found indicative of his intent. For example we learn that he had cancelled a planned trip to Rome where he was to take part in a meeting of the

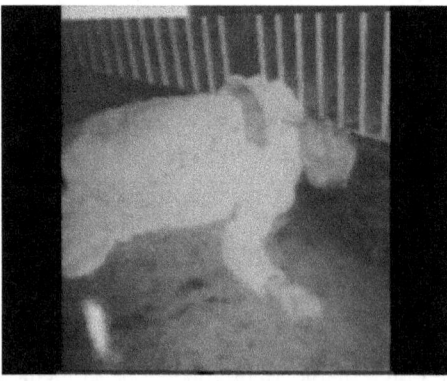

Figure 2.11 Archival still image from *A Sun Sets In* of Bishop Dr. John Joseph after he committed suicide outside the gates of the Sahiwal Sessions Court.
Source: National Commission for Justice and Peace, Lahore, Pakistan.

Legacy of Islamization 67

association of missionary institutes, because he felt it necessary to remain in Pakistan given the threat to the Christian community from Islamic religious fundamentalists.

Commenting on Bishop Joseph's death, Bishop Bonaventure Paul, Chairperson of the NCJP, states in the film that the Christian community considered him a 'saviour'. He rejects that his suicide was an act of frustration, proudly calling it instead an 'act of conviction'. As street protests in support of Bishop Joseph's cause begin to spread countrywide, we see archival footage and photographs of peaceful mourners being beaten up and taken into custody by the police.

Cecil Chaudhry talks about Bishop Joseph's suicide: 'There was not a shadow of doubt that this was a very planned and deliberate act on his part to offer himself as a sacrifice for the millions of other Pakistanis to be set free from discriminatory laws.' Asked by the off-screen interviewer what was the result of the Bishop's sacrifice Chaudhry elaborates: 'Three changes took place. All minorities united on the same platform – Hindus, Sikhs, all joined us. Secondly, a lot of Muslims who had been too scared to speak up before began to take up the issue in newspaper articles in the Urdu and English press. Thirdly, the government was shaken up.'[74]

The film concludes with shots of people paying homage to the Bishop's grave, as a popular Pakistani singer, Shazia Manzur's grieving song, entitled '*Sparrow*', plays to his memory in the background.[75]

A Sun Sets In is a sorrowful and grave comment on Pakistan's climate of religious intolerance and discrimination against its own.[76] It is particularly poignant that it took Bishop Joseph's suicide to bring any meaningful attention to the issue. The film focuses on the unfortunate fact that whereas all religious minorities in Pakistan face low social status and discrimination, the Christian community has been particularly targeted as the lowest class of citizens. Giving her views in the film, human rights lawyer and activist Asma Jehangir points to the inequality meted out to all minorities by the state:

Figure 2.12 Archival image of Bishop Dr. John Joseph from *A Sun Sets In*.
Source: National Commission for Justice and Peace, Lahore, Pakistan.

'All non-Muslims are disadvantaged by the simple act that they are not in the mainstream of electoral politics. If you look at the Christian community, most of them live below the poverty line – that by itself is discrimination. Is it not taken for granted that anyone who sweeps the floor has to be a Christian? As if they were born to take up this occupation. I think it is the most gruesome form of humiliation.'[77]

Perhaps, *A Sun Sets In* will remain the only film to be made in Pakistan by a local filmmaker that takes up the issue of the Blasphemy Law in relation to the Christian minority.[78] It is understandable that given the serious censorship constraints and religious biases, the filmmaker had to work within boundaries that did not afford him the space or the opportunity to address and reject government policies and the sensitive religious aspects that are a hindrance to the review and repeal of this law. These constraints are indicative of state censorship eventually leading to self-censorship, a lingering legacy that can be traced back to Zia's Islamization period.[79] It is little surprise then, that a documentary on the injustices meted out to other religious minority communities under the Blasphemy Law, particularly the *Ahmeddiyya* community, has not even been attempted, despite the fact that they are the biggest targets to be victimized under this law.[80]

In preserving the biographical sketch of Bishop John Joseph, and the events leading to his tragic, yet defiant, end, *A Sun Sets In* remains a topical and poignant historical testimonial to Pakistan's descent into religious intolerance against its own citizens, and the discrimination suffered by all religious minorities under the same law.[81]

The sacrificial, resolute, albeit violent, end of a peaceful, compassionate clergyman remains a distressing reminder of the politicization of religion by Zia-ul-Haq through the Blasphemy Law, one that remains to be repealed or amended. Given the religious sentiments attached to the Blasphemy Law, it has been impossible for successive governments to amend or repeal it. In 2009, the Supreme Court of Pakistan rejected an appeal filed 18 years ago against the Federal *Shariat* Court (FSC) punishment for blasphemy. In doing so, it has ruled that the death penalty is the only punishment that Islamic law provides for blasphemy.[82]

Filmmaker Shahid Nadeem, who himself has been an advocate of social justice and spent his entire career opposing religious extremism and dictatorial regimes, lets his subjects do all the talking onscreen. His own on-screen absence throughout the film provides his minority subjects the rare opportunity to air their views on their marginalization. Regardless of the audience it may or may not have found within Pakistan, the very production of this documentary has played a potentially 'persuasive,'[83] and 'legislative role,'[84] as pointed out by film scholars Michael Renov and Bill Nichols, respectively, that remains influential in pushing for the repeal of the Blasphemy Law.

Here it is pertinent to cite a case in which a Christian woman, Asia Bibi, mother of five, was sentenced to death for blasphemy, the first such conviction of a woman, sparking protests from rights groups. Her case dates back to June 2009 when she was asked to fetch water while out working in the fields. However, a group of Muslim women labourers had objected, alleging that as a non-Muslim her touch had made the water 'unclean'. A few days later the women went to a local cleric and alleged that Asia Bibi had made derogatory remarks about Prophet Mohammad, upon which the cleric approached the police, who opened an investigation. Consequently, Asia Bibi was arrested in the Ittanwalai village, and prosecuted under Section 295-C of the Pakistan Penal Code (PPC), which carries the death penalty. On November 8, 2010, she was handed down the death sentence by a court in the Nankana district in central Punjab. The incident generated significant protests by rights groups who continue to stress that the controversial legislation should be repealed as it is exploited for personal enmity and encourages extremism. Although Pakistan has yet to execute anyone for blasphemy, it is the first time a woman has been sentenced to hang. It remained to be seen if Asia Bibi's conviction would be overturned on appeal.[85]

However, despite the renewed widespread domestic and international pressure to repeal the Blasphemy Law, following the Asia Bibi conviction, Minister for Minorities, Shahbaz Bhatti stated categorically that that would not happen: 'Pakistan will not repeal its controversial Blasphemy Law, but may amend it to prevent abuse because scrapping the legislation could fuel militancy.'[86] Bhatti's words were to prove prophetic.

A series of horrific events that unfolded subsequently point to the controversial nature of the Blasphemy Law, and the strong opposition to any sympathy or move for its review or repeal. In January 2010, Governor of Punjab, Salman Taseer, was shot dead in the capital city of Islamabad by one of his own bodyguards, Malik Mumtaz Hussain Qadri, who opened fire on him and pumped 27 bullets into his body. Qadri later proudly confessed that he had killed the governor because of Taseer's support to Asia Bibi, and his public criticism of the Blasphemy Law as a 'black law'.[87] The division between Pakistan's liberal and radical segments can be judged from the fact that while a large section of civil society and lawyers protested and condemned the murder of Salman Taseer, his murderer Qadri was hailed as a hero by right-wing lawyers who showered rose petals on him as he arrived for his court hearing. Radical religious parties and leaders also gave out a call that no one should attend Taseer's funeral or offer funeral prayers for him as he was an 'infidel'.[88] Similarly, in March 2011, Pakistan's Minister for Religious Minorities, Shahbaz Bhatti, who had been receiving death threats because he supported Salman Taseer and his sympathetic stand for Asia Bibi and the review and amendment of the Blasphemy Law, was gunned down in Islamabad by those claiming to be the 'The *Qaeda* and the Taliban of Punjab'. Two assassins sprayed Bhatti with eight bullets, before scattering pamphlets that described him as a 'Christian infidel'.[89] In the continuing saga of religious hatred, intolerance, and revenge, in August 2011, Salman Taseer's son, Shahbaz Taseer, was kidnapped on his way to work in the provincial capital of Lahore[90] by four armed men allegedly belonging to the *Tehreek-e-Taliban Pakistan* (TTP) militant group. Amid conflicting media reports, Taseer's exact whereabouts and fate remained unknown till his recovery five years later in March 2016.[91]

70 *Legacy of Islamization*

After spending four years on death row for alleged blasphemy, in October 2014, the Lahore High Court upheld Asia Bibi's death sentence.[92] While in another horrific incident in the town of Kot Radha Kishan, in the Punjab province, a young Christian couple were tortured and then burnt to death in a brick kiln where they worked by an angry mob of Muslim men on allegations of desecrating pages of the *Quran*.[93] Given the growing trend of religious intolerance in the country, it remains to be seen if such incidents of violence and injustice targeting religious minorities will ever be taken up by Pakistani filmmakers as subjects for investigative documentaries or narrative films.

Conclusion

This chapter discussed a selection of documentary films that have addressed the intersections of politics, religion, and law as they affected contemporary Pakistani society. Beginning with the period of General Zia-ul-Haq's Islamization process and legal reforms, *Jaloos* (1988) set the tone for the changes and oppositional forces that had begun to take shape during this time – whether it was to confront and oppose *Sharia* laws that jeopardized women's equal rights in the form of the *Zina Hudood* Ordinance and the Law of Evidence, or the Blasphemy Law that have continued to hound and victimize women and religious minorities and sects, as these films examine. Today, these representative films, filmmakers, and organizational affiliations provide a historical filmic testimony to the politicization of Islam under Zia's authoritarian regime, as well as the historical roots and history of the emergence of activist documentary filmmaking practices in Pakistan.

Following from *Jaloos* which was made to be archived as a commemorative film for the women's organizations that participated in the 1988 procession, Sabiha Sumar's three documentaries *Who Will Cast the First Stone?* (1988), *Don't Ask Why* (1999), and *For A Place Under the Heavens* (2003), stand as the pioneering attempt by a Pakistani filmmaker to trace and analyse the roots of religious fundamentalism in Pakistan, addressing issues of politicization of religion, and promulgation of *Sharia* laws on film from within an Islamic state.[94] As they depict a broad cross-section of Pakistani society to give a wide picture of the tensions, conflicts, and contradictions that emerged in the struggle between secular, progressive voices and the fundamentalist elements, we already see religiously connotative words such as *jihad, hijab, burqa*, and *madrasa* entering the Pakistani documentary film vocabulary – terms that were to become subjects of more alarming and grave discussions, as will be apparent in Chapter 3. In particular, Sumar's films call attention to women's rights as human rights, hence equal rights, rather than an issue reserved for feminist enquiry. It is to her credit that as a Pakistani Muslim woman she had dared to launch her filmmaking career with the topic of critiquing the *Zina Hudood* Ordinance during the Islamization period while Zia was still in power. In appropriating what film scholar Thomas Waugh identified as the 'committed documentary' stance,[95] Sumar not only put these sensitive religious and political issues on the cinematic radar internationally, but also set a trend for other Pakistani filmmakers to use this medium as an activist tool, as will become evident further in the following chapters.[96]

As herself a Pakistani Muslim woman who has been part of the history she investigates in her films, Sumar's work underscores the importance of an historical and contextual analysis of all Pakistani filmmakers and their issue-oriented works.[97] This contextual analysis also helps to take into account the filmmakers' own political, personal, historical, social, cultural, and institutional positioning in the process.[98]

In the case of NCSW's documentary film, *Hudood Ordinance 1979: Divine Law, or Law of One Man?* (2005), we see a government–civil collaboration in conducting a critical debate on specific laws, and their validity and implications. For the first time on film, serious critique of the lacunae in the *Hudood* Ordinance and the Law of Evidence are documented through the patronage of a government body as legal experts, politicians, activists, and scholars from both sides join the debate. As the film plays a revisionist role by evaluating the past from a governmental position, it also performs a counter-history role in the context of an activist documentary film movement in contemporary Pakistan.

The NCJP's film, *A Sun Sets In* (2000), is significant in its contribution as it plays a judicial and historical role in documenting the life-sketch of Bishop John Joseph and the events that led to his tragic sacrifice, adding a 'persuasive' stance that draws attention to the harshness of the Blasphemy Law, another horrific legislation that requires reform.[99]

Between the two commemorative films, *Jaloos* (1988), and *A Sun Sets In* (2000), the above filmmakers and organizations can be seen acting as historiographers, stressing accountability for violation of human rights, marginalization of women and minorities, and judicial reforms in the guise of religion.[100] Correspondingly, their films gain their own 'judicial', 'historical',[101] and archival significance as they depict a critical and analytical 'revisionist-history' of the Islamization period through oral accounts and testimonies, and its implications in the present.[102] Making use of archival footage and stills (*Simorgh*), case studies, biographical and personal accounts, observational depictions, interviews (Sabiha Sumar), to interviews and talking heads (NCSW/*Ajoka* Theatre for Social Change), and a biographical life-sketch (NCJP/Shahid Nadeem), we see both individual as well as organizational contributions and collaborations taking on issues of mutual concern for debate, consciousness-raising, and social and judicial reforms.

As post-colonial scholar Homi K. Bhabha pointed out, the process and outcome of delving into the past for answers and guidance for the present, becomes an act of *remembering*, one that 'is never a quiet act of introspection or retrospection, but is a painful re-*membering*, a putting together of the dismembered past to make sense of the trauma of the present'.[103] Correspondingly, it can be argued that the filmmakers discussed in this chapter have *re-membered* and documented their country's painful and complex past to contextualize its threat from religious fundamentalism. The contextual enquiries of progressives (activists, scholars, lawyers, and others) into the roots of religious fundamentalism in Pakistan since 1977, its continuing grip on Pakistani society, and the equally significant resistance by rights activists and women's organizations, can all be defined as a collective activist exercise. This collective activist exercise can be seen as laying the foundation for an '*imperfect cinema*' in the Pakistani context – an '*imperfect cinema*' that not only deviates from the mainstream cinema, but more importantly brings together activist players from a variety of backgrounds and institutional affiliations, including a government body, and seizes the agency to address contemporary issues for social change.[104]

Today, these straightforward, critical films, and their makers occupy a key place in the emergence of an activist documentary cinema in Pakistan as they offer significant historical testimonials through first-hand accounts, views, and perspectives from those directly affected by the transformations in their society as Pakistan struggles to regain its secular origins. Together, this body of work can be seen as bringing Islamic theological debates, religious conflicts and tensions contained in Islamic jurisprudence and *Sharia* laws, and the politics of vested interests to a documentary screen from within a Muslim culture and society that itself had begun to seek accountability from its rulers and policy-makers.

The dominance of *Sharia* laws and legal transformations, the ensuing tilt towards religious fundamentalism, and intersections of religion and politics depicted in these films were to foment future religious extremism, intolerance, and violence not only within Pakistan, but also beyond its borders as illustrated by films in the next chapter – tracking Pakistan's journey from Islamization to the threat of religious militancy, Talibanization, and terrorism.

Notes

1. I have discussed the more general films that deal with the effects of Islamization and judicial reforms on women in this chapter, and those that focus specifically on women and gender-related issues in Chapter 4.
2. Only those organizations, individuals, and fraternities are included in this book whose alliances and collaborative and/or independent productions have made significant contributions to the emergence of an activist documentary film practice in contemporary Pakistan, and whose films will be discussed in the book.
3. The foremost of these was the All Pakistan Women's Association (APWA), formed in 1949 by the wife of Pakistan's first prime minister, Begum Raa'na Liaquat Ali Khan. APWA was formed to tackle the refugee crises that emerged as a result of partition between India and Pakistan in 1947. All Pakistan Women's Association (APWA): Accessed at: http://www.apwapunjab.org/ on April 2, 2015.
4. In the arena of performing arts during the Islamization period a new, defiant, and politically-conscious street and activist theatre of resistance also began to take shape in the country, largely in opposition to the *Sharia* laws, and curtailment of women's rights. Among the significant protest theatre groups that emerged were the *Tehrik-e-Niswan* (The Women's Movement) Theatre Group (1979), *Ajoka* Theatre for Social Change (1983), the *Punjab Lok Rehs* Theatre Group (1986), while the *Rafi Peer* Theatre Workshop (1974), the oldest performing arts company in Pakistan, began combining film, puppet theatre, music, and dance for social awareness and mobilizing resistance. Fawzia Afzal-Khan, 'Street Theater in Pakistani Punjab: The Case of Ajoka, Lok Rehs, and the (So-Called) Woman Question', in Fawzia Afzal-Khan and Kalpana Seshadri-Crooks (eds), *The Pre-Occupation of Postcolonial Studies*, Duke University Press, Durham and London, 2000, p. 171.

For further discussion see Shoaib Iqbal, 'Parallel Theater: Socio-Political Perspective', Kunci Cultural Studies Center: Accessed at: http://kunci.or.id/articles/parallel-theater-socio-political-perscepctive-by-shoaib-iqbal/ on April 2, 2015.

5   Shahla Zia and Farzana Bari, 'Women in Non-Government Organizations', *Baseline Report on Women's Participation in Political and Public Life in Pakistan*. Project of International Women's Rights Action Watch-Asia Pacific. Published by *Aurat* Publications and Information Service Foundation, Islamabad, Pakistan, 1999, pp. 81–2.

6   Thousands of NGOs have emerged in Pakistan since the 1980s that have centred on women's rights and issues. A 2010 USAID study reports that the number of registered and unregistered NGOs in Pakistan stood at 100,000 in 2009, while there were 30,000 registered active NGOs in 2001. Nadia Naviwala, *Harnessing Local Capacity: U.S. Assistance and NGOs in Pakistan*, Harvard Kennedy School Policy Analysis Exercise. Spring 2010.

7   National Commission on the Status of Women, Pakistan (NCSW). Accessed at: http://www.ncsw.gov.pk/index.php on April 2, 2015.

8   *Jaloos (Procession)*, 1988 (VHS. 22 min. 11 sec.). Produced by Ferida Sher for *Simorgh* Productions, Pakistan (Urdu).

9   The *Simorgh* Women's Resource and Publication Centre and Collective, so named after the mythical Iranian bird reputed to have a nest in the Tree of Knowledge, started functioning in 1985 as a part-time initiative, and formalized as a full-time organization in 1995. It was founded by some of the most prominent names associated with the contemporary women's movement and women's rights in Pakistan, including educationist Ms Neelam Hussain who has been serving as its chief coordinator and senior editor for its bi-annual *BAYAN* (Expression), a socio-legal journal that was launched in 2004 to serve as an academic forum on socio-legal issues. As a not-for-profit NGO staffed by educationists, sociologists, and artists, *Simorgh* as a feminist-activist organization has focused on working with students, teachers, media professionals, other national and international NGOs, and Community Based Organizations (CBOs). For details of *Simorgh* projects and publications, visit: http://simorgh.org.pk/.

10 The *Simorgh* Women's Resource and Publication Centre was designated for the co-ordination and preparation of the 1988 procession documented in *Jaloos*, while a number of other major NGOs also participated, including the Pakistan Women Lawyers Association (PAWLA), *ASR* (Impact), Human Rights Commission of Pakistan (HRCP), the *Aurat* Foundation, and *Simorgh* among others.

11 General Zia-ul-Haq was killed in the same year (August 17, 1988) in a plane crash.

12 Khawar Mumtaz and Farida Shaheed, 'Legally Reducing Women's Status', *Women of Pakistan: Two Steps Forward, One Step Back?* Vanguard Books, Lahore, Pakistan, 1987, p. 106.

13 Ibid., p. 108.

14 The first and most significant development in terms of Pakistani women's resistance materialized in response to Zia's gender-discriminatory *Zina Hudood* Ordinance when the case of Fehmida and Allah Bux versus the State came to light in 1981. In this case a sessions judge sentenced a man and a woman to death by stoning and 100 lashes respectively under the provision of the new Ordinance. This judgement served as a catalyst for the swift formation of the Women's Action Forum (WAF) the same year, led by a women's organization, *Shirkat Gah* (Participation Forum), and endorsed initially by five other women's organizations based in Karachi, where it was formed. For the history and formation of WAF see Khawar Mumtaz and Farida Shaheed, 'Zia and the Creation of WAF', *Women of Pakistan: Two Steps Forward, One Step Back?*, pp. 71–5.

For WAF's activism in resistance to Islamization, see ibid. 'WAF and its Growth and Impact', p. 123.

For details of *Shirkat Gah* projects visit: http://shirkatgah.org/.

74 *Legacy of Islamization*

15 For details of this historic February 12, 1983 demonstration see Mumtaz and Shaheed, 'Legally Reducing Women's Status', *Women of Pakistan: Two Steps Forward, One Step Back?*, p. 107.
16 For pictures of police brutalities on women protestors on February 12, 1983 see Asma Jahangir and Hina Jilani, *The Hudood Ordinances: A Divine Sanction?*, Sang-e-Meel Publications, Lahore, Pakistan, 2003, pp. 34–45.
17 February 12, 1984, when the Law of Evidence was implemented, has become the symbol of women's resistance movement and is commemorated countrywide each year as Pakistan Women's Day in memory of the peaceful women's demonstration that was attacked by the police. 'Pakistan Women's Day', Women's Action Forum Press Release, (WAF), Islamabad, Pakistan. February 12, 2004; *The Daily News International*, February 12, Islamabad, Pakistan.
18 The rare video print for *Jaloos* obtained from *Simorgh* Women's Resource and Publication Centre in Lahore, Pakistan, is of rather poor quality. According to sources at *Simorgh*, unfortunately the video print was never preserved through multiple copies, or on DVD.
19 Although these individuals are not identified separately in *Jaloos*, they are featured repeatedly through interviews in later films to be discussed in the book. For example, these include human rights lawyers Asma Jehangir and Hina Gilani, who are also the founding members of *AGHS*, Pakistan's first free Legal Aid Cell set up in Lahore in 1980, besides other prominent names from the legal profession, the Human Rights Commission of Pakistan (HRCP), and various women's rights organizations.

Asma Jehangir also became the first woman to be elected as the president of the Supreme Court Bar Association (SCBA) of Pakistan. 'Asma Wins Thriller to Become First Woman Head of SCBA', *Dawn.com*, October 28, 2010. Accessed at: http://www.dawn.com/news/576333/asma-wins-thriller-to-become-first-woman-head-of-scba on April 2, 2015.
20 Keith Beattie, 'Finding and Keeping: Compilation Documentary', *Documentary Screens: Non-fiction Film and Television*, Houndsmills, Palgrave, 2004, pp. 125–9.
21 Michael Renov, 'The Subject in History: The New Autobiography in Film and Video', *The Subject of Documentary*, University of Minnesota Press, Minneapolis, MN, London, 2004, pp. 109–10.
22 Paula Rabinowitz, 'Wreckage Upon Wreckage: History, Documentary, and the Ruins of Memory', *They Must Be Represented: The Politics of Documentary*, Verso, London, New York, 1994, p. 17.
23 Who *Will Cast the First Stone?* Sabiha Sumar (with Ahmed Alauddin Jamal), 1988 (VHS 52 min.). Retake Film & Video Collective, UK, (Urdu/English/English subtitles). For production details visit: http://ftvdb.bfi.org.uk/sift/title/424112?view=credit.

A separate version and discussion of Sabiha Sumar's three documentary films (*Who Will Cast the First Stone?*, *Don't Ask Why*, and *For A Place Under the Heavens*) has also been published. See Rahat Imran, 'Deconstructing Islamization in Pakistan: Sabiha Sumar Wages Feminist Cinematic Jihad through a Documentary Lens', *Journal of International Women's Studies* (*JIWS*), 9.3, May 2008, pp. 117–54. Access at: http://vc.bridgew.edu/jiws/vol9/iss3/8/.
24 Sabiha Sumar's films include: *Who Will Cast the First Stone?* (1988), *Don't Ask Why* (1999), and *For a Place Under the Heavens* (2003), *Silent Waters* (2003), *Dinner with the President: A Nation's Journey* (2007). Her first narrative feature film, *Silent Waters*, screened at the 2004 Sundance Film Festival, has won seven international awards at various film festivals, including South Africa, France, Argentina, Germany and Australia. At the 2003 Locarno International Film Festival, *Silent Waters* won the Golden Leopard Award for best film, a Leopard for best actress for Indian actress Kirron Kher, and three other awards. Sairah Irshad Khan, 'I've had no support from Pakistanis at home.' Interview with Sabiha Sumar. *Newsline Monthly Magazine*,

Legacy of Islamization 75

  September 2005. Accessed at: http://www.newslinemagazine.com/2005/09/interview-sabiha-sumar/ on January 11, 2016.
25 *Vidhi* Films. Accessed at: http://www.vidhifilms.net/documentaries.htm on April 2, 2015.
26 The film's opening intertitles state that Sumar did not obtain the mandatory No Objection Certificate (NOC) required from the government of Pakistan for exhibition rights in the country, subject to censorship clearance.
  However, having shot the film without the NOC from the Pakistan Ministry of Culture would have automatically barred Sumar from exhibiting her film in Pakistan. Also, because of strict state censorship policies and media curbs, in all likelihood such a film topic at the time would not have been granted an NOC.
  A film unauthorized for exhibition by the Pakistan Censor Board can be punishable with imprisonment for a term which may extend to three years, or with fine which may extend to one *lac* rupees (Rs 100,000), or with both. Central Board of Film Censors, Government of Pakistan: Scroll down to 'Censorship of Films Act 1963' at: https://southasiacommunication.wordpress.com/report-4-film-policy-pakistan/.See under Chapter 1V 'Miscellaneous' # 18 c: 'Penalties and Procedures'.
27 For example, in March 2002, a Nigerian woman, Amina Lawal, was sentenced under the Islamic *Sharia* laws to be stoned to death in Bakori, northern Nigeria. According to reports, she had confessed to having had a child out of wedlock while divorced. Under the *Sharia* laws pregnancy outside of marriage constitutes sufficient evidence for a woman to be convicted of adultery or fornication. The man named as the father of her baby girl reportedly denied having sex with Amina, and his testimony as a man was considered enough for charges against him to be dropped. 'End the Torture of Women in Northern Nigeria', Amnesty International. August 7, 2003. Accessed at: http://www.universalrights.net/news/display.php?id=767 on January 11, 2016. However, following immense international outrage and pressure, an appeals court overturned Amina Lawal's conviction on the basis that her sentence was invalid because she was already pregnant when the *Sharia* law was implemented in her home province. For details of the verdict, see Jeff Koinange, 'Woman Sentenced to Stoning Freed.' *CNN.com*, February 23, 2004. Accessed at: http://edition.cnn.com/2003/WORLD/africa/09/25/nigeria.stoning/ on April 2, 2015.
28 Sairah Irshad Khan, 'I've had no support from Pakistanis at home.' Interview with Sabiha Sumar, *Newsline Monthly Magazine*, September 2005: Accessed at: http://www.newslinemagazine.com/2005/09/interview-sabiha-sumar/ on April 2, 2015.
29 For a critical discussion on the loopholes and implications of the *Zina Hudood* Ordinance and the Law of Evidence, for women in particular through a discussion of two case studies, see '*The Zina Hudood* Ordinance and the Law of Evidence' and 'Legal Injustices' (pp. 87–93). Rahat Imran, 'Legal Injustices: The *Zina Hudood* Ordinance of Pakistan and its Implications for Women', *Journal of International Women's Studies*, 7.2, November 2005, pp. 78–100. Access at: http://vc.bridgew.edu/jiws/vol7/iss2/5/.
30 Under Pakistan's family laws all Muslim divorces, once pronounced, have to be registered by the husband, and ninety days after registration, the divorce becomes effective. Shahida's divorce was not registered as required by law, thereby resulting in an offence. As there is no time bar on registration of the divorce deed, the prescribed offence is ineffective, but the trial court ruled that Shahida's second marriage was illegal, and hence the couple was convicted of committing rape on each other. Since the accused had admitted to living together, it was taken as a form of confession of guilt. Jahangir and Jilani, *The Hudood Ordinances*, p. 58.
31 Following countrywide protests by human rights activists and women's organizations against the verdict, Shahida Parveen and Mohammad Sarwar's convictions were overturned on appeal, and the subsequent re-trial of their case. Ibid., p. 58.
32 For discussion of the Safia Bibi case study, see Mumtaz and Shaheed, 'Legally Reducing Women's Status', p. 103.

76 *Legacy of Islamization*

33 Justice Dorab Patel, belonging to the Zoroastrian faith, was a founding member of the Asian Human Rights Commission [AHRC] in 1987. In 1981 he refused to take a fresh oath under the Provisional Constitutional Order (PCO) promulgated by General Zia-ul-Haq, which deprived the superior judiciary of many of its powers – even though as the second senior-most judge of the Supreme Court, he was certain to be the next Chief Justice of Pakistan. Justice Patel died in 1998. *South Asian Media.Net.* R. John Hinnells and Alan Williams (eds), *Parsis in India and the Diaspora*, Routledge, London and New York, 2008, p. 259.

34 In his inaugural speech as first Governor General of Pakistan after partition from India in 1947, Mohammad Ali Jinnah, the founder of Pakistan, said: '… you will find that in the course of time, Hindus would cease to be Hindus and Muslims would cease to be Muslims, not in the religious sense, because that is the personal faith of each individual, but in the political sense as citizens of the state.' Hector Bolitho, *Jinnah, Creator of Pakistan*, Oxford University Press, Karachi, Pakistan, 2006, pp. 403–4; Muhammad Nadeem Anwar, Raza Ullah, Nazir Ahmad and Muneeb Ali, 'Critical Discourse Analysis of Quaid-e-Azam Muhammad Ali Jinnah's (11th August, 1947) speech in the first Constituent Assembly of Pakistan', *Asian Studies, A Research Journal of South Asian Studies*, 30.1, January–June 2015, pp. 159–73, (p. 171).

35 For discussion on police brutalities and judicial gender-biases against women in prison charged under the *Zina Hudood* Ordinance see 'Rape', 'Role of the Police', 'Gender Bias in the Criminal Justice System', and 'Mistreatment of Victims' in Crime or Custom? Violence Against Women in Pakistan. *Human Rights Watch Report*, August 1999. Accessed at: http://www.hrw.org/reports/1999/pakistan/ on April 2, 2015.

In a 1991 report on Pakistan, Dorothy Q. Thomas of the Human Rights Watch (HRW) explains the status of women confronted with the law enforcement and judicial system in Pakistan: 'Eighty percent of all female prisoners in Pakistan are illiterate. According to a survey conducted in 1988, over 90 percent of the 90 women prisoners interviewed in two prisons in Punjab were unaware of the law under which they had been imprisoned. Over 60 percent had received no legal assistance whatsoever.' Dorothy Q. Thomas, 'Double Jeopardy: Police Abuse of Women in Pakistan', *Human Rights Watch Report*, 1991. Accessed at: http://www.hrw.org/reports/1992/pakistan/ on April 2, 2015.

36 General Zia-ul-Haq had a disability in one of his eyes, and popularly became the target of public ridicule, and later newspaper cartoons and caricatures.

Ironically, Ghulam Sakina's words bore terrible truth seventeen years later in 2005 when the country's best known woman lawyer, Asma Jehangir, also interviewed in the documentary, was publicly roughed up and partially stripped of her shirt while protesting for women's right to participate in a mixed marathon race. The event was largely seen as a test for army dictator General Pervaiz Musharraf's claims of having brought 'enlightened moderation' to Pakistan in his quest to be the chief US ally at the forefront of the 'War on Terror' and supporter against religious fundamentalism. Jehangir, along with numerous other civil society activists, was brutally beaten up in public, arrested, and piled into police vans as a way of deterring any further protests. Patrick Goodenough, 'Pakistan Police Arrest Runners in Mixed-Sex Road Race.' *cnsnews.com*. May 16, 2005. Accessed at: http://www.cnsnews.com/news/article/pakistan-police-arrest-runners-mixed-sex-road-race on January 12, 2016.

37 Sairah Irshad Khan, 'I've had no support from Pakistanis at home.' Interview with Sabiha Sumar. *Newsline Monthly Magazine*, October 13, 2009. Accessed at: http://www.newslinemagazine.com/2005/09/interview-sabiha-sumar/ on April 2, 2015.

38 Bill Nichols, 'What Are Documentaries About?', *Introduction to Documentary*, Indiana University Press, Bloomington, IN and Indianapolis, IN, 2001, p. 70.

39 Within Pakistan, Sumar was still unable to screen her film despite the fact that a democratically elected and progressive woman Prime Minister, Benazir Bhutto, took power after Zia's death.

Legacy of Islamization 77

40 *Don't Ask Why*, Sabiha Sumar, 1999 (VHS 58 min.) Pakistan, Trafik Film Production (Urdu/English/English sub-titles). The film was produced and funded as part of the *Girls Around the World* documentary series first aired on Arte, a German-French cultural channel. For details on the series visit: Women Make Movies (WMM). Accessed at: http://www.wmm.com/filmcatalog/pages/c518.shtml on April 2, 2015.
41 On observational film see Bill Nichols, 'What Types of Documentary Are There?', *Introduction to Documentary*, Indiana University Press, Bloomington, IN and Indianapolis, IN, 2001, pp. 99–138.
42 Asked how much of *Don't Ask Why* is factual, Sumar asserted: 'It's not fiction. It is a documentary based on this young girl's real diary and she plays herself in the film and actually reads aloud from it.' Khan,. 'I've had no support from Pakistanis at home.'
43 Under Islamization, the *sari*, the most popularly worn and internationally recognized dress of Indian and South Asian women, began to be identified by the state and religious fundamentalists as a 'Hindu' dress, and thus discouraged. Extremist forces further translated the *sari* as an anti-Islamic symbol that represented Hindus and Indians as 'infidels.' Khawar Mumtaz and Farida Shaheed, 'The Veiling and Seclusion of Women', *Women of Pakistan: Two Steps Forward, One Step Back?*, Zed Books Ltd., London and New Jersey, 1987, p. 78.
44 Before Islamization, dress codes, marriage of choice, complaints and cases of adultery, etc., were treated as personal matters, and dictated by individual family traditions and the Family Law respectively. For discussion on transformations in Pakistan's civil society and institutions following Zia-ul-Haq's Islamization in 1977, see ibid., pp. 77–98.
45 The *burqa* is a head to toe covering garment with a mesh screen for eyes worn by very conservative Muslim women in the sub-continent. In Afghanistan, the Taliban officially enforced the *burqa* for all women as a symbol of their fundamentalist government and policies.
46 Denying allegations that she resorts to Pakistan-bashing in her film, Sumar said that she had always questioned the system. She claims that when she was in the age group of 17 to 25, she would have never joined a women's conservative organization to understand religion as her character in the film did: 'But things are changing. There was a debate going on in Pakistan about women's rights, and the need to interpret the Koran in a more liberal way.' Khan, 'I've had no support from Pakistanis at home.'
47 The reference is to Indian Bollywood film stars Shah Rukh Khan and actress Rani Mukherjee, both hugely popular among South Asian audiences, and in the Middle East where dubbed and subtitled Indian films are watched by Arab audiences as well.
48 1999 also saw Pakistan return to another era of dictatorship under General Pervaiz Musharraf (1999–2008), following a military coup that deposed the then elected Prime Minister, Mian Nawaz Sharif.
49 *For a Place Under the Heavens*, Sabiha Sumar, 2003 (VHS 53 min.), Pakistan, *VIDHI* Films/Unlimited Production in association with ZDF/ARTE (Urdu/English/English sub-titles).
50 Sumar introduces her friends on screen as Nausheen, a women's rights lawyer with whom Sumar had worked on a women's legal and political education project in prisons; Saba, who runs a women's development think-tank; and Aliya, who works for an independent TV network, and is a doctoral student at the time, pursuing a degree in Islamic Political Thought.
51 Although consumption of alcoholic drinks and all forms of intoxication are considered forbidden by Islam, they were not prohibited in Pakistan till, in a bid to appease religious parties for political gains, Prime Minister Z. A. Bhutto imposed a countrywide prohibition on the sale and consumption of alcohol before he was removed from power in 1977. He also imposed a symbolic ban on gambling and

nightclubs, and announced Friday as the weekly Muslim holiday, replacing Sunday which was identified by religious parties as a Christian holiday, and placed copies of the *Quran* in high ranking hotels and government rest houses. Mumtaz and Shaheed, 'The Evolution of Islam in Politics.' *Women of Pakistan: Two Steps Forward, One Step Back?*, p. 14.

52 Before General Zia-ul-Haq came to power, cabaret performances and dancing, casinos, nightclubs, and bars were a popular and common nightlife feature among Pakistan's urban elites. Zia banned all such activities, proclaiming them 'un-Islamic'.

53 In the Indian sub-continent, as well as Iran before the Islamic Revolution in 1979, and Afghanistan before the Taliban regime took control in 1996, conservative Muslim women who chose to veil wore either a *chador* (shawl worn loosely over the head and shoulders), or the *burqa* that also covered the body and face. The *hijab*, on the other hand is a mandatory head-covering garment worn by women and girls in Saudi Arabia and other orthodox Islamic countries, including Iran following the Islamic Revolution.

54 During Pakistan's independence from India in 1947, the Kashmir state was also divided into two parts, and has since then been a source of conflict between the two countries. Pakistan has continued to claim sovereignty over the Indian Kashmir as a Muslim homeland for the Kashmiris, and thereby a part of Pakistan. The Kashmir conflict can be traced back to 1989, when the Jammu and Kashmir Liberation Front (JKLF) launched an armed struggle against Indian rule. Military and other means of support from within the Pakistani establishment, and independent *jihadist* groups, both within and outside of Pakistan, lend passionate support for what is seen as a 'holy' cause, and account 'in large measure, for the gradual take-over of the armed struggle in Kashmir by militant Islamist groups, mainly based in Pakistan and led, for the most part, by Pakistani nationals'. Yoginder Sikand, '*Islamist Militancy in Kashmir: The Case of the Lashkar-i-Tayyeba*', November 20, 2003. Accessed at: http://www.sacw.net/DC/CommunalismCollection/ArticlesArchive/sikand20Nov2003.html on April 2, 2015.

Since partition, Pakistan and India have fought two full-fledged wars over Kashmir, one in 1965, and the other in 1971 that also resulted in the separation of East Pakistan, and the birth of Bangladesh. For a background to the Pakistan–India conflicts since 1947, see Sumit Ganguly, *The Origins of War in South Asia: Indo-Pakistani Conflicts Since 1947*, Westview Press, Boulder, CO and London, 1986.

55 The concept of martyrdom (*Shahadat*) in Islam is believed to be the ultimate religious offering Muslims can make by giving their life in the service of God. However, in recent times this concept is being distorted by religious fanatics, terrorist organizations, and suicide bombers to serve and justify their extremist religio-political agendas. The themes of *Jihad* and *Shahadat* did not occur in Pakistani textbooks before 1979, but under Zia's Islamization curricula and textbooks openly eulogized *Jihad* and *Shahadat* and urged students to become *mujahids* and martyrs. A. H. Nayyar, 'Insensitivity to the Religious Diversity of the Nation', in A. H., Nayyar, and Ahmad Salim (eds), *The Subtle Subversion: The State of Curricula and Textbooks in Pakistan: Urdu, English, Social Studies and Civics*, Sustainable Development Policy Institute (SDPI), Islamabad, Pakistan, 2002, p. 22.

56 Since 1979, these *madrasas* in Pakistan have also become the hub and training grounds for Islamic fundamentalist ideologies, and the promotion of violent '*jihad*' against non-Muslims. For further discussion see Zahid Hussain, 'Nursery for Jihad', *Frontline Pakistan: The Struggle with Militant Islam*, Columbia University Press, New York, 2007, p. 76.

57 For a discussion on Pakistani women's role in contemporary society see Shimaila Matri Dawood, 'Will the Real Pakistani Woman Please Stand Up?', *Newsline Monthly Magazine,* Karachi, Pakistan, March 2005.

58 Shaheen Sardar Ali was formerly professor of law at the University of Peshawar, Pakistan, Minister for Health, Population Welfare and Women's Development in the Government of the North West Frontier Province (Pakistan), and Chairperson of the National Commission on the Status of Women (NCSW). She teaches Islamic Law at Warwick School of Law, University of Warwick, Coventry, UK. Accessed at: http://www2.warwick.ac.uk/fac/soc/law/staff/academic/ali/ on April 2, 2015.

59 Since its establishment in July 2000, the NCSW has been working alongside legal experts and national and international human rights and women's organizations, including the United Nations. The NCSW has been active in publishing annual reports, documenting socio-legal developments in the country, and holding debates and seminars to review the impact of *Sharia* laws on women's status and rights concerning divorce, inheritance, family laws, child custody, and Islamic concepts of justice, such as *qisas* (equal punishment) and *diyat* (blood money), in criminal procedures. The NCSW has been headed by various prominent women activists, including Ms Khawar Mumtaz as its chairperson, who is a long time women's rights activist, former Executive Director of the *Shirkatgah* Women's Resource Centre, and founder member of the Women's Action Forum (WAF) in opposition to General Zia-ul-Haq's Islamization process. Accessed at: http://www.ncsw.gov.pk/ on April 2, 2015.

60 *Hudood Ordinance 1979: Divine Law, or Law of One Man?*, 2005 (DVD 23.51 min.), *Ajoka* Productions for the National Commission on the Status of Women, Pakistan (Urdu/English sub-titles).

61 Renov, 'The Subject in History', pp. 109–10.

62 Nichols, 'What Are Documentaries About?', p. 70.

63 Documentaries made by the National Commission on the Status of Women on women's issues include:*Prisoners of Circumstances*, 2006 (DVD 22 min. 50 sec.). Produced by National Commission on the Status of Women under UNDP-IS-NCSW Project, 2006, Pakistan (Urdu/English sub-titles).

Mera Bhag, Tiyaag hi Tiyaag (*The Promise*), 2008 (DVD 11 min. 19 sec.). Produced by the National Commission on the Status of Women with assistance from the United Nations Development Fund for Women (UNIFEM), Pakistan (English/Urdu).

64 Shahid Nadeem, screenwriter, journalist, and human rights activist has been associated with Pakistan Television (PTV) since 1973 as producer and playwright. He has also worked with Amnesty International (AI), and has been imprisoned thrice for his writing and non-violent opposition to military rule. With a focus on human and gender rights, Nadeem has written over 40 stage plays, mostly for *Ajoka* Theatre for Social Change that he runs with his wife, Madeeha Gohar, in Lahore, Pakistan. Accessed at: http://ajoka.org.pk/ on September 12, 2014.

65 *A Sun Sets In*, Shahid Nadeem, 2000 (DVD 45 min.), National Commission for Justice and Peace (NCJP) Production, Pakistan. (Produced in both English and Urdu versions. Off-screen commentary in English version by Graham Horn and Rebecca Edge). The film has been shown as part of the 15 films chosen for the Traveling Film South Asia Documentary Film Festival in 2001, and has held 40 shows in different places. *Film SouthAsia*. Accessed at: http://www.filmsouthasia.org/ on April 2, 2015.

66 The Blasphemy laws of Pakistan are considered a relic of the 1860 British colonial criminal law. By 1986, they were 'Islamized' by General Zia-ul-Haq. In 1991, elected Prime Minister Nawaz Sharif made the death penalty mandatory. Abuse of these laws became rampant after Zia-ul-Haq's Islamization of the laws: while there had been only seven cases between 1927 and 1986, the number of cases between 1986 and 2004 increased to more than 4000. *Rationalist International*. Bulletin # 135 (21 November 2004). Accessed at: http://www.rationalistinternational.net on September 13, 2014.

67 Pakistan is a multi-ethnic and multi-religious country. While 96 per cent comprise Muslim *Sunni* (majority) and *Shia* (minority) sects, 4 per cent of its population

represents religious minorities, and includes Christians, Hindus, Sikhs, Buddhists, Parsis, Bahá'ís, Ahmadis, and Kalash. *Franciscans International*. Accessed at: http://www.franciscansinternational.org/node/3037 on September 15, 2014.

68 In 1980, the Zia regime began adding new sections into the Pakistan Penal Code's existing injunctions dealing with offences against Islam. Known generally as the Blasphemy Law, the new inclusions, 298-A and 298-C, proved to be cunning and water-tight legal provisions to rule through fear and punishment.

Inserted into the existing law in 1980, section 298-A made the use of derogatory remarks in respect of persons revered in Islam an offence, punishable with up to three years' imprisonment. In 1986, this was further narrowed down through the insertion of another inclusion, 295-C, that specifically made defiling the name of the Prophet Mohammad a criminal offence, punishable with death or life-imprisonment. *Amnesty International Report on Pakistan*, September 1996 (*ASA* 33/10/96). Accessed at: http://www.amnesty.org/ on September 13, 2014.

69 The National Commission for Justice and Peace (NCJP) was formed by the Pakistan Catholic Bishops' Conference in 1985. As an advocacy and human rights organization the Commission has been defending cases of blasphemy against Muslims, Christians, and Hindus since 1990, in addition to campaigning for the abolition of the Blasphemy Laws. Accessed at: http://www.ncjp-pk.org on September 14, 2014.

70 A reading of the Blasphemy Law in the Pakistan Penal Code clarifies not only the all-encompassing nature of this law, but also the looseness with which it can be, and has been, manipulated or applied, particularly against religious minorities such as Christians and the *Ahmeddiyya* communities, as a means for executing vicious personal vendettas, religious hatreds, and politically motivated agendas through false accusations. For discussion of the Blasphemy Law see *'Blasphemy Laws in Pakistan: A Historical Overview'*, Center for Research and Security Studies (CRSS), Islamabad, Pakistan. Accessed at: http://www.pharosobservatory.com/c/asia/pakistan/pakistan-center-for-research-and-security-studies-report-on-blasphemy-laws-en on January 12, 2016.

71 Three Christian men, Manzur Masih, Rahmat Masih, and Salamat Masih had been arrested in May 1993 accused of blasphemy, under Section 295-C of the Pakistan Penal Code (PPC). They were said to have passed pieces of paper into a mosque in Punjab province. The slips of paper allegedly bore insulting comments about Prophet Mohammad. The three had been accused by a cleric, Maulvi Fazl-e-Haq, who was a leader of the militant group *Sipah-e-Sahaba*, which at that time was not banned. Fazl-e-Haq claimed the three had also scribbled graffiti on the mosque wall. At Lahore High Court, the three were acquitted, and set free, accompanied by another young man who had been falsely accused. Standing on the steps of the courthouse, the four were shot at by gunmen. Manzur Masih was killed. The Lahore High Court judge, Arif Iqbal Husain Bhatti, who had acquitted him was also later gunned down in his office in 1997 by extremists for freeing the Christians. Adrian Morgan, *'Pakistan: Abuse of Christians and Other Religious Minorities'*. Accessed at: http://www.thepersecution.org/news/09/fsm1007.html on September 14, 2014.

72 A Christian man, Ayub Masih, 30, in the Sahiwal district of the Punjab province was sentenced to death on April 27, 1998 on charges of blasphemy under section 295-C of the Pakistan Penal Code (PPC) by a court in Sahiwal. On 14 October 1996, Ayub Masih had been arrested following allegations made by a Muslim that he felt offended when Ayub Masih told him that Christianity was 'right' and that he should read British author Salman Rushdie's *Satanic Verses*, and that they had scuffled after this alleged exchange.

The Catholic Bishop of Faisalabad, Bishop John Joseph, pointed out that the allegations appeared to be motivated by a dispute over property between Muslim and Christian inhabitants of the village. Several families were forcibly evicted and several Christians beaten by villagers following the filing of the complaint against Ayub

Masih. Bishop John Joseph committed suicide in May 1998 in protest against the imposition of the death sentence on Ayub Masih; the death sentence was followed by non-violent countrywide protests of Christian communities. '*Pakistan: Blasphemy Acquittal Welcome But Law Must Be Amended,*' Amnesty International, August 2002. Accessed at https://www.amnesty.org.uk/press-releases/pakistan-blasphemy-acquittal-welcome-law-must-be-amended on January 12, 2016.

After a six year ordeal behind bars Ayub Masih was acquitted by the Supreme Court which ordered his immediate release from the high-security cell in the Multan Central Jail where he had been awaiting execution. Faced with ongoing death threats, Ayub quietly left Pakistan in 2002. Nina Shea, '*Testimony of Nina Shea: Pakistan's Anti-Blasphemy Laws*', Hudson Institute's Center for Religious Freedom, New York, USA, October 8, 2009. Accessed at: http://www.hudson.org/content/researchattachments/attachment/748/sheapakistan108.pdf, p. 6, third para., on January 12, 2016.

73 Linda S. Walbridge, 'Blasphemy', *The Christians of Pakistan: The Passion of Bishop John Joseph*, RoutledgeCurzon, London, 2003, p. 90.

74 At the time of Bishop John Joseph's suicide, the Pakistan Muslim League (PML-N) was in office, led by Prime Minister Mian Nawaz Sharif (1997–1999). Sharif's earlier tenure as prime minister had been from 1990 to 1993. Benazir Bhutto, leader of the Pakistan People's Party (PPP), and the first woman elected as prime minister of a Muslim state, also served twice as PM – 1988–1990 and 1993–1996, after General Zia-ul-Haq's death in an air crash in 1988. Despite being elected twice each to office by popular vote, neither political party, nor their leaders attempted to address the thorny issue of the revision or repeal of the Blasphemy Law.

75 '*Sparrow*' is part of the two-volume collection of 18 songs entitled *Aman Ke Geet* (Songs of Peace) released by the NCJP in 2009. The collection includes songs related to themes of peace and harmony, and are sung by Pakistani singers in all provincial languages including Urdu, Punjabi, Balochi, Seraiki, Sindhi, and Pushto. Personal email correspondence with Peter Jacob, Executive Secretary NCJP, Lahore, Pakistan, on March 20, 2010.

76 For example, in another brutal attack on the Christian community in August 2009, seven people were burnt alive and 18 others injured in the town of Gojra after violence erupted over the alleged desecration of the *Quran*. More than 50 houses were set on fire and a place of worship belonging to the minority community was damaged by an angry Muslim mob. According to sources, most of the houses were burnt by a group of youth who, their faces covered, threw petrol bombs, and fired indiscriminately. Tariq Saeed, 'Seven Burnt Alive in Gojra Violence.' *Dawn Online Newspaper*, August 2, 2009. Accessed at: http://www.dawn.com/news/848930/seven-burnt-alive-in-gojra-violence on January 12, 2016.

77 Historically, the Christian minorities have been associated with the most menial of jobs in the Indian sub-continent, those considered impure and polluting to Hindus and Muslims, and thus treated as the lowest strata of society, i.e. the 'untouchables'. They have been associated with jobs such as removing dead animals from the fields, skinning animals, removing the bodies of the unclaimed dead, executing condemned criminals, and cleaning latrines. They also ate carrion and leftovers. This lower status accorded to them has been a source of discrimination as equal citizens at every level. Walbridge, *The Christians of Pakistan*, p, 16.

Lower class Christians in Pakistan commonly identify themselves by using '*Masih*' as a surname (a reference to Jesus Christ as Messiah) to distinguish themselves from the Muslims. Ibid., p. 90.

Tracing the history of Christian communities in the pre- and post-partition India and the creation of the new Muslim state of Pakistan in 1947, Pieter Streefland notes: 'Already in advance of 1947 there were Christian Punjabis who had migrated to urban areas and taken up sweeping there. They were the forerunners of a predominantly urban grouping of Christian Punjabi Sweepers (CPS) which swelled

82 *Legacy of Islamization*

enormously with the arrival of Christian Punjabi's from the villages of the Punjab during the years immediately following the creation of Pakistan. At the time of partition, *Mazhbi*-Sikhs also joined this grouping. They had either decided not to journey to the new India, or hadn't the means to do so. They resolved to convert to Christianity because they believed as Christians they might live more safely in the midst of Moslems.' Pieter Streefland, 'The Christian Punjabi Sweepers', *The Sweepers of Slaughterhouse: Conflict and Survival in a Karachi Neighbourhood*, Van Gorcum, Assen, The Netherlands, 1979, pp. 10–11.

The Christian sweepers have also been known as *Chuhras*, a derogatory term that distinguishes them as a dark-skinned caste (a visible factor that in itself is looked down upon and stigmatized culturally), associated with impurity, and thus treated as 'Untouchables' by both Muslims and Hindus in the sub-continent. Ibid., pp. 7–8.

78 This is the only film on the Blasphemy Law, made by a Pakistani filmmaker and/or Pakistan-based organization, that has been available for viewing on this topic.
79 Shahid Nadeem, 'Silencing the Nation: Censorship Acts Since 1947', in Neelam Hussain, Samiya Mumtaz and Samina Choonara (eds), *Politics of Language*, Simorgh Women's Resource and Publication Centre, Lahore, Pakistan, 2005, p. 169.
80 For Blasphemy cases against the *Ahmeddiyya* community see *Asian Human Rights Report*: 'Pakistan: The Year 2009 Was Worst for Ahmedis', February 3, 2010. Accessed at: http://www.thepersecution.org/news/10/ahrc1003.html on September 15, 2014.
81 For discussion of victimization and persecution of religious minorities under the Blasphemy Law in Pakistan, see Shea, '*Testimony of Nina Shea: Pakistan's Anti-Blasphemy Laws*'.

For discussion on violations of religious freedom in Pakistan see: *The United States Commission on International Religious Freedom (USCIRF) Annual Report, 2010*. 'Annual Report 2010 – Countries of Particular Concern: Pakistan', April 29, 2009. Accessed at: http://www.unhcr.org/refworld/category,COI,USCIRF,,PAK,4be2840c20,0.html on April 2, 2015.
82 Nasir Iqbal, 'Death Only Punishment for Blasphemy', *The Daily Dawn*, April 21, 2009. Accessed at: http://www.dawn.com/news/458991/ae˜death-only-punishment-for-blasphemyae on January 12, 2016.
83 Michael Renov, 'Towards a Poetics of Documentary', in Michael Renov (ed.), *Theorizing Documentary*, Routledge, New York, London, 1993, p. 21.
84 Nichols, 'What Are Documentaries About?', p. 70.
85 *The Daily Dawn Online*, 'Christian Woman Sentenced to Death in Blasphemy Case', November 12, 2010. Accessed at: http://www.dawn.com/2010/11/12/christian-woman-sentenced-to-death-in-blasphemy-case-2.html on April 2, 2015.
86 *The Daily Dawn*, 'Pakistan Will Not Repeal Blasphemy Law', November 23, 2010. Accessed at: http://www.dawn.com/2010/11/23/pakistan-will-not-repeal-blasphemy-law-minister.html on April 2, 2015.
87 The *News International*, 'Governor Punjab Salman Taseer Assassinated by His Own Guard', January 4, 2011. Accessed at: http://www.thenews.com.pk/NewsDetail.aspx?ID=8689 on April 2, 2015.
88 Saeed Shah, 'Mainstream Pakistan Religious Organizations Applaud Killing of Salman Taseer', *The Guardian*, January 5, 2011. Accessed at: http://www.guardian.co.uk/world/2011/jan/05/pakistan-religious-organisations-salman-taseer on April 2, 2015.
89 Declan Walsh, 'Pakistan Minister Shahbaz Bhatti Shot Dead in Islamabad', *The Guardian*. March 2, 2011. Accessed at: http://www.guardian.co.uk/world/2011/mar/02/pakistan-minister-shot-dead-islamabad on April 2, 2015.
90 Imran Chaudhry, 'Shahbaz Taseer Kidnapped', *The Daily Times*, August 27, 2011. Accessed at: http://archives.dailytimes.com.pk/main/27-Aug-2011/shahbaz-taseer-kidnapped on January 12, 2016.

91 Syed Ali Shah. 'Abducted Shahbaz Taseer rescued from Balochistan after five years.' *The Daily Dawn*. March 9, 2016. Accessed at: http://www.dawn.com/news/1244361/abducted-shahbaz-taseer-rescued-from-balochistan-after-five-years on March 29, 2016.

Salman Taseer's murderer, Mumtaz Qadri, was executed by hanging at Adiala Jail, Rawalpindi, Pakistan, on February 29, 2016. 'Taseer's Killer Mumtaz Qadri Hanged'. *The Daily Dawn*, March 1, 2016. Accessed at: http://www.dawn.com/news/1242637 on March 2, 2016.

92 *The Daily Dawn*, 'LHC Upholds Blasphemy Convict Asia Bibi's Death Penalty', October 17, 2014. Accessed at: http://www.dawn.com/news/1138402/lhc-upholds-blasphemy-convict-asia-bibis-death-penalty on April 2, 2015.

93 *Dawn.com*, 'Christian Couple Lynching Incited by Mullah of Local Mosque: Police', November 5, 2014. Accessed at: http://www.dawn.com/news/1142437/christian-couple-lynching-incited-by-mullah-of-local-mosque-police on April 2, 2015.

94 In 1992, Sabiha Sumar founded her own film production company, *Vidhi* Films, and established the Centre for Social Science Research in Karachi, Pakistan. *Vidhi* Films and the *Vidhi* Film Fund projects include media research for social and political change, film production, outreach and political education, and technical training in filmmaking. As part of its outreach and political education programme, the organization has been arranging mobile film screenings in remote towns and villages, where people do not have access to cinema, to promote awareness and generate discussion and debate on socio-political issues. *Vidhi* Films. Accessed at: http://www.vidhifilms.net/index.htm on April 2, 2015.

95 Waugh, 'Why Documentary Filmmakers Keep Trying to Change the World', p. xiv.

96 For example, an analysis of Sumar's distribution and exhibition records obtained from their US-based distributor Women Make Movies shows that two of her documentaries discussed in this chapter, *Don't Ask Why* and *For a Place Under the Heavens*, have largely been in circulation, both through video rentals and sales, in American universities, colleges, schools, women's organizations, human rights organizations such as the Amnesty International and Human Rights Watch, and various Asian and women's film festivals. These are complemented by several rentals/sales to various academic and similar organizations in Canada, Australia, Sweden, Japan, Taiwan, Lebanon, and Israel. Data on exhibition, sales and rental records obtained by permission of Sabiha Sumar from her distributor Women Make Movies in New York, USA, on July 2, 2007.

97 Viola Shafik, 'Introduction', *Arab Cinema: History and Cultural Identity*. (Revised edition), The American University in Cairo Press, Cairo, Egypt, New York, 2007, p. 4.

98 Chuck Kleinhans, 'Forms, Politics, Makers and Contexts: Basic Issues for a Theory of Radical Political Documentary', in Thomas Waugh (ed.), *"Show Us Life": Toward a History and Aesthetics of the Committed Documentary*, The Scarecrow Press, Inc. Metuchen, NJ, and London, 1984, p. 320.

99 Renov, 'Towards a Poetics of Documentary', p. 21.

100 Ibid., p. 27.

101 Nichols, 'What Are Documentaries About?', p. 70.

102 Renov 'The Subject in History', pp. 109–10.

103 Homi. K. Bhabha, 'Foreword', in Frantz Fanon, *Black Skins, White Mask*. (translated from the French into English by Charles Lam Markmann), Grove Press, New York, USA, 1967, p. xxiii.

104 Julio Garcia Espinosa, 'For An Imperfect Cinema' (1970), in Michael Chanan (ed.), *Twenty-Five Years of the New Latin American Cinema*, BFI Books, UK, 1983, p. 31.

3 Cinema on Terror
Charting the militant mix of politics, religion, and Talibanization

Introduction

While issues of political and judicial transformations set in motion by General Zia-ul-Haq's Islamization process dominate documentaries in the previous chapter, this chapter focuses on the beginning of a new era characterized by a *militant* mix of politics and religion in Pakistan. This is the period of the dictatorship of President General Pervaiz Musharraf (1999–2008), and his alliance with the US in its so-called 'War on Terror'.

By the late 1990s and after, several major developments, both regional and international, were beginning to affect and transform Pakistan's socio-political landscape: the Taliban influence in the region;[1] the 9/11/2001 terrorist attacks in the US; the US-led 'War on Terror' and attack on Afghanistan in 2001; the cross-border (Afghanistan) militancy, and a mass exodus of Afghan refugees to Pakistan; and the emergence of dangerous religious strife and divisions in the region. Another very significant development taking place in Pakistan was the mushrooming of *madrasas* (religious seminaries), facilitated and strengthened by *jihadist* organizations.[2] Espousing an ambitious, and deadly, anti-US and anti-West Taliban and *Al Qaida* agenda for terrorism and destruction, these organizations were beginning to defiantly recruit and train militants and suicide bombers through a call for *jihad*.[3] (For a background on the radicalization of *madrasas* in Pakistan see Appendix 4). Such ideological strife proved to be factors that would alter Pakistan's socio-political fabric for the worse.

The trend towards Talibanization and terrorism also saw the emergence of documentary filmmakers who turned to investigating its roots and implications, seeking accountability from policy makers, religious and political leaders, and others in key positions. One name that dominates the documentary narrative sequence of a body of work that tracks the roots of terrorism in Pakistan that I define as a 'Cinema on Terror' is that of a Pakistani woman filmmaker, Sharmeen Obaid-Chinoy. As Musharraf clung to power, and served as a frontline US ally in the 'War on Terror', a contextual reading of Obaid-Chinoy's thematically related films depict issues of Pakistan's involvement in the conflict in the region: its descent into growing religious extremism; domestic political and ideological rifts;

the spread of *madrasas* as centres for recruiting and training militants; and the threat of Talibanization and terrorism breeding on its own soil.[4] Obaid-Chinoy's filmic depictions of the consequent internal armed conflict, displacements, unrest, and destruction form a connective narrative link between the religious fundamentalism and politicization of religion fostered during the Islamization period, as discussed in the last chapter.

Obaid-Chinoy's six representative films discussed here, albeit overlapping certain historical and socio-political details, not only complete a picture of Pakistan's further plunge into religious extremism, but also highlight the new and expanding trend of a divisive and militant politicization of Islam with an international *jihadist* agenda. Her films illustrate that from Zia to Musharraf, as fresh developments unfolded in the wake of 9/11/2001, there was a new set of names, terms, and facts entering the Pakistani documentary film vocabulary: Taliban; *Al Qaida*; 'War on Terror'; terrorism; suicide attacks; names of various *jihadist* and terrorist organizations, and their involvement in radical *madrasa* education; internally displaced persons (IDPs); and refugee camps.

This chapter discusses the role Obaid-Chinoy's documentaries have played in defining a 'Cinema on Terror' film category that focuses on tracking and documenting the roots and patterns of terrorism – one that investigates, informs, cautions, and warns of Pakistan's impending dangers, and global implications, if extremist forces are not contained, and political leaders and policies held accountable.

Sharmeen Obaid-Chinoy

Sharmeen Obaid-Chinoy began her career as a documentary filmmaker after completing her undergraduate studies in Economics and Government at Smith College, Massachusetts, USA, and two master's degrees from Stanford University in International Policy Studies, and Communication. Working as a documentarist and journalist, her work has covered a variety of subjects with a particular focus on Muslim societies, issues of religious fundamentalism, gender discrimination, and social justice.[5] She began her filmmaking career with the New York Times Television (NYTT) in 2002 where she produced her first documentary film, *Terror's Children* (2003). The film won Obaid-Chinoy several awards that included the Overseas Press Club Award (2004), the American Women in Radio and Television Award (2004), and the South Asian Journalist Association Award (2006). In February 2012, Obaid-Chinoy also became the first Pakistani documentary filmmaker to win an Oscar for her film entitled *Saving Face* (2011) that addresses the topic of victimization of women by acid-attacks in Pakistan. This was followed by a second Oscar win in February 2016 for her film entitled *A Girl in the River: The Price of Forgiveness* (2015) on the topic of honour-killings in Pakistan.[6]

A number of Obaid-Chinoy's films focus on the socio-political consequences of *jihadist* militancy, drift towards terrorism, and indoctrination of extremist ideologies through *madrasas* that have allegedly taken on the role of 'incubators for militants' in Pakistan.[7] Her work, discussed in this chapter, can be seen as a

'Cinema on Terror' that explores the wave of Talibanization sweeping Pakistan in the wake of the US-led so-called 'War on Terror'.[8]

Employing a combination of reportorial, and an investigative-journalistic approach in all her films, Obaid-Chinoy's own appearance, active involvement with her subjects, and on-screen communication with the viewer brings an engaging immediacy to her topics.[9] As she observes and interviews her subjects on critical and sensitive issues, and participates in the lives and events she covers, the filmmaker takes the viewers along on her journeys through what have been some of the most dangerous terrains, and conflict zones in the world. These include the tribal belts in the Khyber Pakhtunkhwa Province (formerly the North West Frontier Province (NWFP)) of Pakistan, and the adjoining Afghanistan borderland that had become a hub for *jihadist* organizations and their operations. This region became increasingly hostile and inaccessible because of the US-led 'War on Terror', particularly for women, and especially so for a Muslim woman filmmaker.[10] While she identifies herself as a Muslim in various on-screen appearances, Obaid-Chinoy crosses various restrictive boundaries to enter dangerous territories dominated by hardened religious militants and orthodox, patriarchal mindsets. Her investigative journeys to unveil the roots of terrorism and the workings of *jihadist* organizations in Pakistan display an undoubtedly courageous stance in reporting conditions, and developments that continue to have a global impact. The following contextual readings of her films illustrate what I define as the new paradigm of 'Cinema on Terror'.

Terror's Children (2003)

Sharmeen Obaid Chinoy's first film, *Terror's Children* (2003), probes the effect of the Taliban influence on children in Pakistan, and neighbouring Afghanistan, and the repercussions this could have for the region in the years to come.[11] The film addresses the plight of displaced Afghan refugee children who were forced to flee their war-ravaged homeland during the Taliban rule as the US launched its 'War on Terror'. We learn that as hundreds of thousands of Afghan refugees, nearly half of them children, began to enter Karachi, Pakistan, after the Taliban regime fell in 2001 in Afghanistan, the city turned into a volatile hub for terrorist activities. These activities included the 2002 kidnapping and brutal murder of American journalist and South Asia correspondent for the *Wall Street Journal* (WSJ), Daniel Pearl, by *Al Qaida* operatives,[12] and the attack on the US consulate in Karachi that killed 10 people, and injured dozens.[13]

Terror's Children revolves around the vast *Jadeed* Refugee Camp in Obaid-Chinoy's coastal home city of Karachi that according to her was already brimming with a population of 12 million. For ten weeks in the summer of 2002, she followed the lives of eight Afghan children in the camp to investigate the changes in their status and livelihood as a consequence of their displacement. The film tracks the activities of these children, mostly boys, as they are caught in a web of hunger, deprivation, suspicion, and alienation in a foreign country. We see some scavenging through garbage dumps near their refugee camp and illegal encroachments to collect bottles and other items they can sell for a meal. Some turn to *madrasas* to secure free sustenance and shelter in return for their allegiance to the 'cause of Islam'. A few work 12-hour shifts in carpet-weaving factories, earning 80 cents a day to support an entire family. Obaid-Chinoy observes and records these children's disturbing transformation, views, and aspirations that range from hatred and vengeance against both the US and the Taliban, to the belief that a global conversion to Islam would end the conflict. Some simply show a keen desire to return home to a peaceful Afghanistan. Obaid-Chinoy engages with her subjects' daily routines to draw attention to the poverty, confusions, and conflicts that are shaping their vulnerable lives and thinking, rendering them easy prey for militant organizations and radical *madrasas* to recruit and indoctrinate. The depiction of their impressionable mindsets is in turns alarming, sobering, at times even comical, but invariably sad.

Terror's Children opens with ten-year-old Khal Mohammad, who is studying in a pro-Taliban *madrasa* for poor children, and learning to recite and memorize the *Quran* by rote without understanding a word of Arabic, saying his prayers. He has no hesitation in sharing his coaching at the *madrasa*:

> 'If God gives us strength, anything can be done. God willing, we will strike. We would strike so that America would repent for Afghanistan. Real Muslim hearts would be glad. America's veins would be cut.'

Figure 3.1 Image of carpet-weavers from *Terror's Children*.
Source: Sharmeen Obaid Films.

His innocent face belying the venom he has been fed, Khal is already critical of Obaid-Chinoy's attire because she does not cover her face completely as Muslim women do in his native Afghanistan.[14] Deeply indoctrinated by a puritan Taliban ideology at a tender age, he states that '*jihad* is our duty', announcing categorically: 'Everyone who believes in God should not use a TV set, VCR, or cable at home. Instead you should give to charity, pray, and fast'.[15]

In contrast, to get a broader view of the *madrasa* system, Obaid-Chinoy visits the *Jamia Islamia madrasa* in the upscale Clifton neighbourhood of Karachi, where a more liberal and enlightened view of Islam and religious teaching is being practiced. Taught by educated religious scholars and professors, the children of the well-to-do are shown learning and playing in comfortable surroundings, where food and other amenities are plentiful, and trips to a games arcade and the beach also figure in their weekly activities. The juxtaposition between the *Jadeed* Refugee Camp, housing more than fifteen thousand refugees who live and work there, and the *Jamia Islamia madrasa* shows that liberal and extremist religious ideologies are shaped not simply by an adherence to, or rejection of, orthodoxy, but also by economic factors – quite simply the role money, food, and shelter can play in forming ideological agendas and beliefs. Factors that *jihadist* organizations continue to exploit to their advantage.

Back to the *Jadeed* Refugee Camp, where garbage dumps abound, and lack of basic facilities such as clean drinking water and sanitation prevail, we meet more '*Terror's Children*': nine-year-old Noor works several jobs to help support his

Figure 3.2 Image of Khal from *Terror's Children*.
Source: Sharmeen Obaid Films.

family; eleven-year-old Bareed picks garbage and sells what he can; Leila, 9, and Anissa 11, the only two girls shown, are confined to working at home, and in their spare time apply the little cheap makeup they have as they playact a doll's wedding ceremony among friends. This is a sad reminder, Obaid-Chinoy notes, of the fact that girls as young as them, or even younger, are commonly sold into marriage in Afghanistan. On the other hand, as we see footage of Afghan children flying kites, an activity that was banned by the Taliban in Afghanistan, it is reflective of the relative freedom they could enjoy as refugees even in the most meagre of circumstances in Pakistan.

Scenes of scores of Afghan children roaming the narrow crisscrossing lanes of the *Jadeed* Refugee Camp, and the streets of Karachi, picking through garbage, working at recycling centres, surrounded by squalor and filth, convey the despair, humiliation, and miserable predicament of the entire refugee community. It is understandable how the uncertain future these children face in a foreign country, where suspicion and hostility combine to house them, makes recruitment by *jihadist* organizations and *madrasas* an attractive option in return for a basic meal and religious education.

The Karachiites Obaid-Chinoy interviews on the street are unanimous in their mistrust and contempt for the Afghan refugees in their city, branding them as 'terrorists', 'drug pushers', and 'arms dealers'.

Terror's Children concludes with a quarter of the *Jadeed* Refugee Camp emptying and mud shacks being torn down as their residents prepare to leave for Afghanistan through a UNHCR repatriation centre.[16] In the last meetings with some of her subjects, Anissa's father tells Obaid-Chinoy that his daughter will 'begin to wear the *burqa* at 12, and get married at 15 or 16'. Bareed says he might get killed on his return to Afghanistan, but if he survives, he will become a fighter. Khal, who will be returning as a *hafiz*, having successfully memorized the whole *Quran*, is confident that this will secure him a 'place in heaven'.[17] As a parting gesture, Obaid-Chinoy takes Khal to an open-air public park where men and women are taking a dip together in the pool. Though the women are fully clothed in 'Pakistani conservative swimwear', as Obaid-Chinoy points out, Khal's shock and horror at the sight of such open mingling are echoed in his stunned response: 'Everyone here is going to hell. I will go to hell now that I have seen such a sight.' He also gives his own verdict: 'Let's have everyone in America follow Islamic law. The whole world should be Muslim, even the US.' Ending her filmic journey with her subjects, Obaid-Chinoy confides that every one of them had asked her if their participation in the film would in some way make their life better? A desperate question the filmmaker leaves her viewers to ponder on.

Terror's Children set the tone for a series of Obaid-Chinoy's films that would investigate the spread of militancy and terrorism being promoted by the fast growing radicalized *madrasa* culture that had begun to take root within Pakistan. We see a 'Cinema on Terror' unfold as Taliban influence grew in the country, supplying *jihadist* organizations with a steady flow of potential recruits that would eventually lead to Pakistan's very own 'Taliban generation', as illustrated in the concluding film in this chapter.

Reinventing the Taliban? (2003)

Obaid-Chinoy's second film, *Re-inventing the Taliban?* (2003), focuses on the impact of radical Talibanization in Afghanistan spilling into Pakistan during General Pervaiz Musharraf's alliance with the US.[18] The film made her the first non-American journalist to be awarded the prestigious Livingston Award (2005), and the youngest recipient of the One World Media Broadcast Journalist of the Year Award (2007) in the United Kingdom.[19] The film also won the Special Jury Award at the Banff Television Festival, Canada, in 2004.[20]

Reinventing the Taliban? begins with Obaid-Chinoy reflecting on her own urban, middle-class up-bringing in a secular and progressive Pakistani environment where she was free to dress as she pleased, enjoy Western music, and go abroad for higher education without being seen to compromise her Muslim identity. Hers is a reflective stance that is reminiscent of Sabiha Sumar's nostalgia in *For a Place Under the Heavens* (2003) as she traced the socio-political and judicial transformations taking root in Pakistan during General Zia-ul-Haq's Islamization phase.

Reinventing the Taliban?, as the sign of interrogation ominously queries in the title, investigates the growing anti-US aggression fostered by the US-led 'War on Terror', and the consequent dangerous tilt towards a radical Taliban-like rule which was officially promoted by religious parties in Pakistan at the time of the film's production.[21]

Obaid-Chinoy's filmic journey takes her to the provincial capital of Peshawar where she sets out to track the Taliban influence now spilling into the North West Frontier Province of Pakistan (NWFP) from neighbouring Afghanistan, dominated by the same *Pakhtun* ethnic group and culture. In Peshawar, she finds 'frightening changes', reflective of the broad, and significant leaning towards religious fundamentalism and abhorrence towards the US. This shift is supported by the growing control of the clergy through the election of the fundamentalist *Muttahida Majlis-e-Amal* (MMA) (United Action Front) political party. It is significant to note that the MMA had played on anti-secular, anti-US sentiments to win an unprecedented popularity and landslide victory in the 2001 elections to form a government in two provinces of the country.[22] We see footage of bearded men, and *mullahs* (Islamic clerics) attending MMA rallies to urge support for the passage of their *Sharia* Bill. Bearing anti-US and anti-Musharraf placards reading 'Osama is our hero', and chanting 'Whoever supports America is a traitor', and 'Musharraf is a dog', on the streets of Peshawar convey the alarming radical political developments that had begun to challenge the dictator's pro-US stance, and threaten Pakistan's socio-political fabric.

Walking through bazaars (markets) in Peshawar, Obaid-Chinoy is visibly horrified at the conflicting scenes and transformations she takes in. We see posters of Osama Bin Laden and other *Al Qaida* leaders, and religious posters of the *Ka'aba* selling alongside revealing posters of a popular Indian film actress, Kareena Kapoor.[23] Images of Pakistani female models on billboards and advertisements with their faces blackened and defaced serve as a sharp reminder of the extent to which the Taliban ideology was being officially promoted by the *Sharia*-led MMA government. Other practices included the banning of music as 'un-Islamic', and a crackdown on musicians. As he walks her down the Akbari Market in the old part of the city, singer and musician Gulzar Alam tells Obaid-Chinoy that he had his business shut down, and was jailed for singing at a wedding party. We learn that for generations musicians had lined the streets of this market making musical instruments, and teaching music. Very few of them remain now. Archival footage shows the police torching thousands of music CDs and video film cassettes on the streets on the orders of the MMA government. Similar crackdowns affected the livelihoods of artists who had for generations painted murals and hoardings for films and cinema houses. Ismail, a mural painter, tells Obaid-Chinoy that his profession had been acceptable when he was hired to make posters and paint hoardings for the MMA leadership during their election campaign. But now, he was banned on the pretext of religion, and was confined to only painting words.[24]

The emerging socio-political environment depicted in *Re-inventing the Taliban?* presents a startling comparison with the changes wrought in Afghanistan by the puritan Taliban regime, and their emulation and 'reinvention' in the Pakistani system. As Obaid-Chinoy is followed by the disapproving gaze of bearded men on the streets of Peshawar, they taunt her for roaming around without her face covered, reminding her that 'the clerics and the Taliban are coming'.

Figure 3.3 Image of musicians from *Reinventing the Taliban?*
Source: Sharmeen Obaid Films.

Unfortunately, this was not an idle threat, as at the time Obaid-Chinoy made her documentary, Pakistan began to be seriously mired in the spread of radical Taliban-style extremism being promoted through *madrasas* as retaliation for Pak–US alliance in the 'War on Terror'.

The tensions and confusions between a secular environment, and the new constraints imposed on the arts, women's rights, and women's participation in public life are reflective of where the new MMA government was headed in social and political terms. This new environment of intolerance is laid bare in Obaid-Chinoy's meeting with the founding member of the MMA, *Maulana* Sami-ul-Haq, Chief of the *Jamiat-e-Ulema Islam* (JUI), and also the patron of the most radical *madrasa* in the country, the *Darul-Uloom-Haqqania*, where the majority of Taliban leaders have reportedly studied. Haq defends the Taliban and their radical ideology, and argues that the US is bent on 'anti-Islam propaganda', and that 'Talibanization' and 'terrorism' are the words it has adopted to malign Islam.[25] He categorically denounces Western/US liberalism as wholly corrupt, immoral, and unacceptable for a Muslim state where he believes state and religion should work in unison: 'We will not tolerate secularism. We will not tolerate the supremacy of the United States. They want to make our women shameless and immoral. This will not be allowed.' He contends that only his party, and its ideology can serve as a viable antidote to the country's problems, including poverty, illiteracy, and corruption. Needless to say, Haq continues to exert tremendous influence among Pakistan's anti-West religious parties.

Eight months after the election of the MMA government, Obaid-Chinoy investigates the effects of the MMA's ideological stance by seeking responses at roadside tea stalls and eateries from ordinary citizens who had voted for the MMA. She draws mixed reactions as to the validity or rejection of women's oppression, ban on the arts, and the state-imposed religiosity that forces men to grow their beards, and women to veil. Many seem to have lost confidence in the ruling party and its forced policies and tactics of governance, although no one denies their religious allegiances.

Depictions of this emerging trend to 're-invent' a Taliban structure of governance in Pakistan warn of the deleterious consequences for Pakistan, and the broader global context. Obaid-Chinoy points out that MMA is backed by thousands of hardened militants, radicalized religious fundamentalists, and extremists who have easy access to weapons. As Obaid-Chinoy takes a journey into Darra Adam Khel, a tribal area that hosts the largest unregulated arms market in the world that began trade in 1897, and is also the thriving arms market catering to the entire NWFP (and which had been the main weapons pipeline for the Taliban during their rule in Afghanistan), we see handguns and automatic rifles being manufactured and sold at $20 and $50 respectively.[26] Scenes from the vibrant, busy, arms bazaar are perhaps the chilling highlight of the film: billboards displaying shop names and their phone numbers; busy arms craftsmen and production units in operation; a ready merchandise of polished, new small sub-machine guns, machine guns, and Kalashnikov rifles; arms neatly displayed in shining glass show-cases; people test-firing their prospective purchases in the air. A shopkeeper proudly tells Obaid-Chinoy that they can 'reproduce anything they can get their hands on', a reference to any foreign arms that may be captured in the region and that can be copied in manufacturing. The filmmaker points out that the most significant and alarming fact is that these arms in the unregulated market are available for sale to anyone, including 'hard-core extremists'.

During her visit to the Peshawar Degree College that houses the MMA *Shabab-e-Milli* (Youth Wing), Obaid-Chinoy listens to its leaders, both students and professors, as they defend their Taliban-like support for the oppression and segregation of women in the name of religion. They declare that it is necessary to blacken out women's faces on billboards, asserting that women cannot even buy anything from male shopkeepers. They believe that women should not be allowed to 'laugh outside their homes', advocating the 'blackening and boarding of windows' wherever women reside. All these measures, they claim, are in compliance with 'Islamic' values and laws. We see a shocking resemblance with transformations during the Taliban era in Afghanistan now being politically endorsed and promoted as an 'ideal model' by the MMA.

Obaid-Chinoy visits a heavily veiled MMA member of the National Assembly named Razia Aziz who agrees with, and endorses the MMA view on women. As Obaid-Chinoy leaves Aziz, she wonders what it would be like to have to wear a *burqa*. Trying one on in a shop, the filmmaker exclaims 'My God! Can't even breathe in here!' This outlook is shared by Bushra Gohar, a social worker and member of the *Awami* National Party (ANP) (People's National Party) and the National Assembly, who tells Obaid-Chinoy she has never veiled, nor will. She deems the practice of veiling 'un-Islamic', regardless of the MMA directives, and prevalent atmosphere of religious fundamentalism in the province. The two opposing points of view filmed between members of the MMA and the ANP political parties exemplify and document the tensions and frictions between the liberal old norms, even in the historically conservative NWFP capital, and the imposition of a new, alien orthodox order imposed by religious parties.

Re-inventing the Taliban? takes a welcome, and encouraging, turn as musician Gulzar invites Obaid-Chinoy to a music concert arranged by the opposition party, ANP. Party president Asfandyar Wali, and Afrasiab Khattak, provincial party president and also member of the Human Rights Commission of Pakistan (HRCP) tell Obaid-Chinoy they arranged the concert to show their opposition to the MMA ideology, and to promote the *Pakhtun* culture. Although the concert is attended by an all-male audience only, the very fact that it is taking place in the MMA stronghold and provincial capital is a significant symbol and documentation of the oppositional forces that have continued to defy and challenge religious fundamentalists in Pakistan.

After concentrating on the hub of the Taliban ideology, Peshawar and the NWFP, the filmmaker sets out to investigate if such extremist ideologies could only prosper in the impoverished zones of the NWFP, or could they spread to mainstream Pakistani society as well. Travelling back to Lahore, the cultural capital of Pakistan, and provincial capital of the Punjab province, she realizes the glaring differences between the two worlds. The film now shows footage of unveiled women freely shopping in the markets; female models preparing for fashion shoots and walking down the ramps at fashion shows; and actress Ayesha Alam narrating her lines for a performance of Eve Ansler's *Vagina Monologues* to be staged in the federal capital city of Islamabad. Defending her right to carry on with her artistic pursuits, Alam tells Obaid-Chinoy that she is also well-aware of grim realities such as acid-attacks on women's faces, and threats to families of artists from extremist factions.[27] Though fundamentalist pockets may consider Alam's artistic stance as nothing more than a corrupting influence of Western cultures on Pakistan's urban life, her defiance is also indicative of an openness in Pakistan to broader cultural and artistic currents.

Jugnu Mohsin, a woman journalist, activist, and managing editor and publisher of the English weekly magazine, *The Friday Times*, tells Obaid-Chinoy during her interview that Pakistani women's are hard-won freedoms, and they will not give them up regardless of political and religious pressures.[28] On the other hand, Mohsin draws attention to the devastating prospects of religious fundamentalist politics and its influence in a 'geo-strategically located nuclear-armed Pakistan'. What emerges is a sobering picture of a country torn between its desire for secularism and modernity, and extremist elements and politics bent on opposing any such progress. No doubt, Obaid-Chinoy's filmic depictions of the dangerous influence of the MMA ideology are a warning to secular elements in Pakistan, and the world, to resist a zealous minority that wants to 'reinvent the Taliban' in its midst, and threaten the world with its fundamentalist dogma.

Obaid-Chinoy ends her film with a visit to the Wagah border near Lahore, which divides India and Pakistan, two nuclear rivals that have fought two full-fledged wars in the past, and remain antagonistic towards each other despite deep-rooted cultural and historical ties. Watching the change-of-guard ceremony, she weighs the possibility of Pakistan's nuclear arms getting into the hands of radicalized extremists, and what this would mean for the world – a threat that has grown increasingly worrying for the international community over the years. Religious, political, cultural, and gender tensions interweave as *Reinventing the Taliban?* ends with a warning from Gulzar, the musician from Peshawar: 'We need to work hard, because if our culture is taken away from us, then the coming generations will stone our graves.'

Reinventing the Taliban? draws attention to the frightening progression of radical and politicized religious ideologies that were taking root at the socio-political levels in Pakistan in 2003. Adding another thematically related sequence to the 'Cinema on Terror', the film pinpoints the alarming trends that were shaping the county's future, and would threaten the world: a strong tilt towards Talibanization; the fundamentalist, militant, and oppressive ideologies being endorsed by religious political parties; the un-checked mass production of arms in Darra Adam Khel; and the vibrant and progressive urban life and cultural activities threatened by Talibanization. As a historical record of a past that continues to influence and shape the present, Obaid-Chinoy's investigative documentation in *Re-inventing the Taliban?* signals and warns of the trend towards religious militancy and extremism that would gain momentum within Pakistan, while espousing an ambitious global agenda for terrorism in the name of *'jihad'*. The sign of interrogation in the title of the film leaves behind alarming and dangerous possibilities.

Pakistan: On A Razor's Edge (2004)

The pattern of terror and Talibanization unfolding in *Reinventing the Taliban?* is further compounded as Pakistan struggled to fight on several fronts, including its persistent uneasy relationship with nuclear-armed neighbour and arch rival, India. In *Pakistan: On A Razor's Edge* (2004), Obaid-Chinoy explores the web of internal strife and conflicts that surrounded President Musharraf's multiple political entanglements: commitment to the West in fighting the 'War on Terror'; making peace with India; the ongoing Kashmir dispute; Pakistan's alleged role in nuclear proliferation abroad; the opposition posed by religious leaders; and the growing religious extremism at home.[29] The aforementioned factors continued to strengthen anti-US and anti-India sentiments in the country, while religious segments pushed for an 'Islamic' state identity. The documentary, accompanied by the filmmaker's commentary and reflections, remains significant in its expository intent,[30] and its account of the complex mix of religion and politics in Pakistan haunting its very stability, and position in the international community.

Pakistan: On A Razor's Edge begins with Obaid-Chinoy boarding a 'peace train' from India to Lahore, a goodwill service that was initiated between both countries to thaw enmities, and foster trust and interaction between its people.[31] Her interviews with travellers depict their joy, and also caution, regarding the new initiative as the train pulls into the Punjab provincial capital of Lahore. Scenes of eagerly awaited reconciliation with long separated families at the Lahore railway station point to what is described in the film as a result of the 'historic handshake' between Pakistan's President Pervaiz Musharraf and Indian Prime Minister, Atal Behari Vajpayee, as they agreed to begin peace initiatives in January 2004.[32]

Symbolic of the new beginning between Pakistan and India, we see scenes of the annual festival of *Basant* (Spring) in Lahore that celebrates the arrival of spring. Featuring kite-flying contests as a main sport, footage depicts a picture of merrymaking, dancing, and joviality very different from the glum realties that otherwise beset Pakistan. Walking through brightly lit streets at night, Obaid-Chinoy asks ordinary citizens if they are hopeful about the new possibility of peace with India. While some show enthusiasm, one old street vendor cautions her: 'Ask me another time. If this interview is aired, we will both be jailed. This is Pakistan!'

Pakistan: On a Razor's Edge, made during one of the most tense, and dangerous periods in President Musharraf's tenure, gives a varied picture of the many mindsets and clashing loyalties that were brewing among segments of civil society, the government, and military factions. In particular, there were prevailing anti-US, anti-Israel, and anti-India sentiments of those who blamed Musharraf for selling out to the West and going against his own people. As she observes the variety of local and Western billboards that advertise fast-food restaurants and

Figure 3.4 Sharmeen Obaid-Chinoy interviews Maulana Sami-ul-Haq in *Pakistan: On a Razor's Edge*.
Source: Sharmeen Obaid Films.

banks, Obaid-Chinoy describes her homeland as 'a country of secrets and paradoxes, still emerging from its recent past, before 9/11, when it was the Taliban's main supporter'. We realize that Pakistan is perched precariously at a crossroads, 'determined to be part of the modern world', as she says, but equally infested by dangerous, oppositional elements at influential and key decision-making positions. These decision-makers strongly opposed the US, and equated modernity and progress with Western 'anti-Islam' designs.

Obaid-Chinoy's interviews with government and military officials develop a critical picture of the balancing act Pakistan is striving to achieve, both in the international arena, as well as domestically – a most vulnerable situation for both extremists and anti-Musharraf elements to exploit. Interviewees include the former Chief of the Army Staff General Aslam Beg; Lieutenant General (late) Hameed Gul, the head of the country's notorious Inter-Services Intelligence Agency (ISI) before 9/11, when Pakistan was openly supporting the Taliban; *Maulana* Sami-ul-Haq, a senator and founding member of Pakistan's powerful fundamentalist political movement who zealously voices his mistrust and opposition to the US, and solidarity with the Muslim world. Others include Jugnu Mohsin, journalist and publisher of *The Friday Times* weekly, and Ahmed

Rashid, a well-known authority on Islamic fundamentalism, the Taliban movement, and the geo-politics of the region.[33] In Lahore, Jugnu Mohsin tells Obaid-Chinoy that 9/11 has benefited Pakistan:

> 'I may be being very unconventional here, but I'll say to you that 9/11 has been very good for Pakistan. Suddenly, overnight, we had to choose which way to go. The state decided to dump the Taliban – not a moment too soon, I can tell you as a woman.'

Mohsin notes that the economy has improved, and that there is growing popular support for peace with India: 'We don't want to fight a thousand-year war with India. Not least because both countries are armed with nuclear weapons.'

Nuclear monuments erected in front of the Lahore railway station that replicate the Chagai Hills in the Balochistan province where Pakistan detonated nuclear devices, take on a critical significance in the film. During Obaid-Chinoy's 2004 trip, Pakistan's nuclear programme becomes an international scandal as Dr Abdul Qadeer Khan, head of the Kahuta Research Laboratories, and architect of Pakistan's nuclear programme, is accused of nuclear proliferation to Iran, Libya, and North Korea.[34] The film documents how, as the controversy heats up, Dr Khan, who was considered a national hero for matching India's nuclear capability, is forced to deliver a televised confession of proliferation, and apologize to the nation and seek forgiveness. Following the public apology, we see footage of President Musharraf, dressed in military uniform, accusing Dr Khan of having acted unilaterally for personal financial gains, but also extending a pardon for Dr Khan in a television speech. Musharraf categorically denies any involvement of the army or the government in the matter. Dr Khan's televised confession and apology in English on Pakistan state-run television on February 4 (after which he was placed under house arrest) prompts Obaid-Chinoy to remark that it was 'meant for audiences far beyond Pakistan'; that is, to appease the international community, particularly the US and the West. However, in his interview journalist Ahmed Rashid rejects Musharraf's accusations and claims:

> 'It is impossible that one man could have carried out such acts of proliferation over 27 years involving weapons, technology, and missiles. It is impossible that Dr Khan acted alone. The military had to be involved. It was the Pakistani army that needed the missiles they got in a nuclear barter deal with the North Koreans. I am sure, as army chief, General Beg was involved.'

Retired General Mirza Aslam Beg, who was Pakistan's Chief of the Army Staff in the midst of Dr Khan's proliferation activities in the late '80s, categorically denies any involvement on his part. At his Rawalpindi residence when Obaid-Chinoy asks him why he has not been arrested despite allegations that he was in the know, the general replies: 'Just to disappoint you, and my American friends and their stooges here in Pakistan, they still want me behind bars for sins which I have not committed.' He goes on to state that the whole matter of nuclear proliferation is an American 'conspiracy to destabilize Pakistan', expressing the anti-US stance at the very core of the Pakistani military leadership.

This anti-US view is seconded strongly by the former Chief of Inter-Services Intelligence (ISI) Lieutenant General (late) Hameed Gul, who was known as one of the most powerful men, and 'spymaster' in Pakistan when the development of the nuclear programme was at its height. Talking to Obaid-Chinoy, he rejects allegations of proliferation outright, and terms them as mere 'fibbing' and 'speculation', and blames America and Israel for trying to subvert Pakistan's nuclear capability. He proclaims that 'Islam is the target, Islam is the new enemy. Islam is the challenge.' He believes that the US wants to dismantle Pakistan's nuclear arsenal: 'If at present the US needs Musharraf it does not mean that they will abdicate their objective of de-nuclearizing Pakistan.'

Obaid-Chinoy's discovery of such deep-rooted beliefs, and reactions at the most important and powerful levels of the Pakistani army and governance, document and highlight the dangerous scenario that was unfolding. She comments:

> 'Gul's strong anti-Americanism, and his paranoia are widespread in Pakistan. More and more the nuclear scandal feels like a Pandora's box. Who knows what would happen to Pakistan if it were opened?'

The nuclear proliferation controversy had deeply divided the Pakistani nation. The majority accused President Musharraf and the army of humiliating a national hero, Dr Khan, and using him as a scapegoat to cover up the army's own involvement.[35]

Maulana Sami-ul-Haq, an old friend of Osama Bin Laden's (though he is careful to state on camera that he has not met Bin Laden lately) whom Obaid-Chinoy goes to meet in the North West Frontier Province (NWFP), defends the sharing of nuclear technology as a 'duty' towards other Muslim countries:

> 'If we gave it to Iran, what's the crime? If we gave it to Libya, what's the crime? If Europe shares this technology, it's the duty of all Muslims to share their knowledge. America has surreptitiously forged an elaborate scheme to strip Pakistan of its nuclear technology.'

Haq blames Musharraf for cutting a deal with the US by allowing the Pakistani army to hunt down Osama Bin Laden and *Al Qaida* in the tribal areas along the Afghan–Pakistan border in what was known as the 'Spring Operation':

> 'They will leave our border in shambles. They want Muslims to be tied up like goats and sheep, so they can slaughter us at their will. Why doesn't Musharraf understand that all this is part of their plot?'

Haq's views and beliefs echo those of General (late) Hameed Gul, and serve as clear evidence of the anti-US and anti-Musharraf convictions shared by the high command of the Pakistan Army and radical religious factions.

We see footage of sites in Rawalpindi where President Musharraf had narrowly escaped two assassination attempts in December 2003. These attacks had been carried out as a result of opposition to his double-game policies to appease both radical Islamists in Pakistan and Western allies in the 'War on Terror'. In the first instance, explosives ripped a bridge apart seconds after his presidential convoy had passed over it. The second attack took place only two weeks later on Christmas Day as two cars filled with explosives, signalled by someone in the presidential convoy, rammed into the motorcade, leaving 17 people dead, and more than 40 wounded.[36] We learn that, reportedly, investigators found one suicide bomber's cell phone with the memory chip still intact. It had phone numbers linking the assassin to 'a Pakistani hardline extremist group' with links to *Al Qaida*, involved in the fighting in Kashmir. On her visit to the site of the second assassination attempt, Obaid-Chinoy finds a strong mix of reactions to the incident as eyewitnesses recount the details, some condemning the incident, while others favour Kashmiri *jihadists* as 'freedom fighters'. She comments:

> 'Their arguments reflected the heart of the struggle going on within Pakistan – the struggle between the progressive majority and a fundamentalist minority whose influence reaches far beyond their numbers.'

Obaid-Chinoy points out that following Musharraf's peace moves with India, he proclaimed the thousands of Kashmiri *jihadists* fighting in the Indian Held Kashmir (IHK) as 'terrorists fighting a proxy war', thereby forcing them to go underground, and opening up yet another dangerous front for confrontation. As Obaid-Chinoy watches an angry group of Pakistani nationalists burning an effigy of India's prime minister, Atal Behari Vajpayee, in Rawalpindi she is reminded: 'Kashmir is not just the cause of extremists, it's a deeply felt issue, embedded in Pakistan's identity. There's even a national holiday, Kashmir Day.'[37]

On conditions that his name, and that of his organization, not be disclosed, a militant from a banned *jihadist* outfit who has been fighting in Kashmir agrees to speak to Obaid-Chinoy. At a secret location, lit only by candlelight, the man, obscuring his face, categorically rejects that his comrades are terrorists. Instead, he blames India for committing atrocities in Kashmir, and defends himself and his organization as fighting for the liberation of Kashmir:

> 'In Kashmir, I witnessed the cruelty, and torture. Hindu religious extremists can come into Kashmir. They commit mass-murder, they loot, rape Muslim women, set our homes on fire. Are these not acts of terrorism? In Indian eyes they are not. Every drop of our blood is dedicated to the Kashmir struggle.'

Denying that Kashmiri *jihadists* are responsible for the attacks on President Musharraf's life, the militant instead blames them on India's intelligence agency, RAW, and Israel's Mossad. Hearing such resolve, and allegations only leave the filmmaker with a gloomy and disturbing conclusion that chances for peace are more fragile than she thought: 'What chance do peace agreements have in the face of such conviction when *jihadists* are prepared to die to make Kashmir a part of Pakistan?'

As the Kashmir dispute has lingered over the decades, the most dangerous factor to emerge is that both India and Pakistan are now also armed with a nuclear arsenal. This fact of nuclear capability may be a source for pride for both countries, but remains a volatile concern for the rest of the world should religious extremists gain power in Pakistan.[38]

Amid the ongoing *Basant* festival, Obaid-Chinoy's last journey in the film once again takes her to the Pakistan–India border at Wagah where each day an elaborate change-of-guard ceremony is watched by crowds from both sides. As she watches Pakistani soldiers in dark green uniforms and their Indian counterparts in khaki brown engage in 'a ritualized shadow play', strutting and outdoing each other, she observes: 'But on this day I saw something different. For the first time, in a gesture of friendship, they shook hands. And the crowd broke out in cheers. On both sides.' An unfulfilled dream of friendship that still lingers for the people of both countries, despite the many political and diplomatic attempts made to normalize relations for over six decades.

As part of a 'Cinema on Terror', *Pakistan: On a Razor's Edge* adds a crucial connective link in tracking and situating the myriad problems, tensions, dangers, and patterns of militancy and terrorism that Pakistan not only faced within its own borders, but also poses for the rest of the world if fundamentalist factions are not contained. By the end of the film, it is evident that the impact and fallout of the US-led 'War on Terror', tensions with India, impact of *jihadist* ideologies, and domestic rifts and instability had ignited many alarming and frightening ideological and political fronts across Pakistan. In retrospect, we get a sobering historical and contextual filmic documentation of the compelling and deteriorating circumstances that had been set in motion despite Musharraf's removal from office in 2008, and the democratically elected government of President Asif Ali Zardari that succeeded him, and continued to serve as a US ally in the region.

Pakistan's Double Game (2005)

In a country already beset with internal strife, conflicts, and oppositional religious forces, as depicted in *Pakistan: On A Razor's Edge* (2004), *Pakistan's Double Game* (2005) focuses on President Musharraf's commitment to the international community regarding the 'War on Terror', and curtailment of religious fundamentalism at home.[39] Sharmeen Obaid-Chinoy travels the breadth of Pakistan to investigate the growing trend of suicide attacks, militancy, and ideological rifts brewing within Pakistan's cities. As American suspicions grew that Osama Bin Laden was in hiding somewhere in Pakistan, her thrust in the film is to investigate Musharraf's 'double game' policies as he played an ally of the US to hunt down militants, while trying to conciliate Islamist opinions among his own people. Obaid-Chinoy notes at the very outset: 'The government has targeted foreign militants but not home-grown ones. Dig a little deeper and you find Pakistan's war against terror has been a limited one.'

Beginning her journey in the high-security Karachi Central Jail that houses some of the most notorious militants, Obaid-Chinoy's comment sets the tone for the rest of the film: 'In Pakistan, nothing is as it seems.' She tells us that cameras are not normally allowed inside the high-security prison, but because the government is eager for the world to see what it is up against, it has permitted filming and interviews. We learn that since 9/11, many high-ranking *Al Qaida* members fled to Pakistan after their bases in Afghanistan were destroyed. The Karachi Central Jail superintendent, Amanullah Niazi, tells Obaid-Chinoy that the resolve and strength of captured terrorists cannot be undermined as they are highly trained and capable militants, and that even within captivity they strive to 'make bombs with sulphur, sugar, and fertilizers' to break out of jail. While talking of the serious and numerous threats he receives through letters and phone calls, Niazi shows his arm that was scarred by inmates who threw boiling water mixed with chemicals at him. He emphasizes that imprisonment does nothing to diminish the eagerness of captured militants to re-join terrorist activities if they get out.

In Lahore, Obaid-Chinoy speaks to members of the *Lashkar-e-Jhangvi* (LeJ) at their office, a militant group fighting for the liberation of Kashmir from India that is operating despite a government ban.[40] A member brazenly states that the government dare not shut them down as they have many friends and sympathizers in Pakistan's intelligence services and the army which support their efforts as 'freedom fighters', and not 'terrorists'. He points out that they are the same people who were propped up by the US as Mujahideen in the 1980s to fight against the Soviets in Afghanistan, but now simply the 'definitions' have changed because they no longer serve American interests. As they reject being labelled 'terrorists', LeJ members vow to keep fighting their war of liberation, one they claim has already taken 80,000 lives. They assert that discontent with President Musharraf's pro-US policies has resulted in the Pakistan Army now being perceived as 'traitors', rather than heroes, by a growing segment of Pakistanis, particularly given that over 700 Muslim militants were captured and handed over to the US since 9/11. Obaid-Chinoy's documentation of this serious ideological divide is reflective of the dangerous divisions now taking root in the Pakistan Army itself. Similarly, such alarming support for religious militancy and *jihadist* organizations from within the army ranks reflects the widening gulf between the Pakistani people and the military rulers.

Obaid-Chinoy arranges to meet with Hafiz Ahsan, a former Guantanamo Bay detainee who has returned home in Lahore, and is now treated as a 'folk hero' among his community because of his tales of torture at the hands of US officials. Ahsan contends:

> 'America is at war with Islam, and the world wants to break up Pakistan because it is a Muslim stronghold of Islam – a nuclear state with trained *jihadis*, and religious schools that preach the will to die for Islam.'

The conciseness of Ahsan's analysis reflects his unwavering beliefs that have only been strengthened despite his horrific experiences in captivity in Guantanamo

Bay. But, most alarmingly, now his 'folk hero' status also carries the power to influence and incite many others towards anti-US hatred and religious extremism. Although kept under surveillance by Pakistani intelligence in the hope that he will lead authorities to the capture of other *Al Qaida* members, Ahsan's outlook speaks of the same unrelenting resolve and mindset of militants in the Karachi Central Jail.

Returning to Karachi, Obaid-Chinoy finds her home city has turned into a hotbed of sectarian clashes, shootings, and car-bomb attacks aimed at destabilizing Musharraf's government. She notes that this growing trend of suicide-bomb blasts that had also begun to target *Shia* mosques is evocative of developments in Iraq, another country afflicted by US presence. Obaid-Chinoy speaks to police superintendent Imtiaz Khoso who is in charge of investigating terrorist attacks in Karachi. He tells her that the sectarian violence is a result of the growing strong belief among *Sunni* extremists that targeting the *Shia* minority, and killing a *Shia* is preferable over killing a 'foreign infidel', and more are joining their ranks every day.[41] Asked to explain the escalating violence that is engulfing the city, Khoso blames Musharraf's post 9/11 pro-US policies, rather than foreign militants or extremists – a view that is supported by the five attempts on the president's life, in one of which his own security personnel were implicated. We learn from Khoso that during investigations, jailed militants vowed to carry on with their terrorist and extremist agenda if, and when, they get out of jail – a population of unrepentant, and committed militants simply biding their time in prison.

Obaid-Chinoy's investigation invariably leads her back to the NWFP. Here, in the Khyber Agency bordering the Afghan border, she meets with tribal elders in the sparse village of Wazirthand as a special guest. She learns of further divisions and opposition in a belt that had remained an autonomous area, where the Pakistan Army had never ventured to enter. But now, because of US pressure, Pakistani forces were targeting the region. Her hosts, a large of group of bearded men, take turns to tell her that they do not take orders from outsiders, even if they belong to *Al Qaida*. Instead, they follow their own tribal codes of *Pashtunwali* that dictates a duty to protect 'guests'.[42] This defiance reflects their rejection of the Musharraf government's 70,000-strong troop deployment to weed out *Al Qaida* and Taliban militants in the area. None of the tribal elders believes that the fight is to capture Osama Bin Laden, but rather it is an excuse to establish control of the area, and install pro-government leaders. Similarly, they believe that 'Osama is a "trump card" that the US is holding till it seizes control of Pakistan, Afghanistan, Syria, Iraq, and Iran'. This conviction and resistance are also resonant with the much wider, and growing, fundamentalist opposition to the US, and its perceived designs to invade and rule the Muslim world. Images of the muddy and unimpressive small tribal village belie the power, influence, and militancy its inhabitants command in their region. Posing a threat to trained armies equipped with the most modern weaponry, these tribal leaders make it clear that it is *their* will that prevails in the tribal belt.

Returning to Peshawar, Obaid-Chinoy's mission is to seek out banned film footage of foreign fighters and tribesmen killing Pakistani troops. She points out

Figure 3.5 Sharmeen Obaid-Chinoy with tribal elders and residents of the village of Wazirthand in the Khyber Agency in *Pakistan's Double Game*.
Source: Sharmeen Obaid Films.

that it was 'here in the 1980s that the CIA had armed and funded the Mujahideen to fight against the Soviet troops occupying Afghanistan. One of those they worked with was Osama Bin Laden'. We are led inside a narrow market selling DVD films depicting wars involving Muslims around the world – extremists' very own 'cinema of terror' and heroism being marketed in an obscure bazaar in Peshawar. Taking films of footage censored and banned by the Musharraf government, Obaid-Chinoy visits a local *madrasa*, the *Darul Uloom Nomania*, where according to her militants often find new recruits. She shows clips of Pakistan Army convoys and trucks set ablaze by militants in the tribal belt to a group of *madrasa* students for their reaction to the sight of 'Pakistanis killing Pakistanis'. Visibly angered and upset at a battle they see being fought 'on behalf of US and European interests', students blame their own army and government for launching an offensive in Wana, the capital of the South Waziristan Agency, reportedly a hub of high ranking Taliban militants and *Al Qaida* operatives.

Returning to Islamabad, Obaid-Chinoy tries to negotiate government access to the tribal areas where the 'War on Terror' was fiercest. She learns that no journalists are being allowed to travel there because of bad weather and cancellation of all helicopter flights. Instead, she is offered a chance to interview the Pakistan Army Inter-Services Public Relations (ISPR) spokesperson Major General

Figure 3.6 Sharmeen Obaid-Chinoy speaking with protestors at a *Jamaat-e-Islami* rally in Islamabad in *Pakistan's Double Game*.
Source: Sharmeen Obaid Films.

Shaukat Sultan. Angered at her question as to 'whether the army's operations in the tribal areas were anything more than "window-dressing" for the Americans?' Sultan vehemently defends the Pakistan Army's position, and commitment to rout out terrorist outfits.[43] He stresses that the Pakistan government is having to walk a very tight rope, as it tries to balance domestic sentiments and international obligations as a frontline state. He tells Obaid-Chinoy that in the last year alone, the Pakistan Army lost 250 soldiers, while more than 500 have been injured – 'a heavy loss for any army', he elaborates. To prove what the army is up against, Sultan shows her footage on his computer of the underground cells and bunkers belonging to militants that could not be destroyed even after the Pakistan Army bombed them. These, he states, had served as underground communication bases from which the militants could jam communications, even on helicopters. He shows footage of the elaborate range of equipment, including computers, night vision devices, and sophisticated cameras, that were captured by the Pakistan Army. These images clearly establish a deadly enemy that is well-equipped, and prepared to fight back, belying their Western media image of primitive, bearded barbarians hiding in caves, with little or no modern knowledge.

Winding up *Pakistan's Double Game*, Obaid-Chinoy attends an emotionally charged rally led by a member of Pakistan's biggest religious party, the *Jamaat-e-Islami*. We see enraged bearded men, and even young children, chanting anti-

Musharraf slogans, branding him and his supporters as 'traitors'. The rally leader demands that it is time for Musharraf to end his alliance with America – a constant refrain that continued to impact Pakistan's internal politics and security, and had been the cause of growing extremism across the breadth of the country. Talking to Obaid-Chinoy, the *Jamaat-e-Islami* activist warns that the religious parties will unite to launch a campaign against Musharraf's pro-US policies if they are not abandoned. Having shown both the government, and extremist points of view on the 'War on Terror', and Musharraf's 'double game' that has resulted in only dividing the nation, and endangering the country's stability, Obaid-Chinoy concludes:

> 'For four years President Musharraf has played his double game – seeking to do America's bidding, while placating his own people. The contradictions in that approach are becoming even more apparent. He is in danger of infuriating both sides. In the war on terror nothing is ever quite as it seems. At the moment, the last thing President Musharraf needs is to inflame Islamic opinions by capturing Osama Bin Laden in Pakistan'.

Developments documented in *Pakistan's Double Game* expose the frightening ideological differences that were spurred by growing mistrust of the Musharraf regime and its pro-US policies, and the resultant growing influence of *jihadist* and extremist factions in the country. As another addition to the 'Cinema on Terror', the film forges a cinematic link with developments in *Re-inventing the Taliban?* (2003), and *Pakistan: On A Razor's Edge* (2004) that were pushing Pakistan closer to a danger of Talibanization.

Cold Comfort (2006)

In her next documentary, *Cold Comfort* (2006), Obaid-Chinoy shifts her focus to give us an insight into the ideological exploitation by a terrorist organization even in the midst of a humanitarian crisis.[44] Here, the filmmaker explores the aftermath of a massive earthquake, registered at 7.5 on the Richter scale, which hit Pakistan's northern areas in October 2005 and killed an estimated 87,000 people, while rendering another 3 million homeless. The film provides a valuable insight into how a militant organization has taken advantage of this natural calamity to promote itself, and win over public loyalty.

Travelling in a Pakistani military helicopter to Balakot, the epicentre of the earthquake in the North West Frontier Province (NWFP), Obaid-Chinoy finds that flattened cities have now turned into refugee camps. Once a vibrant 3,200 feet high tourist destination that served as a home-base for mountaineers and trekkers headed for the Himalayas, Balakot now presents scenes of horrific destruction, rubble, poverty, and distress. We see long lines of refugees standing in freezing weather for handouts from relief organizations, while the fast approaching winter is bringing snow to an already miserable situation. The film captures scenes of unhygienic conditions where up to nine people are cramped into a single small

Figure 3.7 Image of earthquake destruction from *Cold Comfort*.
Source: Sharmeen Obaid Films.

tent, as stench of garbage and human waste engulfs the air. Nasreen Bibi, whose husband and two daughters were buried alive, tells the filmmaker that it is the worst for women. Nasreen shares that she has been propositioned many times by men in return for food and a job.

As government relief supplies begin to arrive, and the projected rebuilding period is estimated in years, we see that it is the religious factions that seize the opportunity to play the religion card by targeting a poor and homeless population that has little or no choice. Obaid-Chinoy's film shows how the highly organized and well-equipped *Jamaat-ud-Dawa* militant religious group, outlawed and banned by the US as a terrorist organization, has stepped in to take advantage of the miserable conditions, and deprivation as a result of the earthquake. The organization is at the forefront of not only providing basic necessities, but even computers for children, and secure, segregated camps for women.[45]

We learn that as an Islamic militant group whose fighters were engaged in *jihad* on the Indian side of Kashmir, their young, radical cadres were the first to reach the badly affected mountainous areas, the massive earthquake changing their roles overnight from militants to relief-workers. Told not to film any of the volunteers in the camp, Obaid-Chinoy points out that the men there have all been involved in some kind of militant activity or struggle, and would not want to reveal their identities on camera.

Invited to visit the *Jamaat-ud-Dawa* camp, Obaid-Chinoy is met with scenes of sharp contrast with the rest of the camps. The *Jamaat-ud-Dawa* camp entrance boasts of a 'handicraft school for women', '*Sharia*-based veiling environment', and 'provision of basic food'. We see that neat computer rooms, sanitary conditions, and provision of meat dishes in the midst of colossal destruction have replaced poverty and despair as a banned terrorist organization makes its mark in the guise of social work. The administrative leader in the camp, Abu Zargam, who at first refuses, then relents, to be filmed sitting next to Obaid-Chinoy, tells her that the earthquake is a 'punishment from God'. He claims that people are realizing that they have been punished for the un-Islamic, and immoral conditions prevalent in Pakistan such as cinema houses, and billboards showing female models in revealing clothes. He tells her that people are thanking the *Jamaat-ud-Dawa* as 'angels' for correcting their ways.[46] Zargam states that the *Jamaat-ud-Dawa* is here to stay, and theirs is a 'long-term commitment' to the victims of the earthquake and the region, and that they are already in the process of re-building facilities in Balakot ahead of the refugees' return. He emphatically conveys the sincerity of his

Figure 3.8 Image from *Cold Comfort* of children receiving *madrasa* education.
Source: Sharmeen Obaid Films.

organization to the earthquake victims as opposed to the government's inadequate efforts and intentions. Talking about the *Jamaat-ud-Dawa* camps, Zargam proudly says that they are built for privacy along Islamic lines – providing segregation for women, with attached bathrooms and boundary walls around each tent. This efficiency, and ability, of a militant group to capitalize on human deprivation, loss, and destruction is reminiscent of the pattern of recruitment by *jihadist* organizations as seen in earlier films.

With the harsh winter season approaching, those put up in makeshift camps have little choice than to applaud the *Jamaat-ud-Dawa*'s efforts, terming them 'angels' sent by God to guide them, and rectify their ways. It becomes evident that the *Jamaat-ud-Dawa*'s calculated capitalization on people's desperation is succeeding in encouraging them to convert to their brand of Islamic ideology. Whether through *madrasas* and free food, or implications of a 'sinful' life that can only be redeemed through a militant recourse to oppose Western-style secular ideologies, it is clear that terrorist organizations in Pakistan have worked strategically to win support and loyalty. Documentation of such desperate

Figure 3.9 Image from *Cold Comfort* of a girl cooking on makeshift arrangements at the refugee camp.
Source: Sharmeen Obaid Films.

circumstances in *Cold Comfort* present another angle to the leverage militant organizations are set to exploit to their advantage.

We are shown a large number of international humanitarian and relief agencies also at work in the camps, including a team of 1700 Cuban doctors, and their 13 mobile units that are treating up to 350 patients per day. Talking to people in Balakot on the last day of her visit, Obaid-Chinoy hears many claiming that the *Jamaat-ud-Dawa* were the first to arrive with relief goods, food, and ambulances. Others tell her that the *Jamaat-ud-Dawa* only helps those who join their organization and support their ideology. As she winds up her visit, Obaid-Chinoy sums up this remote corner of Pakistan that was once the exclusive stronghold of the Islamic militant groups, but where the international relief organizations are also making their mark:

> 'To me it seemed as if a battle was waging in the midst of the relief operations, between the Islamic groups and the international relief organizations. I wonder who will win the minds and hearts of these people as they struggle to survive the first winter after a shattering earthquake'.

In addition to the role of *madrasas* as hubs of recruitment, as depicted in Obaid-Chinoy's earlier films, *Cold Comfort* plays a significant expository role as it depicts the unrelenting resolve and resourcefulness of banned terrorist organizations to compete with the government, and promote themselves through social work as well. It is worth noting the grave effect the promotion and success of *jihadist* agendas has had in the region, given that the area had always been the hub of tourism and tourism-based economy, and its inhabitants had held moderate views. The penetration of *jihadist* organizations and their unchecked operations and oversight by the government speaks volumes for their influence and support from within the Pakistani establishment to help them pursue their agendas and operations with impunity, despite the fact that rescue teams from the government as well as from friendly countries were operating in the region, as depicted in the film.

Pakistan's Taliban Generation (2009)

Pakistan's Taliban Generation (2009), a multi-award winning film, including an Emmy in 2010, makes an alarming connection with the developments covered in Obaid-Chinoy's earlier documentaries as it focuses on Pakistan's unabated drift towards Talibanization, despite the army's resolve to counter it.[47] From the days when Afghans were forced to flee to Karachi for refuge in *Terror's Children* (2003), to a generation of Pakistani children now being prepared for suicide attacks in this film, we see the emergence of Pakistan's very own Taliban generation.[48] We are introduced to horrific and escalating developments despite Pakistan's return to democratic rule, continuing American and Western alliances to fight religious extremism, and its own citizens' aspirations for a secular and progressive state.[49]

110 *Cinema on Terror*

Pakistan's Taliban Generation opens with footage from a Taliban recruitment propaganda video glorifying child-suicide bombers. It shows a class of young boys wearing white bandanas inscribed with the first tenet of Islam, the *Kalma Tayyabah*, saying their prayers in a *madrasa*.[50] Their teacher, dressed in brown military fatigues, with his face covered, is shown instructing them on the justification and merits of suicide-bombings.

Intended to attract young children to join their *jihadist* movement which will prepare them to fight 'in the name of God', the video plays a shocking song in a young boy's voice: 'If you try to find me/ After I have died/ You will never find my whole body/ You will find me in little pieces.' This is followed by archival footage of three teenaged boys, shown smiling jubilantly, who served and died as suicide bombers – Zainullah, who killed six people; Sadiq, who killed 22; and Masud, who killed 28. Together, these images set the tone for *Pakistan's Taliban Generation*, a documentary that focuses on Taliban-run *madrasas* that are preparing a generation of suicide bombers among Pakistan's impoverished areas and populations.

Travelling across Pakistan to map the spread of religious extremism, Obaid-Chinoy visits a paraplegic and rehabilitation centre in the city of Peshawar. Since 2004, the city has become a refugee hub for those caught in the crossfire between the Taliban, and the US-backed Pakistan Army offensive in the North-West Frontier Province (NWFP), and the adjoining tribal areas along the Afghan border. At the centre, we see the horrific toll of this conflict that has left countless

Figure 3.10 Sharmeen Obaid-Chinoy speaks with a patient at a paraplegic and rehabilitation centre in Peshawar in *Pakistan's Taliban Generation*.
Source: Sharmeen Obaid Films.

crippled, maimed, or paralysed for life by roadside bombs and rocket attacks, creating a disabled population with no future and nothing to return to. Accompanied by footage of those confined to wheelchairs, families and children recount atrocities and tales of bombs destroying their homes and watching limbs being blown away in the deadly crossfire between the Taliban and the Pakistan Army. Similarly, a visit by the filmmaker to the Swat Valley, a holiday resort that had been a tourist destination not too long ago, and was dubbed the 'Switzerland of the East', reveals the havoc wrought since the spread of the Taliban influence. As Talibanization arrived on Pakistan's doorstep, and the Pakistan Army offensive took off, Obaid-Chinoy informs us in the film that 400,000 people were forced to flee from their homes, the largest internal displacement Pakistan had ever seen till then. This displacement also included most government officials, as the Taliban beheaded 50 of their colleagues.[51]

We learn that over 200 girls' schools were blown up by bombs as the Taliban banned girls' education. Women were forced to veil, and forbidden to leave home alone – something that had been hitherto alien to the Swati women.[52] Veiling her own face through most of the film, Obaid-Chinoy, talks to two nine-year-old girls, Zarlasht and Rukhsar who, expressing their anger and dismay, take her to see the remains of their destroyed school building where 400 girls had studied. Images of the school's rubble are testimony of the indiscriminate use of power and intolerance espoused by the Taliban ideology against women. Narrating their experiences under the Taliban in turns, one girl tells of a particularly horrifying scene:

> 'We saw the dead body of a policeman tied to a pole. His head had been cut off, and was hanging between his legs. There was a note saying that if anyone moved the dead body, they would share the same fate'.

We learn from Obaid-Chinoy that barbershops, music shops, and cinemas have been forced to close in Swat as Taliban radio broadcasts warn of severe repercussions, including beheading, for those defying their *Sharia* laws. A Taliban broadcast plays in the background, a man's emotionally charged and defiant voice proclaiming:

> '*Sharia* law is our right, and we will exercise this right whatever happens. I swear to God we will shed our own blood to achieve this. We will make our sons suicide bombers! We will make ourselves suicide bombers! I swear to God if our leader orders me I will sacrifice myself, and blow myself up in the middle of our enemies.'

As Obaid-Chinoy hurries through the streets of Swat's main town, Mingora, fresh Taliban attacks on a Pakistani army convoy can be heard in the background, and news spreads that the Taliban are surrounding the area. On her way, she points out the main square that has been renamed the '*Khooni Chowk*' (Bloody Square) by the local population because of the public beheadings carried out there by the Taliban.

It is significant to note, as Obaid-Chinoy points out in the film, that although Swat lies outside the tribal belt, as a measure of political compromise in the face of the Taliban insurgency, the Pakistan government had also made a deal, namely the *Nizam-e-Adl* (System of Justice) Ordinance, with them in April 2009. Under the deal, President Asif Ali Zardari signed the Ordinance imposing *Sharia* law in the Swat Valley, claiming that it was the 'demand of the people'. The Ordinance only served to further empower the Taliban and other groups there and in the surrounding areas of the Provincially Administered Tribal Areas (PATA). This move, potentially providing the Taliban with a new safe haven to operate from, also led to increased incidents of human rights violations, particularly against women.[53] In May 2009, the *Nizam-e-Adl* peace deal fell through as the Pakistan Army launched a massive offensive to oust the Taliban from the Swat Valley.[54]

Focusing on Pakistani children being trained in the country's *madrasas* as the next generation of Pakistani Taliban, specifically as suicide bombers, Obaid-Chinoy interviews several potential recruits and recruiters. Hazrat Ali, a boy from a poor farming family in Swat who was recruited by a *madrasa* at thirteen, has recently returned from fighting alongside the Taliban. He proudly tells Obaid-Chinoy that he is trained to use rocket launchers, grenades, guns, and bombs, and to carry out a suicide attack against 'infidels', and the Pakistan Army that the Taliban view as an enemy because of its pro-US stance. Displaying great pride in the Taliban's strength and numbers at fourteen years of age, Ali is confident of their ability to defeat the Pakistan Army. Asked if he would carry out a suicide attack, he replies simply: 'If God gives me the strength'.

Next, Obaid-Chinoy takes a trip with Pakistan Army officials to Bajaur, the border area ten miles from Afghanistan where hundreds of Taliban and *Al Qaida* militants arrived after they were driven out of Afghanistan, and where the London transport bombers were also allegedly trained.[55] Driven very fast in an army van to avoid a Taliban ambush, Obaid-Chinoy is shown vast areas of the strategic town of Loisam that was once the trading centre of the Bajaur Valley, with a population of 7000. It now lies bombed and flattened by the Pakistan Army. Army officials tell Obaid-Chinoy that the army employed this demolition strategy as the most effective means of getting rid of Taliban militants. Footage of ruin, decaying heaps of rusting iron, and rubble are testimony to the repercussions of the indiscriminate army strategy that also affected civilian populations caught in the midst of these cleansing operations. We learn that, unfortunately, such operations also resulted in thousands of internally displaced citizens fleeing not only the Taliban, but also their own army.

We see the repercussions of the above conflict starkly echoed at the *Kachegori* Refugee Camp in the NWFP where the Pakistan government was struggling to look after its own Internally Displaced People (IDPs), estimated at almost one million. Reminiscent of the displaced Afghan population in the *Jadeed* Refugee Camp in *Terror's Children* (2003), and itself once home to those fleeing the war in Afghanistan, the *Kachegori* camp site is shown to be brimming with more than 30,000 IDPs, half of whom are children, while more families arrive daily.

As Obaid-Chinoy points out that one of the first things that hit her was the sheer number of children running around barefoot, we see vast numbers roaming around the camp aimlessly, their impoverished faces marked by despair. Here, Obaid-Chinoy meets two young boys, Waseefullah and Abdur Rehman, who are also best friends. Both fled their homes in a Taliban-controlled village in Bajaur Agency when Pakistan army offensives destroyed their *madrasa*. Despite their common present predicament, and strong friendship, they are sharply divided in their outlook and plans. Waseefullah recounts a US missile strike in 2006 that killed 80 people, among them his cousin whose dead body he saw being eaten by dogs the day after, and whose only remains, his legs, they brought to the village to bury. Archival footage from October 2006 shows the *madrasa* destruction site become a recruitment rally where Taliban militants are delivering fiery anti-US speeches. Waseefullah remembers being in the crowd that day, where he made up his mind to join the Taliban when he is older. On the other hand, his friend Abdur Rehman who blames the *Al Qaida* as the root cause of the conflict, and the main reason behind all the destruction, expresses his resolve to join the Pakistan Army one day. Asked if they would fight each other if their chosen paths were to materialize, both boys show an immediate resolve to kill each other for their beliefs on the battlefield. Their conflicting outlooks reflect the misplaced enmities sweeping an entire generation of youngsters as the Pakistan Army continued its deadliest offensive against the Taliban in South Waziristan (backed by 30,000 troops, gunship helicopters, and fighter jets), the hub of the Pakistan Taliban leadership. The offensive resulted in the Taliban waging a counter war through suicide attacks in the country's major cities, targeting army bases, educational institutions, law enforcement agencies and their offices, markets and civilian populations, and even highway interchanges.[56] Noticed by Taliban informers in the camp, Obaid-Chinoy is warned to leave – an indication of the Taliban's infiltration, influence, and control even in a Pakistani government-run refugee camp.

Obaid-Chinoy meets with Major General Tariq Khan of the Frontier Corps, in charge of the army's offensive against the Taliban in the tribal belt. He defends the army operations as 'justified', despite heavy casualties of their own population. Talking of the human cost, Khan informs that over 5000 civilians have lost their lives since the Taliban began their insurgency, while the army has suffered the 'death of 1,500 soldiers, and thousands wounded, a number ten times greater than British soldiers killed fighting the Taliban in Afghanistan'.[57] Asked if the army will succeed in eliminating the Taliban threat, Khan is quick to respond: 'We will win it hands down.'

In sharp contrast, hospitalized soldiers visited by Obaid-Chinoy in an army hospital in Peshawar give her a very different picture. Speaking in the presence of five military officers deputed to monitor their interviews, and what they have to say about their injuries, they point to the Taliban's hatred for the Pakistan Army as a consequence of its pro-US policies. Severely physically debilitated for life, having lost limbs, or eyesight, some share their fear of losing the war, saying it is becoming all the more difficult to combat an enemy that melts back into the population.

This fear of failure finds credence as the deputy leader of the *Tehreek-e-Taliban* Pakistan (TTP), Hakimullah Mehsud, filmed for the first time, is shown arriving in a US armoured vehicle, captured in an attack on a NATO convoy headed for Afghanistan, at a girl's school building they have closed down and turned into an operations base.[58] Warned that as a woman she would be killed if she visits the area where the Taliban are openly inviting journalists to show their strength, Obaid-Chinoy employs a local cameraman to film for her in a village in the tribal belt of Orakzai. Footage shows a long-haired Mehsud, flanked by bearded, armed Taliban combatants, some with their faces covered, holding a press conference. Iterating the Taliban's resolve to fight back, Mehsud calmly declares that US strikes in their areas are only reinforcing their beliefs, and warns that they will take over Peshawar as well as other cities, and will topple the government if the Pakistan Army continues to side with the US. Not an empty threat, Obaid-Chinoy comments, as news reports of suicide attacks continued to be on the rise across Pakistani cities, killing 800 people in 2008 alone.

Returning to Karachi, her coastal home city at the other end of the country, Obaid-Chinoy finds an alarming Taliban presence in the city's slum areas. Deputy Superintendent of the anti-terrorist squad responsible for eliminating the Taliban in the slums, Raja Omar Khattab, tells her that the Taliban are using criminal networks to extort money through kidnappings and ransoms to raise funds for their war. Police officials escort her to see the site of a house where a three-hour shootout between the police and the Taliban took place. We learn that rather than surrendering, the militant gang eventually blew themselves up in their hideout.

Footage shows slum neighbourhoods that have turned into Taliban training and recruitment grounds. Here the Taliban are indoctrinating impoverished children and youth, some from even as far away as the tribal areas, in unregulated *madrasas*. Obaid-Chinoy meets Shaheed, a student in one of the *madrasas* she visits. Memorizing the *Quran* in Arabic, a language he cannot understand, Shaheed shares his views on the place of women in Islam, claiming that only the Taliban know how to treat women: 'They should be confined to home as per the dictates of the *Sharia*, and just as the government has banned the use of plastic bags, it should do the same to them', implying that they be banned from being seen in public. Inspired by child suicide bombers' propaganda videos that students regularly watch at his *madrasa*, Shaheed expresses his own heartfelt desire to fight alongside the Taliban when he completes his education. He is keen to carry out suicide attacks abroad some day 'where most infidels are, so I can answer God one day that I carried out His will by eradicating evil for Islam, and thus be redeemed to go to heaven'. Shaheed's teacher, who rejects all accusations of teaching an extremist ideology, tells the camera in calm, calculated tones that only 'love, peace, and harmony' are taught at his *madrasa*. But, as the camera moves away, he is heard stating that 'martyrdom is the greatest achievement for a Muslim'.

Obaid-Chinoy's search for Taliban child recruiters leads her to a Taliban commander, *Qari* Abdullah, who she comments does not even bother to hide his face despite the ongoing government crackdowns in Pakistani cities. Taking pride in his mission and work, the *Qari*, a diminutive man who rocks back and forth as *madrasa* children are taught to do while reciting the *Quran*, shares that he himself went to train as a child in a *madrasa* in Afghanistan.[59] He defends recruiting and using children to carry out suicide attacks and execute spies, saying calmly: 'If you are fighting, God provides you with the means. Children are tools to achieve God's will. And whatever comes your way you sacrifice it. So it's okay.' Talking of their recruitment and training methods, he casually explains how the Taliban convince small children to join them: 'The kids want to join us because they like our weapons. They don't use weapons to begin with. They just carry them for us, and off we go.' On seeing clips from the children's propaganda video that Obaid-Chinoy shows him on her cell phone, the *Qari* looks intently, and then pompously observes that they are much older than the lot he is preparing, who, he proudly claims, range from '5, 6, and 7 years in age'.[60]

Obaid-Chinoy ends her documentation of *Pakistan's Taliban Generation* with a grave realization and comment:

> 'The Taliban are confident of winning the support of the next generation … There are 80 million children in Pakistan. More than a quarter live below the poverty line. If the militants continue to recruit freely then soon Pakistan will belong to them.'

The issues detailed and analysed in *Pakistan's Taliban Generation* are ongoing: growing Taliban influence and recruitment; indoctrination of *jihadis*, and extremist ideologies in *madrasas*; anti-US sentiments; suicide attacks; terrorist organizations and their operations. Obaid-Chinoy's film not only informs of Pakistan's ongoing political, social, and economic upheavals and security challenges but also performs the multiple role of investigating and communicating the consequential present and future threats to Pakistan, and also for the world. The textual reading and analysis of *Pakistan's Taliban Generation* thus completes the sequence of her six films that can be described as a thematically related 'Cinema on Terror' that tracks and contextualizes the multi-faceted roots and complicated patterns of religious extremism and terrorism intensifying in Pakistan.

Conclusion

This chapter discussed Sharmeen Obaid-Chinoy's six representative films that depict and contextualize Pakistan's continuing experience with a militant mix of religion and politics and the looming threat of Talibanization being promoted by extremist organizations and leaderships. Becoming a hub of terrorist activities, *jihadist* organizations, militant ideologies, and pro-Taliban *madrasas* during the period discussed here, we see Pakistan embroiled in combating terror and destruction unfolding within its own borders and cities. What emerges is a 'Cinema on Terror', inspired by the continuum of the political and ideological divisions and conflicts instigated by the 'War on Terror'.

Obaid-Chinoy's films illustrate the socio-political impact and consequences of the transforming nature of the US alliance with Pakistan, as the country journeyed from one US-backed military dictator, President General Zia-ul-Haq (1977–1988), to another, President General Pervaiz Musharraf (1999–2008). This contrast between the Pak–US pro-*jihad* and pro-Mujahideen stance during the Soviet invasion of Afghanistan in the late 1970s, and their current anti-*jihad* and anti-fundamentalism alliance after the *Al Qaida* terrorist attacks on the US in 2001, highlight the internal transformations and challenges that have been shaping Pakistan's own political and socio-economic landscape,and geo-political standing in the world. Together, these six thematically-linked topical documentaries form a filmic historical and contextual narrative of developments and trends towards religious militancy that continue to affect and mould domestic and international politics, and policies.

From *Terror's Children* (2003) where we see victims and refugees of the US-led war in Afghanistan arrive in Karachi, to *Reinventing the Taliban* (2003) that depicts the emerging trend of Talibanization on Pakistani soil, to Obaid-Chinoy's multi-award winning film, *Pakistan's Taliban Generation* (2009), portraying the widespread *madrasa* culture, escalating violence, extremist Taliban ideologies, and recruitment and training of young children to become suicide bombers, we see Pakistan's descent into Talibanization coming full circle. These young and vulnerable 'armies of God' now being mass-produced in Pakistani *madrasas*, ready for export to carry out deadly missions within, and abroad, sound a grim warning for the country's own stability, and security worldwide.

Similarly, in *Pakistan: On a Razor's Edge* (2004), we are given a picture of the complex and intense internal political and ideological strife that was beginning to take root in a nuclear-armed Pakistan during President Musharraf's alliance with the US and the West in the 'War on Terror', and the ongoing complex relationship with neighbouring India. On the other hand, *Pakistan's Double Game* (2005) investigates and exposes the expanding pattern of destruction, unrest, mistrust, and militancy as a result of the failure of Musharraf's policies as he sought to cling to power, and appease both the West as well as extremist segments at home. *Cold Comfort* (2006) presents a vivid example of the successful manipulation and exploitation by a terrorist organization in winning over public opinion and support even in the worst of natural disasters, such as a deadly earthquake.

In all her films, Obaid-Chinoy stresses the growing number of *madrasas*, and their dangerous reach and influence in the country, that continue to spread a culture of intolerance, militancy, and extremism. As they defiantly train large numbers of potential *jihadists*, the threat these pro-Taliban seminaries pose to not only Pakistan's own stability and peace, but to the entire world is a factor that engages the international community in its support for the 'War on Terror'. It is evident that Zia's Islamization strategies of merging the state and religion set a negative and dangerous precedent for Pakistan's future, one that continues to hinder the country's return to a secular and democratic identity, even after a lapse of more than three decades.

Using a reportorial and journalistic style and focus in all her films, complemented by interviews, and her own on-screen active participation and interaction with her subjects, the filmmaker has journeyed through some of the most dangerous territories and environments in Pakistan and borderland with Afghanistan to present an expository narrative. The activist intent of her journalistic documentaries resonates in her repeated attempts to investigate and expose the many factors and conflicts that have been shaping not only her country's destiny and future, but would also threaten global security – a post 9/11 cinema on terrorism that investigates the roots of Pakistan's growing tilt towards Talibanization and those supporting it. In Obaid-Chinoy's films we see members of militant organizations and terrorist networks defending their operations; clerics who take pride in promoting terror and hatred in the guise of '*jihad*' through *madrasa* teachings and indoctrination of extremist ideologies; Taliban recruiters and commanders justifying their recruitment of young children as 'tools to carry out God's will', anti-US religious scholars that even justify Pakistan's nuclear proliferation to other countries; interviews with key government officials and decision makers with conflicting views and beliefs. Similarly, interviews with liberal and progressive voices that shun religious extremism and support a return to moderation complete the picture of a Pakistani nation torn between regressive elements, and its desire for advancement. Together, these filmic enquiries and documentations give a rounded picture of the divisive environment that has continued to threaten Pakistan's stability.

The personal, political, and historical positioning of the filmmaker that film scholar Chuck Kleinhans stresses, is of great importance to contextualize and analyse Obaid-Chinoy's filmmaking.[61] As events related to religious extremism unfold and develop at such rapid speed, not only in Pakistan, but also worldwide, Obaid-Chinoy has sought to investigate and report first hand from the very midst of the people, policy-makers, events, and militant groups and mindsets that were shaping Pakistan's socio-political landscape.[62] In documenting the roots and penetration of militant ideologies over a decade, and the consequent impending disaster and undercurrents that threaten the world, she has given us a contextual documentary 'Cinema on Terror' that captures the history of the escalating trend towards terrorism. In contrast to foreign filmmakers, news anchors, or the many 'analysts' and 'experts on terror' doing the rounds on foreign news networks, Obaid-Chinoy's work provides a view from a native filmmaker who is positioned as an 'insider', both as a Pakistani citizen and a Muslim.[63] Well aware of the nuances, languages, and constraints, she is part of, and placed in the midst of, her country's political, social, and cultural landscape, and its lived history, and the events that unravel in real life in the country she explores and documents.

Obaid-Chinoy's close mapping of developments that illustrate growing religious extremism in Pakistan take on the characteristics of a *developing story,* one that stresses the significance of the fleeting moments depicting militancy, and comments from key players caught on film as precursors of the larger picture that keeps evolving and re-defining itself through new developments in terms of events, international politics, and policy shifts to address these issues. What we see in Obaid-Chinoy's body of work discussed here is a *developing story* of hatred and terror that has, unfortunately, become a *running story* since the 9/11 terrorist attacks in the USA, and has been taking a heavy toll, both physically and mentally, on the Pakistani population that finds itself in the crossfire.[64] Seen in retrospect, this filmic body of work stands as a testimony to the problems, and dangers that have been developing consistently in Pakistan over a long period of time, and today infiltrate and manifest themselves globally through terrorism and Islamic militant's call for *jihad*. For example, an alarming development is the emergence of the fast growing, brutally militant, anti-West and anti-*Shia* Islamic State of Iraq and Syria (ISIS) movement that aims to revive and establish the '*Islamic Caliphate*', and spread its *Salafist* Islamic ideology through force and violent means in South and Central Asian regions, and eventually worldwide.[65] The ISIS movement has also begun to make inroads into Pakistan and Afghanistan, with several hardline extremist organizations, such as the followers of the *Ahrarul Islam* who call themselves *Jamaat-ul-Ahrar*, a splinter faction of the TTP, pledging allegiance to their ideology and aims.[66] ISIS wall chalking has also been spotted in Pakistan's largest city, Karachi, to make its presence felt and elicit support.[67]

As a young Muslim woman filmmaker working her way through the most conservative of societies and dangerous of terrains, such as the tribal belts and the NWFP, and meeting with hardened militants, pro-Taliban commanders, and clerics, we see Obaid-Chinoy defying spatial boundaries that could otherwise limit her appearance in the public sphere in a Muslim society, and access to the people and circumstances she has documented.[68]

Taking religious fundamentalism, militancy, and terrorism as her focus of investigation and expose, Obaid-Chinoy's contribution can be seen as an addition to the political and activist intent that Third Cinema[69] and Cinema Novo[70] manifestos advocated, albeit at a different time and context in history, on a different continent, but this time with global consequences. It is important to note that Third Cinema and Cinema Novo activist perspectives of the 1960s can be re-appropriated, and are relevant in the contemporary documentation of the effects and dangers of Islamic religious extremism and militancy, as in the case of Pakistan.

In Obaid-Chinoy's documentaries – a body of work that investigates and documents the spread of religious fundamentalism and related developments from 2003 to 2009 – we have a Pakistani narrative sequence of a 'Cinema on Terror' that informs, and warns of domestic and international consequences of *jihadist* agendas and influence, as much as it stresses accountability from policy and decision-makers. It would be apt to argue that, today, as the world is confronted by an era defined by a legacy of terrorism long after the 9/11/2001 attacks in the US and *Al Qaida* leader Osama bin Laden's capture and death by US forces in Abbottabad, Pakistan, in May 2011, a 'Cinema on Terror' documentary film category, bridging Cinema Studies, history, politics, and now the many facets of religious extremism, led by a Pakistani woman filmmaker, too has emerged to depict and critique it from within the Muslim world.[71] Obaid-Chinoy's detractors may argue that her foreign-funded films, to be released on foreign channels, dictate a choice of topics that pander to an international audience, inclusion in international film festivals, and chances of winning prestigious awards. Such criticism notwithstanding, her films stand as a valuable historical testimony to the horrific developments of religious extremism and fundamentalist ideologies that have been engulfing not only Pakistan, but also continue to pose a most urgent threat to the world.

Notes

1 Led by Mullah Mohammad Omar as their elected *Amir-ul-Momineen* (Leader of the Faithful), the Taliban had declared Afghanistan as a 'completely Islamic state' after the capture of Kabul in September 1996. As had happened in Pakistan during General Zia-ul-Haq's Islamization process, the first victims of the new puritanical Islamic order in Afghanistan were women, who found their freedoms completely curtailed in the name of a new national religious identity. The very first religious edict issued on Radio Kabul, renamed 'Voice of Sharia', announced a strict Islamic dress code for women, while forbidding them to go out to work, or even to go out alone without a male chaperone. The edict brought to a standstill not only the livelihood of the majority of the female workforce, but also had a crippling effect on the country's educational and healthcare system as women students, teachers, and other employees suddenly found themselves either out of a job, or the right to pursue their profession. Michael Griffin, *Reaping the Whirlwind: The Taliban Movement in Afghanistan*, Pluto Press, London, 2001, pp. 5–8.
2 *Madrasas* and organizations that espouse an extremist, pro-Taliban, and militant education and ideologies, such as recruiting and preparing children for suicide-attacks, are referred to in the book as '*jihadist*'.
3 For a background to the Taliban ideology, and the reforms they introduced in Afghanistan, see Peter Marsden, 'The Warriors of God' and 'The Taliban Creed', *The Taliban: War, Religion and the New Order in Afghanistan*, Oxford University Press, Zed Books, Ltd, London, New York, 1998, pp. 43–66.
4 Other Pakistani filmmakers that have addressed similar issues of growing religious fundamentalism, socio-political unrest, and regional conflict include Maheen Zia, Munizae Jehangir, Samar Minallah, and Sabiha Sumar.
5 Picking on themes of conflict, struggle, gender, and injustices, Sharmeen Obaid-Chinoy's films have also addressed the impact of the US-led invasion and war in Afghanistan on Afghan women (Lifting the Veil/ *Afghanistan Unveiled*, 2007); the US-led invasion and sectarian violence on Iraqi children (*The Lost Generation*, 2008); women's lives, struggles, and an emerging women's movement for equal citizenship rights in the ultra orthodox and conservative Saudi Arabian society (*Women Of The Holy Kingdom*, 2005); issues of religious identity and socio-cultural integration of Muslim immigrants living in Sweden (*Assimilation No, Integration Yes*, 2006); the Aboriginal and First Nations young women who have gone missing in the province of British Columbia, Canada, and the alleged discriminatory treatment and apathy of police by their relatives (*Highway of Tears*, 2006); poverty, illegal abortions, and the tussle between women's and pro-life Catholic Church groups in the Philippines (*City Of Guilt*, 2006); the discriminatory treatment of illegal Zimbabwean migrants who have fled the political and economic turmoil in their home country to seek refuge in South Africa (*The New Apartheid*, 2006); the plight of the transgender community in Pakistan (*Transgender: Pakistan's Open Secret*, 2011); the victimization of women by acid-attacks in Pakistan (*Saving Face*, 2011); women's education in Pakistan (*Humaira: The Dream Catcher*, 2013); and *3 Bahadur* (*The 3 Brave Ones*) (2015), Pakistan's first 3D animation feature-length adventure family entertainment film in Urdu with a primary target audience of children.

Sharmeen Obaid-Chinoy's films are mostly collaborative ventures with foreign media channels such as Channel 4 UK, PBS, CBC, *Al-Jazeera*, CNN, HBO, and the Discovery Times Channel. For details on Obaid-Chinoy's films, awards, and projects visit: http://sharmeenobaidfilms.com/

6 *Saving Face*, Sharmeen-Obaid Chinoy (with Daniel Junge), 2011 (DVD 52 min.), Naked Edge Films (English/English sub-titles/Urdu).

Following her Oscar win for the Best Documentary Film (Short Subject), Sharmeen Obaid-Chinoy has also been included in the Time Magazine's list of '100 Most Influential People' in 2012. *The Daily Times*. 'Sharmeen Obaid-Chinoy in *Time Magazine's* List of 100 Most Influential People'. April 19, 2012. Accessed at: http://archives.dailytimes.com.pk/infotainment/19-Apr-2012/sharmeen-obaid-chinoy-in-time-magazine-s-list-of-100-most-influential-people on January 12, 2016.

Shaimaa Khalil. 'Pakistan's Sharmeen Obaid Chinoy: The Oscar double winner.' BBC News, Islamabad, Pakistan. February 29, 2016. Accessed at: http://www.bbc.com/news/world-asia-35690403 on March 29, 2016.

Discussion of Sharmeen Obaid-Chinoys film *A Girl in The River: The Price of Forgiveness* (2015) is part of the authors' under-progress book on comparative cinemas from Pakistan, Iran, and Afghanistan.

Sharmeen Obaid Films. Accessed at: http://sharmeenobaidfilms.com/ on November 3, 2014.

7 C. Christine Fair, 'Introduction', *The Madrassah Challenge: Militancy and Religious Education in Pakistan*, United States Institute of Peace Press, Washington, DC, 2008, p. 1.

8 Following the 9/11/2001 Al Qaida attacks in the US, the US-led 'War on Terror' was initiated in October 2001 to target the *Al Qaida* leadership, and oust the Taliban regime (1996–2001) in Afghanistan. For details on the emergence of the Taliban movement see Ahmed Rashid, 'Kandahar 1994: The Origins of the Taliban', *Taliban: Islam, Oil and the New Great Game in Central Asia*, I.B.Tauris, London, New York, 2008, p. 17.

9 Erik Barnouw, *Documentary: A History of the Non-Fiction Film*. Oxford University Press, UK, 1974, p. 51.

10 The province's change of name to Khyber Pakhtunkhwa (KP) occurred in April 2010. Within this book I have used the name North West Frontier Province (NWFP), where it was used as such by the filmmakers in their films prior to the name change.

11 *Terror's Children*, Sharmeen Obaid-Chinoy (with Jay Keuper and Mohammad Naqvi), 2003 (DVD 45 min.), Discovery Times Channel (Urdu, Darri, English/English sub-titles).

12 *Committee to Protect Journalists* (CPJ). 'Daniel Pearl'. Accessed at: http://cpj.org/killed/2002/daniel-pearl.php on November 3, 2014.

13 Arman Sabir and S. Raza Hassan, '10 Die in Karachi Car-bomb Blast: Terrorist Act Outside US Consulate'. *Dawn Internet Edition*, June 15, 2002. Accessed at: http://www.dawn.com/news/43175/10-die-in-karachi-car-bomb-blast-terrorist-act-outside-us-consulate on January 12, 2016.

14 In an article in January 2009, South Asia scholar, Pervez Hoodbhoy estimated that as opposed to the official government figures that put the number of *madrasas* at 13,000 where 1.5 million students are acquiring education, the commonly quoted figures range between 18,000 and 22,000 *madrasas*, where the number of students could be correspondingly larger. Pervez Hoodbhoy, 'The Saudi-isation of Pakistan'. *Newsline Monthly Magazine*, Karachi, Pakistan, January 2009. Accessed at: http://www.newslinemagazine.com/author/pervez-hoodbhoy/ on November 3, 2014.

15 The Taliban regime had banned music and TV during their reign. However, in the post-Taliban scenario, television stations made a booming comeback as around twenty TV stations began to operate out of Kabul. *Daily Dawn Online*, 'Afghanistan: Lacking Literacy, Security, But Lots of TV', November 24, 2009. Accessed at: http://www.dawn.com/news/923779/afghanistan-lacking-literacy-security-but-lots-of-tv on November 5, 2014.

16 According to a *Global South Magazine* report, 'According to government estimates, there were some five million Afghan refugees in the country by the end of 2001 including those born inside Pakistan since 1979. ... The UNHCR has not been very

successful in its mission is evident in the most recent repatriation data. It is reflected in the fact that Pakistan also holds the record for the biggest refugee repatriation since 2002–03 when 1.9 million Afghans were sent back to Afghanistan. The 1.5 million who repatriated in 2002 were the largest number of returning refugees anywhere in the world since 1972. A total of 3.5 million Afghan refugees were repatriated by 2007. The repatriations were meant to be voluntary, but the vast majority of refugees who registered in Pakistan never wanted to return to Afghanistan.' For further details see Khalid Hussain, 'What it Means To Be A Refugee.' *Global South Development Magazine*. A Development Quarterly. 6, April–June 2011pp. 16–17.

According to the.UNHCR, The UN Refugee Agency, Pakistan hosts almost 1.5 million registered Afghan refugees – still the largest protracted refugee population globally. Since 2002, UNHCR has facilitated the return of 3.8 million registered Afghans from Pakistan.

17 *Hafiz*: Arabic for 'guardian'. In Islamic cultures, *hafiz* is a title awarded to one who has memorized the entire *Quran*. Normally, this learning practice is facilitated at *madrasas*.
18 *Reinventing The Taliban?*, Sharmeen Obaid-Chinoy (with Ed Robbins), 2003 (DVD 54 min.) Discovery Times Channel (Urdu, English/English sub-titles).
19 Sharmeen Obaid Films. Accessed at: http://sharmeenobaidfilms.com/ on November 7, 2014.
20 The Internet Movie Database (IMDb). Accessed at: http://www.imdb.com/title/tt1078921/awards on November 7, 2014.
21 For a list of 'Taliban laws' imposed in Afghanistan, which included even a ban on white socks, perceived as an insult to the white Taliban banner, and were inclusive enough to place a ban on caged birds, see: Shaista Wahab, 'The Taliban Era: 1996–2001', in Shaista Wahab and Barry Youngerman, *A Brief History of Afghanistan*, University of Nebraska at Omaha, Arthur Paul Afghanistan Collection, and Barry Youngerman. Facts on File, Infobase Publishing, USA, 2007, p. 218.
22 The *Muttahida Majlis-e-Amal* (MMA) (United Action Front) religious alliance won the majority vote in the October 2001 regional elections, and ruled the North West Frontier Province (NWFP) and Balochistan. Following its sweeping success, on November 25, 2002 the MMA formed its government in NWFP at both the provincial and national level. In June 2002, the NWFP parliament approved legislation to make *Sharia* (Islamic teachings) the governing law in the province. The MMA government issued directives to ban music on public transport, medical examinations of women by male doctors, male coaches for women athletes, and male journalists from covering women's sports. *Global Security.org*. Accessed at: http://www.globalsecurity.org/military/world/pakistan/mma.htm November 11, 2014.
23 The *Ka'aba* is the symbolic house of God for Islam and Muslims, and site of the holiest Muslim pilgrimage in Mecca, Saudi Arabia.
24 It is important to mention here that the art of human representation in fundamentalist Islam, whether through figural art or painting, has historically been considered a means that undermines the authority and unity of God as the sole creator of the universe, and thus the sole entity with the power to give life. As Islamic scholar Muhammad Marmaduke Pickthall elaborates, 'painting and sculpture were restricted by universal consent to conventional designs, because of the association of the forms of living creatures with idolatrous worship'. On the subject and place of painting, music, and drama in Islam, Pickthall points out that although 'There is no direct command that I can discover in the Quran or in our Prophet's recorded sayings, only he refused the request of a Persian painter to be allowed to paint his portrait and take it back to the Persian people, for fear lest it might be idolized.' Mohammad Marmaduke Pickthall, 'Science, Arts, and Letters', *The Cultural Side of Islam*, Ashraf Press, Lahore, Pakistan, 1961, pp. 76–7.
25 *Maulana* Sami-ul-Haq, also known as the 'Father of the Taliban', has served as the director and chancellor of the *Darul-Uloom-Haqqania madrasa* since 1988, after the

death of his father, *Maulana* Abdul Haq, who founded the *madrasa*. The *madrasa* is considered the launching pad for the Taliban movement in the early 1990s. Located in Akora Khattak, near Peshawar, the *Darul-Uloom* is reputed to have trained top Taliban leaders, including *Mullah* Omar, now in hiding. Haq, a long time religious politician, was among the founders of Pakistan's *Muttahida Majlis-e-Amal* (MMA) (United Action Front), a coalition of six Islamic religious parties. Imtiaz Ali, 'The Father of the Taliban: An Interview with Maulana Sami-ul-Haq', *Global Terrorism Analysis. Spotlight on Terror*, 4.2, May 23, 2007, The Jamestown Foundation. Accessed at: http://www.jamestown.org/programs/gta/single/?tx_ttnews%5Btt_news%5D=4180&tx_ttnews%5BbackPid%5D=26&cHash=2feb32fe98 on November 14, 2014.

26 Darra Adam Khel is reputed to be the largest illegal arms market in Asia. *Indiatvnews.com*. Accessed at: http://www.indiatvnews.com/print/news/pakistan-s-darra-adam-khel-is-world-s-largest-illegal-arms-marke-14283-2.html November 14, 2014.

27 For reasons of security, the performance was confined to invitees only. For details of Eve Ansler's *Vagina Monologues* performances in Pakistan, see 'Staging It In Pakistan Was Tough.' Accessed at: http://www.vday.org/node/1200.html#.VpUE_9bFFPM on January 12, 2016.

28 *The Friday Times* weekly magazine has been known for its liberal and progressive stance and opposition to martial law and dictatorial regimes since its first publication in 1989.

29 *Pakistan: On A Razor's Edge*, Sharmeen Obaid-Chinoy (with Ed Robbins), 2004 (DVD 24 min.). Public Broadcasting Corporation (PBS), (Urdu/English/English sub-titles).

This film was made while Obaid-Chinoy was a graduate student at Stanford University, USA, as well as a reporter for New York Times Television (NYTT).

In a lecture at the University of Oxford in 1907, Lord Curzon, the Viceroy of India, which then included Pakistan, had described India's border as 'the razor's edge on which hang suspended the modern issues of war and peace, of life and death to nations'. Muhammad Saleem Mazhar and Naheed S Goraya, 'Border Issue between Pakistan & Afghanistan', *Journal of South Asian Studies*, 24.2, July–December 2009, pp. 204–20 (p. 204).

30 Bill Nichols, 'What Types of Documentary Are There?', *Introduction to Documentary*, Indiana University Press, Bloomington, IN and Indianapolis, IN, USA, 2001, p. 105.

31 The *Samjhauta* Express (Friendship Express) train service was restored between Pakistan and India on January 15, 2004. The two countries broke off most ties in 2001 after India blamed Pakistan for involvement in an armed attack on the federal parliament in Delhi. 'India, Pakistan Resume Train Link', *British Broadcasting Corporation* (BBC), January 15, 2004. Accessed at: http://news.bbc.co.uk/2/hi/south_asia/3395901.stm on November 14, 2014.

The biweekly *Samjhauta* Express train, launched on July 22, 1976 following the Shimla Agreement, served as a symbol of the historical ties between India and Pakistan following the 1947 partition of India, and the creation of Pakistan as a Muslim state. Running between Amritsar and Lahore, a distance of about 42 kilometres, it was used by people of both countries with meagre resources to visit relatives and friends across the border. Due to disturbances in the Punjab in the late '80s, Indian Railways terminated the service at Attari, where customs and immigration clearances take place. The *Samjhuata* Express was discontinued on January 1, 2002 in the wake of a terrorist attack on the Indian Parliament on December 13, 2001, for which India accused Pakistan. After resumption of service in 2004, the train service travelling from New Delhi to Lahore was made a terrorist target in India on February 18, 2007, leaving 68 people dead, and dozens injured. Sarath Kumara, 'Train Atrocity in India Targets "Peace Process"', *World Socialist Web Site* (WSWS). February 24, 2007. Accessed at: http://www.wsws.org/articles/2007/feb2007/indi-f24.shtml on November 15, 2014.

32 At the 2004 South Asian Association for Regional Cooperation (SAARC) summit in Islamabad, Pakistan, President Pervaiz Musharraf and the Indian Prime Minister, Atal Behari Vajpayee, had held talks and shook hands on promoting peace between the two

Cinema on Terror 123

nuclear rivals. Ramesh Randeep, 'Musharraf and Vajpayee Pledge Peaceful Links'. *The Guardian*. January 6, 2004. Accessed at: http://www.guardian.co.uk/world/2004/jan/06/pakistan.india on November 15, 2014.

33 Among Ahmed Rashid's various writings on the rise of Islamic fundamentalism, and the Taliban, are *Taliban: Militant Islam, Oil and Fundamentalism in Central Asia*, Yale University Press, New Haven, CT, USA, 2000; *Jihad: the Rise of Militant Islam in Central Asia*, Yale University Press, New Haven, CT, USA, 2002; and *Descent into Chaos: How the War Against Islamic Extremism is Being Lost in Pakistan, Afghanistan and Central Asia*, Allen Lane Press, London and New York, 2008.

34 On May 28, 1998, Pakistan exploded five underground nuclear devices in response to India's nuclear tests two weeks earlier. The Pakistani response triggered worldwide condemnation, and fears of nuclear conflict between the arch-rivals. Pakistani officials disclosed the devices were detonated underground in the Chagai Hills in the Balochistan province. '1998: World Fury at Pakistan's Nuclear Tests', *British Broadcasting Corporation* (BBC). Accessed at: http://news.bbc.co.uk/onthisday/hi/dates/stories/may/28/newsid_2495000/2495045.stm on November 15, 2014.

For further details on Pakistan's nuclear programme see: Andrew Koch, 'Pakistan's Nuclear Test: The Other Shoe Drops in South Asia', Centre for Defense Information, *Weekly Defence Monitor*, May 28, 1998. Accessed at: http://www.bu.edu/globalbeat/nuclear/southasia/koch052898.html on January 12, 2016.

35 On February 6, 2009 the Islamabad High Court (IHC) declared detained nuclear scientist, Dr Abdul Qadeer Khan, a 'free citizen' but kept secret the terms regulating his limited 'freedom' agreed to by the government and the petitioner. The IHC imposed a ban on the publication of the secret agreement. Following his relative freedom, Khan changed his position, claiming that he was forced by General Pervaiz Musharraf into making the televised statement. The military government continued to maintain that Khan had supplied centrifuges, equipment, and other information to Iran, Libya, and even North Korea. 'Nuclear Scientist AQ Khan Declared 'Free Citizen'', February 6, 2009. *Dawn.com* Accessed at: http://www.dawn.com/news/443278/nuclear-scientist-aq-khan-declared-ae~free-citizenae on November 21, 2014.

36 President Musharraf has recounted the assassination attempts on his life in his memoir entitled: Pervez Musharraf, *In the Line of Fire: A Memoir*, Free Press, New York, 2006.

37 Since 1991, Pakistanis from around the world have observed February 5 as a day to express solidarity with the people of Kashmir, and their struggle for independence from India.

38 Citing US non-government analysts, a 2011 report in the *Washington Post* stated Pakistan has doubled its nuclear weapons stockpile over the past several years. As opposed to 30–60 weapons only four years earlier, it had increased its arsenal to 110 deployed weapons, edging ahead of India which has 60–100 weapons. 'Pakistan Nuclear Arsenal Tops 100', *Daily Dawn Online*. January 31, 2011. Accessed at: http://www.dawn.com/news/602834/pakistans-nuclear-arsenal-tops-100 on January 12, 2016.

39 *Pakistan's Double Game*, Sharmeen Obaid-Chinoy (with Claudio Von Planta), 2005 (DV. 24 min.), Channel 4, UK (English/Urdu).

40 The *Lashkar-e-Jhangvi* (LeJ) (Army of *Jhangvi*) is an extremist *Sunni* Muslim, and anti-*Shia*, militant organization affiliated with *Al Qaida* and the Taliban. It was banned by the government of Pakistan in 2001, and the US in 2003 as a Foreign Terrorist Organization under US law. Formed during the mid-1990s, the LeJ, is said to be an offshoot of the Islamic extremist group known as the *Sipah-e-Sahaba* (SSP). The parent group of the LeJ, *Sipah-e-Sahaba*, was co-founded by *Maulana* Haq Nawaz Jhangvi, in whose honour the new organization was named. The LeJ has also been held responsible for the January 2002 kidnapping and killing of US *Wall Street Journal* journalist Daniel Pearl. For further history and details of the LeJ organization, see *South Asian Terrorism Portal*: '*Lashkar-e-Jhangvi*'. Accessed at: http://www.satp.org/satporgtp/countries/pakistan/terroristoutfits/LeJ.htm on November 21, 2014.

41 *Sunni* extremists consider *Shias* as 'non-Muslim', hence 'infidels'.
42 *Pashtunwali* (also referred to as *Pakhtunwali*) is the tribal code of honour and revenge among the *Pashtuns*. Serving as much as a tribal law as a code of honour, it includes norms governing revenge (*badal*), hospitality (*melmastia*), and sanctuary (*nanawati*). Rizwan Hussain, 'The Pakistan–Afghanistan Relationship in a Historical Perspective', *Pakistan and the Emergence of Islamic Militancy in Afghanistan*, Ashgate Publishing Limited, Hampshire, UK, 2005, p. 34.
43 There have been grave concerns in the US administration regarding the mismanagement of $11 billion of US aid given to the Musharraf regime since 9/11 for its role and alliance in the 'War on Terror'. It is alleged that 'Pakistan has used the money to purchase helicopters, F-16s, aircraft-mounted armaments, and anti-ship and antimissile defense systems – weapons that Indian officials and others have deemed of questionable relevance to the counter-terrorism mission. A June 2008 report from the U.S. Government Accountability Office found widespread accounting irregularities with Pentagon spending.' For further details see Greg Bruno and Jayshree Bajoria, 'US–Pakistan Military Cooperation', *Council on Foreign Relations* (CFR), June 26, 2008. Accessed at: http://www.cfr.org/publication/16644/uspakistan_military_cooperation.html on November 25, 2014.
44 *Cold Comfort*, Sharmeen Obaid-Chinoy (with Michael Fuller), 2006 (DVD 21 min.), PBS (Urdu/English/English sub-titles).
45 *Jamaat-ud-Dawa* (JuD) is a Pakistani *Wahhabi* militant organization, founded in 1985. Initially called *Markaz Daw'a wal Irshad*, it changed its name after the US declared *Lashkar-e-Tayyaba* (LeT) a terrorist organization, and a ban imposed by the Pakistani government. Known as a front for the LeT, the JuD publicly rejects this association. In April 2006, the US State Department announced the inclusion of JuD to the Specially Designated Global Terrorist Designation (SDGT). *New Delhi Television* (NDTV). Accessed at: http://www.ndtv.com/convergence/ndtv/mumbaiterrorstrike/Story.aspx?ID=NEWEN20080076123&type=News on November 25, 2014.

LeT is a Pakistan-based *Sunni* extremist organization that was formed in 1989 as the military wing of the Islamic fundamentalist movement, *Markaz al-Daw'a wal Irshad* (MDI) (Centre for Religious Learning and Propagation, also known as the *Jamaat-ud-Dawa*). The LeT adheres to an extreme *Salafist* interpretation of Islam, a *Wahhabi* version followed by *Al Qaida* and the Taliban.

Originally, the LeT was formed to wage *jihad* against the Soviet occupation of Afghanistan. After the withdrawal of the Soviet troops, in the 1990s the LeT concentrated on the insurgency in Indian-Administered Kashmir (IAK). The banned LeT continues to operate in Pakistan under the alias *Jamaat ud-Dawa* 'Commonwealth Numbered Regulations-Explanatory Statements', *Australasian Legal Information Institute*. Accessed at: http://www.austlii.edu.au/au/legis/cth/num_reg_es/ccar200915n214o2009414.html on November 25, 2014.
46 In an interview Obaid-Chinoy recounted her experience of the religious indoctrination that was taking place in the refugee camps. During her visit, she lived in a tent by the roadside, and got the chance to experience first hand religious sermons that started daily with the morning prayers at 5.00 a.m.: 'Every morning for about 20 minutes there would be a sermon by the local cleric talking about how the people in this earthquake zone were suffering because they had not been in touch with God and because they were not following Islam properly', Jackie Bennion, 'Rough Cut: *Pakistan: Cold Comfort*. Interview With Sharmeen Obaid-Chinoy', *Public Broadcasting Service* (PBS). Accessed at: http://www.pbs.org/frontlineworld/rough/2006/02/pakistan_cold_cint.html on November 25, 2014.
47 *Pakistan's Taliban Generation* (also entitled *Pakistan: Children of the Taliban*), Sharmeen Obaid-Chinoy (with Dan Edge), 2009 (DVD 47 min.), October Films for Channel 4 UK (Urdu/Pushto/English/English sub-titles).

The film won the 2009 Association for International Broadcasting (AIB) Award for Media Excellence in the Best Current Affairs Documentary category. Accessed at: http://sharmeenobaidfilms.com/awards/ on November 27, 2014.

Pakistan's Taliban Generation, which has been aired on Channel 4/PBS/CBC/Arte/SBS, was also awarded the 2010 Alfred duPont-Columbia Award in New York, USA. For Sharmeen Obaid-Chinoy's list of awards see: http://sharmeenobaidfilms.com/awards/. Accessed on January 12, 2016.

On September 27, 2010, *Pakistan's Taliban Generation* won Sharmeen Obaid-Chinoy and Dan Edge the International Emmy in the Current Affairs category at the Lincoln Center in New York, USA. *Dawn Online*. '"Pakistan's Taliban Generation" wins Emmy.' September 28, 2010. Accessed at: http://www.dawn.com/news/922409/pakistans-taliban-generation-wins-emmy on January 12, 2016.

48 Since the 9/11/2001 terrorists attacks on the USA particularly, it has become a common practice for Muslim extremist and fundamentalist forces to train young children along the lines of their *jihadist* ideologies in religious seminaries in Pakistan and Afghanistan. For example, an Associated Press (AP) story in April 2007 reports the circulation of a video of a 12-year-old Pakistani Muslim boy beheading another Muslim man accused of being an American spy in the name of *jihad*. Abdul Sattar, 'Jihadist Video Shows Boy Beheading Man', The Associated Press, *The Washington Post*, April 21, 2007. Accessed at: http://www.washingtonpost.com/wp-dyn/content/article/2007/04/20/AR2007042001160.html on January 12, 2016.

49 High profile terrorist attacks within Pakistani cities have included an attack by masked gunmen, armed with grenades and rocket launchers, on the visiting Sri Lankan cricket team in broad daylight in the Punjab provincial capital, Lahore, in March 2009. *BBC News Online*, 'Hunt for Lahore Cricket Attackers'. Accessed at: http://news.bbc.co.uk/2/hi/south_asia/7921430.stm on November 27, 2014.

Other attacks that have included public places, markets, 5-star hotels where foreigners stay, and offices of law enforcements agencies, including those among the country's most important and guarded areas such as the Pakistan Army General Head Quarters (GHQ) in October 2009 in the city of Rawalpindi, are significant indicators of how committed, organized, and powerful radical extremists have become. The attack on the GHQ was claimed by the *Tehreek-e-Taliban* Pakistan (TTP) in response to the Pakistan military's offensive to flush out their hideouts in the tribal areas. *Thaindian News*, 'TTP Group Claims Responsibility for Rawalpindi GHQ Attack'. Accessed at: http://www.thaindian.com/newsportal/south-asia/ttp-group-claims-responsibility-for-rawalpindi-ghq-attack_100258753.html on November 29, 2014.

50 The first tenet of Islam, *Kalma Tayyabah* (The Word of Purity) states: '(There is) none worthy of worship except Allah. Mohammad is Messenger of Allah'. Accessed at: http://www.khwajagharibnawaz.net/Kalma.htm November 29, 2014.

51 Following their infiltration into the Swat Valley in late 2008, less than 100 kilometres from the capital, Islamabad, the Taliban declared the establishment of Islamic rule through rigid *Sharia* laws. These included public amputations, floggings, and stoning, besides forcing religious minority groups such as the Sikhs living in the Orakzai Agency to either leave the region, or pay the Islamic poll-tax, *jizya*, if they wished to stay. In mid-May 2009, the Pakistan military launched an operation to expel the Taliban from Swat, with the long-term aim of completely wiping them out. Within weeks, the military operation succeeded in driving out the Taliban from the main towns of the Swat Valley. On 5 August 2009, the Taliban commander, Baitullah Mehsud, was killed in a US drone attack as a result of Pak-US intelligence-sharing. For further details see: Ishtiaq Ahmed, 'Talibanisation of Pakistan: Threat Abated!', *South Asia*, 14, October 2009, South Asian Studies Publication, National University of Singapore (NUS).

52 It may be mentioned here that in Afghanistan the Taliban had gone as far as throwing acid on the faces of young schoolgirls to deter them from attending school. *BBC*

126 *Cinema on Terror*

Online News, 'Acid Attack on Afghan Schoolgirls', November 12, 2008. Accessed at: http://news.bbc.co.uk/2/hi/south_asia/7724505.stm on November 29, 2014.

53 For example, in April 2009 a reportedly secretly filmed two-minute cell phone video clip released on the Internet showed the public flogging of a woman by the Taliban in Swat. The veiled woman, face down on the ground, screamed as two men held her arms and feet and a third man whipped her repeatedly. The clip created a public outrage, both within the Pakistani civil society, and internationally. YouTube: *Swat Girl Punished by Taliban* (2009). YouTube clip accessed at: https://www.youtube.com/watch?v=H2i0YkZ74_c on January 12, 2016.

President Asif Ali Zardari signed the *Nizam-e-Adl* (System of Justice) Ordinance in 2009. The Ordinance followed the peace deal signed by the government of NWFP with the Taliban to end hostilities in the area between Pakistan and the *Tehreek-e-Taliban* Pakistan (TTP) which had been ongoing since the summer of 2007. *Human Rights Watch*, 'Pakistan: Swat Deal Grave Threat to Rights'. Accessed at: http://www.hrw.org/en/news/2009/04/15/pakistan-swat-deal-grave-threat-rights on November 29, 2014.

For further discussion on the *Nizam-e-Adl* deal, see A. Mukhtar Khan, 'The Return of Shari'a Law to Pakistan's Swat Region', *Terrorism Monitor*, 7. 4, March 3, 2009. Accessed at: http://www.jamestown.org/single/?no_cache=1&tx_ttnews%5Btt_news%5D=34576&tx_ttnews%5BbackPid%5D=7&cHash=081b812552 November 29, 2014.

54 Pamela Constable, 'Pakistan Announces Army Offensive Against Taliban: Move Solidifies Collapse of Peace Accord', *The Washington Post Foreign Service*. Accessed at: http://www.washingtonpost.com/wp-dyn/content/article/2009/05/07/AR2009050703130.html November 30, 2014.

55 The London transport system was hit by a series of coordinated terrorist suicide attacks on July 7, 2005 that killed dozens of people and injured hundreds. *BBC Special Report*, 'London Attacks'. Accessed at: http://news.bbc.co.uk/2/hi/in_depth/uk/2005/london_explosions/default.stm November 30, 2014.

56 The *Tehreek-e-Taliban* Pakistan (TTP) (The Pakistani Taliban Movement) has also been highly active in conducting and claiming responsibility for suicide attacks on Pakistani law enforcement agencies, including army bases, police academies, and intelligence headquarters such as the Inter-Services Intelligence (ISI), and the Military Intelligence (MI) in retaliation for the Pakistan Army's US-backed offensive against their hideouts in the northern and tribal areas of the country. 'TTP Claims Responsibility', *The Daily Times* Online Edition, November 15, 2009. Accessed at: http://archives.dailytimes.com.pk/main/15-Nov-2009/ttp-claims-responsibility on January 12, 2016.

57 The *Pakistan Institute of Peace Studies* (PIPS), a terrorism monitoring organization, reports that in 2009 alone 12,632 lives were lost in Pakistan to suicide attacks, terrorist bombings, predator drone attacks and military operations against militants – only a few hundred less than the lives lost in Afghanistan. Neha Khator, 'Pakistan: On the Razor's Edge', *The Deccan Herald*, December 30, 2010. Accessed at: http://www.deccanherald.com/content/49033/pakistan-razors-edge.html on November 30, 2014.

58 Hakimullah Mehsud succeeded Baitullah Mehsud as the TTP leader after the former was killed in a US CIA-missile strike in August 2009 in his stronghold of South Waziristan. The Baitullah Mehsud-led TTP has also been suspected of ordering the assassination of Pakistan's former Prime Minister Benazir Bhutto in December 2007. Declan Walsh, 'Air Strike Kills Taliban Leader Baitullah Mehsud', *The Guardian*, August 7, 2009. Accessed at: http://www.guardian.co.uk/world/2009/aug/07/baitullah-mehsud-dead-taliban-pakistan November 30, 2014.

On November 1, 2013, Hakimullah Mehsud was also killed in a US drone attack. 'Hakimullah Mehsud Killed by Drone, Pakistan Taliban Say', *British Broadcasting Corporation*, November 2, 2013. Accessed at: http://www.bbc.com/news/world-asia-24776363 on November 30, 2014.

59 *Qari* is a status awarded to those who have learnt to read and recite the *Quran* with the proper rules of pronunciation and rhythm, known as *Tajwid*. *Tajwid* is believed to be the codification of the sound of the revelation as it was revealed to Prophet Mohammad, and as he subsequently rehearsed it with Angel Gabriel. Thus the sound itself has a divine source and significance, and, according to Muslim tradition, is significant to the meaning. For detailed definitions, and further discussion see Kristina Nelson, '*Tajwid*'. *The Art of Reciting the Qur'an*, The American University in Cairo Press, Cairo, Egypt, 2002, p. 14.

60 There remained grave concerns about displaced Taliban fighters and militants who have begun to move into the main cities of the Punjab province and Karachi to form smaller cells as a result of the Pak–US attacks on their hideouts in the NWFP, and the tribal belt. Griff Witte and Joby Warrick, 'Insurgents Forced Out of Pakistan's Tribal Havens Form Smaller Cells in Heart of Nation', *Washington Post Foreign Service*. Accessed at: http://www.washingtonpost.com/wp-dyn/content/article/2009/12/18/AR2009121804334.html on November 30, 2014.

61 Chuck Kleinhans, 'Forms, Politics, Makers and Contexts: Basic Issues for a Theory of Radical Political Documentary', in Thomas Waugh (ed.), *"Show Us Life": Toward a History and Aesthetics of the Committed Documentary*, The Scarecrow Press, Inc. Metuchen, NJ and London, 1984, p. 320.

62 Asked in an interview how she was able to acquire the trust of the people she filmed, Sharmeen Obaid-Chinoy explained her approach, saying that the only way to gain the confidence of strangers is to spend considerable time with them: 'I camped in Afghanistan, Balakot, and in the Philippines while filming. You have to become part and parcel of their world because there are no re-enactments in documentaries – you have to be there to capture the action at all times'. Ali Asghar, Interview with Sharmeen Obaid-Chinoy, *Herald Monthly Magazine*, Karachi, Pakistan, October, 2008, p. 118.

63 Trinh T. Minh-ha, 'An All-Owning Spectatorship', *When the Moon Waxes Red: Representation, Gender, and Cultural Politics*, Routledge, New York, 1991, p. 81.

64 For example, in 2010 law enforcement officials in New York's Times Square averted another terrorist attack, links to which have been traced back to the TTP in Pakistan. Faisal Shahzad, a naturalized Pakistani-American, arrested as the man behind the failed New York car-bomb incident, admitted to Taliban links in Pakistan. 'Pakistan Taliban Group Claims NY Bomb Attempt', *Dawn Online Newspaper* May 3, 2010. Accessed at: http://www.dawn.com/news/915083/pakistan-taliban-group-claims-ny-bomb-attempt on January 12, 2016.

The unrecognized, and often ignored, psychological toll on Pakistan's own population remains an alarming factor. For example, as religious extremism, suicide bombings, and militancy became a common occurrence, particularly in public places in the conflict-ridden Khyber Pakhtunkhwa Province (formerly the North West Frontier Province), cases of mental health due to anxiety attacks, paranoia, and post-traumatic stress disorder (PTSD) were on the rise. One report points out that as many as ten to fifteen new patients suffering from violence, and related trauma were being admitted daily in hospitals in the city of Peshawar. Out of them, it is estimated that at least ten new patients suffering mentally from violence-related incidents arrived daily at Peshawar's Sarhad Psychiatric Hospital alone. 'Psychologists Issue Health Warning'. *Dawn Online Newspaper*, May 14, 2010. Accessed at: http://www.dawn.com/news/893725/psychologists-issue-health-warning on January 12, 2016.

65 For a history and discussion of the Islamic State of Iraq and Syria (ISIS) movement see Patrick Cockburn, *The Jihadis Return: ISIS and The New Sunni Uprising*, OR Books, New York, 2014.

66 Shamim Shahid, 'Spillover Effect: ISIS Making Inroads into Pakistan, Afghanistan', *The Express Tribune*. September 3, 2014. Accessed at: http://tribune.com.pk/story/757186/spillover-effect-isis-making-inroads-into-pakistan-afghanistan/ on December 2, 2014.

67 *The Nation*, 'ISIS Performs Wall Chalking in Karachi'. October 16, 2014. Accessed at: http://nation.com.pk/national/16-Oct-2014/isis-performs-wall-chalking-in-karachi?utm_source=feedburner&utm_medium=feed&utm_campaign=Feed%3A+pakistan-news-newspaper-daily-english-online%2FBreaking+(The+Nation+%3A+Breaking+News)on December 2, 2014.
68 Fatima Mernissi, 'The Meaning of Spatial Boundaries', in Reina Lewis and Sara Mills (eds), *Feminist Postcolonial Theory: A Reader*, Routledge, New York, 2003, p. 489.
69 Fernando Solanas and Octavio Getino, *Towards a Third Cinema'* (1969), in Bill Nichols (ed.), *Movies and Methods*, University of California Press, Berkley, CA, USA, 1994, pp. 55–6.
70 Glauber Rocha, 'The Aesthetics of Hunger' (1965), in Michael Chanan (ed.), *Twenty-Five Years of the New Latin American Cinema*, BFI Books, UK, 1983, p. 13.
71 *Canadian Broadcasting Corporation* (CBC), 'Bin Laden Death Ends 10-Year Manhunt', May 1, 2011. Accessed at: http://www.cbc.ca/news/world/story/2011/05/01/us-obama.html on December 2, 2014.

4 Victims of a vicious system
Women, violence, and human rights

Introduction

While there is tremendous diversity among Muslim women from various regions, there is also a common thread as they share gender-based and patriarchy-driven oppressions and violence across cultures. As Iranian human rights activist and scholar Mahnaz Afkhami points out, over half a billion Muslim women live in vastly different socio-cultural and socio-political environments, and yet, their oppressions are similar due to their gender-specific abuse and marginalization meted out in the name of culture:

> The infringement of women's rights is usually exercised in the name of tradition, religion, social cohesion, morality, or some complex of transcendent values. Always, it is justified in the name of culture. Nowhere is this better demonstrated than in the Muslim societies, where over half a billion women live in vastly different lands, climates, cultures, societies, economies, and politics.[1]

This cross-cultural predicament of Muslim women is exemplified by the prevalence of extreme forms of gender-specific violence found across Muslim societies such as a recourse to, and brazen justification of, crimes such as honour-killing, honour-rape, forced marriages, acid-attacks, and burning of women to resolve disputes, settle scores, and avenge and redeem so-called 'honour'.

As General Zia-ul-Haq's Islamization process supported state-sponsored gender-discrimination in Pakistan through its fundamentalist approach to religion and legal transformations, the subsequent periods of democracy also saw a surge in violence against women, encouraged by what Pakistani journalist Abbas Jalbani attributes to the culture of 'brutalization', a culture initiated by the Zia-ul-Haq regime that included public executions and lashings, and a system of summary punishments for alleged moral deviations.[2]

Today, human rights violations and gender-specific violence against women continue to be widespread in Pakistan. Despite the fact that Article 25 of the 1973 Constitution of Pakistan, which deals with the fundamental rights of Pakistani citizens, states clearly that nothing 'shall prevent the State from making any special provision for the protection of women ...'[3] and Pakistan's ratification of the CEDAW convention (the UN Convention on the Elimination of all Forms of Discrimination Against Women) in 1996,[4] violence and discrimination against women is commonplace.[5] It is believed that the majority of the incidents go unreported altogether due to a lack of faith in the police and justice system, or because of socio-cultural restraints, such as in the case of reporting marital/domestic violence and rape to law-enforcement agencies.[6]

In the tribal areas of Pakistan, patriarchal tribal customs, traditions, and honour codes continue to dictate an oppressive parallel legal system, known as the *jirga* and *panchayat* (tribal juries and councils), headed by tribal chiefs and supported by feudal landlords. Under the guise of custom and tradition, these tribal councils have been at the forefront of supporting and carrying out horrific human-rights violations and gender-specific punishments such as *karo kari* (honour-killings), *Swara* (giving away of minor girls in forced marriages as compensation to settle disputes or avenge murders), and honour-rape to settle scores.[7] According to data released by Pakistan's Interior Ministry, since 2009 over 11,789 cases of violence against women have been registered, while the numbers grow.[8] But despite the establishment of women's police stations, countless cases also go unreported due to lack of faith in the country's law enforcement machinery, and fear of police corruption.[9]

It is important to note that various non-governmental organizations, legal-aid cells, lawyers, activists and women's rights groups in Pakistan have continued to focus on issues of various forms of violence against women, and have brought to bear pressure on successive governments and policy makers to amend or promulgate laws that would specifically address these rights issues.[10]

This chapter will extend the 'Cinema of Accountability' category to focus on representative documentary films, filmmakers, and organizations that address particular gender-specific issues affecting Pakistani women from their standpoint.[11] It will examine the violation of human rights and personal security as a result of various forms of violence, physical abuse, exploitation, marginalization, and denial of women's equal rights through a contextual reading of a selection of documentaries.[12]

Numerous Pakistani activist organizations and independent filmmakers have drawn attention to the widespread forms of violence and discrimination detailed in this chapter, with a particular focus on 'honour' and revenge through extreme acts of violence such as 'stove-burning', 'acid-attacks', '*karo kari*' (honour-killing), 'honour-rape', and *Swara*. It is pertinent to evaluate the activist intent and contribution of the following films in raising awareness, and seeking accountability for the inhumane treatment meted out to women, and the failure of the state, laws, and the law-enforcement machinery to provide them with security and justice. To facilitate the contextual reading of the honour-related issues depicted in these films, the section entitled 'Perspectives on Notions of 'Honour' and 'Shame'' in this chapter will give an introductory socio-cultural background to tribal notions of 'honour', the patriarchal parallel tribal justice system in Pakistan, and the role these play in the violent victimization of women in particular on the pretext of 'tradition', and delivering 'justice'.

Stove Burning: Neither Coal Nor Ashes (*Na koella bhye na raakh*) (*Simorgh* Productions 1993)

Made by the *Simorgh* Women's Resource and Publication Centre and Collectives' *Simorgh* Productions, *Stove Burning: Neither Coal Nor Ashes* (1993) focuses on the issue of gendered domestic violence against women whereby wives are burnt by husbands or in-laws and the incident is made to look like an accident as a result of a kerosene oil or gas cooking-stove explosion.[13] Supported by testimonies, interviews, and off-screen commentary, *Stove Burning* stands as a significant critical documentary that investigates and contextualizes the sociocultural aspects involved in the issue of burning women by simulated stove-bursts in Pakistan. Produced in 1993, in the early stages of Pakistani activist documentary cinema, the film demonstrates that over the intervening years, incidents of violence against women have been on the rise throughout Pakistan, and continue to be the result of greed, demand for dowry or money by in-laws, desire of the husband to re-marry, salvaging so-called honour or ego, domestic rifts, or the desire to get rid of a woman who may be a wife, daughter-in-law, sister-in-law,

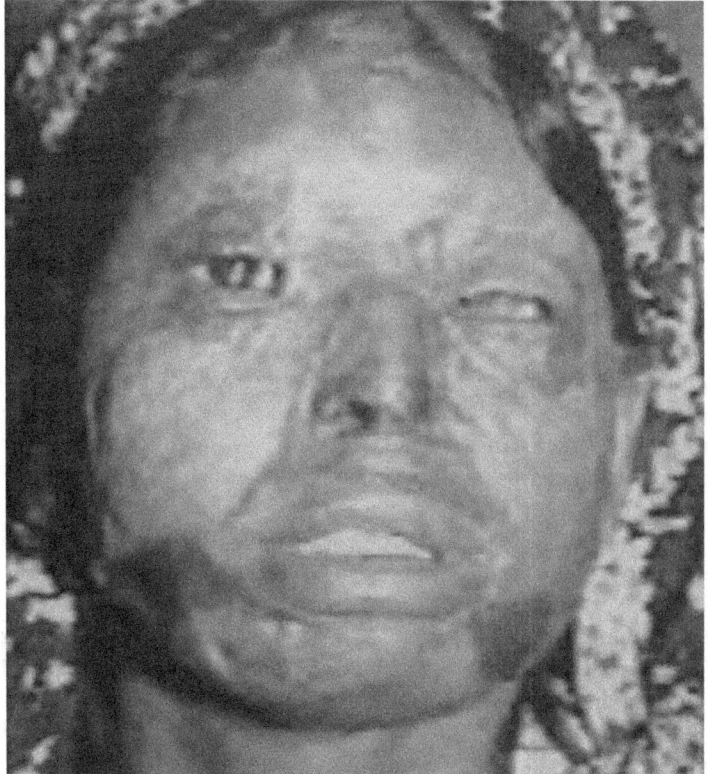

Figure 4.1 Image of burn victim from *Stove Burning: Neither Coal Nor Ashes*.
Source: *Simorgh* Productions.

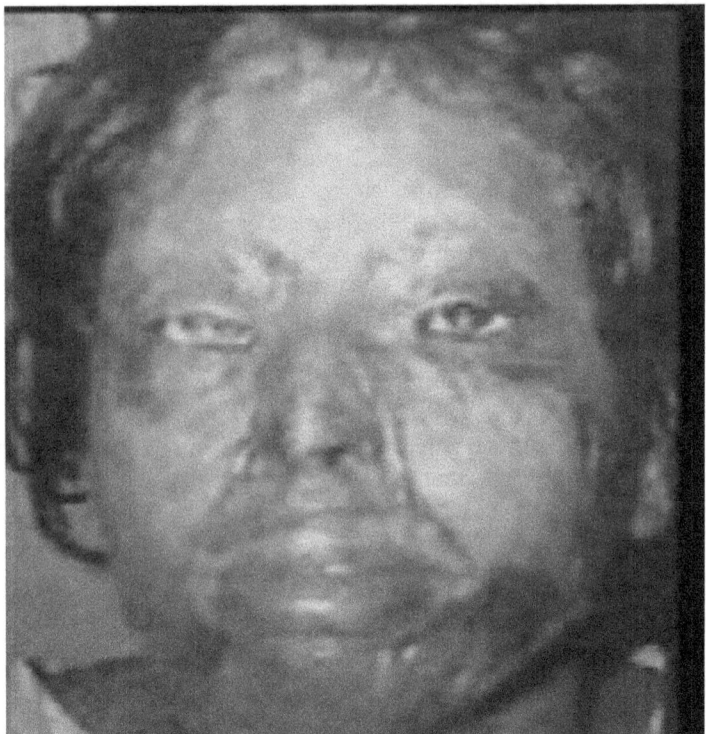

Figure 4.2 Image of burn victim from *Stove Burning: Neither Coal Nor Ashes*.
Source: *Simorgh* Productions.

and even daughter. The usual pattern of these crimes involves women being attacked by their husbands and in-laws who pour oil on them in the kitchen and set them on fire due to domestic quarrels, and then, if the women survive, blackmail them to take the blame for the 'accident' or else risk losing the custody of their children. Besides this method, a leaking gas-stove is also used to start a simulated explosion and fire by unsuspecting women who light them.[14]

With a focus on the Punjab province, *Stove Burning* opens with disturbing images of defaced and disfigured women who have been burn victims as the voice-over informs us that each year up to 1200 such burn cases by kerosene oil stove-bursts are reported in the Punjab provincial capital of Lahore alone, and on average five cases are brought to hospitals on a daily basis. Whether the reasons for burn-related deaths of these victims are accidental, suicide, or murder, the sheer figures of the widespread practice in Pakistan are devastating. Hospital staff interviewed in the film reveals that most women patients who are admitted say that the stove burst accidentally while they were cooking, although most of the incidents are instigated by domestic violence. We learn that despite the knowledge of rising figures of such violence, the Punjab province, with a population of

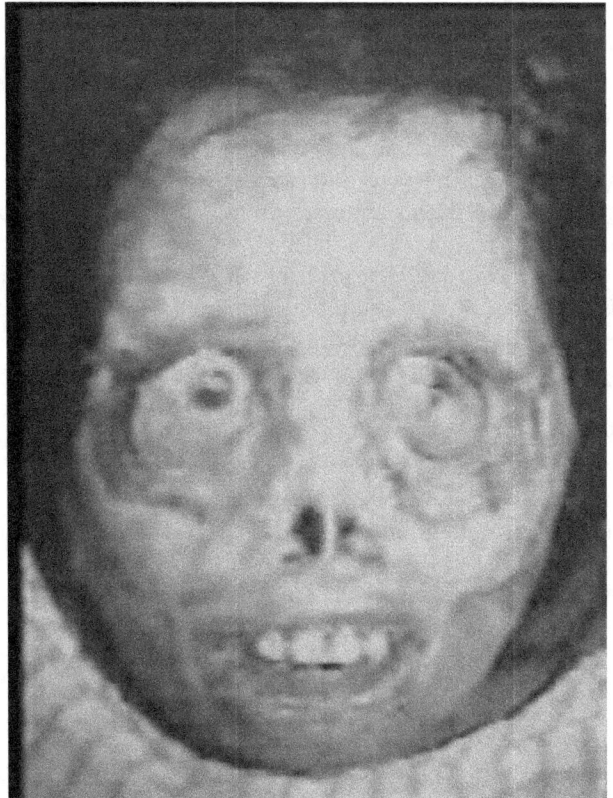

Figure 4.3 Image of burn victim from *Stove Burning: Neither Coal Nor Ashes*.
Source: *Simorgh* Productions.

70 million at the time, and growing, has only one burn unit located at the government Mayo Hospital in Lahore, and that too with inadequate facilities.

Figures for 2015 remain disappointing as only four burn units are reported to be fully functional in the Punjab province.[15]

Interviews with doctors at the Mayo Hospital reveal a horrific picture of gender violence and criminal levels of victimization. Stressing the need for public awareness about the dangers and risks of using faulty oil and gas stoves, and the danger of wearing synthetic clothing near them that easily catch fire, Dr Zafar Aziz argues in the film that if the burns in such cases are accidental only the front part of the body and face is likely to be burnt, not the back or the entire frame as happens in pre-meditated incidents. He points to the need for checks on the manufacturers of these cooking units to ensure safety standards. On the other hand, Dr Abdul Babar contends that with adequate facilities even 60 per cent burn victims can also be saved leading to an 80 per cent survival rate, but with inadequate facilities the mortality rate in such cases stands at 95 per cent.

Speaking out on the dearth of medical facilities to deal with burn cases, he points out that as opposed to the mushrooming of costly, private, specialized cardiac centres catering to the rich elite, these stove-burning incidents occur among the poor sections of society, and the setting up of burn units holds little or no importance even for the government as the singular burn unit at the Mayo Hospital exemplifies.[16] Dr Babar reveals that contrary to what might appear in the press, most stove-burn incidents are cases of 'homicide' carried out by husbands and in-laws and made to look like 'accidents', a view that is seconded by various nurses and other hospital staff who explain that it is easy to recognize homicide cases because the whole body is burnt, including the back, and not just the front as would be the likely case in an 'accident'.

As voice-over highlights the judgment passed by the Lahore High Court in 1991 regarding the mandatory 24-step safety testing of oil and gas stoves, and accountability of manufacturers, we are told that despite this court directive substandard stoves continue to be sold in the market due to a serious lack of stringent law enforcement mechanisms to check their manufacturing.

Hina Jillani, an advocate of the Supreme Court of Pakistan, interviewed in the film highlights the social, cultural, and legal limitations and pressures that women burn victims face in speaking out. Jillani points out that in many cases such victims cannot give testimony or details of the incident because they die. Other victims, who by the time they make it to the hospital, have no idea whether they will even survive, and if they do, they fear to speak the truth because to begin with they have no witnesses to prove their case since such incidents normally take place at the in-laws' or the husband's' house, nor do they have any idea what their future will be. As well, these women are pressured by their in-laws not to turn them in or else they will lose custody of their children. Given the rising rate of stove-blast incidents, Jillani emphasizes that legislation be passed in which it should be made mandatory for the police to investigate these cases along specific procedures, and ensure that no lacunae are left for perpetrators to get away. She points out that the more such cases make it to court, they will serve as a deterrent and basis for accountability.

In voice-over we learn that in 1991 on the directions of presiding Justice Munir A. Sheikh, the Lahore High Court legislated that investigating officers in stove-blast cases should not be below the rank of Deputy Superintendent Police (DSP). These DSPs were directed to take the stoves into custody, and record the testimony of the dead woman's parents, and, in the case of a married woman, also take testimony from her in-laws. The directive also stated that the faulty stove-maker would be required to take responsibility under the Pakistan Penal Code (PPC). Additionally, in such cases it would be the duty of the hospital superintendent to immediately record the statement of the doctor on duty. Although such directives at the state level seem promising, we learn in voice-over that only two victims of stove-burn cases could be traced, Sakina and Martha Parveen, for fear of being killed by in-laws/husbands, or losing their children if they spoke out publicly. Of these two women, we learn that contact could only be established with the latter. By documenting such a situation, *Stove Burning* exposes the lack of faith in Pakistan's law-enforcement machinery by the victims, and the fears and insecurity these women continue to live with.

Adding a testimonial value to the bleakness of *Stove Burning*, Martha, a burn case victim from 1986 who still carries visible burn scars and facial disfigurement, narrates how she was beaten by her in-laws while cooking in the kitchen, and while being threatened and abused she had kerosene oil poured over her and was set alight. She recalls that as she screamed and tried to run out, her in-laws closed all the doors, while only her brother-in-law came to her rescue. After she got burnt, her in-laws informed her parents of the incident as an 'accident'. Her mother-in-law told Martha to treat the whole incident as an 'accident', and threatened her that if she spoke out against her husband, they would retaliate against her maternal family. Martha shares her consequent fears and details of her severe and lasting injuries following the incident. Recalling her treatment as that of a 'slave' at her in-laws' house, Martha points to the socio-cultural pressure and aspects of women's subordination and suppression in the Pakistani society: 'When parents marry off their daughters, they tell her that now only her corpse can return to her parental home.' Having initially told her parents that she had been burnt accidentally while putting oil in the stove, Martha encourages all burn victims to come forward and speak out against their perpetrators. However, Martha's remains a lone voice in the film as *Stove Burning* shows images of more burnt women howling in pain on hospital beds, and the reality of their helplessness and despair. The film makes a critical point by showing the fact that only one survivor from the hundreds of women victimized each year in Punjab could be found to speak out publicly. Clearly, the victims of these vicious and violent acts are paralysed by fear, a fact exacerbated by government indifference to women's security and rights.

The film provides insights from the Mayo Hospital staff in terms of the contradictory statements of female burn victims and their families. In particular, comments focus on, and detail, how police are bribed by perpetrators to produce contradictory evidence that helps culprits get away with even murder. We learn that the filmmakers were unsuccessful in their attempts to have police officials speak on camera.

Doctors, hospital staff, and a victim in the film try to explain the complex social factors, lack of justice, and the plight of women in Pakistani society as the main cause of such heinous domestic violence. Lawyer Jillani points to the fact that although many cases are reported, very few make it to court because of a variety of socio-cultural factors as well as the failure of the police to conduct an unbiased enquiry. Giving a broad overview of the situation, Jillani states that a woman's death is not a 'big deal' in Pakistani society because her economic dependence renders her 'dispensable, and replaceable'.

Stove Burning ends with a list of women's names scrolling down the screen who were subjected to stove-burns from January to July in 1993 (the year the documentary was filmed) and admitted to one hospital in Lahore alone. Their average age is listed as 23 years, including those as young as 10, 11, 13, and 14 years of age. In conclusion, the lamenting ironic Punjabi couplet that is recited off-screen evokes the human cost of the barbaric intent and result of 'burning' women alive as a convenient and 'cost-effective' method of eliminating them: 'Burnt wood becomes coal, coal becomes ash/ Though I am burnt, I become neither coal nor ash.'

In exposing and drawing attention to the criminal intent of perpetrators of stove-blast incidents, compounded only by the apathy of the Pakistani state and police corruption, *Stove Burning: Neither Coal Nor Ashes* remains a significant activist filmic documentation of the realities of women's victimization through horrific cases of domestic abuse and violence. As well, the film stands as a documentary testimony to the 'legislative and deliberative'[17] aspects of a 'Cinema of Accountability' taking shape regarding violence against women in Pakistan.

Burnt Victims: Scars on the Society (AGHS Legal Aid Cell 2002)

While stove-burning remains a catastrophic form of violence against an increasing number of women in Pakistan, another means of violence and revenge that has been rapidly on the rise is throwing acid on women's faces and bodies. *Burnt Victims: Scars on the Society*, made by the AGHS Legal Aid Cell as a consciousness-raising and educational film for the purpose of training its staff to deal with cases of violence against women, also stresses the alarming situation of violence against women in the form of stove-burning and acid-attacks.[18] Whereas this expository film, narrated mostly through voice-over, stresses much of the same socio-cultural factors and implications for women regarding stove-burning as in the previous film (*Stove Burning: Neither Coal Nor Ashes*, 1993), it additionally addresses the practice of 'acid-burning' or 'acid throwing' as the practice has come to be known – the act of throwing acid on a woman's face and body to disfigure her as violent revenge for a number of reasons or perceived transgressions including insufficient dowry, infertility or inability to produce a son, bringing 'dishonour' to the family, suspicion of illicit romantic or sexual relations, rejected marriage proposals, or simply a husband's desire for a second marriage.[19]

The film begins with off-screen commentary on the lack of essential facilities such as air-conditioning even at the Mayo Hospital Burn Unit, the only one in Punjab. It is pointed out that in January 2002 alone the hospital received 40 burn victims of which 37 per cent were young women. The film is interspersed with disturbing images of charred bodies of women, and testimonies of badly disfigured and traumatized female burn victims, suffering extreme pain in meagre hospital facilities, who recall their experiences of being burnt by stove-blasts or having acid poured over them by family members.[20] Whereas stove-bursts are normally blamed on faulty stoves, the film points out that acid-burns are never an accident. Once again, the overwhelming majority in such cases are women. Off-screen commentary informs viewers that according to data an acid-burn victim is brought to the Mayo Hospital every week, while four out of the six victims being treated in the third week of July 2002 alone were acid-burn victims. Dr. Intesar-ur-Rashid, a surgeon at the Mayo Hospital, points out that those with 40 per cent or less burns have a good chance of survival if treated. However, because of the high cost of the treatment, 20 per cent of the patients leave the hospital despite doctor's orders to stay. Given the economic reasons, he points out that 50 per cent of those who leave early succumb to their wounds.

On the one hand, the film highlights the April 1991 directives of the Lahore High Court that specifically addressed the issue of burn-accidents and state assistance to victims such as expenses to be paid by the state for the burial of a victim, or free medical care. However, through testimonies of actual victims and their families who refute having received any such assistance, the film draws attention to state apathy in the actual execution and effectiveness of these directives. As well, the lack of actual implementation of the directives also explains why many burn patients who do make it to hospital, either leave dead or without proper treatment due to economic constraints.

Most importantly, *Burnt Victims* addresses and highlights the issue of the unchecked and easy availability of acid to anyone for purchase. Although one acid-seller speaks of the procedure to get approval for a government license to sell acid that includes the inspection of a proposed shop site by a magistrate and the police, footage of rows and rows of huge, unmarked and unnumbered drums of acid lying in unsecured open lots and premises of sellers belies his claims. Off-screen commentary points out that 'there is no procedure to register the sellers of acid, leave alone a listing of buyers, and that whoever wants acid, for whatever purposes can simply go to one of the stores and have their fill.'[21] The film ends with founding member of AGHS Legal Aid Cell, lawyer and human rights activist Asma Jehangir stressing the need for the application of stringent regulations and laws and accountability measures that would serve as protection for women, and deterrents in both the illegal sale and misuse of acid.

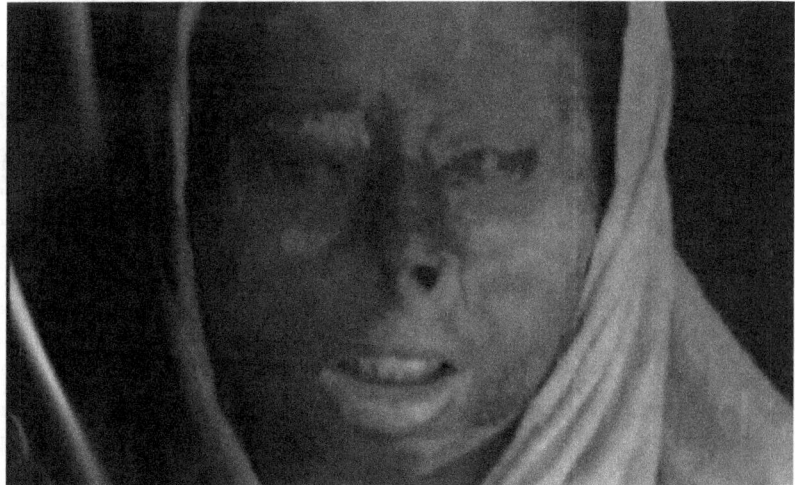

Figure 4.4 Image of burn victim from *Burnt Victims: Scars on the Society*.
Source: Film director Ahmar Rehman.

Although both *Stove Burning: Neither Coal Nor Ashes* (1993) and *Burnt Victims: Scars on the Society* (2002), made almost a decade apart, are most disturbing and difficult films to watch because of the images they depict of victims, they are nevertheless invaluable as documentary testimonies that exhort a legislative and deliberative response to horrific crimes of violence that more often than not go unpunished, even unreported.[22] It may be mentioned here that on continued pressure from women's and rights organizations, both within Pakistan and abroad, a Domestic Violence (Prevention and Protection) Act 2009 had been passed by the National Assembly on August 4, 2009. However, due to the objections raised by the Council of Islamic Ideology (CII), the Senate failed to do the same within three months as required by the Constitution, opting to let the bill lapse.[23] Another bill entitled the 'Acid Control and Burn Crime Prevention Act 2010' drafted by the Acid Survivors Foundation (ASF) of Pakistan, on the directives of the then Chief Justice, Iftikhar Muhammad Chaudhry, was presented to the Ministry of Women Development (MoWD). This detailed bill that covers all aspects of burn related crimes and punishments, and sale, purchase, and manufacture of acid, also awaited approval and passage at the time by the National Assembly.[24]

However, it was once again the private sector and civil organizations that filled in for governmental neglect. Given the rising incidents of extreme domestic violence directed at women, clinical psychologist Shahnaz Bokhari founded the Progressive Women's Association (PWA) in 1990. Since its inception, her organization has been involved with providing shelter, securing medical care, and arranging legal assistance to female victims and survivors of domestic abuse and violence such as acid-attacks and stove-burning, honour related rape, and other physical attacks.[25] Since 1994, the PWA has held various workshops on domestic violence against women at provincial levels, and sought to include participation from government and law enforcement officials, NGOs, and the legal fraternity to foster alliances and channels of legal accountability against these issues. Shahnaz Bokhari and the PWA's has been a most valuable and significant struggle against these most violent and horrific of acts directed at women, considering that despite personal threats and harassment by victim's families, and a corrupt law enforcement system, the PWA has remained resolute in opposing and highlighting governmental and societal biases against protecting women through state legislation.[26] The PWA also runs a shelter for victims by the name of *AASRA* (Support), founded in 1999 as a home for destitute female victims of domestic violence. *AASRA* accommodates 30 residents at a time, and has supported up to 150 women annually since it started in spite of police interference and raids, as victims are hounded and continue to face threats from relatives and the police for escaping their abusers.[27]

There are other organizations as well that focus on the treatment, support, and advocacy for burn victims, such as the Acid Survivor's Foundation of Pakistan (ASF), founded in 2006, with the support of the UK-based Acid Survivors Trust International (ASTI).[28] Similarly, in the face of unabated domestic violence against women, the non-governmental AGHS Legal Aid Cell established a separate violence and burn victims project in 2007, the AGHS Burn Unit and

Monitoring Cell, to document and research case studies of burn victims.²⁹ It was reported that as many as 122 women were burnt in Lahore from April to June in 2009, according to the second three-month monitoring and follow-up by AGHS. Of the 122 women, 21 were attacked by acid and 101 were set on fire. From this alarming number, 82 burnt women survived and 40 died. This figure of burnt women, including those burnt by acid-attacks, had doubled since the first three-month monitoring. According to the AGHS Monitoring Cell, the above statistics pertain to Lahore alone, but it is suspected that the situation is the same countrywide. The Acid Survivors Foundation reports that 114 cases of acid-attacks were reported in 2014, while only eight convictions took place.³⁰

Saving Face (Sharmeen Obaid-Chinoy 2011)

At the 84th Academy Awards ceremony in Los Angeles, USA on February 26, 2012, Sharmeen Obaid-Chinoy also became the first Pakistani documentary filmmaker to win an Oscar for her film entitled *Saving Face* (2011).³¹ Recipient of the coveted award in the Best Documentary (Short Subject) category, Obaid-Chinoy's observational film addresses the widespread practice of acid-attacks on women across Pakistan, including the Seraiki belt in Southern Punjab, a major cotton growing area where industrial acid is readily available as it is used for cleaning cotton.³² Winning the Oscar for the film, Obaid-Chinoy's documentary has brought this form of violence to centre-stage prominence, both globally and within Pakistan. It can very well be argued that the horrific issue of acid-attacks has been key in winning the recognition and acclaim rather than the quality of the film itself.

Although not the first film on the topic of acid-attacks to be made in Pakistan, as this chapter illustrates, the award-winning prominence *Saving Face* has achieved, and its international premiere on the HBO channel, are factors that together have contributed immensely to establishing the utility of documentary cinema as an activist tool for consciousness-raising, resistance, cross-cultural communication, and social change in Pakistan.

Supported by the ASF in Pakistan, *Saving Face* revolves around the stories of two Pakistani women, Rukhsana and Zakia, who have been victims of acid-attacks, and their struggle in the process of rehabilitation, seeking justice, and undergoing reconstructive surgery by a Pakistani London-based plastic surgeon, Dr Mohammad Jawad, who returns to his homeland to treat them.³³

It is to Obaid-Chinoy's credit that she has been able to encourage her two main female subjects to come forward and speak of their experiences on film. We learn that when 39-year-old Zakia attempted to divorce her husband he retaliated by dousing her with acid, while Rukhsana, 25, was burned with acid and set on fire by her husband and his family. However, Rukhsana's ordeal did not end with this attack. She had no choice other than to continue living with her husband as she became pregnant after the acid-attack.

The encouraging note in the film is that for the first time we actually see acid-attack victims not only receiving reconstructive surgery, but also justice as

Figure 4.5 Image of filmmaker Sharmeen Obaid-Chinoy during the filming of *Saving Face*.
Source: Sharmeen Obaid Films.

Zakia's husband is convicted of assault and sentenced to two life sentences under the new Acid Control and Acid Crime Prevention Bill 2010, and The Prevention of Anti-Women Practices (Criminal Law Amendment) Bill 2008, that legislates severe punishment for physically harming women with corrosive substances.[34]

Obaid-Chinoy's film covers most of the same factors and trauma related to acid-attacks on women as the previous two films discussed in this chapter, *Stove Burning: Neither Coal Nor Ashes* (1993) and *Burnt Victims: Scars on the Society* (2002), although her film is rather weak in providing an adequate background to the socio-cultural and socio-economic contexts as the two aforementioned films do. The activist focus in *Saving Face* seems to tilt towards highlighting the courage of the two victims to come forward with their stories, as well as Dr Jawad's willingness and ability to offer reconstructive surgery. However, in the absence of a grounded socio-cultural and socio-economic contextualization as in the earlier films on similar subjects, despite its very difficult and crucial topic, not to mention scenes of the victims physical disfigurement that require tremendous courage to watch, in retrospect as a film *Saving Face* seems to convey a hasty promo-like quality both for the victims' predicament and the good doctor's noble inclination to help them, which may not have been the filmmaker's intent.

However, despite what maybe the film's weaknesses, or the viewer's personal take, the very fact that another film is made on the subject of heinous acts of acid-attacks, and the international acclaim *Saving Face* has garnered because of its topic, has renewed the urgent need for accountability through the new laws and the prosecution of offenders.

It is particularly encouraging that given the enthusiasm with which Obaid-Chinoy's achievement has been received within Pakistan, there are plans afoot to dub *Saving Face* in regional languages for screening as an educational tool on local TV channels, as well as in educational institutions, and other venues in villages and towns across Pakistan for consciousness-raising, and encouraging social activism against acid-attacks.[35] Obaid-Chinoy has also used the success of her film as a platform to launch an Anti-Acid Campaign (Project SAAVE) that would reach out to victims across the country and help them come forward to seek justice.[36] It is also a welcome prospect that for the first time the government of Pakistan decided to confer the second most prestigious civilian award, the *Hilal-e-Imtiaz* (Crescent of Excellence) on a documentary filmmaker. In recognition of her work, the president of Pakistan, Asif Ali Zardari, awarded Sharmeen Obaid-Chinoy the *Hilal-e-Imtiaz* on Pakistan Day in 2012.[37]

It can be argued that whereas *Saving Face* may lack in contextualizing the issue of acid-attacks in any great depth, it has proven the successful ability and utility of documentary film to project crucial issues in reaching out to wide cross-cultural audiences to foster solidarity and garner support against gender violence.

Perspectives on notions of 'honour' and 'shame'

In order to understand how tribal and cultural notions of 'honour' and 'shame' play out in Pakistani society, it is pertinent to contextualize their significance and symbolism in tribal and feudal societies. The following discussion will facilitate in the reading and understanding of the honour-related violence, crimes, and discrimination against women as represented in the following films.[38]

The notion of 'honour' in tribal societies has very specific meaning and implications, and is closely tied to the notion of 'shame' that may be endured by a family, tribe, or community due to a person's behaviour or acts. Primarily, both shame and honour are associated with the conduct of women that may or may not be deemed honourable, thus becoming a source of honour or shame for the entire tribe. The higher the status of the tribe, the greater its stakes in preserving its honour and the powers of its members sitting in a *jirga* or *panchayat* (tribal juries or councils).[39] Treatment of women as objects that can be traded or victimized to avenge shame or regain honour also translates into the tribal patterns and means of retaining honour. Although honour-killings have come to be associated with Islamic societies as an Arab-Islamic practice, these murders have been occurring in all regions of the world, including the West.[40] While motives behind extreme acts of violence against women such as stove-burning and acid-attacks are instigated by hatred, revenge and greed, honour–related crimes such as honour-killing and honour-rape are supported by a moralistic stance. These acts are justified and carried out on the pretext of the patriarchal perception of protecting family and tribal honour, and the victimization of women whose bodies are seen to be the repository of this honour.[41]

However, although honour-killings in Pakistan are largely associated with tribal and feudal areas where 'honour' is a driving force in relationships and social standing, these killings occur across the country. As opposed to victims of stove-burning and acid-attacks who are seen as blameless and innocent, women victimized by honour-killing are seen to have brought on the violence upon themselves due to their own allegedly inappropriate 'dishonourable' conduct and deeds such as an alleged affair, extra-marital sexual relations, elopement or a marriage of choice against family consent, or desire for divorce, and even employment, hence incurring the justification for their killing and death.[42] In all cases, this 'dishonourable' conduct is judged either as a woman's actual or perceived involvement with a man who is not her husband or is not acceptable to her family as her husband, or defiance of tribal codes of behaviour and subservience, thereby giving all male members of a woman's immediate, extended, and marital family in a tribal and feudal setup the justification to take her life to redeem family and tribal honour.[43] In many cases, even a mere rumour about a woman's infidelity or extra-marital sexual conduct or relations is enough to serve as the basis for honour-related crimes.

Additionally, whereas stove-burning and acid-attacks are usually not carried out by a woman's own family but rather husbands, in-laws, and rejected lovers or suitors, honour–killings are carried out by her own male relatives such as father, brothers, and cousins to redeem and uphold family and tribal honour. The fact that a woman's own family members carry out such killings further legitimizes the act as her relatives are seen to have an integral bond with her that can only be severed due to extreme circumstances. Although the concept of such killings predates Islam, and is neither sanctioned by religion nor restricted to Islamic or tribal societies or rural and uneducated regions and segments of society, these acts are commonly justified in the name of religion because they are seen to enforce morality and uphold patriarchal family power structures.[44]

Because of deeply ingrained notions of males as the guardians of a woman's chastity and moral conduct, honour-killings occur in all the provinces of Pakistan and are accepted as an act of redemption that is also sanctioned by tribal councils and tribal chiefs in tribal areas. For example, known as '*karo kari*' in the tribal belts of the Sindh province, tribal custom prescribes death for both a '*kari*' woman (blackened woman) who is suspected of immoral activity and illicit sexual relations, and her male partner '*karo*' (blackened man).[45] Blackness in this case symbolizes shamefulness and immorality, particularly regarding the extra-marital sexual conduct of women.[46] As well, there are many instances where even fake honour-killings have taken place to serve vested interests. Amnesty International notes that 'reports abound about men who have killed other men in murders not connected with honour issues who then kill a woman of their own family as an alleged *kari* to camouflage the initial murder as an honour killing.'[47]

Pakistan also has a long tradition of the *jirga* (Pashtun word for the tribal justice-system based on a gathering of all-male community representatives for decision-making) and *panchayat* system (village councils in South Asia that have the power to call a *jirga* (jury)) in which crimes or affronts to dignity and perceived 'honour' are punished outside the framework of Pakistani law. It is pertinent to mention here that despite their status and importance in the tribal setup, these tribal councils have no official legal standing in Pakistan, and yet the government authorities have failed to take adequate measures to contain this parallel legal system and prevent such bodies from taking the law into their own hands, and hand down judgments. The *panchayat* comprises elders from the higher tribe and caste in a tribal community, and has the power to call a *jirga* (jury), which again comprises other male members from the higher tribe and caste as well. The tribal council is approached by members of the lower tribes/castes to give judgment in their feuds, and resolve conflicts and problems. The tribal council meets in public and the final judgments are passed down by all members collectively, and are treated as final. Although this system is used to settle all kinds of scores, from murder cases to property disputes to minor disagreements between members of different or the same tribes and castes, its most horrific effects are felt by women because in any case they are subservient to the patriarchal order and codes of conduct in a tribal setup. Any judgment passed by these tribal councils and juries becomes an uncontestable order in the tribal society.[48]

Given the above situation, Pakistani state legislation such as the *Diyat* law (compensation by blood-money), as well as the *jirga* and *panchayat* system operating in Pakistan, empowers tribal society in such a manner that women's status and security remain subservient to the male order of morality and social values, and permeates all classes in these communities regardless of economic or tribal status.

It is in the backdrop of this mentality that men, mostly in Pakistan's tribal setup, see the subjugation of women not only as lesser beings in terms of gender, but more importantly as a means of preserving their own status within their communities. As a means to this end, raping, killing, trading, and humiliating a rival's women is also considered a legitimate means of vengeance and preserving one's own and the tribe's honour. The contextual reading of the following representative documentary films illustrates how notions of 'shame' and 'honour' are used as pretexts for committing violence and crimes against women with impunity.

Shame: A Tale of Karo Kari (*Dastak* Society for Communication 2005)

Shame: A Tale of Karo Kari (2005) focuses on the custom of *karo kari* (honour-killing) as it is practiced and justified in the feudal and tribal society in the rural areas of the Sindh province and southern Punjab where the practice is most rampant in Pakistan.[49] Accompanied by off-screen commentary, interviews with government officials, lawyers, journalists, human rights activists, clerics, and rural men who actually condone the custom as a just means of regaining family honour by killing women suspected of illicit relations with men, the filmmakers, Sharjil Baloch and Dr Iftikhar Ahmed, provide insight into the practice and motives that instigate it. Views, perspectives, analyses, and stories of the custom of *karo kari* and related incidents from a cross-section of society reveal the socio-cultural complexities, customs, traditions, deep-rooted gender biases, and patriarchal and feudal power that support, protect, and preserve the practice.

Funded by the Global Opportunity Fund of the Foreign and Commonwealth Office of the British Government through the British Council of Pakistan, *Shame: A Tale of Karo Kari* is an investigative and expository film produced by the *Dastak* Society for Communications as part of an awareness-raising campaign in rural Sindh and southern Punjab.[50] The film opens with footage of a '*karion jo qabristan*' (graveyard of *karo* (male) and *kari* (female)), an unmarked graveyard located near the bustling cosmopolitan city of Karachi. As the camera pans the vast sad and forlorn, dusty graveyard dotted with a series of raised patches where the buried lie, we learn from voice-over that victims of *karo kari* are buried here without a 'bath, a shroud, a prayer' in unmarked graves where no one, even relatives, visit to offer a prayer. This treatment is reserved for *karo karis* to mark their humiliation and ostracization from their society, as they are denied the rites and rituals of traditional or religious funeral services otherwise accorded to honour the dead.

Kalpana Devi, an advocate of the Sindh High Court recounts an incident when a man who had stopped by a fresh grave of a *kari* to say a prayer was perceived by the community as her *karo* (male lover), and hence killed. We learn that the unknown number of dead buried in the graveyard, mostly women, were 'axed, shot, or beaten to death in public by their own fathers, brothers, or sons on the

Figure 4.6 Image of unmarked graveyard for *karo kari* victims from *Shame: A Tale of Karo Kari*.
Source: Film director Sharjil Baloch.

pretext of "honour"'. These opening scenes set the tone for the film's contextual investigation into the socio-cultural causes, and so-called justifications for honour-killing.

Shame: A Tale of Karo Kari raises questions about the prevalence, and origins, of the practice of honour-killing, and the socio-economic, political, and cultural roots that support it. Shown talking to a congregation of his tribesmen, Sardar Ashiq Khan Buzdar, a tribal chief and politician from Rajanpur, Punjab, reflects on the history and origins of 'honour-killing'. He points out that the practice of honour-killing was unknown in matriarchal societies, but came into existence in patriarchal and class-based feudal societies which reduced women's status to that of 'chattel' that was no more than a commodity like land and gold that is to be protected, but is stripped of all human qualities such as love, tenderness, and feelings: 'Instead, a woman came to be valued as no more than a "good cow" in the courtyard.' Spoken by a tribal chief to his followers, this clip is a rare and highly effective footage of the awareness-raising and consciousness-raising effort that the film seeks to fulfil.

On the other hand, a Sindhi journalist, Ikhlaq Jokhio, points out that it is misleading to claim or give the impression that *karo kari* is a Sindhi custom alone: 'The fact is that historically this custom did not exist here, even before the advent of Islam. It does not belong to this land.' But taking an opposing view, activist and lawyer Zia Awan, advocate of the Sindh High Court and president of the Lawyers for Human Rights and Legal Aid (LHRLA), points out that when a community condones a practice, it is highly difficult to curb it. Shedding light on the socio-cultural aspect of honour-killing, Awan stresses that it is a 'community-sanctioned' violence whereby the perpetrator is appreciated as a man of honour

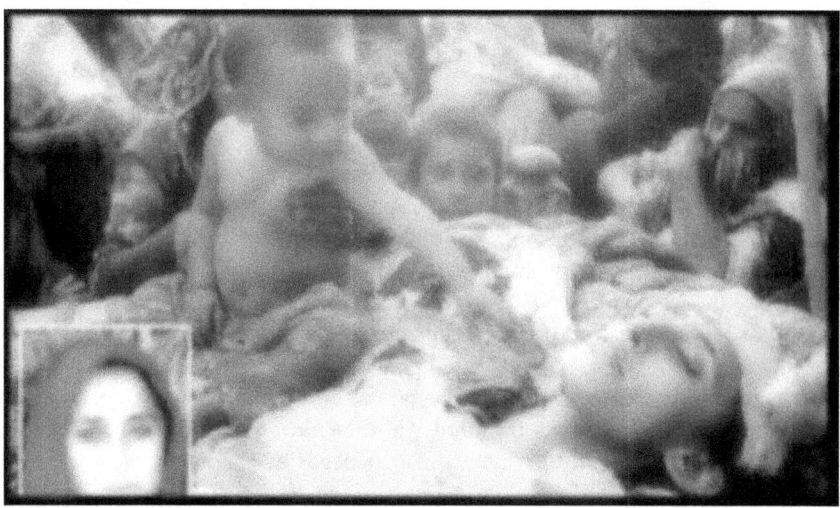

Figure 4.7 Image of female victim of *karo kari* from *Shame: A Tale of Karo Kari*.
Source: Film director Sharjil Baloch.

who can walk tall among his community. Views from ordinary rural men and villagers who defend the practice of *karo kari* as an 'honourable and good Sindhi tradition' illustrate Awan's concerns. One man puts it like this:

> 'We cannot throw a woman out of the house, but we can kill her. In Sindh we still have honour enough to kill if we witness *karo kari*.'

Asked if a woman also has the right to kill a *karo* or husband if she suspects him of infidelity, most say she has no such right as she is a woman. One man who argues that if a *kari* is not killed, other women will be enabled to follow her example, goes as far as to state: 'A woman is like a fly. She will sit on food, and just as happily on dung.' Asked what is a man, he responds: 'A man is fine. He is a human being.'

In documenting such perturbing arguments and gender biases at the very roots of tribal society, *Shame: A Tale of Karo Kari* highlights in broad, but disquieting, terms the socio-cultural complexities and contradictions that plague Pakistani society while the nuclear-armed county aspires to a modern and progressive future and place in the international community.

Shame: A Tale of Karo Kari takes a turn from socio-cultural aspects of honour and honour-killing to the more worldly socio-economic factors that also serve as a premise for such violence. Journalist Nisar Khokhar illustrates the economic gains to be made from honour-related issues when he narrates the story of a merchant who accused another man of his brother having illicit relations with the merchant's wife. However, the merchant agreed to drop the case if a compensation of Rupees 300,000 was paid him under the *Diyat* law provisions. Highlighting the utility and financial gain tied to the application of the *Diyat* law (compensation by blood-money), Khokhar raises the question of redeeming and cashing the notion of 'honour' at a price. What emerges is the material motive, and validity of avenging 'honour' as no more than a threat to extract money. (For an explanation of the *Diyat* law see Appendix 5).

Next, the film turns to the religious factors that are also alluded to as a justification for committing honour-killings. Those interviewed on the Islamic aspect of honour-killing include ordinary rural men, political leaders, and clerics. Spinning a religious twist, one man defends the upholding of honour as a supreme task for Muslims, citing Prophet Mohammad as saying that a man without honour is not a member of the Muslim *ummah* (Muslim brotherhood), and that He (the Prophet) would not look at the face of such a dishonourable man. Another says that genuine *karo kari* is recognized in Islam as punishment is prescribed for it. This is a claim that advocate Kalpana Devi refutes in the film, asking for any mention, and hence validity, of such claims for murder in the *Quran* itself. She blames people for hiding behind religion to whitewash their deeds and motives, a view that is shared by Asad Ullah Bhutto, a *Jamaat-e-Islami* leader and a member of the Sindh National Assembly, who categorically states in the film that the *Quran* and *Sunnah* do not give anyone the right to murder a woman. Although coming from a lawyer and a religious leader and politician, these clarifications do little to appease the rampant beliefs among the tribal and feudal mindsets, and the failure of the state to address the issue effectively by ensuring the rule of law and justice. Also interviewed in the film, academic and activist Amar Sindhu of the Department of Philosophy at the University of Sindh rejects the premise of 'cultural custom' as justification for honour-killings. Instead, she stresses that the majority of *karo kari* cases that she has studied point to economic reasons. She cites the failure of the state for abandoning social institutions, and using them only for self-aggrandizement and as a political tool. Additionally, Sindhu holds the tribal *jirgas* (tribal juries) responsible for playing a fundamental and institutional role in promoting such violence.

Off-screen commentary points out that in most cases honour-killing has little to do with honour. Instead, financial needs, property disputes, tribal enmities, and family feuds are often the reason behind such killings and violence against women that serves as a convenient cloak for monetary and personal gain. This is a view that is also shared by member of Sindh parliament, Sassi Palejo, who agrees on-screen that the state has completely failed to enforce the writ of law, and that more than 'honour', honour-killings are an outcome of revenge, and property claims and disputes.[51]

As the film turns to legal complexities and limitations in Pakistan's law enforcement machinery, Zia Awan categorically points out that in Sindh, where most of such honour-killing incidents occur, the feudal and tribal clique is so strong that the police, courts, lawyers, and municipal authorities, etc., are rendered helpless even if they wish to investigate. Awan blames this on the entrenched power the tribal and feudal elites enjoy in these areas:

> 'The law enforcement and court systems all fail if a *wadera* (landlord or tribal chief) calls a meeting in his constituency and forbids them from becoming witnesses or a complainant. If no one goes as a complainant, what will you do? How will the police prove its case when there are no witnesses or complainants? So, the whole official machinery will fail when the *wadera* and the parallel *jirga* system is there.'

An ordinary rural man (in the film) confirms Awan's analysis: '*karo kari* is an honour issue that can only be resolved through a *jirga*'. On her part, Amar Sindhu believes that the institution of the *jirga* system not only justifies honour-killings but has been sustaining it: 'As one of our *sardars* (tribal chief) said about the *jirga* system on the record "these are our income-generating units."'

Refuting any claims for the justification of the *jirga* system, Asad Ullah Bhutto points out in the film that there is no such concept in Islam, as instead Islam has a judicial and legislative system. He asserts that the *jirga* system enjoys government protection and support, therefore no one can stop their functioning. Bhutto informs of an incident where no less than the Chief Minister of Sindh himself participated in a *jirga* meeting to settle a dispute.

The former Chief Justice of the Sindh High Court, Nasir Aslam Zahid, clarifies for the audience that the *jirga* system is a tribal social custom established over the centuries that the Pakistan government does not recognize. However, he points out that despite two judgements by the Sindh High Court in 2004 that termed *jirgas* as unconstitutional even in the tribal areas, a study conducted by the Human Rights Commission of Pakistan (HRCP) reported that up to 40 *jirgas* had been held even after this decision.[52] Zahid also confirms that these *jirgas* have been presided over by ministers, bureaucrats, members of national and provincial assemblies, and others. The most significant legal point that he turns the viewer's attention to is that women have no audience in *jirgas*: 'A woman cannot appear before a *jirga*. How can you decide a case relating to *karo kari* or any other immoral conduct against a woman unless you hear that woman?'

Sarfraz Khan Jatoi, an advocate of the Sindh High Court, also agrees in the film that the government is supporting the *jirga* system because it has weakened other law-enforcement and legal institutions so much that people have no other avenue than to turn to *jirgas* for speedy decisions: 'Even government functionaries have lost faith in their institutions.' This view is shared by politician Jani Mohammad who also asserts that he has received letters from local level magistrates admitting their inability to settle disputes: 'Courts are unable to settle a dispute even after 15 years. Those decisions have been taken by us.' This reveals an insight into the limitations and apathy of the Pakistani judicial system yet again, and its process of litigation that is too lengthy, ineffective, and expensive.

Journalist Nisar Khokhar sheds light on yet another aspect of *karo kari* and its implications for women, one that belies all claims of justice and 'honour' on the part of the *jirga* system, and those claiming to mete out justice on the pretext of upholding morality. Khokhar points out that *sardars* have courts in various areas of Sindh right next to their houses, and it is here that *kari* women are kept in the servant quarters where they remain as long as she is with the *sardar*: 'If the sardar's son fancies the *kari*, he will not marry her, but will maintain illicit relations with her forcefully.' This exposé of hypocrisy, moral corruption, and exploitation of women already tainted by a tribal system that has condemned them to death in any case as a *kari*, is reflective of the doubly neglected rights and marginalized status of Pakistani women by both the state judicial system, as well as tribal customs and legal system. This state of affairs is vehemently denied by *Sardar* Himat Kumharo, chief of the Abro tribe, who dismissively claims that it is only particular 'dissatisfied groups' in society that want to malign *sardars* and families of good standing for no reason.

Explaining a tribal *sardar's* psyche regarding the *jirga* system, Dr Saeed Buzdar, a provincial union council representative, explains that the *sardar*, well aware of the fact that disputing parties and infighting will only strengthen his position as the peacemaker, will never banish any practice that will increase the power of others at the expense of his own. Danish Zuberi, advocate of the Sindh High Court, argues that although President Pervaiz Musharraf's government has termed *karo kari* as murder under the Criminal Law Amendment Act 2004,[53] the 'waiver' is still there which complicates and weakens the application of the law. She stresses that giving the *wali* (legal heir or guardian) the right to go free in an honour-crime, despite accepting it as a murder, by waiver laws and provisions

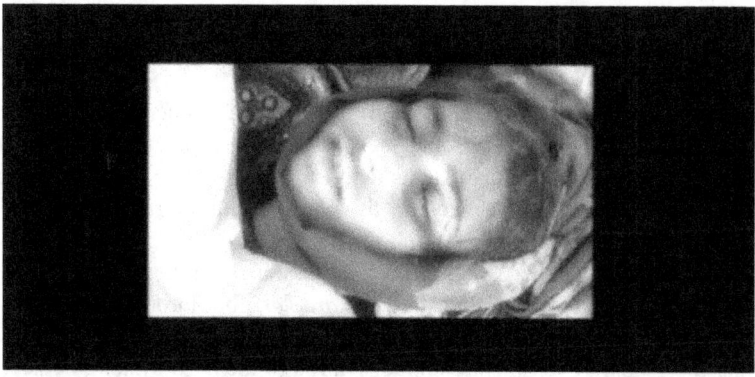

Figure 4.8 Image of female victim of *karo kari* from *Shame: A Tale of Karo Kari*.
Source: Film director Sharjil Baloch.

renders the amendment ineffective, because after all, it is the family members that commit the murder in such cases and can resort to the waiver provision.

Seconding Zuberi's critique of the Amendment Act 2004, Asad Ullah Bhutto expresses his rejection of the concept of the state as '*wali*' as a provision in the Act as it is liable to lead to injustice. He points out that if someone of high standing commits a murder, the prime minister can simply issue a brief directive stating that 'in the name of public interest', a particular case of *karo kari* crime is withdrawn, and the killers go free just because they were well-connected people.

Turning to the clergy, Saeed Buzdar raises a most important point when he stresses that religious clerics can play a significant and positive role in educating people by condemning the practice of *karo kari* as a 'non-Islamic' act. Similarly, he points to the local government representatives such as district councillors that have access to the grassroots level to check the practice of honour-killings in their respective areas: 'If it wants, the state can play a positive role', a view shared by an ordinary rural man in the film: 'If the government provides no law, unjust laws will prevail. If it wants, the government can stop injustice.' Commenting on the vast number of committees otherwise formed by the government such as 'peace committees', Narjees Batool, coordinator for the *Sangtani* Women Rural Development Organization in Rajanpur, Punjab, points to the need for formulating committees at all levels of the law enforcement machinery such as the lower and upper levels of the police department. These, she argues, would act as deterrents by investigating, recording, and following up on cases of *karo kari* to track down culprits and mete out punishment. But, perhaps it is Zia Awan who lays out the practical roadmap to eliminating the practice of *karo kari* and honour-killings by stressing the need to eliminate the feudal, patriarchal *jirga* system that is the root cause of promoting and supporting such practices. Expressing confidence that powerful laws can eliminate this problem, Awan stresses that political and religious parties have to realize the gravity of the problem, and 'use their respective platforms and mosques to preach that elimination of such practices as honour-killings is the real *jihad*, and not those fought at the behest of international donors.'

Shame: A Tale of Karo Kari ends with footage of a women's procession carrying placards, demanding justice and legal reforms as a poem by revolutionary Urdu poet, journalist, and human rights activist, the late Faiz Ahmad Faiz, sung by classical singer Iqbal Bano, plays in the background: '*Lazim hai ke hum bhi dekhen ge* ...' (For certain, we too shall see the day...).[54]

In *Shame: A Tale of Karo Kari*, for the first time on film the filmmakers do not simply explain the socio-cultural custom of *karo kari*, but through interviews and talking heads pinpoint the host of factors responsible for its unabated continuation including the feudal-government complicity through the *jirga* system; neglect and failure of the state to address the issue; lacunae in the *Diyat* law and the concept of the state as *wali*; and socio-economic reasons and excuses. All these factors explain the prevalent exploitation and victimization of women in particular by both the tribal and feudal systems on the pretext of 'honour' and socio-cultural customs, and state apathy to check or penalize such practices effectively.

However, what is significantly missing from the film are any views on the topic of honour-killing from rural Sindhi women, or the female relatives of those implicated in *karo kari* cases. This omission in itself is indicative of the feudal and tribal power in the region, and its hold on the population they rule over as chiefs – a hold on power that can only be countered through a strict execution of state legislation, and promulgation of stringent laws and punishments as many point out in the film. As we hear views from various levels of Pakistani society who are united in their criticism of the state's failure to implement adequate legislation and machinery to check and discourage honour-killings, it becomes apparent that this neglect is responsible for the increasing number of such cases across the country. As pointed out by advocate Danish Zuberi in the film, NGOs and the civil society cannot take on the responsibilities of the state as it is too huge a task. For example, as the film informs viewers at the time, there is still no shelter home for women implicated in such cases in Sindh, where most cases of *karo kari* occur.

As 'honour' becomes a relative issue, Pakistan continues to see a surge in 'honour killings' carried out with impunity despite the act being considered murder under state laws. It is alarming that according to a UN report on Violence Against Women, 4,000 women and men were killed in Pakistan in the name of honour between 1998 and 2003 alone. Of these, the number of women was more than double that of men.[55] Although the media, NGOs, and civil society activists have begun to play a significant role in bringing the issue of *karo kari* and honour-killings in general to public notice, as a documentary film that probes the various factors involved in such crimes from a number of socio-cultural and economic angles, *Shame: A Tale of Karo Kari* plays a 'legislative' and 'deliberative' role in drawing attention to the dismal state of affairs that still prevail with regard to violence against women in Pakistan.[56]

Shame (Mohammad Ali Naqvi 2006)

Mohammad Ali Naqvi's[57] multi award-winning feature length documentary film entitled *Shame*, a biographical film supported by interviews, talking heads, intertitles, and off-screen commentary, documents the shocking ordeal, and defiant and courageous ongoing struggle of Mukhtaran Mai over a period of five years (2002–2006) in detail.[58] Over the years, Mai, an uneducated tribal woman, who was subjected to 'honour-rape' – in this case gang-rape – on the orders of a *panchayat* (village council) in June 2002 in the Punjab village of Meerwala, Pakistan, has emerged as an internationally acclaimed champion of women's rights, and pioneer of education in her remote village. Although not an isolated case of rape or tribal oppression of women, it was Mai's decision to seek justice through the Pakistani judicial system and the accompanying media attention that highlighted the complexities of the intersection of gender, culture, class, and caste/tribe in its most horrendous form.[59] Details of Mai's gang-rape first broke in the local media, and soon made international headlines.[60]

The 'Meerwala gang-rape' story, as it became known in the media worldwide, gained unprecedented attention in Pakistan and abroad, not only because a gang-rape of this nature had taken place, but because this time instead of self-victimization by committing suicide, as is the normal expectation from female rape victims in tribal societies such as Mai's, an uneducated, poor, peasant woman from a lower caste who taught the *Quran* decided to fight back and take her case to court. In

Figure 4.9 Image of filmmaker Mohammad Ali Naqvi (first left in back row) with Mukhtaran Mai (third from left in back row) during the filming of *Shame*.
Source: Film director Mohammad Ali Naqvi.

doing so, she also challenged the government, the state law-enforcement machinery, and the judicial system to deliver justice. As *Shame* gives Mai and her family the opportunity to record their own version of events and testimonies as opposed to the various differing, and sensationalizing, stories that appeared in the media at the time of the event, we see a biographical and chronological sequence of events and developments emerge.

Shame begins with Mai's earliest recorded interview in June 2002 in which, her face partially covered, with only her eyes conveying her misery, she narrates her ordeal in soft, collected but poignant tones. Between her account and her father Ghulam Fareed's narration we learn how Mai, a woman of the lower caste *Gujjar* tribe, was mercilessly gang-raped on June 22, 2002 in Meerwala by four men, including one of the jurists, on the orders of the local tribal council.[61] The gang-rape was a punishment meted out by a *panchayat* to avenge the alleged illicit relationship between Mai's 12-year old brother, Shaqoor, with a woman of the higher-ranking *Mastoi* tribe. As punishment and to avenge their 'honour', Mai's father was ordered by the *Mastoi* tribal council to bring a daughter from his house to beg for forgiveness as per the tribal tradition. As Mai was the eldest at 28 years of age, her father and uncle chose to take her to beg for forgiveness in front of the tribal council. Her voice breaking down, Mai narrates that in response to her pleas for forgiveness, Khaliq, one of her rapists told her 'God is forgiving you' as he dragged her away to a nearby farmhouse where two men were already present. Here, Mai was raped repeatedly as scores of *Mastoi* men stood outside laughing and applauding at what they perceived as justice in the form of 'honour rape', hence justifying their concept of 'honour for honour'. During her ordeal witnessed by as many as 200 witnesses, Mai recalls crying out 'Will any brother save my honour?' to which no one responded or intervened. As a mark of her final humiliation and the *Mastoi's* revenge and victory, Mai was made to walk home barely clothed with her father and uncle as the villagers looked on.

Footage of the dusty, narrow road shows the route to Meerwala, lined by a few roadside village vendors, small shops, and fields and huts – a quiet, remote village described as undeveloped and lacking in basic facilities such as a school, roads, telephone connection, and a police station, the nearest one being 18 kilometres away. Off-screen comments describe the village, with a population of five to six thousand, as cut off from the rest of Pakistan where only 'jungle law' prevails, and all that matters is 'family honour'. We see Mai's house that was to become the focus of such tremendous national and international attention as a simple, sparse rustic structure at the time with a cow and a few goats tied outside. Located only a hundred yards away from hers, the residence of Mai's rapists, the *Mastois*, shows their large estate surrounded by lush fields, indicative of their relative wealth, power, and higher status in the community.

In addition to the fate suffered by his daughter, Mai's father narrates the background that started it all when his son, Shaqoor, was taken away by the *Mastoi* tribesmen and sodomized and tortured. He recalls that when registering his son's case with the police, the *Mastois* had threatened to kill him, and he had known little that seeking justice would instead lead to the gang-rape of his daughter. Mai had later told an inquiry team on July 4, 2002 that the accusation against her brother was concocted by the *Mastoi* tribe after he had threatened to tell his parents that three *Mastoi* men had sodomized him.[62] Denying any relationship with a woman of their tribe, we see Shaqoor speak of the horrific physical abuse at the hands of the *Mastois*. What is apparent is that two crimes had taken place – one against Shaqoor (sodomy), the other the revenge exacted from his sister (rape). Mai's mother and father speak of their daughter's suffering, revealing how they were pressed by visitors from the village to repeat the gory details of the incident, and continued to receive death threats from the *Mastois*.

As the camera slowly pans the Meerwala village, we hear Mai talk of her frame of mind, despair, and humiliation after the rape as village women told her to keep quiet because she was not 'special' and other women had also suffered the same fate – a course of action that she eventually rejected. She talks of the initial days when she contemplated suicide knowing that no one would come forward to confront the *Mastois*. But realizing that 'the worst had already happened' gave her strength and a sense of purpose to seek justice. At this juncture, Mai remembers the point of realization that something in her changed, a change that was to be the beginning of her long, arduous journey through the apathetic Pakistani judicial system.

We see Mukhtaran Mai's journey begin with the local cleric, Abdul Razzaq, who offered to help her by speaking on her behalf during his Friday afternoon sermon, and later escorted her personally to the nearest police station to file a complaint while her own family members refused to press charges or testify. After spending hours at the *Tehsil Jatoi* police station and giving statements to three different officers, we see Mai returning home at 11 pm after failing to register her case with the police – a revelation that is reflective of the wider tribal influence and power of the *Mastois* as a higher tribe. Even though the gang-rape took place on June 22, 2002, the police registered the case as late as June 30 because of pressure from the socially powerful *Mastoi* tribesmen. Thus another crime was committed by the law enforcement agencies as in a rape case valuable medical evidence was lost by a delay in the medical examination of the victim. It was only when the incident made international headlines that it was dealt with in an appropriate manner and action was taken by the police. As the story drew intense media attention, and rights organizations built pressure for justice, we learn the police arrested 14 people, including members of the tribal council who had issued the verdict.

Clips from Mai's first interview in 2002 by Mureed Abbas, a local journalist who was the first to report the story in the media, shows her as a frail, broken woman who introduces herself as '30 years old', and a teacher of the *Quran*, which she has memorized by heart.[63] When asked what punishment her rapists should get, she replies without hesitation: 'death'. As for what would be the single most effective tool of defence against such violations and abuse of women, her reply is 'education'.[64] In the years that were to follow, it was these two objectives that were to transform Mai's life from a docile, broken woman to a vocal, defiant rights activist and educationist who would be acclaimed and honoured internationally for her courage and struggle, becoming a symbol for women's rights and education.

It is pertinent to mention here that in her memoir entitled *In the Name of Honour*, written in collaboration with Marie-Thérèse Cuny, first published in French and subsequently translated into 23 languages, Mai recounts her transformation from a frightened, docile rape victim to a strong-willed survivor:

> 'Nothing will be "as usual" from now on ... I have suffered for days, contemplated suicide, cried my heart out. I am changing, behaving differently, which I would never have thought possible ... When I begin this journey into the legal system, a path from which there is no turning back, I am hampered by my illiteracy and my status as a woman. Aside from my family, I have only one strength to call upon: my outrage ... Before, I had lived in absolute submission; now my rebellion will be equally relentless.'[65]

Her 'outrage' led to her unfailing pursuit of her quest for justice, which was to eventually lead to the arrest of her rapists. Footage shows Mai making a second trip to the police station, and this time managing to register her case. After the story broke in the international media as well, we see foreign media units, journalists, photographers, and representatives of various NGO's descending on Meerwala, turning the once unknown village into a hub of intense curiosity, activity, and focus of interest because of one woman's courageous decision to speak out and be heard. In the midst of such publicity, as the Pakistan government is forced to launch an investigation, we see the Punjab provincial Minister for Women's Development and Social Welfare at the time, Shaheen Attiq-ur-Rehman, visit Meerwala and extend help such as the deployment of guards to protect Mai and her family. Whereas earlier no one had come forward to testify to the horrific crime against Mai, what we now see is a breakdown of barriers of stigma as villagers begin to add their voices of concern, and question the police neglect in not registering the gang-rape case in the first instance.

Footage shows Mai's rapists, now under arrest, being brought to court in shackles as six weeks after the incident the trial begins amidst heavy Pakistani and international media presence such as CNN, Reuters, and the BBC. Indicative of the line of intimate questioning in a rape case, Mai comments off-screen of her unease and fear, and at being questioned by the defence lawyers: 'The lawyers asked horrible things, and then I understood why women are afraid of going to court.' Journalist Nadeem Saeed pays tribute to Mai in the film for not backing away from pursuing her case: 'For three days Mai stood in court answering all kinds of questions. Even men would sweat at doing this.' Eventually, six of Mai's rapists were sentenced to death.

Although the *Mastois* never registered a police case against Mai's brother for allegedly raping their daughter, Naqvi shows us their clan giving their version of events. They accuse Mai of concocting the entire episode of the gang-rape, terming it the 'biggest lie in the history of Pakistan'. However, ten weeks after Mai's rape, we see Yaqoob Khan, defence attorney for the *Mastois*, informing the

Women, Violence, and Human Rights 155

media persons that the judge has reached a verdict: of the fourteen arrested, six men are given the death penalty – four for rape and two for abetting the crime – besides a fine of Rupees 40,000 each. Eight men have been set free. Nevertheless, the attorney expresses hope for a better verdict on appeal by the *Mastois*.

As *Shame* moves into 2003, Naqvi gives us footage of the changes and developments that have taken place a year later. Though still her frail self, Mai is picking up her life but her anger has subsided little as she voices that the only punishment that would satisfy her is the death of her rapists which she will believe only when the verdict is carried out: 'I keep thinking their spirits are going to return from the gallows to haunt me.' This was to prove an ominous thought that, in retrospect, would materialize some years later. Mai informs us that after her trial, other women in the area have begun to come forward and report cases of abuse against them to the police. Footage shows the construction of a girl's school in progress, a police check-post with four officers on duty, and a 24-hour police security outside Mai's house – provided by the government due to continuing death threats from the *Mastois*. Speaking of her trip to Spain, where she was invited to the International Women's Rights Forum as a delegate in February 2003, Mai regrets that her lack of education proved to be a hurdle in participating and interacting with others, stressing once again her belief that education is the strongest tool against oppression. Of the Rs 500,000 cheque that the government of Pakistan gave her to honour her bravery she says: 'I could have

Figure 4.10 Image of Mukhtaran Mai from *Shame*.
Source: Film director Mohammad Ali Naqvi.

left Meerwala, but the people would have stayed the same forever. So I started a school.' Clips show the lively environment of the Government Mukhtar Mai Girls School in session, where up to a hundred girls are now receiving free education. Further, journalist Nadeem Saeed informs us that the village has been renamed after Mai's father, a dual carriageway is under construction, electricity has been provided, and plans are afoot for the construction of a boy's school as well. Intertitles confirm that the government built the Ghulam Fareed Government Primary School for Boys in 2003.

Against these transformations, and the return to comparative normalcy, for the first time we also hear the *Mastois'* version of events. Despite the fact that the *Mastois* never filed formal charges against Shaqoor, Salma Mastoi maintains that she was raped by six men, the last being Mai's brother Shaqoor. Accusing a child of 12 from a lower caste of rape is in itself an incredible exposé of tribal power that is exercised by the *Mastois* to influence and manipulate events and decisions by using their own women to testify and support them. We see Taj Mastoi in her surprisingly impoverished domestic surroundings despite belonging to a higher caste and status, who tells us that three of her sons are rotting in jail for the alleged gang-rape of Mai, and she now has no help with the crops, or the cattle. She vents her bitterness against Mai:

> 'She is free to meet President Musharraf or the governor. She now travels on a plane, with cars, special bodyguards … I am a widow. Mai is fighting with a widow … Let Mai's father come to my face. I will ask him who are the real criminals here, you or us? Which side committed a crime first? You or us? They have made us suffer. God will soon return the favour.'

Naqvi's depiction of a woman left to fend for herself is reflective of the fact that, unfortunately, as tribal women in a patriarchal society Salma Mastoi, Taj Mastoi, Mukhtaran Mai, and others like them, all have an uphill task regardless of their caste, truth of the case, and verdicts reached.

On his part, Mai's father, while acknowledging the positive changes that have taken place in the village such as the construction of schools and roads, says that he still has to live with the stigma and comments about his daughter and son. Similarly, Mai too says that the local village women still look down on her and don't understand her, while it is the urban, educated women who look on her as a symbol of integrity and courage in a male-dominated society.

As *Shame* progresses to 2004, we see the arrival of Naseem Akhtar, an educated woman who has joined Mai in her educational and welfare work. Akhtar points out that Mai's efforts have changed the destiny of the people of Meerwala despite the firm control of the feudal lords who resist any progress such as schools, electricity, roads, and police presence. Nicholas D. Kristoff, the *New York Times* journalist who was present in Pakistan on other business as Mai's story broke in 2002, also makes an appearance. He speaks of writing about Mai's ordeal in the *New York Times* that resulted in a massive outpouring of support, and donations to the tune of $130,000 which went towards the development of

Figure 4.11 Image of filmmaker Mohammad Ali Naqvi (centre), Mukhtaran Mai (left), and Mai's friend Naseem Akhtar (right) during the filming of *Shame*.
Source: Film director Mohammad Ali Naqvi.

her educational efforts. Clips show bare classrooms where earlier children had sat on the floor replaced by neat rows of tables and chairs. The enrolment stands at 350 girls now, and a growing staff, while plans are underway for an expansion to include a high school, and eventually, a college.

In a sudden twist of events, perhaps the worst was yet to come in 2005. Three years after Mai's ordeal, we learn that on appeal five of the six men sentenced to death in her gang-rape case will be freed in a fortnight by the Lahore High Court Multan Bench due to lack of evidence. As media frenzy grows, NGO activists once again rally to Mai's support, both in Pakistan and abroad. The court ruling attracts support from the New York-based Asian-American Network Against Abuse of human rights (ANAA) and its founder Dr Amna Buttar. Mai says she fears for her life even more now. Talking to the press, she breaks down as she appeals to the prime minister of Pakistan for help. She says she finds this court decision more disturbing as this time it has been passed by 'educated people' as opposed to a tribal council that had sentenced her to gang-rape in 2002.

In addition to her appeal in the High Court, we see Mai meeting the then Prime Minister of Pakistan, Shaukat Aziz, who orders four of the accused to be re-arrested.[66] Against these developments, we see Mai being invited by ANAA and Amnesty International (AI) to speak at a Women's Rights Forum in the US. Once again, the government steps in but this time to detain her from leaving the country. We learn that Mai has been put under house arrest, and later taken to an undisclosed location in Islamabad while her passport has been confiscated. In footage added by Naqvi to expose government hypocrisy, Mai reappears after 48 hours, making an appearance at a press conference accompanied by Nilofer Bakhtiar, the then Pakistan government Advisor on Women's Development who carefully orchestrates the event, and displays a guarded stance on behalf of her government. Bakhtiar dismisses any intervention in Mai's disappearance, and regards the entire episode as a 'misunderstanding', saying that Mai had postponed the US trip herself because of her mother's illness. On her part, Mai does not hesitate to contradict Bakhtiar to her face during the press conference, informing them that she had been forcefully put under 'house arrest', a point that a reporter pursues ('Madam, she is saying in front of you that she was under house-arrest') but to little avail as Bakhtiar hurriedly concludes the press conference.

In a later interview in the film, Bakhtiar admits that President Pervaiz Musharraf stopped Mai from visiting the US as he felt that her case would go against the image of the country. It is pertinent to point out in retrospect that the president had felt no remorse at his actions. This is evident from his callous remarks in an interview he gave to the *New York Times* in September 2005, enraging rights activists and the international community. Musharraf stated: 'You must understand the environment in Pakistan. This has become a money-making concern. A lot of people say if you want to go abroad and get a visa for Canada or citizenship and be a millionaire, get yourself raped.' In reply, Mukhtaran Mai had told the BBC: 'I offer all the riches I've made out of the *panchayat*-enforced gang-rape to the president in return for justice.'[67]

As life moves on, clips now show a confident and highly motivated Mai running her own NGO, the Mukhtar Mai Women's Welfare Organization (MMWWO), as work continues on a girls' high school in the village from donations.[68] Besides the schools, the MMWWO board now also lists the Mukhtar Mai Community Dairy Farm and the Women's Crises Relief Centre. Future projects list a health centre, shelter home, and a women's resource centre. By contrast, clips of the *Mastoi* home depict a gloomy and forlorn picture as their family members continue to blame Mai for minting money from their misfortune.

Eventually allowed to travel to the US under growing pressure on the government, we see clips showing Mai receiving international acclaim for her efforts and struggle as she is given a standing ovation by Hollywood celebrities such as Catherine Zeta-Jones, Brooke Shields, and others at the 2005 Glamour Awards in the US. Attending a glittering ceremony at New York's Lincoln Center, dressed in her national dress – a simple white *shalwar kameez* – and receiving the Glamour magazine's 'Bravest Woman of the Year Award 2005', Mai shyly utters a one line speech in Urdu: 'My message is to eradicate oppression with education.' CNN journalist Christiane Amanpour applauds Mai's courage in travelling and telling her story despite discouragements. Other engagements and recognition show Mai as a guest at the closing of the NASDAQ Stock Market in New York, and receiving an award at the 'Vital Voices' Global Leadership Award Ceremony in Washington DC with Hillary Clinton in attendance.[69]

Mai, now visibly plump, relaxed, and smiling easily, is shown sightseeing in New York and meeting the Mayor of Las Vegas. We also see a still photograph of Mai holding a copy of her memoir *In the Name of Honor*, first published in France.[70] Adding to her achievements and recognition, *Time* magazine cites her on its 2006 list of the 100 most influential people in the world. Mai shared this distinction with President Pervaiz Musharraf, a man who had earlier accused her of opportunism in 2005.[71] However, despite the remarkable strides Mai may have made in her individual capacity, how much still remains unchanged is conveyed from the clip of a phone call between the filmmaker and Mai on her return to the village. She is shocked to learn that a nine-year-old student from her school has been raped. But this time, we learn that Mai has acquired the capacity to get the girl's rapists arrested.

As *Shame* enters 2006, we see Mai's Welfare Centre now turned into a hub of activity where a steady stream of women visit her to seek advice on their problems. A school poetry recitation ceremony with girls and boys from Mai's schools also includes a boy from the *Mastoi* tribe who is enrolled there. As she continues with her social work despite constant death threats from the *Mastois*, she reflects: 'Had I left and not struggled, there would have been no schools, electricity, and people's lot would have been the same.' As *Shame* ends its biographical journey in 2006, we learn that Mai, enrolled in her own school, is now in grade five while her case is pending in the Supreme Court of Pakistan.

Whereas Naqvi's film has shown us Mai's personal ordeal push her into the limelight because of her unrelenting defiance, her struggle at the hands of the Pakistani legal system was to bring her back to square one. Mai's case had been pending in the Pakistan Supreme Court since 2005, while six of the fourteen men sentenced to death in connection with the gang-rape were still in custody pending a retrial. In February 2009, the case hearing was again postponed indefinitely. As she continued to fight for justice, Mai's lawyers suspected political interference from influential tribal leaders as the cause for delay.[72]

Despite Mukhtaran Mai's determined, arduous struggle through Pakistan's legal system, it became a cause of national and international shock when on April 21, 2011 the Supreme Court of Pakistan upheld the decision of the Lahore High Court that had cited lack of adequate evidence, and acquitted five of the six men charged in her gang-rape in 2002.[73] The Supreme Court also upheld the decision of the lower court that had included commuting the death penalty of the sixth man to life imprisonment. Although Mai once again filed an appeal in 2011 (the case is still pending), she had said in an interview to the BBC minutes after the verdict that she had lost all faith in the Pakistani legal system, and now feared for the security of her family and her life:

'The police never even recorded my own statements correctly. I don't have any more faith in the courts. I have put my faith in God's judgement now. I don't know what the legal procedure is, but my faith [in the system] is gone. Yes, there is a threat to me and my family. There is a threat of death, and even of the same thing happening again. Anything can happen.'[74]

Shame is as much about the parallel tribal legal system, as it is reflective of the miscarriage of justice through the gender-biased Pakistani state legal system. In *Shame* we see the story of an uneducated, peasant woman's lonely struggle against all odds – yet the Pakistani legal system has let her down repeatedly after waiting for justice for nine years. The significant point in the Meerwala gang-rape case is that this was a solitary incident that received unprecedented coverage and attention in the local and international media, as compared to the countless cases that go unreported altogether in the face of tribal and class power, which is further compounded by women's inferior status in the patriarchal society of Pakistan.[75]

Although Mukhtaran Mai's struggle has today become symbolic of a simple woman's courage and resolve to fight back, and seek triumph over a tribal system that continues to sacrifice and humiliate women as symbols of their 'honour', I am reminded of Pakistani poetess, writer and women's rights activist, Kishwar Naheed, who had expressed her serious doubts and fears despite the initial just and favourable verdict in the Meerwala gang-rape case:

> 'The Meerawala case is not the first such case which has taken place in Pakistan. Rather, every day several such cases occur but are not reported. I still fear that any day Mukhtar Mai will be killed and after a while the culprits will be freed on some pretext or the other. The system in Pakistan has gone back from feudalism to tribalism. Women have become the symbol of revenge, whether it is Benazir Bhutto or Mukhtar Mai.'[76]

Mohammad Naqvi's film *Shame* is significant in its filmic exposé and contextualization of the role caste, customs, patriarchal power structures, notions of honour and shame, the *jirga* and *panchayat* system, tribal modes of revenge, and tribal mindsets play in the victimization of women to exert and uphold their power and status. The film pays tribute to a lone woman's courage in taking on all these marginalizing, victimizing, and discriminatory practices and attitudes, allowing Mai the space and empowerment to offer a filmic testimonial of her ordeal from her perspective and press for accountability. In retrospect, *Shame* today holds authenticity value as what can be termed as a *judicial history* of the earliest days of Mai's trial, and the subsequent dismal performance of Pakistan's judicial and state players. Spanning several years since the horrific Meerwala gang-rape incident took place, this biographical film remains significant in its activist intent of documenting and exposing tribal gender-specific violence, and state apathy and failure in such matters, particularly through the gender-biased judicial process and law enforcement machinery in Pakistan.[77]

Samar Minallah: Ethnomedia & Development

Samar Minallah, graduated and returned to Pakistan with an M.Phil. degree in Anthropology and Development from the University of Cambridge, in 1999, and took up documentary filmmaking as her main vehicle for activism in 2003 mainly to address issues pertaining to social and tribal practices and oppressive traditions that affect women and young girls in rural areas and the Khyber Pakhtunkhwa Province (KP), formerly known as the North West Frontier Province of Pakistan (NWFP).[78] An ultra-conservative *Pakhtun* tribal region, the KP is historically associated with rigid socio-cultural customs that operate in accordance with notions of 'honour', particularly in the treatment and status of women. Minallah has the distinction of being one of the first Pakistani filmmakers who used video to give voice to marginalized groups, especially in the region, by making socially relevant documentaries.

For over two decades now, as an anthropologist, journalist, freelance writer, human rights activist, and now documentarist, Minallah, a multi-award-winning independent filmmaker, and a *Pakhtun* woman herself, has focused on investigating and critiquing tribal customs, and women's rights issues that had traditionally been ignored and remained out of public view and debate in the region and adjoining Afghanistan that shares the *Pakhtun* cultural norms and languages.[79] With a distinctly activist focus, Minallah's Islamabad-based non-governmental organization, Ethnomedia & Development, of which she is the executive director, was founded in 2004 as an independent media think tank that uses media for social change, and specializes in producing advocacy and consciousness-raising films that challenge patriarchal practices and mindsets.[80] The organization continues to collaborate with local and international civil society as well as government and non-governmental organizations to produce documentaries with an activist focus, besides engaging in public forums, workshops, and advocacy campaigns on culturally controversial and sensitive issues that have included honour-related tribal customs and practices such as *Swara*, violence against women, girls' and women's rights, and taboo health issues such as tuberculosis and HIV/AIDS.

For the scope and length of this chapter, I will specifically discuss Minallah's widely screened film *Swara: A Bridge Over Troubled Waters* (2003) that was part of her initiative against the tribal practice of *Swara* and made legislative history in Pakistan as it forced the government to criminalize the practice of giving away of minor girls and women through forced marriages as compensation to settle disputes.[81] Other films by Ethnomedia & Development, some made in collaboration with international NGOs such as ActionAid, the Heinrich Böll Stiftung Foundation, Befare, and the International Labour Organization (ILO), will be discussed briefly to give a sense of the variety of social and rights issues the organization has taken up for filmic representation to raise awareness.

Swara: A Bridge Over Troubled Waters (Samar Minallah 2003)

In addition to being the lead researcher for the first statistical research on the custom of *Swara* in various districts of the Khyber Pakhtunkhwa (KP) Province in Pakistan which was shared with policy makers, media, law enforcement agencies, and other stake holders, Minallah's outstanding achievement has been her ground-breaking 40-minute expository documentary *Swara: A Bridge Over*

Troubled Waters (2003) that put the issue on the national radar.[82] In Pakistan, the documentary served a political purpose as well as it was a catalyst in pushing a law against the custom of *Swara*, and was used as evidence in the first ever Supreme Court case highlighting the issue.[83]

Minallah's documentary challenged the age-old tribal custom of *Swara* as practiced in the KP Province that allows minor girls, even newborns, or in some cases even unborn ones, to be exchanged as commodities and compensation in marriage between rival or disputing groups as a peace-making arrangement to settle feuds, regain lost 'honour', and avenge murder.[84] Under this practice, through forced marriage the '*Swara*' female is condemned to a life of misery and victimization in her in-laws' home as the daughter of the enemy household. In her extensive study on the topic published in 2006, Minallah describes the practice of *Swara*:

> Swara is known to many in Pakistan as an alternative dispute resolution mechanism whereby disputes (often murders) are resolved by traditional peace keeping institutions (jirga, local council of elders) without having to invest time and money in lengthy judicial processes. The price of this dispute settlement is paid by the women/girls from the family of the aggressor who

Figure 4.12 Image of filmmaker Samar Minallah during the filming of *Swara: A Bridge Over Troubled Waters*.
Source: Film director Samar Minallah.

enter the household of the bereaved family, by way of unceremonious wedlock, to remind the aggressors of the injustice their men bestowed upon the bereaved family.[85]

The film documents the stories of several minor girls in the KP Province who were given away under the *Swara* custom, depicting the oppressed, and humiliating lives they have been made to lead as '*Swara*' women, and the views of their male elders and community members, most of whom support the practice as a legitimate tribal custom. Interviews with tribal leaders, human rights activists, journalists, lawyers, and *Swara* victims and their families reveal the complex layers of tradition, tribal law, and gender biases that exist in the tribal set up.

Religious clerics interviewed in the film point out that the proposed marriages of minor girls, whose consent is not part of the *Swara* deal, amount to *nikah-bil-jabr* (forced marriages), which are forbidden by Islam, thus also rendering them illegal in religious terms.[86] They also emphasize that as *Sharia* laws already give the provisions of *Diyat* (blood-money) and *Qisas* (execution of the murderer) for murder and revenge, *Swara* is a purely tribal practice, and has no legal or religious sanction under Islam, or the tribal code of conduct of the *Pukhtuns* known as *Pukhtunwali*.[87] As off-screen commentary explains the tribal customs and

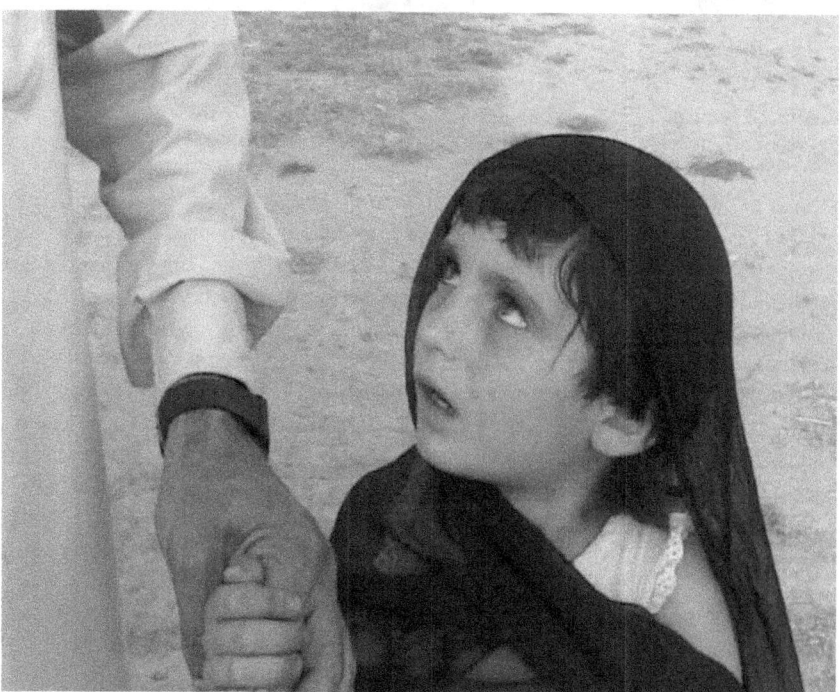

Figure 4.13 Image of *swara* girl from *Swara: A Bridge Over Troubled Waters*.
Source: Film director Samar Minallah.

Figure 4.14 Image of *swara* girl from *Swara: A Bridge Over Troubled Waters*.
Source: Film director Samar Minallah.

notions of honour, and the dynamics of *Pukhtunwali*, the native tribal unwritten code of law (as opposed to *Sharia* laws in Islamic jurisprudence which are regarded by Muslims as divine laws derived from the *Quran*), interspersed heart-rending images of minor *Pukhtun* girls being led by their fathers to be offered as compensation to enemies through *jirgas* bring to life the callous practice of sacrificing females to appease the acts of men in their societies.

Malik Bilal, a tribal chief from Darra Adam Khel, explains that when the *Sharia* laws of *Qisas* and *Diyat* prove insufficient for revenge, tribal wisdom dictates that a woman be given away as *Swara* so that someday her children will belong to both warring families, and hence the dispute would be settled permanently. (See Appendix 5 for an explanation of the *Qisas* and *Diyat* laws). We learn that under the *Swara* custom, a woman from the aggrieved family goes to the aggressor's/murderer's home to select a girl who would be given away at maturity, and once the settlement is reached goats are slaughtered and a feast held to commemorate the occasion, although the marriage ceremony itself would not be commemorated by any festivities. Bilal points out that in the case of an influential person's murder, instead of one, two *Swara* girls are given away as a status symbol. We learn that this act of 'forgiveness' or resolution of a dispute is known as '*nanawatay*' in the tribal code of *Pukhtunwali*.

Figure 4.15 Image of *swara* girl from *Swara: A Bridge Over Troubled Waters*.
Source: Film director Samar Minallah.

Addressing the legal foundations for *Sharia*, Justice Dr Fida Mohammad Khan of the Federal *Shariat* Court, Islamabad, explains in the film that punishment according to the *Sharia* law should have four characteristics – it should be punitive, retributive, reformative, and a deterrent – none of which are embodied by the custom of *Swara* since the criminal himself goes free and an innocent female is made to pay the price. Nevertheless, an old tribal man defiantly defends the custom, and does not hesitate to display his contempt in the film for *Swara* women:

> 'I may accept a *Swara* girl as payment for my son's murder, she will get food and clothing but I will find it very difficult to have any feelings of kindness towards her in my heart. I will not accord her any marriage ceremony. I will simply whisk her away by hand or on horseback. She is the price for my son's death and will be treated accordingly. This is our custom. Of course I will taunt her and humiliate her. After all, she is the price paid for my son's death.'

These comments demonstrate the oppression, ill-treatment, and discrimination suffered by *Swara* women in their in-laws' homes and in society because they are treated as nothing more than constant reminders of the crimes their male family

166 *Women, Violence, and Human Rights*

Figure 4.16 Image of *swara* girls from *Swara: A Bridge Over Troubled Waters*.
Source: Film director Samar Minallah.

members have committed – hatred and crimes they are not personally responsible for. First-hand accounts in the film from *Swara* women stress the helplessness and despair suffered by them at the mercy of tribal customs. Adding anguish and poignancy to the subject of the film, these tribal women's voices support the filmmaker's intent of raising awareness and opposition to the practice of *Swara* as an illegitimate and brutal means of justice. As the film ends with a small girl being led away by her father to a *jirga* – an image that is repeated throughout the film to endorse the unjust nature of the *Swara* custom – women's testimonies of abusive lives, and views from men that support the practice as an 'honourable' tribal practice establish the fact that the custom of *Swara* is mere revenge, and anything but a genuine and effective form of resolving issues, or eradicating hatred and enmities. There have also been media reports about *Swara* girls being killed by in-laws once they are given away in marriage.[88]

In depicting views and personal stories from a cross-section of society, particularly from *Swara* women themselves, Minallah's *Swara: A Bridge Over Troubled Waters* can be seen as offering a rare empowerment to female victims to come forward and speak out against the unjust custom for the first time. Doing so on film is even more rare considering the conservative environment of the tribal regions and their marginalizing treatment of women, particularly in the public arena. It is no doubt the filmmaker's cultural and gender-sensitive approach has been instrumental in establishing trust and confidentiality with her subjects and female victims of *Swara*, resulting in the investigation of a most neglected, yet significant, issue. Given her own *Pukhtun* ethnicity, knowledge of languages spoken in the region (Pushto/Darri), and her focus on an investigation of specific tribal customs and socio-cultural issues, Minallah's filmic exercise can also be seen as auto-ethnography that film scholar Bill Nichols points to.[89]

It is to her immense credit that in a country notorious for government apathy towards human rights issues, particularly regarding women's rights as we have seen in earlier films, Minallah's activist documentary and persistent campaigning were a key factor in playing a significant legislative and deliberative role[90] by raising countrywide awareness and mobilization against the custom of *Swara*, also practiced by the names of *Khoon Baha, Chatti, Ivaz*, or *Vanni* under the same dynamics in other tribal regions of the country through the tribal legal system.

Minallah's documentary on *Swara* was used as evidence and resource material by the Supreme Court of Pakistan in its case regarding the criminalization of the custom. As a result of the nationwide pressure exerted by Minallah's efforts through the media, her film compelled the Pakistan Supreme Court in 2005 to deliver a benchmark decision that renders the practice of offering and accepting by way of compensation any child or woman against her free will as a criminal offence under Section 310-A inserted into the Pakistan Penal Code (PPC).[91] Minallah has continued to highlight similar tribal customs as *Swara*, known as *Vani, Sungchatti*, and *Irchai* in other tribal regions and provinces of Pakistan, through her activist documentary *The Plagued Mindset* (2008).[92]

Minallah's other filmic topics have included the issue of human smuggling and human trafficking for the purpose of bonded-labour, slavery, prostitution, and children sent as camel jockeys to the Middle East through organized criminal networks operating in Pakistan and abroad (*The Dark Side of Migration* (2009)).[93] This documentary has been widely used for advocacy and educational purposes by the Federal Investigation Agency of Pakistan (FIA) and various non-government organizations. Minallah has also focused on the largely overlooked and neglected long-term emotional impact of war on the lives of Afghan refugee women living in refugee camps in Pakistan's KP Province from their perspectives on the impact of conflict, war, and resultant personal loss (*Dar Pa Dar: Afghan Refugee Women (Where the Heart Lies)* (2008)), and internally displaced *Pakhtun* populations from Bajaur Agency in the province due to the often indiscriminate Pak-US-led aerial strikes on *Al Qaida* and Taliban hideouts that often targeted civilian populations as well in the process (*Da Bajaur Galoona (Homeless at Home)* (2008)).[94] Minallah has also led awareness campaigns, and produced documentaries on issues of health-related stigmas in Pakistani society such as HIV/AIDS, its transmission by migrant workers, and the impact on socially shunned AIDS victims and their families (*The Silver Lining: HIV and AIDS* (2007)), and tuberculosis (*Rays of Hope: A Documentary on Tuberculosis* (2008)) in the most backward areas of the KP region where discussion and seeking treatment for these diseases remains largely taboo.[95]

Besides television talk-shows in local languages such as Pushto and Darri (spoken both in the KP Province of Pakistan, and Afghanistan), Minallah has also conducted her filmic activism through the potential music and songs have in promoting and popularizing ideas and views. These issue-oriented productions have included a music video that emphasizes the importance of girls' education (*Allaho: A Lullaby for You My Daughter* (2009)).[96] This music video makes a significant break with tradition as lullabies in the region are traditionally sung and dedicated to boys as only they are perceived to be precious as heirs, whereas girls are seen as an unwanted burden by parents. Sung by an Afghan woman singer, Naghma, to a lively tune and music, the lullaby is dedicated to girls. Referring to them as the 'jewel of the mother's cradle', the song urges girls to seek education and do well in life in their own right, as opposed to living a sheltered life under male domination. The music video, launched by the Human Rights Commission of Pakistan (HRCP) in Islamabad, Pakistan, has acquired significant importance and popularity as an advocacy tool since hundreds of schools were burnt down in the Northern Areas of Pakistan such as in the Swat Valley, and Afghanistan by religious fundamentalists and the Taliban who oppose girls' education.

The diversity and richness of the *Pakhtun* culture and women are explored and represented in other video songs also such as *Shinwarey Lawangeena: Where the Waters Meet* (2006), and *Warwaee Lasoona: The Dance of Unity* (2008).[97] In particular, the lyrics of *Bibi Shireenay: Where Honour Comes From* (2007) sung by a male singer, Gulzar Alam, pays tribute to the struggles and contribution of rural *Pukhtun* women to their society.[98] The folk song video, made as part of the awareness-raising campaign regarding violence against women in collaboration with a women's organization, the *Aurat* Foundation, Peshawar, raises awareness on how women are culturally deprived of their right to inherit property, as well as basic health facilities in the rural areas of Pakistan.

Minallah's productions have been shown in Pakistan's rural areas through mobile screenings, and broadcast on national and regional television channels to generate national debate, while her song videos have met popular demand in the Pushto-speaking regions. Besides film production and publications, Minallah's organization also serves as an outreach research and resource centre that provides sensitizing workshops on local and tribal issues to religious leaders, media persons, and tribal *jirga* leaders.[99]

Most of Minallah's documentaries, especially the award winning *Swara: A Bridge Over Troubled Waters* (2003), are being used for pedagogical, educational, and consciousness-raising purposes around socio-cultural and tribal practices in Pakistan and abroad, including at Amnesty International, while *Bibi Shireenay: Where Honour Comes From* (2007) has also been screened at the United Nations Headquarters in New York, USA.[100] Today, Minallah's filmic contributions present a body of work from an independent Pakistani woman filmmaker who is driven by a strong activist intent to conduct an expository, issue-oriented cultural investigation into a range of neglected and taboo topics that prevail and undermine gender and human rights in conservative tribal societies such as the Khyber Pakhtunkhwa Province of Pakistan.

Conclusion

The contextual reading and discussion of a selection of documentary films in this chapter, both by organizations and independent filmmakers, illustrates the various issues pertaining to extreme forms of violence and honour-related crimes against women, gender-discrimination and biases, and violation of their individual and human rights. Collectively, these investigative, expository, observational, and biographical films draw attention to the inadequate legislative measures, corruption in the Pakistani law enforcement-machinery, and state apathy in dealing with the aforementioned issues, and the socio-cultural and tribal agendas and customs that support and strengthen the brutalization of women in Pakistani society, rendering them victims of a vicious system. Particularly, these productions and their makers illustrate the activist spirit of the documentary film practices taking root in Pakistan, with a distinct focus on social and political 'accountability', legal reforms, and law enforcement that would ensure justice and security for women, and protect their rights as human rights.[101]

Beginning with *Stove Burning: Neither Coal Nor Ashes* (*Na koella bhye na raakh*) (1993) and *Burnt Victims: Scars on the Society* (2002), we get a chilling insight into the patriarchal power structures and mindsets that invoke and justify the victimization of women, domestic violence, even murder, with impunity. By documenting and showing the plight of actual female victims of stove-blasts and acid-attacks, as activist and rights organizations both *Simorgh* and the AGHS Legal Aid Cell have given the subjects of their films a rare voice and chance to exhibit their predicament, highlighting the dangers and cruelty meted out to women in a society and legal system that offers them little protection, and almost no justice. Images of ghost-like disfigured and badly burnt women are testimonies of ruined lives with a bleak future and poor ability to lead independent lives, while ineffective legal directives, and state indifference to the widespread menace of burning, defacing, and murdering women for revenge, monetary gains, or as acts of sheer hatred continue to act as facilitators for such crimes. On the other hand, the wide international success of Sharmeen Obaid-Chinoy's Oscar-winning film, *Saving Face* (2011), and the subsequent Anti-Acid Campaign launched by the film team, have not only been instrumental in bringing the brutal crime of acid-attacks on women to centre-stage prominence, both in Pakistan as well as internationally, but also stresses the legislative and pedagogical value of documentary cinema as a cross-cultural tool in the service of consciousness-raising, justice, and social change.

Shame: A Tale of Karo kari (2005) makes a valuable contribution in tracing not only the roots and practice of honour-killings, but also in holding the state accountable as the final authority in promulgating and expediting adequate laws, and protecting its citizens. As a filmic exposé of problematic legislative lacunae, tribal power, and government apathy that tends to aid brutal murders to be committed with impunity in the name of perceived 'honour', the film holds a historical and legislative significance as it pieces together the many complex and urgent socio-legal factors that need to be addressed by society and the state. In presenting the many aspects relating to the crime and issue of honour-killing, the documentary serves its activist intent as it brings together and exposes the key underlying factors of economic gain, cultural and tribal power structures, failure of state laws and institutions, state complicity with the tribal and feudal system, judicial and state gender-biases, and the victimization of women in particular on the pretext of 'honour' and morality that instigate such murders. In doing so, the film plays a deliberative and legislative role by identifying areas where changes in laws and law-enforcement mechanisms need to be revised and applied.[102]

It may be mentioned here that Sharmeen-Obaid Chinoy's documentary film, *A Girl in the River: The Price of Forgiveness* (2015) garnered tremendous attention, both at home and worldwide, for the crime of honour-killing. Winning in the Best Documentary (Short Subject) category at the 88th Academy Awards held in February 2016 in the US, the film renewed focus on honour killings with Pakistani Prime, Mian Minister Nawaz Sharif, declaring his government's resolve to bring in appropriate legal measures to contain the practice.[103]

Compressing a tribal woman's struggle against all odds into 90 minutes, we see Mohammad Naqvi's documentary *Shame* (2006) play an important archival role by documenting the timeframe and sequence of Mukhtaran Mai's gang-rape case over a period of five years. Naqvi's biographical approach, compilation of media footage and stills, and documentation of the sequence of key events surrounding Mai's case and the developing story carefully pieces together the transformation of an unknown woman into an internationally acclaimed rights activist, and the obscure village of Meerwala into a hub of social welfare activity. As opposed to the many sensationalizing print media stories that have abounded in both the local and international media about the Meerwala gang-rape case, *Shame* brings to life the voices and sights of actual victims, and the locales, courthouses, and the changing landscape as developments such as new schools and social welfare activities begin to emerge. In doing so, Naqvi's observational and participatory documentation acquires the activist value of the 'committed documentary' that is positioned to seek accountability and justice for its subject.[104] As *Shame* acquires its own archival significance in a case that remains unresolved, it also plays a deliberative and judicial role in highlighting not only the brutality of tribal customs and practices, but equally the gender-biases prevalent in the state law-enforcement machinery, drawing attention to the dangers, limitations, and hurdles that prevail and need to be addressed.[105] The film can be seen as a critical cultural-judicial study of the Pakistani tribal legal system versus the state criminal justice system in the Meerwala gang-rape case as it draws attention to the wider issue of marginalization of women's rights and their oppression.

Similarly, the filmic body of work being produced by Samar Minallah's Ethnomedia & Development today stands as a strong and significant ally in pushing for social change, and legislative reforms. Minallah's film entitled *Swara: A Bridge Over Troubled Waters* (2003) addresses the oppressive tribal custom of *Swara* whereby females and minor girls are given away as compensation through forced marriages to settle disputes and avenge murders. As a documentary film that actually aided in the criminalization of such customs,[106] *Swara* testifies to the

Women, Violence, and Human Rights 171

utility of documentary cinema in the service of human rights and social change.[107]

Minallah's activist filmmaking style that focuses on case studies and testimonies of victims of tribal practices embodies a cultural sensitivity to the regional conservative environment, its customs, traditions, and socio-political landscape. As a *Pakhtun* woman conversant in the regional languages, and the socio-cultural nuances and constraints of the people and culture she investigates, as an 'insider' Minallah has been successful in encouraging her subjects, particularly women, to confide and open up about controversial and personal issues in a most conservative society.[108] Today, Minallah's films and her organization stand as significant human rights advocacy tools and educational forum that continue to address and investigate crucial socio-cultural issues with an emphasis on social change and reform.

Together, these documentary films, filmmakers, organizations, and collaborations represent women's gender-violence issues, and the abuse and violation of their human rights both as individuals and as Pakistani citizens, while the contextual analysis also situates their makers' own political, personal, historical, social, cultural, and institutional positioning as activists in the process for change.[109] In addition to independent filmmakers and collaborations between rights and activist organizations in the preceding chapters, films in this chapter illustrate that production of issue-oriented films from non-governmental organizations, as well as the emergence of new documentary filmmaking organizations, such as Ethnomedia & Development, with a focus on advocacy and consciousness-raising continue to add to a committed 'Cinema of Accountability' category in Pakistan, as identified in this study. Collectively, these films and their makers call attention to the pressing need for accountability from the government, policy makers, law-enforcement bodies, the judicial system, and society for reforms and legislative measures to contain the horrific violence and indignities suffered by women on the pretext of culture, tribal customs, and so-called 'honour'.

Serving as visual testimony to the ruthless forms of violence committed against women with impunity, these films remain valuable in upholding and fulfilling the activist intent of documentary film to a) record, reveal or preserve; b) to persuade or promote; c) to analyse or interrogate; and d) express the urgent need for checking and penalizing negative and violent patriarchal and tribal mindsets and cultural practices in the ill-treatment of women.[110]

Film discussions in this chapter demonstrate that Western conceptualizations and terminology of 'feminist' are not wholly applicable to the Pakistani situation, as stated in Chapter 1 (endnote 20) of this book. This is primarily so because of Pakistani women's distinctly unique blend of socio-cultural, historical, political, religious, and tribal backgrounds that is specific to them and their national identity and realities. These complex factors cannot be overlooked if a meaningful contextual analysis of Pakistani women's oppressions, marginalization, and victimization through laws, cultural practices, and subjugation in a patriarchal system are to be conducted. Pakistani women's rights and issues primarily remain human rights issues till such time they are granted and ensured equal status, rights, and protection as individuals and citizens under the state laws. In fact, it is near impossible to contain and evaluate the representation of widespread brutal violence depicted in films in this chapter in particular within the diverse or neat divisions and frameworks of Western feminist film studies, and feminism.[111] Hence, these Pakistan-specific issues, films, and filmmakers necessitate contextual analyses that situate them within their own particular socio-cultural, political, and historical ground realities, as well as the contributing factors of economic contradictions, and gender-specific constraints that are also dictated by class, and influenced by patriarchal notions of morality.[112]

Discussions in this chapter emphasize the invaluably crucial and activist utility of documentary cinema to continue to identify, document, and highlight pressing issues of violence against women and violation of gender and human rights for debate, consciousness-raising, and social change in countries like Pakistan – as indeed they do for building cross-cultural and cross-class communication for solidarity, and encouraging activist alliances that the contextual reading of films in this book illustrates.

Correspondingly, the use of talking heads as a strategy to forge a direct subject–viewer connection,[113] and autobiographical accounts of ordinary people that offer counter-historical and anti-patriarchal versions of the same events, render these films as significant archival records that seek accountability for their human rights violation.[114] As well, we see and experience the common beliefs and convictions for justice held by both the filmmakers, and the subjects and victims they empower to speak out.[115] Together, the filmmakers and their subjects give the viewer not only an insight into the gender-specific predicaments faced by the subjects, and potentially by women in general, they also invoke action for justice, and accountability for such crimes and maltreatment, not only in Pakistan but also in the broader sense of gender/women's rights, and protection from violence globally.

Notes

1 Mahnaz Afkhami, 'Gender Apartheid, Cultural Relativism, and Women's Human Rights in Muslim Societies', in Marjorie Agosin (ed.), *Women, Gender, and Human Rights: A Global Perspective*, Rutgers University Press, USA, 2001 p. 234.
2 Abbas Jalbani, 'A Return to Tribalism?', *Dawn Weekly Review,* September 12–18, 2002, p. 7.
3 Ardeshir Cowasjee, 'Injustice to Women', *The Daily Dawn*, Pakistan, February 5, 2004. Accessed at: http://www.dawn.com on February 5, 2011.
4 For details see Shahla Zia, and Farzana Bari, 'Women in Non-Government Organizations', *Baseline Report on Women's Participation in Political and Public Life in Pakistan.* Project of International Women's Rights Action Watch – Asia Pacific. Published by *Aurat* Publications and Information Service Foundation, Islamabad, Pakistan, 1999, p. 11.
5 According to the *State of Human Rights in 2008 Report* prepared by the Human Rights Commission of Pakistan (HRCP) at least 1,210 women were killed for various reasons in Pakistan, including at least 612 killed for honour; there were 808 sexual harassment cases of which 350 were rape cases, 445 gang-rape cases and 13 cases of stripping. At least 221 victims were minors. *State of Human Rights in 2008 Report.* 'Women', Human Rights Commission of Pakistan, Maktaba Jadeed Press,

Lahore, Pakistan, p. 115. Similarly, a monitoring exercise conducted by the Lahore-based law firm AGHS Legal Aid Cell shows that from April to June in 2009, 122 cases of women being burnt were reported in the city of Lahore alone. Of them, 21 women had acid burns while the rest were injured by direct exposure to flames. Of these, 40 victims died. *The Daily Dawn*, 'Violence Against Women Unchecked', July 4, 2009. Accessed at: http://www.dawn.com/news/879454/violence-against-women-unchecked on April 2, 2015.

6   For 2014 data on violence against women in Pakistan, see 'Rights of the Disadvantaged: Women', *State of Human Rights in 2014*, Human Rights Commission of Pakistan. U. B. Printers, Lahore, Pakistan, 2014, p. 201. Accessed at: http://hrcp-web.org/hrcpweb/data/ar14c/5-1 women - 2014.pdf on April 18, 2015.

For detailed discussion on factors that can hinder reporting of cases of violence against women in Pakistan, see 'The State Response to Violence Against Women'. *Crime or Custom?: Violence Against Women in Pakistan*, Human Rights Watch World Report, New York, August 1999, p. 33. Accessed at: http://www.hrw.org/reports/1999/pakistan/ on April 2, 2015.

7   The Human Rights Commission of Pakistan (HRCP) 2010 report released in April 2011 states that at least 1,790 women were murdered in 2010 as a result of honour-killings and other forms of violence. Of these, 791 women were killed in incidents of so-called honour killing or *karo kari*, and the killers were often related to the victim. According to statistics provided by the police departments in the four provinces, cases of rape of 2,903 women, nearly eight women a day, were reported to the police. These included at least 51 cases of gang-rape. These figures were believed to be only a fraction of the actual problem as cases are often not reported or are hushed up. *State of Human Rights in 2010*,, 'Violence Against Women', Human Rights Commission of Pakistan, Maktaba Jadeed Press, Lahore, Pakistan, 2010, pp. 206–7.

8   *The Daily Dawn Online*, 'Over 11,000 Cases of Violence Against Women Registered Since 2009', February 21, 2011. Accessed at: http://www.dawn.com/news/607746/over-11000-cases-of-violence-against-women-registered-since-2009 on January 15, 2016.

9   Given the alarming rise in violence-related cases, up to nine women's police stations, staffed by women police officers, have also been established in the cities of Karachi, Larkana, Hyderabad, Peshawar, Abbottabad, Islamabad, Lahore, Rawalpindi, and Faisalabad. Ibid. Accessed at: http://www.dawn.com/news/607746/over-11000-cases-of-violence-against-women-registered-since-2009 on January 15, 2016.

10 For discussion of Pakistani family laws that address and affect women's rights, see Rubya Mehdi, *The Islamization of the Law in Pakistan*, Routledge Library Edition: Politics of Islam, UK, 2013.

For the AGHS Legal Aid Cell 2009–2010 statistical figures of violence against women in Pakistan, see Huma Patrick, 'Cases of Violence Against Women in Pakistan: November 2009–October 2010', *AGHS Legal Aid Cell Publications*, Lahore, Pakistan, 2011.

11 Nancy C. M. Hartsock, 'The Nature of a Standpoint', *The Feminist Standpoint Revisited and Other Essays*, Westview Press, Boulder, CO, 1998, p. 107.

12 Chuck Kleinhans, 'Forms, Politics, Makers and Contexts: Basic Issues for a Theory of Radical Political Documentary', in Thomas Waugh (ed.), *"Show Us Life": Toward a History and Aesthetics of Committed Documentary*, The Scarecrow Press, Inc. Metuchen, NJ and London, 1984, p. 320.

13 *Stove Burning: Neither Coal Nor Ashes* (Punjabi title: *Na koella bhye na raakh*), 1993 (28 min.). Produced by Nadia Shah for *Simorgh* Productions, Pakistan. (Urdu/Punjabi).

14 A. A. Hayat. *Women: Victims of Social Evil*, Pakistan Institute of Security Management, Press Corporation of Pakistan, 2002, pp. 32–3.

15 For the Burn Units situation in the Punjab province, see 'Only Four Burn Units in Punjab Fully Functional', *The Daily Dawn* e-paper *'Metro Lahore'* section May 12, 2015. Accessed at: http://www.dawn.com/news/1181484 on January 15, 2016.

16 Since the making of *Stove Burning* in 1993, till 2011 there was only one other burn unit under installation in Jinnah Hospital in Lahore, Punjab, but the progress was slow because of lack of funds and the amount of expenditure involved in the establishment of such units. Personal communication with Ms Huma Patrick, Coordinator AGHS Legal Aid Cell Burn Unit and Monitoring Cell, Lahore, Pakistan, June 28, 2011.

For the situation in Lahore, also see: Iqtidar Gilani, 'Only Two Burn Units Functional in City', *The Daily Nation* September 13, 2012. Accessed at: http://nation.com.pk/lahore/13-Sep-2012/only-two-burn-units-functional-in-city on April 2, 2015.

The situation remains grim for burn patients as even major government hospitals in the capital city of Islamabad, and its twin city of Rawalpindi, lack adequate facilities. For details see: Muhammad Qasim, 'Pakistan Lacks Burn Treatment Facilities', *The News International*, April 1, 2014.

17 Bill Nichols, 'What Are Documentaries About?', *Introduction to Documentary*, Indiana University Press, Bloomington, IN and Indianapolis, IN, 2001, p. 70.

18 *Burnt Victims: Scars on the Society*, Ahmar Rehman, 2002. (20 min. 38 sec.) AGHS Legal Aid Cell in collaboration with Katholische Frauea Deutchland, Pakistan (Urdu/Punjabi/English/English sub-titles).

19 According to a report by the UN Women, while acid-attacks are most prevalent in Bangladesh, Cambodia, India, and Pakistan, they have also been reported in Afghanistan and in parts of Africa and Europe. In 2002, Bangladesh became the first and only country that instituted a law to address acid production business. In 2002 the Bangladesh government passed the Acid Crime Prevention Act 2002 and Acid Control Act 2002 that regulate the import and sale of acid in open markets, and treat acid-attacks as a serious punishable crime. 'Acid Attacks', *UN Women: United Nations Entity for Gender Equality and the Empowerment of Women*. Accessed at: http://www.endvawnow.org/en/articles/607-acid-attacks.html on April 2, 2015.

It is encouraging that, due to the unwavering struggle and pressure by women's rights activists and women parliamentarians, an Acid Control and Acid Crime Prevention Bill, 2010 was presented and passed in the National Assembly of Pakistan on May 10, 2011. The Bill sought to deter incidents of acid-attacks on women, and to compensate and rehabilitate victims. The Bill recommended the punishment of either life-imprisonment or imprisonment for a minimum of 14 years, besides a minimum fine of Rupees 1 million. *The Daily Times*, 'NA Passes Bill to Prevent Acid Attacks Against Women', May 11, 2011. Lahore, Pakistan. Accessed at: http://archives.dailytimes.com.pk/main/11-May-2011/na-passes-bill-to-prevent-acid-attacks-against-women on January 15, 2016.

20 The Pakistani Women's Human Rights Organization (PWHRO) describes the life-altering physical and psychological effects of acid-attacks on survivors: 'Acid burns through eyes, skin tissue, and bone. Usually, the victims are left blind and with permanent scar tissue. Their bones are often fused together – jawbones sealed tight, chins locked to chests, hands left permanently contorted in the position they held as they tried to deflect the splash. The psychological scars are even worse. Depression, anxiety and shame would be part of the emotional aftermath of any scarring injury. Victims of acid-attacks are also often ostracized by their communities and even held responsible for incurring the attack they suffered.' For case studies of acid-attacks see: 'Recent Victims of Inhuman Attacks with Acid', *Pakistani Women's Human Rights Organization* (PWHRO). Accessed at: http://pakistaniwomen.org/acid_pwhro.html on April 2, 2015.

21 According to a survey conducted by a Pakistani English newspaper, *The Daily Times*, there were around 1,000 chemical and acid dealers running their business without any checks on sale and purchase of acid. A bottle of acid could be bought for domestic use by anyone as the district administration failed to enforce any checks on the sale of the item. Nadia Usman, 'Acid Accessibility Behind Increase in Burn Cases', *The Daily Times*. April 6, 2008. Lahore, Pakistan. Accessed at: http://archives.

dailytimes.com.pk/national/06-Apr-2008/acid-accessibility-behind-increase-in-burn-cases on January 15, 2016.

22 Nichols, 'What Are Documentaries About?', p. 70.

23 For further details see: *Human Rights Watch*. 'Pakistan: Expedite Domestic Violence Legislation'. Accessed at: http://www.hrw.org/en/news/2010/01/11/pakistan-expedite-domestic-violence-legislation on April 2, 2015.

24 For details of the Acid Control and Burn Crime Prevention Act 2010 see: Myra Imran, 'First Major Step Towards Legislation Against Burn Crimes: Bill Titled "Acid Control and Burn Crime Prevention Act 2010" Presented to the Ministry', *The News International*, August 12, 2010, Lahore, Pakistan.

Similarly, a Prevention of Anti-Women Practices (Criminal Law Amendment) Bill was passed by the National Assembly of Pakistan on November 15, 2011, and approved by the Senate to become law in December 2011. Sumera Khan, 'Women-specific Bills Passed: Fourteen Year Jail Term for Acid-Throwers', *Express Tribune*, Islamabad, Pakistan. Accessed at: http://tribune.com.pk/story/305482/unanimous-vote-senate-passes-women-protection-anti-acid-throwing-bills/ on April 2, 2015.

25 According to the Pakistani Women's Human Rights Organization (PWHRO), Shahnaz Bokhari, chief coordinator and clinical psychologist at the Progressive Women's Association (PWA) in Rawalpindi, states that PWA has counted 8,000 victims burned by acid as well as kerosene and stoves since 1994 just from the cities of Rawalpindi, Islamabad, and a 200-mile radius, and not Pakistan as a whole. The *Aurat* Foundation has documented 53 cases of acid-attacks in 2009 in Pakistan (42 in Punjab; 9 in Sindh; 1 in NWFP; 0 in Balochistan; 1 in Islamabad). The organization also points out that the scenario in 2010 seemed to be no better, while women's activists believe that only 30 per cent of acid-attack cases are reported. *Pakistani Women's Human Rights Organization* (PWHRO). 'Recent Victims of Inhuman Attacks with Acid'. Accessed at: http://pakistaniwomen.org/acid_pwhro.html on April 2, 2015.

26 In one decade alone, the PWA has uncovered over 5,675 stove-death victims as part of the 16,000 cases they have documented of violence against women. The data is available at: http://womensenews.org/story/21-leaders-the-21st-century/031223/seven-who-stretch-their-reach-across-cultures. Accessed on January 17, 2016.

27 Ibid. Accessed on January 17, 2016.

The PWA is now available on Facebook: https://web.facebook.com/Progressive-Womens-Association-111315255588748/info?tab=page_info. Accessed on January 17, 2016. There does not seem to be a direct PWA website any longer. This is most probably because of security reasons for both those working there and the victims. For example see this site: http://womensenews.org/story/domestic-violence/021027/pakistans-fiery-shame-women-die-stove-deaths.

28 The Acid Survivors Foundation (ASF) in Pakistan is a branch of the Acid Survivors Trust International (ASTI), a UK-based charity that supports a network of partners who provide surgical treatment and rehabilitation to around 1,000 survivors every year. Acid Survivor's Foundation of Pakistan. Accessed at: http://acidsurvivorspakistan.org/about on April 2, 2015.

29 Data available from the AGHS Legal Aid Cell reveals that 68 women were burnt in the city of Lahore in the first three months of 2009. A statement issued by the cell said eight women were burnt in acid attacks, while 60 were set ablaze. It said the figures were probably a tip of the iceberg, as 49 cases in Lahore alone were reported in the local press, while most went unreported for various reasons. *The Daily Times*. '68 Women Burnt in City in 3 Months', April 15, 2009. Accessed at: http://archives.dailytimes.com.pk/lahore/15-Apr-2009/68-women-burnt-in-city-in-3-months on January 15, 2016.

30 For further details and figures see Yumna Rafi, 'An Unforgiving Scar', *The Daily Dawn*. March 26, 2015. Accessed at: http://www.dawn.com/news/1153480/unforgiving-scar-2014-a-year-of-horrific-acid-attacks on April 2, 2015.

31   *Saving Face*, Sharmeen Obaid-Chinoy (with Daniel Junge), 2011 (52 min), Naked Edge Films (English/English sub-titles/Urdu).
32   For Sharmeen Obaid-Chinoy's list of awards see: http://sharmeenobaidfilms.com/awards/. Accessed on January 17, 2016.
33   Acid Survivors Trust International (ASTI). Accessed at: http://www.acidviolence.org/index.php/news/Saving-Face-trailer-and-the-Press-Release/ on April 2, 2015.
34   The Bill legislates a punishment of 14 years to life imprisonment for crimes involving the disfiguring of human organ/body by a corrosive substance. *The News International*, 'President Gives Assent to Bills on Crimes Against Women', December 22, 2011.
35   Saira Agha, 'Pakistani Women are Brave and Fearless', *The Daily Times*, March 18, 2012. Accessed at: http://archives.dailytimes.com.pk/infotainment/18-Mar-2012/pakistani-women-are-brave-and-fearless on January 15, 2016.
36   *Business Recorder*. 'Sharmeen Chinoy Launches Anti-Acid Campaign', February 28, 2012. Accessed at: http://www.brecorder.com/top-news/1-front-top-news/47514-sharmeen-chinoy-launches-anti-acid-campaign.html on April 2, 2015.

   For details of the Anti-Acid campaign visit Project SAAVE at: http://projectsaave.org/ Accessed on April 2, 2015.
37   *Dawn.com*. 'President Confers Civil Awards on 67: Top National Award for Nusrat Bhutto, Salman Taseer', March 24, 2012. Accessed at: http://dawn.com/2012/03/24/president-confers-civil-awards-on-67-top-national-award-for-nusrat-bhutto-salman-taseer/ on April 2, 2015.

   Pakistan Day is commemorated each year on March 23.
38   In the Pakistani context, honour and shame assume the terms of *ghairat* (honour/pride) and *izzat* (respect/honour), and *sharm* (shame). However, the tribal concepts of punishment for related violations of perceived honour remain similar in all tribal and feudal societies. A. A. Hayat elaborates on the gender-specificity of these terms: '*Ghairat* is masculine. A man must be able to hold up his head with pride and stand tall in public. If his pride is compromised in any way realistically or imagined, it dishonours him. To revive his honour and live with pride in his society he must kill or avenge the insult. Shame is feminine. If a woman is shamed it makes her bow her head and hide her face due to which her public reputation and social position is compromised, and therefore she must be killed.' In the case of women, who are treated as material wealth in such societies and whose worth depends on their 'chastity', Hayat points out that 'Rape or murder committed is not considered to be the actual crime, it is the loss of chastity which is considered to be central to the issue. This code of tribal honour transcends the laws of the land and its influence proves even stronger than that of religion.' A. A. Hayat 'Honour-Killings', *Women: Victims of Social Evil*, Pakistan Institute of Security Management, Press Corporation of Pakistan, 2002, p. 88.
39   The word *Jirga* (also known as *Loya Jirga*) has its roots in the Turkish word meaning 'circle'. In many tribal societies even now, these tribal councils sit in a circle to decide matters. Rahimullah Yusufzai, 'Circled in Controversy', *Newsline Monthly Magazine*, Karachi, Pakistan. August, 2002.
40   Reports submitted to the United Nations Commission on Human Rights show that honour-killings are also committed in Bangladesh, Great Britain, Brazil, Ecuador, Egypt, India, Israel, Italy, Jordan, Pakistan, Morocco, Sweden, Turkey, and Uganda. Even though Iraq, Iran, and Afghanistan have not submitted reports to the UN in the past, the practice of honour-killings has been reported in all three countries. 'Marital Law & Customary Practices: "Honour-Killings"', *Bayan Bi-Annual Socio-Legal Journal*, Vol. IV, September 2005, *Simorgh* Women's Resource and Publication Centre, Lahore, Pakistan, p. 92.

   For detailed discussion on violence against women on the pretext of 'honour', see *Amnesty International*: 'Pakistan: Violence Against Women in the Name of Honour', London, 1999.

For examples of first-hand accounts of honour-killings in the UK, and the reasons behind them as narrated by men who committed these acts, see Ayse Onal. *Honour Killing: Stories of Men Who Killed*, Saqi Books, London, San Francisco, CA, Beirut, Lebanon, 2008.

41 Hayat, 'Honour-Killings', p. 91.
42 In 2008, a brutally shocking incident of a tribal group-murder of women came to light in Pakistan's Balochistan province. The HRCP reports: 'Perhaps the most extreme example of violence in the name of tradition was witnessed in Balochistan, in August, when five women were shot and killed for wanting to marry of their own choice. The women, three of whom were teenagers, belonged to the Baba Kot village in the remote district of Jafferabad. The three young girls, aged between 16 and 18, had dared to defy tribal norms in wanting to marry of their own choice and reject the tribal elders' marriage commands. They were kidnapped and arrangements made to kill them. Two elder female relatives tried to intervene and they too were shot along with the younger 'offenders'. All five of them were then thrown in a ditch and covered with mud. Some NGOs claimed that at least some of the women were alive when they were buried. The decision to murder the women was made and its enforcement overseen by village elders, the head of whom was said to be the brother of a provincial minister. When Senator Yasmin Shah raised the issue in parliament a month after the incident, saying that no action had been taken against the perpetrators, it was followed by an outrageous reaction from two senators from the Balochistan province. Senator Israrullah Zehri defended the gruesome deed adding that it was part of "our tribal custom" and that "these are centuries-old traditions and I will continue to defend them"'. *State of Human Rights in 2008*, 'Violence Against Women: The Hold of Tradition', Human Rights Commission of Pakistan Maktaba Jadeed Press, Lahore, Pakistan, p. 120.

For further details on this case of tribal group-murder see: Noor Akbar Khalil, 'Honour Killing in Pakistan: The Case of 5 Women Buried Alive', *Human Dignity and Humiliation Studies*, University of Gothenburg Sweden, 2010. Accessed at: http://www.humiliationstudies.org/whoweare/coreteamlong.php - akbar on April 2, 2015.

43 Yasmeen Hassan, *The Haven Becomes Hell: A Study of Domestic Violence in Pakistan*, Special Bulletin August 1995. Published by *Shirkat Gah*, WLUML Coordination Office Asia, Lahore, Pakistan, p. 22.
44 Ibid., p. 22.
45 Hayat, 'Honour-Killings', p. 90.

For a tribal perspective on the concept of 'blackened face' that corresponds to the concept of loss of honour, and 'shame', see Raphael Patai, 'The Bedouin Ethos and Modern Arab Society', *The Arab Mind*, Charles Scribner's Sons, New York, 1983, p. 101.

46 In the Sindh province of Pakistan the practice of honour-killing is known as *karo kari*; in the Balochistan province as *siya-kari*; in Punjab by the name of *kala-kali*; in the Khyber Pakhtunkhwa (former North West Frontier Province) as *tora-tora*. All the terms denote 'black' as indicative of the dark and dishonourable nature of the crime for which the offenders are punished. Rashida Patel, 'The Menace of Honour Killing', *Gender Equality and Women's Empowerment in Pakistan*, Oxford University Press, Karachi, Pakistan, 2010, pp. 73–4.
47 *Amnesty International*. 'Pakistan: Honour Killings of Girls and Women: Fake Honour Killings'. Accessed at: http://www.academia.edu/9872947/Honour_killings_of_girls_and_women on January 14, 2016.
48 For detailed discussion on the workings of the *jirga* system see Hassan M. Yousufzai and Ali Gohar, 'The Context of Jirga', *Towards Understanding Pukhtoon Jirga*, Just Peace International Publishers, Peshawar, Pakistan, 2005, p. 23; and Ali Wardak, 'Concept and Definition of Jirga', *Jirga – A Traditional Mechanism of Conflict Resolution in Afghanistan*, University of Glamorgan, UK, 2003, p. 3.

49 *Shame: A Tale of Karo Kari*, Sharjil Baloch and Iftikhar Ahmed, 2005 (33 min.), 2005, *Dastak* Society for Communications (Urdu/Seraiki/English/English sub-titles).

Sharjil Baloch has been making films as a freelance director since 2011, and also works as an actor and writer. He was associated with the *Dastak* Society for Communication as a film director. Dr Iftikhar Ahmad is a social scientist. *Shame: A Tale of Karo Kari*, his first film venture with Sharjil Baloch, was screened at the 6th International Karafilm Festival in Karachi, Pakistan, in 2006. 6th International Kara Film Festival, 2006. Accessed at: http://www.karafilmfest.com/KaraFilm2006/films_documentaries_02.htm on April 2, 2015.

Sharjil Baloch works as a video producer with the BBC Urdu Service in Karachi, Pakistan. His work can be viewed at Culture Unplugged: http://www.cultureunplugged.com/storyteller/Sharjil Baloch - /myFilms Accessed on April 2, 2015.

Given the rising figures of *karo kari* in the Sindh province, the Sindh Police initiated setting up helplines and anti-*karo kari* cells in four districts of the province: Sukkur, Ghotki, Khairpur, and Naushero Feroz. Human Rights Commission of Pakistan. Accessed at: http://www.hrcp-web.org on June 26, 2010.

50 'Karachi: British Council's Drive Against Honour Killing.' *The Daily Dawn*, Karachi. June 10, 2006. Accessed at: http://www.dawn.com/news/196250/karachi-british-council-s-drive-against-honour-killings on March 16, 2016.

51 For a high profile case of *karo kari* in which an accused woman, Haleema Bhutto, and her family have been seeking government help to provide them protection and justice, and the state's apathy to address their problem, see Mahtab Bashir, 'Karo Kari Victim Announces Hunger Strike Unto Death', *The Daily Times*. June 3, 2011. Accessed at: http://archives.dailytimes.com.pk/islamabad/03-Jun-2011/karo-kari-victim-announces-hunger-strike-unto-death on January 15, 2016.

In a rare development, after camping outside the National Press Club, Islamabad, for 15 months Haleema Bhutto's ordeal was taken up as a *suo moto* case by the Supreme Court of Pakistan and she was given protection, while the tribal *jirga* members who had ordered her honour-killing were to be arrested and put on trial. Accessed at: http://www.youtube.com/watch?v=D_zg6n-3CEs on November 22, 2011.

52 For details on the Sindh High Court ruling see *IRIN*, 'Pakistan: Focus on Court Decision Banning Jirga Trials', April 26, 2004. Accessed at: http://news.irinnews.org/Report.aspx?ReportID=24213 on April 2, 2015.

53 For details of the Criminal Law Amendment Act 2004 see: Ministry of Women Development, Government of Pakistan, 'Acts and Regulation on Women Issues in Pakistan'. Accessed at: http://www.niew.gov.my/contents/PDF/acts%20&%20regulations/Pakistan/GOVERNMENT_OF_PAKISTAN.pdf on May 17, 2011.

54 This poem by the late Faiz Ahmed Faiz became a rallying point for rights and political activists since it was first sung by the late Iqbal Bano to a packed and emotionally charged auditorium at the Alhamra Hall in Lahore in 1988 while General Zia-ul-Haq was still in power. Zia's death in a plane crash the same year rendered this poem a symbol of struggle and victory against oppressive regimes, laws, and practices, and is sung widely at crucial activist junctures and events in Pakistan.

55 For further details see: *UN Entity for Gender Equality and the Empowerment of Women*: 'Facts and Figures on Violence Against Women: Honour Killings'. Accessed at: http://www.unifem.org/gender_issues/violence_against_women/facts_figures.php?page=4 on June 15, 2011, p. 4.

According to an *Aurat* Foundation report, 3,000 people have been killed for 'honour' since 2008. *Dawn.com*. 'Murder for 'Honour': Over 3,000 Victims in Seven Years', November 17, 2014. Accessed at: http://www.dawn.com/news/1145062/murder-for-honour-over-3000-victims-in-seven-years on April 2, 2015.

The *Human Rights Commission of Pakistan 2013* report states that in 2013, 869 women were murdered as a result of honour-killings, and 359 were killed in cases of *karo kari. State of Human Rights in 2013 Report*. 'Honour Crimes', Human Rights Commission of Pakistan Publication, Lahore, Pakistan, p. 180.

56 Nichols, 'What Are Documentaries About?' p. 70.

57 Mohammad Naqvi is an independent Pakistani/Canadian filmmaker, writer, producer, and director. Among the many awards and honours he has received are: Television Academy Honor, Academy of Television Arts and Sciences (Special Emmy group) 2008; Development In Literacy Honoree 2007, 2009; San Diego International Film Festival, Best Documentary 2008. For further details on Naqvi's productions and work visit: http://www.linkedin.com/pub/mohammed-naqvi/6/773/b98 Accessed on April 2, 2015.

For details of Mohammad Naqvi's current productions and projects visit: http://monaqvi.com. Accessed on January 19, 2016.

58 *Shame*, 2006, Mohammad Ali Naqvi (96 min.), Pakistan/USA, Showtime in Association with Mü Nân Pictures. Showtime Networks, Inc. (Seraiki/Urdu/English subtitles).

Shame has won several international documentary film awards such as the Humanitarian Award – Chicago International Documentary Film Festival; Women in Leadership Award – Full Frame Documentary Festival; American Film Institute (AFI) Project 20–20 Participant. *Shame* has been shown at various international film festivals. These include: Toronto International Film Festival 2006, World Premier; American Film Institute Film Festival 2006; International Documentary Film Festival of Amsterdam 2006 (IDFA); Dubai International Film Festival 2006; Tribeca Film Festival 2007: and many others around the world. Accessed at Mohammad Naqvi: http://www.myspace.com/shamefilm on June 4, 2011.

59 It is pertinent to mention here that within South Asian societies, even the non-tribal ones, there is a strong prevalence of the caste system quite independent of religion, culture, and economic class. Sociologist Chris Smaje points out that the *jati* (caste system) is a dominant force, not only in the tribal communities, but generally also, and it is around this social structure and caste differences that marriages and socialization are based and class distinctions made. He elaborates that people who marry and procreate among themselves pass on their particular *jati* identification to their offspring, so that the *jati* can be regarded as a closed, ascriptive social group. Smaje's analysis of the caste system is also pertinent to present South Asian societies, and reflects on the inequalities inherent in the interaction between castes underlying the Meeerwala gang-rape case. Chris Smaje, 'Race, Caste and Hierarchy', *Natural Hierarchies: The Historical Sociology of Race and Caste*, Blackwell Publishers, Oxford, 2000, p. 12.

60 In the Meerwala case, a local journalist first reported the incident after which the international media picked it up. Widespread international publicity of the case, as well as pressure from Pakistani rights organizations and activists was instrumental in forcing the Pakistan government to take up Mukhtaran Mai's case, and seek a fair trial and judgement.

61 Mukhtaran Mai is also referred to as Mukhtar Mai elsewhere. The filmmaker refers to her as Mukhtaran Mai in the film.

Pakistani journalist Abbas Jalbani describes the tribal parallel justice system as one governed by the tribal/feudal lords, and an integral part of such societies that dominate the rural areas of the country where the majority of the population lives. Jalbani notes that 'in most of the decisions of these traditional courts women have to pay for the sins committed (or even not committed, as was the case with the Meerwala victim) by men'. Abbas Jalbani, 'A Return to Tribalism?', *The Dawn Weekly Review*. September 12–18, 2002, p. 1.

62 Saleem Sheikh, 'Shame in the Name of Justice', *The Daily News Weekly Magazine*, Lahore, Pakistan, July 16, 2002.

63 Discrepancies in knowing exact ages or dates of birth are common in the lower, uneducated, or peasant classes in tribal societies as births that do not take place at hospitals are not officially registered.

64 Mukhtaran Mai not only survived her ordeal, but also courageously spoke to the media (a rarity itself in Pakistan considering the nature of her ordeal and the stigma attached to a raped woman in an orthodox society) on how she thinks the lot of Pakistani women can be improved. In her first interview to the Pakistani media after her trial she said: 'Education is the key to awareness ... This is the most that parents in rural areas can offer their daughters, I still feel deprived of education. The Meerwala incident only strengthened my convictions on the significance of education. For it was educated urban women who supported my decision to take a firm stand in bringing the perpetrators to justice, while I was vilified by the illiterate village women who saw my decision as nothing more than the washing of dirty linen in public ... Women should start their struggle against injustice from their homes by resisting domestic violence. Their silence and tolerance encourages men to further suppress them. They should muster courage to resist the hand raised against them.' Nadeem Saeed, Interview excerpts from 'Life After the Verdict', *The Daily Dawn*, Lahore, Pakistan. December 9, 2002.

65 Mukhtar Mai, *In the Name of Honor: A Memoir*, with Marie-Therese Cuny. Translated by Linda Coverdale. Atria Books, New York, London, Toronto, Sydney, 2006, p. 31.

Mai's book was first published in French and translation rights were sold to Brazil, Czech Republic, Germany, Greece, India, Holland, Hungary, Indonesia, Israel, Italy, Egypt, Japan, Korea, Latin America, Portugal, Spain, Sweden, Taiwan, the US, Canada, and the UK. For details see: 'After Musharraf, it's Mukhtaran Mai's Book', *Rediff India Abroad*, October 12, 2006. Accessed at: http://www.rediff.com/news/2006/oct/12mai.htm on April 2, 2015.

66 BBC. 'Pakistan Rape-case Men Rearrested', March 18, 2005. Accessed at: http://news.bbc.co.uk/2/hi/south_asia/4361289.stm on April 2, 2015.

67 *BBC News*, 'Outrage at Musharraf Rape Remarks', September 16, 2005. Accessed at: http://news.bbc.co.uk/2/hi/south_asia/4251536.stm on April 2, 2015.

It is ironic that Mai's memoir, *In the Name of Honor: A Memoir*, was also published in 2006 in the US by the same publisher, Simon and Schuster, that published President Pervaiz Musharraf's biography, *In the Line of Fire*. Stop Honour Killings!, 'Musharraf's US Publisher to Bring Out Mukhtaran Mai Book'. Accessed at: http://www.stophonourkillings.com/?q=es/node/728 on June 18, 2011.

68 For details on the Mukhtar Mai Women's Welfare Organization (MMWWO) visit: http://www.mukhtarmai.org/ Accessed on April 2, 2015.

69 Among other honours and awards that Mukhtaran Mai has received over the years were an invitation to address an assembly at the UN Headquarters in New York in May, 2006.

In 2006, the Council of Europe awarded Mukhtaran Mai the North South Prize 2006. Accessed at: http://wn.com/North-South_Prize on June 4, 2011.

In 2010, the Laurentian University, Sudbury, Canada conferred an honorary doctorate degree on Mukhtaran Mai in recognition of her struggle for women's rights. *Geo Television Network*. 'Mukhtar Mai to Receive Honorary Doctorate Degree', June 11, 2010. Accessed at: http://www.geo.tv/6-11-2010/66495.htm on April 2, 2015.

70 Her memoir entitled *In the Name of Honor: A Memoir* was published in New York in 2006. According to the *New York Times*, it became the number three bestseller in France and has been translated into twenty-three languages. For further details see: *Oslo Freedom Forum*. Accessed at: http://www.oslofreedomforum.com/speakers/mukhtar_mai on June 4, 2011.

71 President Pervaiz Musharraf of Pakistan and Mukhtaran Mai both shared the distinction of being listed among the 100 most influential people of the world by *Time*

magazine in 2006. While Musharraf was listed under the 'Leaders and Revolutionaries' category, Mai was honoured in the 'Heroes and Pioneers' list. *The Daily Times*, 'Musharraf, Mai on Time Magazine's 100 List', May 2, 2006. Accessed at: http://www.dawn.com/news/190210/musharraf-mukhtaran-on-time-100-list on January 15, 2016.

72 Nicholas Kristof, 'Mukhtar Mai's Case in Pakistan', *The New York Times*. March 2, 2009. Accessed at: http://kristof.blogs.nytimes.com/2009/03/02/mukhtar-mais-case-in-pakistan/ on April 2, 2015.

73 *BBC News South Asia*. 'Pakistan: Acquittals in Mukhtar Mai Gang Rape Case', April 21, 2011. Accessed at: http://www.bbc.co.uk/news/world-south-asia-13158001 on April 2, 2015.

74 Ibid.

75 *The Human Rights Commission of Pakistan 2002 Annual Report* concluded on the status of Pakistani women: 'Despite making up almost 51 percent of the population, women continue to face a discriminatory status within society. Most alarmingly, it was found that violence against them, in almost every form, was on the rise. A woman was raped every two hours somewhere in the country, while hundreds became victims of 'honour' killings and rape, domestic violence, burnings and murder. Perhaps the most distressing part of focusing on women's rights in Pakistan is the fact that many cases that are brought to the limelight, with media attention and involvement of non-governmental organizations (NGOs) at some stage peter out. They make the headlines for a few days – and then are forgotten. Other women suffer abuses in silence for years, die violent deaths and get buried in unmarked graves', *Human Rights Commission of Pakistan Annual Report*. Pakistan, 2002. Accessed at: http://hrcp-web.org/hrcpweb/ on April 27, 2011.

76 Personal communication with Ms Kishwar Naheed, September 20, 2002.

77 By April 2016, Mai's appeal filed in 2011, remained pending in the Supreme Court of Pakistan.

78 Personal email communication with Samar Minallah. June 22, 2015.

79 Samar Minallah has received both national and international recognition for her work for civil rights and support of disadvantaged groups, particularly women in Pakistan. Among the many awards she has received are: The UNICEF Child Rights Award 2005; Perdita Huston Activist for Human Rights Award 2007 for her film *Swara: A Bridge Over Troubled Waters* (2003); UNESCO Best Documentary Filmmaker Award 2007 for her film *The Silver Lining: HIV and AIDS* (2007) on HIV/AIDS and women in Pakistan; International Roberto Rossellini Award 2009 (Italy); Cannon Award 2009 at the International Film Festival (Italy); Center for Civic Education Pakistan Civic Courage Award 2010; and the Pakistan Women's Day Award 2011 for challenging patriarchal traditions through media documentaries. This award was given to her by the National Commission for the Status of Women (NCSW), Government of Pakistan. Personal communication with Samar Minallah.

For further details on Samar Minallah's work and projects visit: http://www.ethnomedia.pk/ Accessed on April 2, 2015.

80 Julia Lesage, 'The Political Aesthetics of the Feminist Documentary Film', in Patricia Erens (ed.), *Issues in Feminist Film Criticism*, Indiana University Press, Bloomington, IN and Indianapolis, IN, 1990, p. 224.

81 It may be mentioned here that although Pakistan ratified the *United Nations Convention on the Rights of the Child* in 1990, this ratification has had little or no bearing on children's rights in the country given government apathy in such matters, and tribal and socio-cultural traditions and practices that remain unchecked. *United Nations Treaty Collection: Convention on the Rights of the Child*. Accessed at: http://treaties.un.org/Pages/ViewDetails.aspx?src= TREATY&mtdsg_no=IV-11&chapter=4&lang=en on April 2, 2015.

182 *Women, Violence, and Human Rights*

Pakistan's ratification of the UN Convention on the Rights of the Child in 1990 prohibits child marriages. In addition, under the Muslim Family Law Ordinance 1961, a girl must have attained the age of 16 and a boy must have attained the age of 18, and both need to consent before the marriage can take place. Pakistani laws such as the Marriage Restraint Act 1929 and the Pakistan Penal Code (articles 310 & 338-E) also prohibit and criminalize the sale and underage marriage of girls. For further discussion see: Berti Stefano, *Rights of the Child in Pakistan, Report on the Implementation of the Convention on the Rights of the Child by Pakistan*, World Organization Against Torture, Geneva, Switzerland, 2003, p. 11. Accessed at: http://www.refworld.org/pdfid/46c190b40.pdf on January 17, 2016.

Society for the Protection of the Rights of the Child, *Child Marriage*. Accessed at: http://www.sparcpk.org/Other-Publications/CM.pdf on January 17, 2016.

Women Living Under Muslim Laws, *Child, Early and Forced Marriage: A Multi-Country Study*, December 2013, p. 32. Accessed at: http://www.wluml.org/resource/child-early-and-forced-marriage-multi-country-studyon January 17, 2016.

The Institute for Social Justice, *Child Marriages in Pakistan*, Accessed at: http://www.isj.org.pk/child-marriages-in-pakistan/ on January 17, 2016.

82 *Swara: A Bridge Over Troubled Waters*, Samar Minallah, 2003 (40 min.), *Ethnomedia & Development* for the *Mera Ghar* (My Home) Project of GTZ and the *Aurat Foundation* of Peshawar, Pakistan (Pushto/ Urdu/ English sub-titles).

Swara: A Bridge Over Troubled Waters has been aired in various districts and far flung areas of the Khyber Pakhtunkhwa Province to create discussion within civil society. It has also been shown at conferences and workshops, as well as aired on various Pakistani television channels such as the state-owned Pakistan Television, Peshawar, and PTV World, as well as independent channels such as Geo Television, and the ARY channel. This film has also been included in the Amnesty International New York archives because of the strong influence it has had in communication for social change.

Pakistani and international screenings of *Swara: A Bridge Over Troubled Waters* have included: The Regent Park Film Festival, Toronto 2003; South Asian Human Rights Film Festival, New York 2004; Sussex University, UK 2004; Pittsburgh University, USA 2004; Amnesty International USA On Campus Film Festival 2004; Syracuse University, USA 2004; Travelling Film South Asia, Columbia University, USA 2004; Mateela Film Festival, Pakistan 2004; South Asian Film Festival, Nepal 2003; Kara Film Festival, Karachi, Pakistan, 2003; The South Asian Film Education Society International Film Festival, Vancouver, Canada, 2013. Email correspondence with Samar Minallah, July 5, 2011.

83 Lesage, 'Political Aesthetics', p. 224.
84 In her study on *Swara*, Samar Minallah points out cases where a *jirga* gave a two-month-old girl in marriage to a one-year-old boy. Some girls are promised in marriage to men substantially older than them. Similarly, even unborn girls were promised as compensation. Ethnomedia & Development, 'Types of *Swara*', *Swara –The Human Shield: A Study on the Custom of SWARA in North West Frontier Province*, Ethnomedia Publications, Islamabad, Pakistan, 2006, p. 57.
85 Ibid., 'Introduction', p. 2.

Similarly, Muhammad Ali Baba Khel notes in his study entitled '*Swara*: Women as Property' that modes to practice *Swara* can vary due to geographical and cultural variations in different societies, for example in the various provinces and regions of Afghanistan and the tribal belts in Pakistan. For further details see Muhammad Ali Baba Khel, '*Swara* in Practice', *Swara: Women as Property*, *Aurat* Foundation Publications, Peshawar, Pakistan, 2003, p. 9.

86 *Nikah-bil-jabr* (forced marriage) is prohibited in Islam. The consent of a woman in *nikah* (Islamic marriage contract) is obligatory. For details see: Baba Khel, 'Status of *Swara* in Islam', p. 14.

87 Samar Minallah points out that not only is the practice of *Swara* un-Islamic but it is also against the basic principles of the *Pukhtunwali* code which considers women as a symbol of honour who are meant to be kept away from the sight of strangers, and more so from the gaze of enemies. 'Dynamics of Swara', *Swara – The Human Shield: A Study on the Custom of SWARA in North West Frontier Province*, Ethnomedia Publications, Islamabad, Pakistan, 2006, p. 53.
88 Zofeen T. Ebrahim, 'Death Penalty: 'Swara' Killings in Pakistan Continue', *Inter Press Service News Agency*, September 27, 2005. Accessed at: http://www.ipsnews.net/africa/interna.asp?idnews=34896 on April 2, 2015.
89 Bill Nichols, 'Why Are Ethical Issues Central to Documentary Filmmaking?', *Introduction to Documentary*, Indiana University Press, Bloomington, IN and Indianapolis, IN, 2001, p. 18.
90 Ibid., p. 70.
91 In 2003, Samar Minallah filed a petition that requested the court to declare the handing over of a female as compensation in any form of settlement, as well as a forced marriage under the custom of *Swara*, as illegal marriage. The case against *Swara* was heard by the Chief Justice of Pakistan, Justice Iftikhar Mohammad Chaudhry, and a *suo moto* notice was taken in December 2005, whereby under landmark orders on December 16, 2005 the Supreme Court of Pakistan instructed the inspector generals of police in all four provinces and in the Northern Areas to act against any incidents of *Swara*-related practices as a criminal offence. 'Progressive Directions Under the Supreme Court', *Swara – The Human Shield: A Study on the Custom of SWARA in North West Frontier Province*, Ethnomedia Publications, Islamabad, Pakistan, 2006, pp. 26–35.

It may be mentioned here that under Islamic laws of *Qisas* and *Diyat*, only exchange of property, and blood-money are allowed as compensation, not the exchange of human beings. Ibid., 'Petition filed by Ethnomedia in Supreme Court', p. 126.
92 *The Plagued Mindset*, Samar Minallah, 2008 (15 min.), Ethnomedia & Development, Pakistan (Urdu/Punjabi/English/English sub-titles).
93 *The Dark Side of Migration*, Samar Minallah, 2009 (25 min.), Ethnomedia & Development, Pakistan. Developed and produced in collaboration with ActionAid and Befare with financial assistance from the European Commission. (Urdu/Punjabi/English sub-titles).
94 *Dar Pa Dar: Afghan Refugee Women. (Where the Heart Lies)*, Samar Minallah, 2008 (15 min.), Ethnomedia & Development, Pakistan (Pushto/Darri/English sub-titles).

Da Bajaur Galoona. (Homeless at Home), Samar Minallah, 2008 (17 min.), Ethnodmedia & Development, Pakistan (Pushto/English sub-titles).
95 *The Silver Lining: HIV and AIDS*, Samar Minallah, 2007 (15 min.), Ethnomedia & Development, Pakistan (Pushto/English/English sub-titles).

Rays of Hope: A Documentary on Tuberculosis, Samar Minallah, 2008 (35 min.), Ethnomedia & Development, Pakistan. Made in collaboration with the Provincial TB Control Programme, Health Department of NWFP, and the Ministry of Economic Cooperation and Development (BMZ), Government of the Federal Republic of Germany (Pushto/English sub-titles).
96 *Allaho: A Lullaby for You My Daughter*, Samar Minallah, 2009 (5 min.), Ethnomedia & Development, Pakistan. Made in collaboration with HBS Afghanistan, WCLRF, and the Heinrich Böll Stiftung Foundation, Afghanistan (Pushto/English sub-titles).
97 *Shinwarey Lawangeena: Where the Waters Meet*, Samar Minallah, 2006 (7 min.), Ethnomedia & Development, Pakistan. Made in collaboration with the Heinrich Böll Stiftung Foundation, Afghanistan. Pakistan (Pushto/English sub-titles).

Warwaee Lasoona: The Dance of Unity, Samar Minallah, 2008 (8 min.), Ethnomedia & Development, Pakistan. Made in collaboration with the Heinrich Böll Stiftung Foundation, Afghanistan (Pushto/Darri/English sub-titles).

98 *Bibi Shireenay: Where Honour Comes From*, Samar Minallah, 2007 (6 min.), Ethnomedia & Development, Pakistan. Made in collaboration with the *Aurat* Foundation, Peshawar, and GTZ (Pushto/English sub-titles).
99 For details on Samar Minallah's filmography and Ethnomedia & Development projects visit: http://www.ethnomedia.pk Accessed on April 2, 2015.
100 Email correspondence with Samar Minallah, July 5, 2011.
101 Susan Moller Okin, 'Feminism, Women's Rights, and Cultural Differences', in Uma Narayan and Sandra Harding (eds), *Decentering the Centre: Philosophy for a Multicultural, Postcolonial, and Feminist World*, Indiana University Press, Bloomington, IN and Indianapolis, IN, 2000, p. 28.
102 Nichols 'What Are Documentaries About?', p. 70.
103 Sharmeen Obaid's Second Documentary Nominated for Oscar', *The News International*. January 14, 2016. Accessed at: http://www.thenews.com.pk/latest/90311-Sharmeen-Obaids-second-documentary-nominated-for-Oscar on January 19, 2016.
104 Thomas Waugh, 'Why Documentary Filmmakers Keep Trying to Change the World, Or Why People Changing the World Keep Making Documentaries', in Thomas Waugh (ed.), *"Show Us Life": Towards a History and Aesthetics of the Committed Documentary*, The Scarecrow Press, Inc. Metuchen, NJ, and London, 1984, p. xiv.
105 Nichols 'What Are Documentaries About?', p. 70.
106 Section 310-A inserted into the Pakistan Penal Code (PPC) Criminal Law (Amendment) Act now states the following penalty for exchange of girls or women as compensation: 'Whoever gives a female in marriage or otherwise in *badl-e-sulh* (compensation) shall be punished with rigorous imprisonment which may extend to ten years but shall not be less than three years.' Samar Minallah, 'Judiciary as Catalyst for Change', p. 5. Accessed at: http://supremecourt.gov.pk/ijc/Articles/9/2.pdf on April 2, 2015.
107 According to Samar Minallah, around 70 girls had been saved from being forced into *Swara* forms of marriages in cases where the Supreme Court of Pakistan intervened based on the petition filed by her, while many others continued to be recovered as cases are reported to the police. Email correspondence with Samar Minallah on July 31, 2011, and January 15, 2015.
108 Trinh T. Minh-ha, 'An All-Owning Spectatorship', *When the Moon Waxes Red: Representation, Gender, and Cultural Politics*, Routledge, New York, 1991, p. 81.
109 Kleinhans, 'Forms, Politics, Makers and Contexts', p. 320.
110 Michael Renov, 'Towards a Poetics of Documentary', in Michael Renov (ed.), *Theorizing Documentary*, Routledge, New York, London, 1993, p. 21.
111 The *Human Rights Commission of Pakistan (HRCP) 2014 Annual Report* released in April 2015 states: 'The Aurat Foundation estimates that more than 3,000 have been killed for "honour" since 2008 in Pakistan. HRCP database recorded that 923 women and 82 minor girls fell victim to "honour" killings in 2014. The count included 21 deaths in Gilgit-Baltistan. The total number of victims of these crimes is usually higher as both men and women are targeted in such incidents. The predominant cause of these killings in 2014 was alleged illicit relations where both the boy and girl believed to be involved in the relationship were murdered as a result. Firearms were the most commonly used method of carrying out these killings ... Acid attacks have been rising in Pakistan despite the criminalization of this offence in 2010. According to HRCP's database seven women died in acid attacks on 92 women and 13 minors in 2014. Sixty women expired in other incidents like cylinder blast, stove burning and setting on fire. Between 2007 and 2014 the Acid Survivors Foundation (ASF), an NGO supporting acid attack victims, has recorded 1,090 incidents of acid attacks. 43 cases were recorded in 2009, 55 cases in 2010, 150 in 2011, 93 in 2012, 143 in 2013 and 161 cases were recorded from January–October 2014. The number of cases has increased since last year, which makes it all the more necessary to have a comprehensive law in place in each province to protect the victims. This is

particularly essential for Punjab where 56 per cent of the cases took place in 2013 according to ASF', *State of Human Rights in 2014*. 'Honour Crimes and Acid Attacks', *Human Rights Commission of Pakistan 2014 Report*. U. B. Printers, Lahore, Pakistan, 2014, pp. 217–18.
112 Ella Shohat, 'Post-Third-Worldist Culture: Gender, Nation and the Cinema', in Anthony R. Guneratne and Wimal Dissanayake (eds), *Rethinking Third Cinema*, Routledge, New York and London, 2003, p. 52.
113 Barbara Halpern Martineau stresses the use of talking heads as a style particularly effective for conveying a feminist message: 'It seems useful at this point to make a general distinction between the use of talking heads to represent some official or authoritative position, and the use of talking heads of people who are telling their own stories. Another, more formal three-part distinction can be made among: 1) Interviews where the subject addresses someone who is either off-screen or on; 2) candid or informal discussions filmed in close-up; and 3) direct address to the camera, where the subject appears to be talking to the audience.' Barbara Halpern Martineau, 'Talking About Our Lives and Experiences: Some Thoughts About Feminism, Documentary and "Talking Heads"', in Thomas Waugh (ed.), *"Show Us Life": Toward a History and Aesthetics of the Committed Documentary*, The Scarecrow Press, Inc. Metuchen, NJ, and London, 1984, p. 259.
114 Diane Waldman and Janet Walker, 'Introduction', in Diane Waldman and Janet Walker (eds), *Feminism and Documentary*, University of Minnesota Press, Minneapolis, IN, 1999, pp. 1–2.
115 Ibid., p. 17.

Conclusion

The detailed contextual and inter-disciplinary readings of representative films in preceding chapters illustrate the emergence of an activist documentary film category in contemporary Pakistan that is identified as a 'Cinema of Accountability' in this study. This category is positioned to investigate, expose, take to task, and press for accountability from the state, judiciary, policy makers, and society regarding the historical and ongoing violation of human rights. Chapters on films, divided thematically, discuss various socio-political, historical, and cultural issues, developments, and problems that contemporary Pakistani documentarists have depicted for consciousness-raising, advocacy, and social change from within a Muslim state. These issues include politicization of religion, women's issues, minority issues, human rights abuses, complex and controversial impact of *Sharia* laws, Islamic fundamentalism and extremism, terrorism, and consciousness-raising about gender-specific tribal and cultural practices, including violence against women.

As a first and introductory academic study on Pakistani activist documentary cinema, and hence absence of pre-existing critical scholarship on the subject, Chapter One discusses a combination of various relevant activist documentary film-studies themes and perspectives, including feminist documentary perspectives and frameworks, which could be borrowed to explore the issues and topics covered in this book. These overarching themes and perspectives include 1) Perspectives on the Contextual and Historical Approach to Documentary Filmmaking; 2) Perspectives on the Activist and Political Intent of Documentary Film; 3) Feminist Perspectives on Documentary Film and Activism; 4) Parallels with Other Activist Film Currents (perspectives on Third Cinema, Cinema Novo, and a post-Third-Worldist approach). Together, the application of key theoretical frameworks and thematic perspectives on documentary cinema serve as building blocks in defining a new theoretical framework for an issue-oriented activist documentary 'Cinema of Accountability' in contemporary Pakistan that has its roots in the Islamization period of military dictator General Zia-ul-Haq (1977–1988).

The concept of 'spatial boundaries' in Islamic societies offers perspectives on the gender-specific constraints and hurdles that Pakistani women filmmakers can face, and have yet managed to work around or defy, as films made by women documentarists such as Sabiha Sumar, Sharmeen Obaid-Chinoy, and Samar

Minallah illustrate. Additionally, a brief background to the developments in the Pakistani film industry during the Islamization period contextualizes the emergence of activist documentary filmmaking practices in Pakistan as a consequence of religious fundamentalism and authoritarian state directives and policies.

Additionally, a brief synopsis of the deterioration of Pakistani cinema under Islamization reveals the suffocating political conditions and environment that were affecting the growth of the cinema industry.

Chapter Two discusses films that focus on the legislative reforms, state-directives, and socio-political transformations that were shaping Pakistan during General Zia-ul-Haq's dictatorship and Islamization period (1977–1988). Rooted in the Islamization period that saw the beginning of Pakistan's descent into religious fundamentalism, these films, filmmakers, organizations, and collaborative productions represent the emergence of a 'committed'[1] activist documentary filmmaking practice in Pakistan as it investigates and reflects on the suffocating environment of fear, coercion, punishment, and oppression of the Zia regime. Giving voice and space to rights activists, lawyers, scholars, and others, films discussed in this chapter highlight the intersection of politics, religion, and law, and their consequent, and continuing, impact on women's legal status, religious minority groups, and the violation and curtailment of individual and human rights. Most significantly, these films and their makers lay the foundation for a 'Cinema of Accountability' in Pakistan, and its activist intent by documenting and archiving the critical testimonies and views of marginalized sections and victims of Zia's legislative reforms.

As the contextual reading of these films reveals the deleterious impact of Zia's Islamization and sweeping transformations in the name of religion, they serve as a valuable archival filmic counter-history of the roots of religious fundamentalism in Pakistan, and the emerging strong and defiant voices of resistance, particularly women's. Further, the chapter illustrates the oppositional forces that were also beginning to take shape, and mobilize civil society for resistance and social change such as the emergence of women's resistance groups and organizations.

Together, films in this chapter depict the foundation for an activist *'imperfect cinema'* in the Pakistani context that brings together defiant voices and views from a variety of backgrounds (professionals, rights activists, government officials, policy makers, legal experts, clerics, women, and ordinary people) and institutional affiliations to address contemporary issues for social change.[2] Significantly, this body of filmic work also introduces us to a pioneering independent Pakistani Muslim woman documentarist, Sabiha Sumar, whose films stand at the forefront of investigating and critiquing the impact of Zia's legislative reforms, politicization of Islam, *Sharia* laws, and religious fundamentalism in Pakistan. Collectively, the productions discussed here set the foundation for an activist documentary 'Cinema of Accountability' from within a Muslim state that is entrenched in the critique of the Islamization period, and extends to discussion of films and issues in subsequent chapters.

Forming a connective link between the developments during the Islamization period in Chapter Two, Sharmeen Obaid-Chinoy's six representative films in

Chapter Three constitute a 'Cinema on Terror' that investigates Pakistan's continued descent into religious fundamentalism as the country now finds itself confronted by a new trend of religious extremism and militancy in the form of Talibanization, and the brutal and violent *jihadist* ideologies fostered through mushrooming radical *madrasas*. As the Pakistani government, civil society, and anti-US and anti-West religious factions become embroiled in internal strife and divisive ideologies, Obaid-Chinoy's topical films present a body of work that explores the phenomenon of sweeping *jihadist* sentiments and terrorist organizations, and the recruitment and training of potential terrorists through pro-Taliban *madrasas*. These thematically related films address the period in which Pakistan became a frontline state in the US-led 'War on Terror' during President Pervaiz Musharrraf's tenure (1999–2007) following the 9/11 terrorist attacks on the US in 2001, and the subsequent US attack on Afghanistan in 2001 that resulted in cross-border militancy and a mass exodus of Afghan refugees to Pakistan.

Obaid-Chinoy's investigative and reportorial films that cover a wide range of locations, views, and reflections from a vast cross-section of society, including members of terrorist organizations, radical clerics, and potential *jihadists* being trained at *madrasas*, among others, conjure a sobering picture of a nuclear-armed Pakistan dominated by a growing domestic influence of militant Islamic factions such as the Taliban and the *Al Qaida*. Through her historical and contextual filmic works, the complex patterns of religious extremism that have been shaping and impacting Pakistan's domestic socio-political and socio-economic landscape are detailed.

Today, Obaid-Chinoy's films present a 'Cinema on Terror' – a cautionary body of work that is also an archival testimony of the militant mix of religion and politics, and radical patterns and changes instigated by religious extremism that now pose a serious threat to global security. Collectively, the filmmakers and productions discussed in Chapters Two and Three identify an anti-Islamic fundamentalism film category from within a Muslim society itself.

The focus in Chapter Four is on consciousness-raising and expository documentary films that address extreme forms of violence against women, and their 'honour'-related victimization in Pakistan. These films made by independent filmmakers and organizations cover a range of vicious and violent practices such as stove-blasts, acid-attacks, honour-killing, honour-rape, and the tribal custom of *Swara* that sanctions the giving away of minor girls in forced marriages as compensation to avenge murders and settle feuds. A contextual reading of films in this chapter, supported by data from human rights organizations, and a discussion on notions of 'honour' and 'shame', reveals a culture of horrific forms of violence against women, and murder on the pretext of so-called 'honour' and morality, such as in the practice of *karo kari*.

Further, as Samar Minallah's film *Swara: A Bridge Over Troubled Waters* (2003) illustrates, documentary film has played a most significant and successful deliberative and legislative role[3] in the criminalization of the practice of forced marriages, and giving away of minor girls against their wishes to settle disputes as per tribal customs. Hence, these films stand as a valuable activist contribution to a 'Cinema of Accountability' from Pakistan that calls for urgent and serious attention and reforms from the state, the legal system, law-enforcement bodies, and policy-makers to address violence perpetrated against women.

It is pertinent to mention here that in a significant move in December 2011 the then President of Pakistan, Asif Ali Zardari, signed into law the much awaited Criminal Law (Second Amendment) Bill 2011. An outcome of persistent pressure and demand from rights organizations and activists, this Bill includes The Acid Control and Acid Crime Prevention Bill 2010, and The Prevention of Anti-Women Practices (Criminal Law Amendment) Bill 2008, that prohibits forced marriages, gives women inheritance rights, and legislates severe punishment for physically harming women with corrosive substances.[4] Although the success of this legislation will depend on its effective application, its passage is in itself a significant victory for rights activists, and particularly Pakistani women. However, it is significant to add that Sharmeen Obaid-Chinoy's Oscar-winning documentary film, *Saving Face* (2011), on the topic of acid-attack victims in Pakistan has brought much needed attention, both in Pakistan and internationally, to the hideous crime of acid-attacks through consciousness-raising. It can be hoped that more victims will be encouraged to come forward and press for accountability now that the Criminal Law (Second Amendment) Bill 2011 that includes the Acid Control and Acid Crime Prevention Bill 2010, and the Prevention of Anti-Women Practices (Criminal Law Amendment) Bill 2008, mentioned above, are also in place.

On her part, Sharmeen Obaid-Chinoy has initiated Project SAAVE (Stand Against Acid Violence) with an aim to screen her film at various forums worldwide to spread public awareness, involve rights organizations, and mobilize public opinion for justice and reforms.[5] These developments affirm the significance and potential of a documentary 'Cinema of Accountability' that can be instrumental in enforcing legal reforms and social change. Similarly Obaid-Chinoy's second Oscar win for her documentary film entitled *A Girl in the River: The Price of Forgiveness* (2015) on the topic of honour-killings has brought very significant international, and renewed national, attention to the issue. Within Pakistan, the film has garnered much-needed government and social pressure for enforcement of stringent legal measures to check the practice.

In addition to a reading of individual films, Chapter Four provides an overview of the various topics, themes, and advocacy projects that independent filmmaker Samar Minallah and her non-governmental organization, Ethnomedia & Development, have taken up for filmic representation and consciousness-raising in the Khyber Pakhtunkhwa Province (KP), one of the most conservative regions of Pakistan where tribal laws and customs hold immense power and control. The success of portrayal of topics in *Saving Face, A Girl in the River: The Price of Forgiveness* and *Swara: A Bridge Over Troubled Waters* stand testimony to the utility of documentary film as an activist, pedagogical, and legislative tool for intervention in issues of human rights that can extend its reach through cross-cultural communication to build solidarity, and push for long neglected social and legal reforms.

190 *Conclusion*

Together, films, filmmakers, organizations, and collaborative ventures discussed in the preceding chapters introduce the emergence of an activist documentary cinema in contemporary Pakistan that has so far remained neglected and absent in academic discourse. Covering a vast range of topics since the Islamization period, these representative documentary films identify critical issues, developments, events, practices, and consequences that continue to impact Pakistani society, as they call for accountability, reforms, and social change. Identified as 'Cinema of Accountability', these productions illustrate the pedagogical utility and responsibility of documentary cinema to raise critical issues and consciousness, empower victims to speak out, expose social and political shortcomings, highlight oppressions, promote socio-political resistance and human rights, and press for reforms.[6]

The interdisciplinary contextual reading approach, and 'Cinema of Accountability' paradigm presented here can be applied to discuss similar film practices beyond Pakistan as well where cinematic productions, both documentaries and features, take on issues of human rights and social injustice to expose societal neglect and biases, and governmental apathy such as in matters of gender issues, racism, and ethnic and religious marginalization, among others.

Documentary film practices in Pakistan: a critical overview

It is significant to note that a discussion of independent Pakistani documentary filmmakers, rights organizations, and their collaborative productions also highlights their similarities – most of these filmmakers have received Western education, belong to progressive urban segments of the Pakistani society, and have taken up topical issues that have secured donor funding from Western agencies and media outlets.

Certainly, questions arise in this relationship with Western funders, channels, and influences: How much power and control can independent filmmakers in a Third World country like Pakistan exert in their choice of topics, themes, representations, and production when working with foreign capital and organizations? And, consequently, do their depictions then need to be modified to Western audience's tastes and network demands in order to secure distribution, exhibition, and screenings at international film festivals?

Some may argue that foreign funding, and class privilege such as a Western education, greatly affects choice and treatment of topics for documentary filmmakers from the developing/Third World, and that they tend to pick and package their 'Pakistan bashing' topics and productions to pander to foreign audiences to gain recognition.[7] On the other hand, one also needs to consider if these filmmakers could have produced and exhibited their critical films *without* such support and privilege, particularly given the religion and gender-sensitive and controversial topics they have broached in their films, and the authoritarian political environments they have challenged, exposed, *and* worked within?

Certainly, domestic funding and exhibition opportunities for these films would have either been non-existent, as in the case of the government-controlled PTV, or rare to secure on other subsequent channels at the time of their production, given the subjects of many of these films that critique religious fundamentalism, controversial *Sharia* laws, and other culturally sensitive or taboo subjects such as rape.

It can also be seen from discussion of films in this study that many of these productions were either first shown abroad on the foreign channels that collaborated in their funding and production (e.g. Sabiha Sumar and Sharmeen Obaid-Chinoy's films) (and then made their way back to domestic Pakistani audiences, however limited these might be through access to personal copies or privately arranged screenings); or were produced by collaborative non-governmental organizations (local and foreign) as advocacy, consciousness-raising, and training tools for particular audiences (limited again), and/or their staff (e.g. *Simorgh, Dastak* Society for Communication, AGHS).

Considering Pakistan's historical and socio-political environment as detailed in films in this study, particularly the advent of activist filmmaking that took root in, and against, the Islamization era, the fact remains that with limited training, production, and screening opportunities for documentary cinema within Pakistan, especially in an environment of authoritarian regimes and rigid censorship policies, as well as absence of any national organizations to provide monetary subsidies to independent documentary filmmakers, as in the West (e.g. as the British Film Institute (BFI) in UK, and the National Film Board (NFB) in Canada), collaborative ventures with foreign organizations and media networks have played a significant role as a launching pad in the growth and progress of the activist documentary genre within the country, and promotion of Pakistani documentarists and their productions on the international scene.[8] As well, it needs to be acknowledged that Western collaborations and channels have led to significant exhibition possibilities, and screenings and awards at international film festivals, leading to broader recognition of Pakistani filmmakers and their issue-oriented work, including Pakistan's first Oscar win by Sharmeen Obaid-Chinoy for her documentary film that focuses on violence against women.

As discussions of various films in this book reveal, I maintain that despite availing foreign funding for many of their projects, Pakistani documentary filmmakers have managed to address crucial subjects and problems, including those of global interest and implications such as religious extremism, Talibanization, and terrorism, while keeping the sensitive balance between their own religious identities, ideological beliefs, socio-cultural, political, and religious constraints, historical experiences, activism, and the monetary realities of film production, distribution, and exhibition. As is apparent from the contextual discussions of documentary films on various topics, Pakistani documentary filmmakers have used foreign collaborations and funding as significant *allies* in strengthening the activist role and contribution of their productions to promote their agendas for reform and social change in their home country. For example, the enthusiasm with which Sharmeen Obaid-Chinoy's Oscar-winning documentaries *Saving Face* (2011), and *A Girl in the River: The Price of Forgiveness* (2015) have been received in Pakistan is a clear indication that although the topics of acid-attacks and honour-killings have been in the media all along, including the three similar activist documentary films discussed in Chapter Four that had very limited private screening opportunities (*Stove Burning: Neither Coal Nor Ashes* (1993); *Burnt Victims: Scars on the Society* (2002); *Shame: A Tale of Karo Kari* (2005)), what is urgently needed are wider screening opportunities for documentary cinema within Pakistan for consciousness-raising to muster public support for social change, accountability, and the successful implementation of the rule of law.

No doubt, given the growth of domestic television media outlets, for the future it would be an ideally welcome change if limited domestic exhibition opportunities, and viewership could gradually be expanded through Pakistani channels to create a broader impact of the activist intent of Pakistani documentary productions and their makers. However, in practical terms the possibilities for this to happen are also fraught with various political and censorship policies, as well as sensitive socio-cultural factors, particularly in the case of religion-related and gender issues.

Another issue that arises with Pakistani documentarists is that considering the Western-educated and/or liberal middle-class urban backgrounds of most filmmakers, what level of insight and commitment do they have to understand the plight of underprivileged and marginalized segments of their society? I have argued in this book that given their shared socio-political and cultural history and commonalities with those whose oppressions and problems they depict, Pakistani documentarists, particularly women filmmakers, are uniquely positioned as 'insiders' to identify and depict the transformations and suffering inflicted by religious fundamentalism, harsh state directives and *Sharia* laws, and various human rights abuses. Instead of creating a class hierarchy between themselves and the marginalized groups/individuals whom they empower and give the chance to speak out in their films, Pakistani documentarists' own participation in their films breaks these hierarchies through identification with shared histories and experiences of religious fundamentalism, and its potential effects for other Muslim nations in the region (for example in neighbouring Afghanistan and Iran). Hence, the growth of a 'Cinema of Accountability', regardless of foreign funding sources, with a critical focus on themes of religious fundamentalism, extremism, rigid *Sharia* laws, abuse of human rights, gender-specific violence and discrimination, and women's rights has the potential to serve as an effective tool for both cross-class and cross-cultural communication, and consciousness-raising to build solidarity for reforms and social change in Pakistan in the future.

As the documentary film culture grows in Pakistan, it would also certainly be a welcome development to see the emergence of a national funding organization in the future that would encourage and enable new Pakistani filmmakers to take advantage of subsidies, and greater screening opportunities domestically.

Emerging directions for documentary cinema in Pakistan

Documentary cinema in Pakistan demonstrates a considerable potential to make a substantial and enduring contribution to the advancement of human rights and social change, and consciousness-raising through an audio-visual medium, particularly in the far-flung rural areas where literacy rates are poor. There are several new and emerging avenues and sites through which documentary cinema is gaining prominence, and being promoted in Pakistan.

Film Studies institutes:

A growing interest in film production and documentary film has led to an emergence of film studies degree programmes in some prominent institutions in Pakistan.[9] Among those now offering Bachelors and Masters degrees in film and television production are the Karachi University (KU), the Beaconhouse National University (BNU), the National College of Arts (NCA), and the *Shaheed* Zulfikar Ali Bhutto Institute of Science and Technology (SZABIST).[10]

In 1999, the Karachi University in the Sindh province established its Department of Visual Studies. The department offers a four-year Bachelor's degree programme in Design and Media Arts that includes courses in electronic media production and animation.[11]

The Lahore-based Beaconhouse National University in the Punjab province, established in 2003, is the first liberal arts institution in the country. Its Department of Theatre, Film, & Television offers BA Honours programmes with majors in Theatre, and TV Studies. This includes courses in screenwriting, production, and cinematography.[12]

Established in 1875 as the Mayo School of Industrial Art in Lahore, and renamed the National College of Arts in 1958, NCA is one of the oldest arts colleges in the sub-continent with campuses in the cities of Lahore and Rawalpindi. Beginning in 2005, the college started its first offering of a four-year Bachelors degree programme in Film and Television Studies designed to cater to local requirements, and address socio-political and cultural topics, besides a one-year postgraduate diploma programme in Script, Screenplay & Digital Film Production.[13] Similarly, the Karachi-based Indus Valley School of Art and Architecture (IVSAA) offers a one-year diploma in Digital Film and Video.[14]

The Karachi-based *Shaheed* Zulfikar Ali Bhutto Institute of Science and Technology (SZABIST), established in 1995, offers a four-year Bachelors of Media Sciences degree that includes a major in digital Film and Television Production. Teaching and visiting faculty includes filmmakers and professionals from the Pakistani film and media industry. Since 2008, the SZABIST has also been holding the all-Pakistan inter-university ZAB Film Festival and awards ceremony, renamed in 2011 as the ZAB Media Festival.[15] This private institution is also equipped with advanced studios, auditoriums, cameras, lighting, and sound equipment, editing facilities, and computer labs for graphic designing.[16]

Television and media organizations:

Following the deregulation of the Pakistani media in 2002 under the Pakistan Electronic Media Regulatory Authority Ordinance (PEMRA), there has also been a steady growth of independently owned television channels in the country.[17] As a result of the PEMRA Ordinance, as many as 55 new TV channels were set up, including seven 24/7 news channels, as opposed to the sole state-run Pakistan Television Corporation (PTV) which held complete monopoly over news dissemination and programming content before de-regulation. During the years following deregulation, these numbers grew to 90 independent channels, besides the 28 foreign channels, catering to the Pakistani audience.[18] Currently, there are well over 100 independent TV channels operational in the country.[19] Some of these commercial media outlets such as the Urdu and English language stations *Hum* TV, *Geo* Newsgroup TV, and the *Dawn* Media Newsgroup TV, among others, have also taken up documentary and telefilm productions to address socio-political and socio-cultural issues.

Newsline Publications, a print media organization founded in 1989 that has remained an outspoken and critical voice at the forefront of investigative reporting about crucial socio-political and cultural issues in Pakistan, also launched its film division under the banner of *Newsline* Films in January 2004. Equipped with its own film production unit that specializes in the production of documentaries, *Newsline* Films has produced films in collaboration with ActionAid, the British High Commission, Asia Foundation, and the Human Rights Commission of Pakistan on social and political issues that have been screened on national television channels as well as at film festivals in Pakistan and abroad.[20]

As a result of new communication technologies, another development on the Pakistani documentary scene emerged through the Interactive Resource Centre (IRC), an NGO that releases its research, films, and plays on its web TV portal, *Maati* TV, and YouTube.[21] Founded and headed by Mohammad Waseem in 2000, a former member of the Lahore-based activist Punjab *Lok Rehas* Theatre Group founded in 1986,[22] the IRC interactive theatre productions and training workshops for social change incorporate the interactive 'theatre of the oppressed' forum theatre philosophy promoted by Brazilian theatre director Augusto Boal.[23] Boal's audience-inclusive interactive 'forum theatre' approach as its defining characteristic, the IRC has been actively training small theatre companies in remote rural areas of Pakistan, as well as holding major annual theatre festivals.[24]

Encouraged by the public response and interest in their audience-inclusive and public theatre approach, the IRC has combined its 'theatre of the oppressed' approach with documentary filmmaking, and community video and training workshops at the grassroots level. Issues covered by the IRC productions have included bonded-labour, child-labour, sexual harassment of women at the workplace, minority rights, gender and religious rights and discrimination, and environmental issues, among others. Since its inception, the IRC has developed into a resource centre that is producing participatory community videos, documentaries, video profiles and talk shows, and mobile videos using cable networks, TV channels, radio, and web-based TV to disseminate its advocacy and activist productions.

The IRC has been holding participatory training workshops in rural areas as well as schools and colleges to train children, youth, and those already involved in theatre, in basic filmmaking and production techniques through its Community Film School and Media Unit. The organization has conducted much of its work in collaboration with other local and foreign human rights and welfare NGOs including the Canadian International Development Agency (CIDA), ActionAid, Oxfam, and the United States Institute of Peace. The result has been the emergence of a growing number of new independent documentary filmmakers in small districts and rural areas, and a volume of community and participatory videos. A selection of 14 of these documentaries have been broadcast on the BBC Urdu Service Online's *Shehar Kahani* (City Stories) series in one year, while more continued to be posted on the BBC's website for mass-dissemination.[25]

Taking advantage of mobile phone technologies, the IRC has proceeded to train youth and students as part of its collaborative ventures with local universities through its Film and Citizen Journalism Workshops and the IRC-*Umeed Jawan* (Fresh Hope) collaborative series in the production of mobile phone videos on various socio-cultural and economic issues.[26]

Film festivals and screening sites:

There has also been a growing trend towards film festivals and related activities in Pakistan to introduce audiences to current local and foreign productions. These nascent efforts have included the involvement of independent filmmakers, as well as academic institutions and student film clubs and societies. While some venues have not been sustainable, a film festival culture has nevertheless developed in the country that is likely to gain strength given the trend towards Cinema and Film Studies in academic programmes, and the emerging number of independent filmmakers looking for avenues to showcase their work.

In 2001, Pakistan became host to a successful international film festival, the non-political and non-profit *KaraFilm* Festival. Held annually in the country's port city of Karachi, through a competitive process the festival began to exhibit and promote alternative documentary cinema, shorts, and feature films by established as well as emerging independent filmmakers from within Pakistan, and abroad.

Founded by prominent names in Pakistani filmmaking circles such as Hasan Zaidi, Mehreen Jabbar, and Maheen Zia, the KaraFilm Society was also established with an aim to develop, improve, and protect film as an art form in Pakistan, and promote it on the international scene. The organization sought to encourage quality filmmaking and alternative voices, introducing audiences to current film trends and practices, both at home and abroad. Towards this end, the KaraFilm Club has been engaged in organizing screenings and talks by Pakistani and foreign visiting filmmakers, and workshops running throughout the year.[27] However, due to financial constraints, and the deteriorating security situation in Karachi the International *KaraFilm* Festival has had to defer its annual event since 2010.

The five-day *Vasakh* Documentary Film Festival, an initiative of the IRC, held for the first time in April 2008 in the Punjab provincial capital of Lahore is a continuation of the *Mateela* Film Festival that came into existence in 1998. The

Vasakh festival provided an exhibition venue for selected documentaries, by Pakistani filmmakers as well as international submissions that included award-winning films from the Travelling Film South Asia as a special feature. Other organizations that collaborated with the *Vasakh* festival include the Human Rights Commission of Pakistan, offering its auditorium for the screenings, as well as the Forman Christian College University (FCC) in Lahore where the IRC held screenings for students as part of their 'Urban Youth' participatory video training programme.[28] The 5th *Vasakh* film festival in 2012, held in collaboration with the Department of Mass Communication, Forman Christian College (FCC), Lahore, screened over forty documentaries. In addition to film screenings from 25 educational institutions from across Pakistan, the three-day festival also showed submissions from six international universities including Australia, Norway, and India.[29]

The *Vasakh* Film Festival 2015, now in its eighth year, showcased student films from across Pakistan as well as international documentary films on the themes of peace, tolerance, and cultural heritage.

Extending the emerging popularity and interest in filmmaking practices to children, in 2008 the Lahore-based Ali Institute of Education (AIE) hosted the first International Children's Film Festival (LICFF) in Lahore, Pakistan.[30] During its nine–day run, the LICFF screened films selected from its filmmaking workshop programme for children and young people (ages 13–18) that aimed at fostering arts education through the film medium.[31] The new batch of films produced in this workshop were to be presented in the 2nd LICFF to be held in October 2009, while selected films were sent to other international festivals for young filmmakers. Screening 263 films from 37 countries, the 2nd LICFF also had collaboration with other international children's film festivals, such as the Los Angeles International Children Film Festival; Little Big Shots International Film Festival for Kids; Kids for Kids International Film Festival; Toronto International Children's Film Festival; and the Prix Jeunesse Festival, Munich.[32] The second LICFF also included three mini documentary films selected through collaboration with the *Dawn* News TV channel.

It is significant to note that within a short span of time since its inception in 2008, the LICFF made remarkable progress, attracting submissions from across the world, and in July 2011 also took its festival to Hunza, one of the oldest settlements in Pakistan, in the far-flung new province of Gilgit-Baltistan (GB), located at an altitude of 12,000 feet, where people had no access to TV or cable at the time.[33]

Since its launch in 2008, the LICFF has screened close to 367 films from 45 countries to an audience of children and young people numbering over fifty thousand. These screenings have included shorts, feature lengths, and documentaries in the major cities of Pakistan, besides 15 smaller festivals and other events in schools and communities across the country.[34] By 2012, over 1,891 schools and organizations had participated in LICFF events. Extending its operations, the LICFF also created the Islamabad International Children's Film Festival (IICFF) and the Karachi International Children's Film Festival (KICFF). Additionally, the organization also developed a new programme by the name of Film *Sewa* (Film Help) that takes film screenings to public schools and marginalized communities.[35]

In 2014, the 6th LICFF, held in the cities of Lahore and Karachi, screened a selection of 169 films from 45 countries from a submission of 1,160 films from 60 countries, with an attendance of a 42,000 strong audience.[36]

In 2009, a collaborative project entitled 'Focus on Pakistan: Filmmaking for Social Change' was launched by the funding support of the British High Commission, Pakistan, in association with the London International Documentary Festival (LIDF),[37] and the US-based Eckova Productions that specializes in advocacy and consciousness-raising productions that address social issues.[38] Under this initiative, 30 young filmmakers, aged between 17 and 22 and affiliated to higher education institutions in Karachi and Lahore, were recruited for hands-on training workshops by UK and Pakistani film teachers in the field of documentary with the aim of training them to make films on topics of their choice that would explore the experiences and views of ordinary Pakistanis at the grass-roots level. Ten of these productions were screened at the London International Documentary Festival held at the British Museum in 2010.[39]

Under the LIDF initiative, 16 documentaries were produced by 45 emerging Pakistani filmmakers focusing on individual stories and experiences of bomb blasts, riots, effects of extremism on arts and culture, interfaith harmony, and poverty in Pakistan.[40] This access to explore crucial issues, and exhibit their work on an international platform at the London International Documentary Festival, that continued through the 2011 LIDF festival as well, provided a valuable chance to a new generation of Pakistani documentary filmmakers to build cross-cultural affiliations and solidarity for social change in their home country.[41]

A similar venue for cross-cultural and cross-class communication and exhibition was provided to a group of Pakistani women in Karachi by training them to project their experiences of violence and abuse online (YouTube) through documentary film by the Women's International Shared Experience project (WISE) initiated by the Asian Human Rights Commission (AHRC), and the Asian Legal Resource Centre (ALRC).[42] The WISE training workshop, held by the Pakistan Institute of Labour Education and Research, taught these women the basics of filmmaking and computer skills. Under this initiative, for 14 days the WISE project worked with nine women, some illiterate, from across the Sindh province of Pakistan who had been victims of domestic and sexual abuse, training them in basic video film production to develop a documentary to tell their own stories of suffering, and those they interviewed.[43] The result, a 10-minute participatory production entitled 'Half Face', aimed to empower women to share their experiences and tell their stories of abuse and human rights violation from their angle.[44]

Adding women's voices to the emerging trend of using documentary film for consciousness-raising and advocacy for social change, the *Shirkat Gah* Women's Resource Centre, Lahore, in collaboration with the Women Living Under Muslim Laws (WLUML) – Women Reclaiming and Redefining Culture (WRRC) programme, held an inter-university film competition and festival in March 2011 to create awareness about Violence Against Women (VAW), and to commemorate 100 years of the International Women's Day (1911–2011).[45]

Entitled 'Violence Is Not Our Culture' and made under *Shirkat Gah's* technical assistance, students from four leading universities in Lahore such as the Lahore University of Management Sciences (LUMS), the Lahore College for Women University (LCWU), the Punjab University (PU), and the Beaconhouse National University (BNU), showed seven films that highlighted topics of various gender-specific forms of physical, emotional and sexual violence against women, including acid-attacks and workplace harassment, with the objective of encouraging the reporting of violence-related cases.[46]

The *Shirkat Gah*-WLUML initiative and sponsorship is reflective of the growing importance and use of documentary film as a pedagogical and activist tool by activist organizations in contemporary Pakistan for spreading awareness, and highlighting areas that need urgent government and societal attention and intervention for reform.

In view of the contextual discussions of documentary films in Chapters Two, Three, and Four, and the related developments discussed in this conclusion, it is encouraging to see the promising opportunities that the emergence of new filmmaking institutes and departments, film festivals, film clubs, television media, and online film exhibition sites hold for the future development and growth of the activist documentary film scene in Pakistan.

Expanding exhibition sites:

It can be argued that with the advent of contemporary cost-effective and accessible film production technologies and exhibition possibilities, we can see the activist aesthetics of Third Cinema extending to Pakistan.[47] Such advancements have also expanded the exhibition and circulation opportunities for Pakistani documentaries.

Today, communication technologies are facilitating the transportability of films through highly compact means such as DVDs, and exhibition possibilities via the Internet, web TV portals, and YouTube, thereby providing documentary cinema a valuable means of expanding and communicating its activist content cross-culturally to offer an audio-visual platform to build broader cross-cultural, as well as cross-class, alliances for resistance and reform.[48] These technological advancements can be seen as extending the geographical boundaries for an international and cross-cultural reach of the socio-politically activist documentary medium much along the lines of the 'third cinema, third video, and even third television'.[49] Additionally, these developments offer the potential to strengthen and promote the activist intent of Pakistani independent filmmakers, and collaborative ventures by allowing them to reach out to wider audiences globally.[50]

Similarly, the expanding number of filmmaking institutes and academies, as mentioned earlier, have the potential to play a significant role in inspiring new activist Pakistani documentary filmmakers who are familiar with their socio-cultural and political issues to create a cinema that aims to spread awareness, and encourage resistance, particularly among youth, against the spread of religious fundamentalism and extremism, and highlights crucial human rights issues. Given the growth of media outlets in Pakistan after deregulation, access to the cost effective technologies and web-based exhibition possibilities discussed earlier, new filmmakers can continue to press for judicial reforms, policy changes, women's empowerment, and improvements in human rights.

This study has identified two emergent areas of activist documentary cinema in Pakistan. Firstly, we can see the emergence of a new paradigm in activist documentary cinema from within an Islamic society – a 'Cinema of Accountability' – that blurs the boundaries between aesthetics of documentary film and its utility as a vehicle for promoting social change. This Pakistani 'Cinema of Accountability' that has emerged from within an Islamic society serves as a significant model that is culture-sensitive, even religion sensitive where applicable, and yet incisive and bold in its investigation, critique, and deliberations for legal reforms and social change from within its own society.

Secondly, the 'Cinema on Terror', as identified in this research, provides a new documentary category of filmic representations and enquiry that has emerged from within Pakistan in the wake of rising religious fundamentalism, extremism, Talibanization, and militancy as a result of the post 9/11/2001 US-led 'War on Terror' – a new filmic category that can also be applied to, and be inclusive of, other cinemas that broach similar issues in other parts of the world, and their critique. For example, a 'Cinema on Terror' could also include films such as the multi award-winning Pakistani feature film *Khuda ke Liye* (*In the Name of God*) (2007),[51] and Indian Bollywood feature films such as *New York* (2009),[52] and *Kurbaan* (*Sacrificed*) (2009)[53] that address issues such as the post-9/11 victimization of Muslims in the US, religious extremism, and terrorism respectively.

It is promising that despite the gaps that may still need to be addressed, we can see the resonance of Third Cinema aesthetics of activism, and the arrival of a Cinema Novo in the Pakistani documentary cinema context that has the potential to play an active and crucial role in the service of human rights and social change.[54] Poised as a documentary 'Cinema of Accountability', Pakistani activist documentary cinema has also imbibed and extended the evolving resistant and revisionist-historiography essence and reach of the post-Third-Worldist cinema's political struggle (not only feminist) to include contemporary issues and topics impacting not only Pakistan's own socio-cultural and political landscape, but also those that address the global concerns of religious fundamentalism, extremism, terrorism, and Talibanization.[55]

However, although exhibition sites such as film clubs and film festivals are a much welcome development in Pakistan, their access remains largely limited to educated elites and urban areas. There remains a significant need for more venues and exhibition outlets for the promotion of issue-oriented documentaries at the grassroots level to target a larger spectatorship potentially whose problems and predicaments these films seek to address. It is imperative that screening of Pakistani activist documentaries be extended to remote and backward areas of the country by filmmakers through mobile screening units to target and educate audiences where consciousness-raising and advocacy are most needed about socio-political and socio-cultural issues, particularly where literacy levels are also lowest. These efforts could be further enhanced by government sponsorship, inclusion of issue-oriented documentary screenings through the education system, and government–NGO collaborations to promote the activist documentary film culture in Pakistan. Given the low literacy rates, particularly in the far-flung and rural areas of the country, as a visual medium documentary film offers a tremendous potential for acting as a watchdog, imparting education and advocacy, and building pressure for social reform.

The future for a committed 'Cinema of Accountability' that will continue to grow from within Pakistan, and foster the development of the Pakistani activist documentary movement looks promising, but its ultimate success will depend in its ability to reach out and raise consciousness in its own society at the grassroots level to motivate audiences, and press for social change. Given the increasing trend towards film as an effective pedagogical tool and intermediary, and the expansion of Film and Cinema Studies at university levels in Pakistan, the picture looks more than promising for cinema and filmmaking to take flight in an era of cross-cultural media expansion supported by technological advancements.

Notes

1 Thomas Waugh, 'Why Documentary Filmmakers Keep Trying to Change the World, Or Why People Changing the World Keep Making Documentaries', in Thomas Waugh (ed.), *"Show Us Life": Towards a History and Aesthetics of the Committed Documentary*, The Scarecrow Press, Inc. Metuchen, NJ, and London, 1984, p. xiv.
2 Julio Garcia Espinosa, 'For An Imperfect Cinema' (1970), in Michael Chanan (ed.), *Twenty-Five Years of the New Latin American Cinema*, BFI Books, UK, 1983, p. 31.
3 Bill Nichols, 'What Are Documentaries About?', *Introduction to Documentary*, Indiana University Press, Bloomington, IN and Indianapolis, IN, 2001, p. 70.
4 The Bill seeks to punish offences against women, namely, giving them in marriage in *badl-e-sulh, wanni* or *swara*; depriving them from inheritance; forced marriage; and marriage with the Holy *Quran*. The Bill also legislates a punishment of 14 years to life imprisonment for crimes involving the disfiguring of human organ/body by a corrosive substance. *The News International*, 'President Gives Assent to Bills on Crimes Against Women', December 22, 2011.
5 For details on Project SAAVE (Stand Against Acid Violence) visit: http://projectsaave.org/mission/ Accessed on April 2, 2015.
6 Paula Rabinowitz, 'Wreckage Upon Wreckage: History, Documentary, and the Ruins of Memory', *They Must Be Represented: The Politics of Documentary*, Verso, London, New York, 1994, p. 17.
7 Sairah Irshad Khan, 'I've had no support from Pakistanis at home', interview with Sabiha Sumar, *Newsline Monthly Magazine*, September 2005: Accessed at: http://www.newslinemagazine.com/2005/09/interview-sabiha-sumar/ on April 2, 2015.
8 For example, foreign NGOs such as the Heinrich Böll Foundation; CIDA; UN agencies such as the UNDP and UNIFEM; ActionAid; Retake Film & Video Collective; Katholische Frauea Deutchland; and Oxfam, among others, have been donors in the production of various documentary films in Pakistan.
9 There are a number of filmmaking institutes in Pakistan today, most of which at present provide technical instruction in film production and television journalism, such as filming, editing, lighting, etc. For a list of some of these institutes visit: Filmmaking.net, 'Film Schools in Pakistan', http://www.filmmaking.net/filmschools/film_schools_browse.asp?country=Pakistan Accessed on April 2, 2015.

10 Degree programmes and courses at these film studies departments have been designed and taught by leading documentary filmmakers, writers, journalists, theatre actors, drama professors, and those involved in the visual arts, performing arts, television, and advertising industry in Pakistan.
11 For further details on the Karachi University Department of Visual Studies visit: http://www.uok.edu.pk/faculties/visualstudies/index.php Accessed on April 2, 2015.
12 For further details on the Beaconhouse National University Theatre, TV & Film Studies programmes visit: http://www.bnu.edu.pk/bnu/TFT.aspx Accessed on April 2, 2015.
13 For further details about the National College of Arts Department of Film and Television visit: http://www.nca.edu.pk/Dept-Film-tv.html Accessed on April 2, 2015.
14 Indus Valley School of Art and Architecture (IVSAA). Accessed at: http://www.indusvalley.edu.pk/website/programmes/digital-film-and-video/ on March 20, 2016.
15 The *Shaheed* Zulfikar Ali Bhutto Institute of Science and Technology. Accessed at: http://khi.szabist.edu.pk/bs-mediasciences.html on April 2, 2015.
  For SZABIST Media Festival 2015 visit: http://www.zmf.szabist.edu.pk/ Accessed on May 19, 2015.
16 Personal email communication with Head of Department of Media Sciences at ZABIST, Mr Shehram Mokhtar. February 18, 2015.
17 For further details of the Pakistan Electronic Media Regulatory Authority Ordinance and the PEMRA Ordinance 2002 visit: Pakistan Press Foundation, September 28, 2011. Accessed at: http://www.pakistanpressfoundation.org/2011/09/pemra-ordinance-2002/ on January 15, 2016.
18 Riaz-ul-Hassan, 'Media Boom: 90 Channels, 106 FM Stations in 10 Years', *Viewpoint Online Issue 14*, September 28, 2010. Accessed at: http://viewpointonline.net/vp230/media-boom-90-channels-106-fm-stations-in-10-years on January 15, 2016.
19 For a listing of independent and official Pakistani TV channels visit: http://insider.pk/world/media/owns-pakistani-television-channels/ Accessed on February 20, 2015.
20 For details on Newsline Films and productions visit: http://www.newslinemagazine.com/newsline-films/ Accessed on February 20, 2015.
21 For further details on the Interactive Resource Centre (IRC) mission and projects visit: http://irc.org.pk/portal/?page_id=29 Accessed on April 2, 2015.
  The IRC is also disseminating its work and films on *Maati* TV, Pakistan's first web TV. Access at: http://www.maati.tv/
22 For a discussion of the activist resistance theatre movement in Pakistan that emerged in opposition to General Zia-ul-Haq's dictatorship and the Islamization process initiated by him, see: Fawzia Afzal-Khan, *A Critical Stage: The Role of Secular Alternative Theatre in Pakistan*, Seagull Books, Calcutta, New Delhi, India, 2006; and Shoaib Iqbal, 'Parallel Theater: Socio-Political Perspective', Accessed at: http://kunci.or.id/articles/parallel-theater-socio-political-perscepctive-by-shoaib-iqbal/ on April 2, 2015.
23 *First Step*. 'Introduction', Interactive Resource Centre Publication, Lahore, Pakistan, 2004.
24 The IRC's has also been a significant contribution in terms of research, advocacy campaigns, publications, and consciousness raising by extending its operations to involve untrained people from all segments of the Pakistani society, including school children and minority groups to come together on public forums to identify their particular problems, and through an interactive approach, devise possible solutions. Along the way, the IRC has trained over 80 theatre groups in 88 Pakistani cities and given more than 3,000 theatre performances in 86 districts of Pakistan, as well as abroad, on issues of poverty, violence against women, workers' and minority rights, and political education and awareness. Comprising a membership of 800 theatre and social activists, their performances and theatre techniques are further disseminated to community organizations through DVDs and other recordings, and accompanied by publications to enable other theatre groups to develop their own productions using an audience-inclusive and interactive 'theatre of the oppressed' approach. Interactive Resource Centre. Accessed at: http://irc.org.pk/portal/?page_id=29 on April 2, 2015.

25 *Interactive Resource Centre (IRC) Annual Report – 2005–2007*, Interactive Resource Centre Publication, Lahore, Pakistan.
26 IRC Mobile Videos. Accessed at: http://www.maati.tv/mobile-videos/ on April 2, 2015.

   The IRC-*Umeed Jawan* collaboration held its Documentary Film Festival in Lodhran, Pakistan, in April 2015. For details of other collaborative festivals and events visit: http://www.maati.tv/videos/?sort=latest&slg=umeed-jawan-documentary-film-festival-2015. Accessed on April 22, 2015.

   For further details, also visit the IRC–*Umeed Jawan* collaborative venture at: http://irc.org.pk/umeed-jawan/facebook-page/ Accessed on June 29, 2015.
27 For details of the KaraFilm Society visit: http://www.karafilmfest.com/about.htm Accessed on April 2, 2015.
28 *Vasakh* Film Festival. Accessed at: http://www.vasakhfilmfest.com on January 15, 2016.
29 *The Daily Times*, 'FCC Vasakh Film Festival Kicks Off Today', April 2, 2012. Accessed at: http://archives.dailytimes.com.pk/lahore/02-Apr-2012/fcc-vasakh-film-festival-kicks-off-today on January 15, 2016.

   For details of the 8th *Vasakh* Film Festival 2015 visit: http://vasakhfilmfest.com/ Accessed on May 19, 2015.
30 *The Daily Nation*, 'Children's Film Festival Begins at Ali Auditorium', Accessed at: http://nation.com.pk/lahore/15-Jun-2008/Children-Film-Festival-begins-at-Ali-Auditorium on April 23, 2015.

   For details on the Ali Institute of Education (AIE) visit: http://www.aie.edu.pk/ Accessed on April 2, 2015.
31 For details on events and programmes at the Lahore International Children's Film Festival (LICFF) visit: http://lahorechildrenfilm.com/ Accessed on April 2, 2015.
32 For details of the 2nd LICFF in 2009 visit: http://www.lahorechildrenfilm.com/index.php?option=com_content&view=article&id=68&Itemid=215 Accessed on April 23, 2015.
33 For images of the LICFF held in the province of Gilgit-Baltistan visit: https://www.facebook.com/media/set/?set=a.212777792102766.47296.116089451771601 Accessed on April 2, 2015.
34 The 2011 LICFF received and screened submissions from the following countries: Argentina, Australia, Bangladesh, Belgium, Brazil, Canada, China, Ecuador, Finland, Germany, Hong Kong, Iceland, India, Iran, Ireland, Israel, Italy, Japan, Kenya, Macedonia, Mexico, Mongolia, Nepal, Netherlands, Pakistan, Palestine, Poland, Singapore, South Africa, South Korea, Spain, Sri Lanka, Sweden, Taiwan, UK, USA, and Vietnam. Email correspondence with LICFF Director, Shoaib Iqbal on April 16, 2012.
35 Ibid.
36 For details of the 2014 LICFF visit: http://thelittleart.org/2014-lahorekarachi-intl-childrens-film-festival-season-report/ Accessed on April 21, 2015.
37 See 'Filmmaking for Social Change: Prevent and Resolve Conflict', The London International Documentary Festival. Accessed at: http://www.lidf.co.uk/lidf09/feature-events/filmmaking-for-social-change/ on January 15, 2016.
38 Eckova Productions is a US-based production company with offices and facilities in Los Angeles, Nova Scotia, Vancouver, Dubai, Mumbai, and Karachi. For further details on Eckova Productions and their projects visit: http://www.eckova.com/html/welcome.htm Accessed on April 2, 2015.
39 Email correspondence with Patrick Hazard, Director, London International Documentary Festival (LIDF) on October 12, 2010.
40 See: Patrick Hazard, 'LIDF Media Forum: Karachi: Filmmaking for Social Change', http://www.lidf.co.uk/highlights/2011/02/lidf-media-forum-karachi-filmmaking-for-social-change/ Accessed on January 15, 2016.
41 For the London International Documentary Film (LIDF) visit: http://www.lidf.co.uk/ Accessed on April 2, 2015.

   For details on the 'Focus on Pakistan: Filmmaking for Social Change' 2011 LIDF festival visit: http://www.lidf.co.uk/event/focus-on-pakistan/ Accessed on April 2, 2015.

42 WISE – Women's International Shared Experience Project. See: https://itbeginswithme.wordpress.com/2010/08/24/wise-the-womens-international-shared-experience-project/ Accessed on January 15, 2016.
43 Asian Human Rights Commission (AHRC). Accessed at: http://www.humanrights.asia/resources/journals-magazines/eia/eiav4n4/the-wise-women-of-pakistan/?searchterm=wise women project on April 2, 2015.
44 Samia Saleem, "Half Face' Brings 9 Women Full Circle', *The Express Tribune*, July 27, 2010. Accessed at: http://tribune.com.pk/story/31412/'half-face'-brings-9-women-full-circle/ - comment-43417 on April 2, 2015.

   The WISE Women of Pakistan documentary 'Half Face' can be viewed at the following YouTube websites: Part 1: https://www.youtube.com/watch?v=Cr6vRR8Yoo; Part 2: https://www.youtube.com/watch?v=GHHn5DooORo

   For the AHRC WISE training videos visit: http://www.humanrights.asia/news/ahrc-news/AHRC-ART-076-2010?searchterm=wise+women Accessed on May 19, 2015.
45 Women Living Under Muslim Laws (WLUML). 'Pakistan: Inter-University Film Festival: 'Violence Is Not Our Culture'', Accessed at: http://www.wluml.org/node/6994 on April 2, 2015.
46 *Shirkat Gah* Visual Collection. Accessed at: http://shirkatgah.org/visual-collections/ on April 2, 2015.
47 Michael Chanan, 'The Changing Geography of Third Cinema', *Screen*, 38.4, Winter 1997, pp. 383–4.
48 Jack C. Ellis and Betsy A. McLane, *A New History of Documentary*, Continuum, New York, London, 2005, pp. 258–9.
49 Chanan, 'The Changing Geography of Third Cinema', pp. 383–4.
50 For example web resources such as Culture Unplugged, and Vimeo Documentary Film offer a vast selection of issue-oriented documentary films from across the world that can be accessed online free of charge.

   For online films at Vimeo Documentary Film visit: http://vimeo.com/documentaryfilm Accessed on April 2, 2015.

   For a selection of Pakistani documentaries on Culture Unplugged visit: http://www.cultureunplugged.com/documentary/watch-online/festival/gsearch.php-q=pakistan&label=movies Accessed on April 2, 2015.
51 *Khuda ke Liye* (*In the Name of God*), Shoaib Mansoor, 2007 (168 mins), Geo TV/Shoman Production, Pakistan (Urdu/English/Punjabi/English sub-titles).
52 *New York*, Kabir Khan, 2009 (153 mins), Yash Raj Films, India (Hindi/English/English sub-titles).
53 *Kurban* (*Sacrificed*), Rensil D'Silva, 2009 (161 mins), Dharma Productions/UTV Motion Pictures, India. (Hindi/English/English sub-titles).
54 Glauber Rocha, 'The Aesthetics of Hunger' (1965), in Michael Chanan (ed.), *Twenty-Five Years of the New Latin American Cinema*, BFI Books, UK, 1983, p. 13.
55 Ella Shohat, 'Post-Third-Worldist Culture: Gender, Nation and the Cinema', in Anthony R. Guneratne and Wimal Dissanayake (eds), *Rethinking Third Cinema*, Routledge, New York and London, 2003, p. 55.

Appendix 1: The *Hudood* Ordinances

Promulgated in 1979 and enforced in 1980, the *Hudood* laws were a collection of five criminal laws, collectively known as the *Hudood* Ordinances. These included the Offences Against Property Ordinance which deals with the crime of theft and robbery; the Offence of *Zina* Ordinance relates to the crime of rape, abduction, adultery and fornication, while the word '*Zina*' covers adultery and fornication. The Offence of *Qazaf* Ordinance relates to false accusation of *Zina*; the Prohibition Order prohibits use of alcohol and narcotics. The last is the Execution of Punishment of Whipping Ordinance, which prescribes the mode of whipping for those convicted under the *Hudood* Ordinances.[1]

The *Zina Hudood* Ordinance

The punishable by death *Zina Hudood* Ordinance considered all sexual conduct outside the confines of marriage as an offence against the state. These offences included rape, adultery, fornication, and abduction for the purpose of sexual intercourse. Laying down the punishments for adultery, fornication and extra-marital sex, the formulation of the *Zina Hudood* Ordinance has tended to disfavour women, particularly in rape cases where it was applied alongside the Law of Evidence (*Qanun-e-Shahadat*), which further diminished women's legal status in a court of law by admitting a woman's testimony as half of that of a man's. The following is a description of the *Zina Hudood* Ordinance as contained in the Government of Pakistan *Hudood Ordinance* of 1979 *Sharia* laws:

1. The *Hudood* Ordinance criminalizes *Zina*, which is defined as extra-marital sex, including adultery and fornication.
2. It also criminalizes *Zina-bil-jabr,* which is defined as rape outside of a valid marriage.
3. The *Hudood* Ordinance further defines *Zina* and *Zina-bil-jabr* on the basis of the assigned criminal punishment.
4. Hence there is *Zina and Zina-bil-jabr* liable to *Hadd* (punishment ordained (supposedly) by the Holy *Quran* or *Sunnah*).
5. And there is *Zina* and *Zina-bil-jabr* liable to *tazir*, that is, any punishment other than *Hadd*. The *Hadd* punishment is stoning to death, and the *tazir*

punishment for *Zina* is up to ten years of imprisonment and whipping – up to thirty lashes and/or a fine. The *tazir* punishment for *Zina-bil-jabr* is up to twenty-five years of imprisonment and whipping up to thirty lashes.[2]

Notes

1 Asma Jahangir and Hina Jilani, *The Hudood Ordinances: A Divine Sanction?*, Sang-e-Meel Publications, Lahore, Pakistan, 2003, pp. 23–24.
2 *Enforcement of Hudood Ordinance, 1979 (VI of 1979), the Offence of Zina (Enforcement of Hudood) Ordinance, 1979 (VII of 1979), Presidential Order- No. 4 of 1979.* Ministry of Law, Justice and Human Rights, Islamabad, Government of Pakistan. Accessed at: http://www.infopak.gov.pk on November 13, 2013. For detailed explanation of the *Zina Hudood* Ordinance 1979 visit: http://www.pakistani.org/pakistan/legislation/zia_po_1979/ord7_1979.html Accessed on April 2, 2015.

Appendix 2: The Law of Evidence

As a further measure to Islamize the Pakistani criminal justice system under the Zia-ul-Haq regime, the Council of Islamic Ideology (CII) proposed the Law of Evidence (*Qanun-e-Shahadat*) legislation in April 1982, and introduced it into the criminal justice system as law in 1984, causing horrific consequences for women in particular.[1]

The enforcement of the Law of Evidence further strengthened the reach of the *Zina Hudood* Ordinance by dictating that a woman who has been raped could be imprisoned or subjected to corporal punishment if unable to provide an adequate number of witnesses to the incident. The Law of Evidence stated that the testimony of two women is admissible only as one reliable source; i.e., the testimony of a female is to be considered half that of a man's in a Pakistani court of law. The law required that an equivalent of four Muslim male witnesses of 'good repute'[2] verify a woman's claim to sexual penetration and consequent rape.[3] Otherwise, a rape victim is considered guilty of fornication or adultery under the *Zina Hudood* Ordinance.[4]

As further injustice, the *Sharia*-based *Zina Hudood* Ordinance not only governed the sexual conduct of Muslim men and women, but ironically was also extended to religious minorities in Pakistan.[5]

Notes

1 Khawar Mumtaz and Farida Shaheed, 'Legally Reducing Women's Status', *Women of Pakistan: Two Steps Forward, One Step Back?*, Vanguard Books, Lahore, Pakistan, 1987, p. 106.
2 The Pakistan Commission of Inquiry for Women Report of 1997 notes that Muslims of 'good repute' as witnesses is an unfair criterion as they are not likely to watch a rape take place as bystanders. On the other hand, a woman's complaint of rape in a Pakistani court is itself considered a confession of illicit sexual intercourse, and a subsequent pregnancy can serve as evidence against her. For further details and discussion see: *The Commission of Inquiry for Women Report of 1997*, Ministry of Women's Development, Social Welfare, and Special Education, Islamabad, Pakistan, 1997.
3 For further discussion see: Mumtaz and Shaheed 'Legally Reducing Women's Status', pp. 106–10.
4 Explaining the gender-discriminatory nature of the law, feminist scholar Shahnaz Khan points out: 'The onus of providing proof of rape rests with the victim under the *Hudood*

Ordinance and there are severe ramifications if she does not provide that proof. If she is unable to convince the court, her allegation of rape is in itself considered as confession of *Zina* and the victim effectively implicates herself and is liable to *Tazir* punishment. Furthermore, the woman can be categorized as the rapist herself since it is often assumed that she seduced the man.' Shahnaz Khan, 'Implications of the *Hudood* Ordinance', *Gender, Religion, Sexuality and the State: Mediating the Hudood Laws in Pakistan*, Centre for Research and Violence Against Women and Children, London, Ontario, Canada, 2001, p. 3.

5 This development served as yet another violation of human and gender rights that Zia's Islamization and the above-mentioned law facilitated. Whereas the 1973 Constitution of Pakistan, and the *Sharia* Act of Pakistan passed later, did not place religious minorities under the ambit of Islamic laws, with the promulgation of the *Hudood* laws these minorities ceased to be exempted on their religious basis and were instead subjected to the *Sharia* laws of the country. Naeem Shakir, '*Women and Religious Minorities under the Hudood Laws in Pakistan*', Article 2. Vol. 03, No. 03, June 2004. Accessed at: http://www.article2.org/mainfile.php/0303/144/ on April 2, 2015. For a detailed discussion of the *Hudood* Laws, see ibid.

Appendix 3: The Blasphemy Law

The following are a selection of provisions related to religion, and the Blasphemy Law as contained in the Pakistan Penal Code[1]:

1. Offences related to religion (original text)

Section 295

Injuring or defiling place of worship, with intent to insult the religion of any class:

Whoever, destroys, damages or defiles any place of worship, or any object held sacred by any class of persons with the intention of thereby insulting the religion of any class of persons or with the knowledge that any class of persons is likely to consider such destruction, damage or defilement as an insult to their religion, shall be punished with imprisonment of either description for a term which may extend to two years, or with fine, or with both.

Section 295-A

Deliberate and malicious acts intended to outrage religious feelings of any class by insulting its religion or religious beliefs:

Whoever with deliberate and malicious intention of outraging the religious feelings of any class of the citizens of Pakistan by words, either spoken or written or by visible representations, insults or attempts to insult the religion or the religious beliefs of that class, shall be punished with imprisonment of either description for a term which may extend to 10 years, or with fine, or with both.

2. Blasphemy Laws

Section 295-B

Defiling, etc., of copy of Holy Koran:

Whoever wilfully defiles, damages or desecrates a copy of the Holy Koran or an extract therefrom or uses it in any derogatory manner or for any unlawful purpose shall be punishable with imprisonment for life.

Section 295-C

Use of derogatory remarks etc., in respect of the Holy Prophet:

Whoever by words, either spoken or written or by visible representation, or by any imputation, innuendo, or insinuation, directly or indirectly, defiles the sacred name of the Holy Prophet Muhammad (peace be upon him) shall be punished with death.

Section 298

Uttering words, etc., with deliberate intent of wounding religious feelings:

Whoever, with the deliberate intention of wounding the religious feelings of any person utters any word or makes any sound in the hearing of that person or makes any gesture in the sight of that person or places any object in the sight of that person, shall be punished with imprisonment of either description for a term which may extend to one year, or with fine, or with both.

Section 298-A

Use of derogatory remarks, etc., in respect of holy personages:

Whoever by words, either spoken or written, or by visible representation, or by any imputation, innuendo or insinuation, directly or indirectly, defiles the sacred name of any wife (Ummul Mumineen), or members of the family (Ahle-bait), of the Holy Prophet (peace be upon him), or any of the righteous Caliphs (Khulafa-e-Raashideen) or companions (Sahaaba) of the Holy Prophet (peace be upon him) shall be punished with imprisonment of either description for a term which may extend to three years, or with fine, or with both.

Section 298-B

Misuse of epithets, description and titles, etc., reserved for certain holy personages or places:

1. Any person of the Qadiani group or the Lahori group (who call themselves 'Ahmadis' or by any other name) who by words, either spoken or written, or by visible representation: (a) refers to, or addresses, any person, other than a Caliph or companion of the Holy Prophet Muhammad (peace be upon him), as 'Ameer-ul-Mumineen', 'Khalifat-ul-Mumineen', 'Khalifat-ul-Muslimeen', 'Sahaabi' or 'Razi Allah Anho'; (b) Refers to, or addresses, any person, other than a wife of the Holy Prophet Muhammad (peace be upon him), as Ummul-Mumineen; (c) refers to, or addresses, any person, other than a member of the family (Ahle-bait) of the Holy Prophet Muhammad (peace be upon him), as Ahle-bait; or (d) refers to, or names, or calls, his place of worship as Masjid (mosque); shall be punished with imprisonment of either description for a term which may extend to three years, and shall be also liable to fine.
2. Any person of the Qadiani group or Lahori group (who call themselves 'Ahmadis' or by any other name) who by words, either spoken or written, or by visible representation, refers to the mode or form of call to prayers followed by his faith as 'Azan' or recites Azan as used by the Muslims, shall be punished with imprisonment or either description for a term which may extend to three years and shall also be liable to fine.

Section 298-C

Persons of Qadiani group, etc., calling himself a Muslim or preaching or propagating his faith:

Any person of the Qadiani group or the Lahori group (who call themselves 'Ahmadis' or by any other name), who, directly or indirectly, poses himself as a Muslim, or calls, or refers to, his faith as Islam, or preaches or propagates his faith, or invites others to accept his faith, by words, either spoken or written, or by visible representations or in any manner whatsoever outrages the religious feelings of Muslims, shall be punished with imprisonment of either description for a term which may extend to three years and shall also be liable to fine.

Note

1. *Pakistan Penal Code. Blasphemy Law*: 'XV: Of Offences Relating to Religion.' Accessed at: http://www.pakistani.org/pakistan/legislation/1860/actXLVof1860.html on April 2, 2015.

Appendix 4: Background to the radicalization of *madrasas* in Pakistan

Once centres of basic religious learning, usually attached to local mosques, *madrasas* in Pakistan began to mushroom after military dictator General Zia-ul-Haq (1977–1988) usurped power after a coup in 1977 and launched his Islamization process.[1] Granting them state-sponsorship, the Zia regime actively encouraged and supported the spread of *madrasas* across the country, funding them from the Islamic taxes of *Ushr* and *Zakat* that he imposed and made mandatory through the banking sector.[2] Since 1979, these seminaries in Pakistan have also become the hub and training grounds for Islamic fundamentalist ideologies, and the promotion of violent '*jihad*' against non-Muslims. Since the 1990s, a growing number of radicalized *madrasas* have been instrumental in fostering Taliban and *Al Qaida* ideologies, as well as recruiting and training terrorists, suicide-bombers, and militants as depicted in Sharmeen Obaid-Chinoy's documentary films in Chapter 3.

The Zia regime encouraged *madrasa* education by declaring *madrasa* certificates equivalent to normal university degrees.[3] Such state patronage and promotion of *madrasas* during the Islamization process ensured them official sanction as valuable and legitimate organs for the spread of Zia's fundamentalist 'Islamic' ideology.

Additionally, the rise of the '*jihad* culture' since the 1980s gave *madrasas* a distinct purpose and status, as a result of which not only did their numbers dramatically multiply, but consequently the clergy also emerged as a powerful new political and social force that also began to incite sectarian violence.

Today, these radicalized *madrasas* play a significant role in attracting and recruiting Muslims from across the globe, and imparting and nurturing fundamentalist and anti-West ideologies, as in the case of preparing the radical Taliban government in Afghanistan, and training *Al Qaida* militants from across the world. These *madrasas* are also key players in leading and supporting renewed religious fundamentalist activity within Pakistan following the 9/11 attacks in the USA in 2001.[4] According to a Pakistani media survey by the *Jang* Group of Publications in 2006, it was estimated that there were 11,221 *madrasas* in Pakistan in the year 2005. This number had grown from 6,761 in 2000, indicating that since the terrorist attacks of 9/11, their number had almost doubled in Pakistan. These figures also included 448 *madrasas* for women.[5] Tracing the steady increase in the numbers of *madrasas* in Pakistan since its independence from India, Zahid Hussain notes:

At independence in 1947, there were only 137 *madrasas* in Pakistan; in the next ten years their number rose to 244. After that they doubled every ten years. A significant number remained unregistered and therefore it was hard to know precisely how many there were. Government sources put the figure at 13,000, with total enrolment close to 1.7 million. According to the government's own estimates, ten to 15 percent of the *madrasas* had links with sectarian militancy or international terrorism. The trail of international terror often led to the *madrasas* and mosques.[6]

However, it is difficult to state an exact figure in Pakistan, as large numbers of unregulated *madrasas* continue to flourish, such as in the slums and poor neighbourhoods of Karachi, or the Khyber Pakhtunkhwa Province (KP) (formerly the North West Frontier Province (NWFP)), and the tribal belts adjoining Afghanistan where the Taliban influence has been growing steadily.

On US pressure, during his tenure President Pevaiz Musharraf made an attempt to regulate the *madrasas* by having all foreign students expelled, and forcing them to register their institutions and the names of their Pakistani pupils.[7] However, the reforms could not be realized because of continued resistance by religious parties, and the non-compliance of *madrasas* and clerics. In 2009, the Pakistan Ministry of Education reported that the government had virtually shelved a US-aided, multi-million dollar plan to reform *madrasas* as it has failed to garner the support of clerics.[8]

Notes

1 Zahid Hussain, 'Nursery for Jihad', *Frontline Pakistan: The Struggle with Militant Islam*, Columbia University Press, New York, 2007, p. 78.
2 In the economic and banking sectors, Zia introduced reforms that would require banking transactions to conform to the Islamic financial concepts of *Zakat* (wealth tax), *Ushr* (agricultural tax), and *Riba*, (interest). Grace Clark, 'Pakistan's Zakat and 'Ushr as a Welfare System', in Anita M. Weiss (ed.), *Islamic Reassertion in Pakistan: The Application of Islamic Laws in a Modern State*, Syracuse University Press, New York, 1986, p. 63. For further background and discussion on the significance and debate on the Islamic taxation system of *Zakat* and *Ushr* see: ibid., p. 79.
3 A. H. Nayyar and Ahmad Salim (eds), *The Subtle Subversion: The State of Curricula and Textbooks in Pakistan: Urdu, English, Social Studies and Civics*, Sustainable Development Policy Institute, (SDPI), Islamabad, Pakistan, 2002, pp. 3–4.
4 Similarly, in Afghanistan *madrasas* have mushroomed despite the US-led so-called 'War on Terror', and the fall of the Taliban government in Afghanistan, as Zahid Hussain elaborates: 'Not only are the *madrasas* harbouring and aiding existing Afghan warriors, they are also creating new ones. More than 8,000 new pupils have enrolled in the seminaries in the border areas alone since the fall of the Taliban.' Zahid Hussain, 'Nursery for Jihad', *Frontline Pakistan: The Struggle with Militant Islam*, Columbia University Press, New York, 2007, pp. 87–8.
5 Khalid Ahmed, 'The Madrasa Puzzle in Pakistan', *The Daily Times*, June 21, 2009. Accessed at: http://archives.dailytimes.com.pk/editorial/21-Jun-2009/book-review-the-madrassa-puzzle-in-pakistan-by-khaled-ahmed on January 17, 2016.
6 Hussain, 'Nursery for Jihad', pp. 79–80.

Appendix 4: Background to the radicalization of madrasas *in Pakistan* 213

7 In August 2001, the Pakistan government created a Pakistan Madrasa Education Board (PMEB) to establish a network of 'model *madrasas*' and regulate others. In 2002, General Musharraf's government announced the *Deeni Madaris* Ordinance (Voluntary Registration and Regulation), and promised to reform *madrasas* by cracking down on those that preached violence, while pushing others towards moderation, and integrating them into the public school system under the scrutiny of the Education Ministry. Sanchita Bhattacharya, 'Madrasa Policy in Pakistan: Strategies from Within', *International Journal of South Asian Studies*, Vol. 2, July–December 2009, No 2. *Madanjeet Singh Institute for South Asia Regional Co-operation (MISARC)*, Centre for South Asian Studies Department of Politics & International Studies Pondicherry University, Puducherry, India, pp. 185–6.
8 *The Daily Times*, '*Madrasa* Reform in Tatters', July 17, 2009. Accessed at: http://defence.pk/threads/madrassa-reforms.31248/ on January 14, 2016.

Appendix 5: Laws of *Qisas* and *Diyat*

Further to the tribal sanction of honour-related murders, the Pakistani legal system itself had proven to be a facilitator for such crimes by introducing the Islamic concepts of justice, compensation, and retaliation through the laws of *Qisas* (compensation by equal punishment) and *Diyat* (compensation by blood money) in 1990 into the Pakistan Penal Code (PPC) 1860 Chapter XV1 under the title 'Offences Affecting the Human Body'. Till the clause was removed under the Criminal Laws (Amendment) Act 11 of 1997, under the Pakistani law honour-killings were not viewed as 'pre-meditated killing' (*Qatle-Amd*), but rather as committed due to 'grave and sudden provocation', or as 'self-defence', thereby favouring the perpetrator.[1] Given these lacunae, the law actually tended to provide legal cover to the brutal crime of honour-killing, and leniency in facilitating compromise and resolution through pardon by the family members of the victim and perpetrator themselves. Needless to say, such a legislative situation allowed murderers to act with impunity on the pretext of safeguarding 'honour'.[2]

Honour-killings are now criminalized as murder in Pakistan under the Criminal Law Amendment Act 2004[3] that was adopted by the National Assembly without debate amidst an opposition walkout in October 2004.[4] Although honour-killing cases are handled by courts and the justice system, here too they are largely seen as 'provocation murders' by a gender-biased police and judicial system.[5] Lawyer and advocate of the Supreme Court of Pakistan, the late Justice Rashida Patel, points out that despite the removal of the 'grave and sudden provocation' clause 'courts continue to accept violation of "male honour" as a valid basis for awarding token punishment for murders that are termed "honour killings"'.[6]

Similarly, the Pakistani National Commission on the Status of Women (NCSW) notes that the promulgation of the *Qisas* and *Diyat* laws has seen an increase in violence against women including 'honour killings, and *swara/vani* (i.e. giving away of girls to rival parties as *badl-e-sulh* (compensation to victim's family to settle disputes)) with a high rate of acquittal or award of lighter punishment to the male offenders of these crimes.[7] Hence, in essence the state has been a party in sanctioning violence and threat of violence against women because through the *Qisas* and *Diyat* laws murder, among other offences relating to physical injury, is no longer a crime against the state that it would automatically prosecute.[8] Instead, such violence and murder stand as a crime against the person of the victim, hence becoming a private matter.[9] Rabia Ali of the *Shirkat Gah* Women's Resource Centre explains how the *Qisas* and *Diyat* laws have proven to be instrumental in the rising rate of violence against women and honour-killings:

> In real terms it means that a father may kill his daughter, a husband his wife, a brother his sister, with impunity; the heirs of the victim – the killer's own family – will 'pardon' him; and the state will not intervene but 'assist' them in 'exercising their rights'. If ever a *carte blanche* to honour-killings was codified into law, it was done here in Pakistan.[10]

Hence, the negotiable aspect of the *Qisas* and *Diyat* laws provides perpetrators of honour-killing and other physical violence the provision to not only commit such crimes with impunity, but also the legal cover to avoid punishment.[11]

Notes

1 Rashida Patel, 'The Menace of Honour Killing', *Gender Equality and Women's Empowerment in Pakistan*, Oxford University Press, Karachi, Pakistan, 2010, pp. 66–7.
2 A. A. Hyat., 'Legal Aspects', *Women: Victims of Social Evil*, Pakistan Institute of Security Management, 2002, p. 156.
3 For details of the amendment see Maliha Zia Lari, 'The Criminal Law (Amendment) Act 2004', *'Honour Killings' in Pakistan and Compliance of Law*, Aurat Publication and Information Service Foundation, Islamabad, Pakistan, November, 2011, p. 31.
4 For details see *Asian Centre for Human Rights Report*, 'Confronting Honour Killing', October 29, 2004. Accessed at: http://www.countercurrents.org/hr-achr291004.htm on April 2, 2015.
5 Yasmeen Hassan, *The Haven Becomes Hell: A Study of Domestic Violence in Pakistan*, Special Bulletin August 1995. Published by *Shirkat Gah*, WLUML Coordination Office Asia, Lahore, Pakistan, p. 23.
6 Rashida Patel, 'The Menace of Honour Killing', *Gender Equality and Women's Empowerment in Pakistan*, Oxford University Press, Karachi, Pakistan, 2010, p. 67.
7 National Commission on the Status of Women (NCSW), *The Concept of Justice in Islam: Qisas and Diyat Law*, 2005, Islamabad, Pakistan, p. v.
8 For further details on the nature of honour-killings in Pakistan, and the legal implications in dealing with the issue see: *Amnesty International, Pakistan: Honour Killings of Girls and Women*. Accessed at: http://www.academia.edu/9872947/Honour_killings_of_girls_and_women on January 14, 2016.
9 A. A. Hayat describes the brutal modes by which honour-killings are carried out: 'In Sindh and Balochistan victims are ritualistically hacked to pieces before the open view of the family, community and tribe with their implicit/explicit sanction. One of the ways in which a *kari* is killed adopted by the Rind tribe is: *kari* is attired in new clothes like a bride and fed lavishly. A kinswoman (*a'ai godi*) informs the *kari* that it is a religious obligation to kill an adulteress. The *kari* is asked to kneel and bow her head, which is severed from behind in one stroke. In Punjab, these killings are usually carried out by shooting, and are an individual decision and normally not executed in public.' A. A. Hayat., 'Honour-Killings', *Women: Victims of Social Evil*, Pakistan Institute of Security Management. 2002, p. 94.

In another example, the Human Rights Commission of Pakistan (HRCP) cites the following incident of honour-killing in 2010 as a case-study that highlights the mode of the murder: 'In January, media reports highlighted the murder of a girl and a boy by the girl's family in a village of Mian Chunnu sub-district of Punjab. The girl, Sonia, and the boy she wanted to marry were clubbed to death and their bodies publicly hanged for the villagers to see that the family had redeemed its honour. The girl had tried to run away from home after her parents arranged her marriage with a man against her will.' *State of Human Rights in 2010*, 'Violence Against Women: Limits of Free Will', Human Rights Commission of Pakistan, Maktaba Jadeed Press, Lahore, Pakistan, 2010, p. 207.

10 Rabia Ali, 'Society, State and Law', *The Dark Side of 'Honour'*, *Shirkat Gah* Special Bulletin 2004. Published by *Shirkat Gah* Women's Resource Centre, Lahore, Pakistan, p. 36.

11 The *Amnesty International* (AI) report on Pakistan explains the legal complexities and provisions that can be utilized to evade convictions or lengthy sentences in cases of honour-killings, particularly for men: 'Among statutory laws, it is particularly two laws which disadvantage women in Pakistan, both introduced in the name of the Islamization of law. The 1990 law of Qisas and Diyat covers offences relating to physical injury, manslaughter and murder. The law reconceptualized the offences in such a way that they are not directed against the legal order of the state but against the victim. A judge in the Supreme Court explained: "In Islam, the individual victim or his heirs retain from the beginning to the end entire control over the matter including the crime and the criminal. They may not report it, they may not prosecute the offender. They may abandon prosecution of their free will. They may pardon the criminal at any stage before the execution of the sentence. They may accept monetary or other compensation to purge the crime and the criminal. They may compromise. They may accept *qisas* [punishment equal to the offence] from the criminal. The state cannot impede but must do its best to assist them in achieving their objective and in appropriately exercising their rights." This reconceptualization of offences has sent the signal that murders of family members are a family affair and that prosecution and judicial redress are not inevitable but may be negotiated.' *Amnesty International*, 'Gender Bias in Law', *Honour Killings of Girls and Women*, Amnesty International, 1999, p. 12. Accessed at http://www.academia.edu/9872947/Honour_killings_of_girls_and_women on January 14, 2016.

Glossary

Aasra Urdu word for *support*

Ahmeddiyya A minority Muslim religious sect that was declared constitutionally non-Muslim in Pakistan by the Z. A. Bhutto government in 1974

Al Qaida An international terrorist organization founded in the late 1980s by Osama bin Laden

Ahrar-ul-Islam A *Deobandi* pre-Partition religious political party founded in India in 1929

Amir-ul-Momineen Leader of the faithful

Asr Impact

Aurat Woman

Awami **National Party** People's National Party

Badal Pashtun term for *revenge*

Badl-e-sulh Compensation given to a victim's family in Pakistan's tribal societies to settle disputes

Basant Spring kite-flying festival held across the Punjab provinces in Pakistan and India

Burqa Garment worn by conservative South Asian and Afghan Muslim women that covers the face and body

Chador A shawl worn loosely over the head and shoulders

Darul -Uloom House of Knowledge

Dastak (Knock) Name of women's shelter in Lahore, Pakistan

Deobandi Followers of the radical *Deoband* Islamic Movement that includes the Taliban

Dhimmi Non-Muslims according to Islam that follow a sacred religious text, such as Jews and Christians

Diyat *Sharia* law pertaining to blood money

Fatwa Islamic religious edict

Fidaeen Arabic term for soldiers that sacrifice themselves for a cause. In modern Arabic terms, the word normally refers to guerrilla soldiers. (singular: *fidai'i*)

Fiqh Islamic jurisprudence

Gujjar Name of lower-caste tribe in Punjab in the Indian sub-continent

Hadd Literally means the 'limit.' The concept is used in Islamic jurisprudence to denote that punishment which has been prescribed in the *Quran* for a particular crime and is therefore deemed as the maximum punishment awardable. (plural: *hudood*)

Hafiz   Title given to one who has memorized the entire *Quran* by heart

Hijab   Headscarf worn by conservative Muslim women and girls

Hilal-e-Imtiaz **(Crescent of Excellence)**   The second most prestigious civilian award conferred by the Government of Pakistan in recognition of outstanding achievement and performance

Ijtihad   Reinterpretation of Islamic doctrines by analogy as per the need for applying them to particular situations or problems

Imam   Muslim leader of mosque prayers

Islam   A monotheistic religion founded by Prophet Muhammad in Arabia in 7th century CE

Jamaat-ul-Ahrar   A *Tehreek-e-Taliban* Pakistan (TTP) splinter group formed in August 2014 that pledges allegiance to the Islamic State of Iraq and Syria (ISIS), and formation of a global Islamic Caliphate

Jaloos   Procession

Jamaat-e-Islami   A right wing religious political party in Pakistan

Jamaat-ud-Dawa   A *Wahhabi* organization in Pakistan

Jamia   A Muslim place of religious learning and worship, such as the mosque

Jamiat-e-Ulema Islam **(Assembly of Islamic Clergy)**   A far-right, conservative religious Islamic political party in Pakistan

Jatoi   A county in southern Punjab in the Muzaffargarh district of Pakistan

Jihad   Defined as a moral, or physical struggle and resistance encouraged and sanctioned by Islam when faced with a threat to one's life, faith, or rights. This struggle can be non-violent or assume the form of warfare

Jirga/Loya Jirga   Pashtun word in the tribal justice-system for juries comprising a gathering of all-male community representatives for decision-making

Jizya   An Islamic head or poll-tax to be paid by non-Muslims (considered as *dhimmis*) as demanded by early Islamic rulers from their subjects

Ka'aba   Holy shrine in Mecca toward which Muslims turn to pray

Kalma Tayyabah   First tenet of Islam

Karo kari   (blackened man and woman) Honour-killing

Lashkar-e-Jhangvi   (Army of *Jhangvi*). An extremist *Sunni* Muslim, and anti-*Shia*, militant organization affiliated with the *Al-Qaida* and the Taliban

Lashkar-i-Tayyaba **(Army of the Righteous)**   A *Sunni* Islamic extremist organization in Pakistan

Madrasa   Religious seminary. (plural: *madaris*)

Mastoi   A high status Baloch tribe located in the Balochistan, Sindh, and Punjab provinces of Pakistan

Maulana   Title given to an Islamic religious leader

Melmastia   Pashtun term for *hospitality*

Mossad   Name of the Israeli Intelligence Agency

Muslim   Followers of Islam and Prophet Muhammad

Mufti   An expert on Islamic *Sharia* law who is empowered to give rulings on religious matters

Mujahideen 'Soldiers of God.' During the Mujahideen era in Afghanistan (1992–1996) the West came to refer to members of the Afghan resistance as 'freedom fighters,' but they called themselves mujahideen, a word derived from *jihad* for 'soldiers of God.' (singular: *mujahid*)

Mullah Islamic cleric

Muttahida Majlis-e-Amal (United Action Front). A coalition of six Islamic religious parties formed in Pakistan in 2002

Nanawatay Pashtun term for granting refuge or sanctuary/resolving a dispute

Nikah-bil-jabr Forced marriage

Nikah Islamic marriage contract

Nizam-e-Adl Islamic System of Justice

Panchayat Village councils in South Asia that have the power to call a *jirga* (jury)

Pukhtun/Pashtun Members of the predominantly *Pushto*-speaking ethnic group of Afghanistan and the Khyber-Pakhtunkhwa Province of Pakistan. (Formerly, the North West Frontier Province of Pakistan (NWFP))

Pukhtunwali/Pashtunwali The code of conduct of the *Pukhtuns/Pashtuns*

Pushto/Darri Languages spoken both in the Khyber-Pukhtunkhwa Province of Pakistan, and Afghanistan

Tehsil County

Qanun-e-Shahadat Law of Evidence

Qari A status and title awarded to those who have learnt to read and recite the *Quran* with the proper rules of pronunciation and rhythm, known as *Tajwid*

Qisas *Sharia* punishment equal to the offence. For example, execution of the murderer

Quran Holy text of Muslims

Rajam Arabic word for *stoning*

Riba Islamic financial concept of interest in banking

Sardar Tribal chief

Sari Traditional, popularly worn, and internationally recognized dress of Indian and South Asian women

Shabab-e-Milli Youth Wing of the *Jamaat-e-Islami*

Shahadat Concept of martyrdom in Islam

Shaheed Martyr

Shalwar kameez Traditional unisex dress comprising loose trousers and tunic worn in the Indian sub-continent

Sharia Islamic socio-religious laws, based upon the *Quran* which dates back more than 1400 years and is believed by Muslims to be the Divine word of God

Shia Members of the *Shiite* Muslim sect that regards Hazrat Ali as the legitimate successor to Prophet Mohammed

Shirkat Gah Participation Forum

Sipah-e-Sahaba A militant *Sunni Deobandi* Islamic organization in Pakistan affiliated with the *Al Qaida*

Sunnah The Islamic Traditions based on Prophet Muhammad's life

Sunni Members of the *Sunni* Islamic sect that regards the first four caliphs as the rightful successors to Prophet Muhammad

Swara, Khoon Baha, Chatti, Ivaz, **or** ***Vanni*** Tribal customs and practices of giving away of minor girls in forced marriages to settle disputes or avenge murders

Tajwid *Tajwid* is believed to be the codification of the sound of the revelation of the *Quranic* verses as it was revealed to Prophet Muhammad, and as he subsequently rehearsed it with the Angel Gabriel. Thus the sound itself is believed to have a divine source and significance, and, according to Muslim tradition, is significant to the meaning of the *Quran* and its message

Taliban A fundamentalist Islamic militia originating from Afghanistan

Tehreek-e-Taliban Pakistan **(Pakistani Taliban Movement.)** An alliance of militant groups formed in 2007 in Pakistan to fight against the Pakistan army, and attack and expel Western coalition forces from the region

Tehrik-e-Niswan Women's Movement

Ulema Religious scholars (singular title: *Alim*)

Ummah Muslim brotherhood

Ushr Islamic financial concept of agriculture tax

Urdu National language of Pakistan

Wadera Landlord, or tribal chief

Wahabiism A literal interpretation of Islam introduced by the Saudi cleric Muhammad ibn Abd al-Wahab in the eighteenth century

Wali Legal heir or guardian under *Sharia* law

Zakat Islamic financial concept of wealth tax

Zamindar Landlord

Zina Concept of extra-marital sex under *Sharia* laws that includes both adultery and fornication

Index

AASRA (Support) 138
Abbas, Mureed 153–4
Abdullah, Qari 114–15
accountability in Pakistan, cinema of 3–4, 6–7, 31, 199, 200
acid-attacks 85, 94, 119n5, 129, 130, 136, 138–42, 169, 174n19–20, 175n25, 175n30, 188, 189, 191, 198
Acid Control and Acid Crime Prevention Bill (2010) 140
Acid Control and Burn Crime Prevention Act (2010) 138
Acid Survivors Foundation (ASF) of Pakistan 138, 139
Acid Survivors Trust International (ASTI) 138
ActionAid 194, 195
activism-oriented women's movement 24, 41–2, 43
activist film practices, accountability and perspectives on 7, 14–39, 186–7; activist and political intent of documentary film, perspectives on 14, 18–20, 34; activist documentaries, emergence of 17; authoritarian suppression, opposition to 17–18; auto-ethnography in film 18; autobiographical representations, relevance of 25–6; censorship and socio-political constraints 18, 37n45; channels of activism, innovation in 17; Cinema Novo 7, 15, 28, 29, 30, 31, 34, 118, 186, 199; *cinéma vérité* 24; collective revolution, facilitation of 16–17; committed documentary, concept of 19; connections between socio-political conditions and events in films, importance of 15; consciousness-raising 17, 19, 20, 21, 23, 24, 26, 29, 31, 33, 37n43; contextual and historical approach to documentary filmmaking, perspectives on 14, 15–18, 34; democratization of art, advocacy for 16; discussion, documentaries and facilitation of 19; documentary techniques, implications of 24; environmental issues 21; feminist film theory 22–3; feminist frameworks, theoretical application of 21, 35n20, 171–2; feminist perspectives on documentary film and activism 14, 20–26, 34; feminist realism 24; film video work, importance of context in 15–16; gender oppressions 20, 27; historical facts, state-enforced manipulation of 37–8n46; *For an Imperfect Cinema* (Espinosa, J.G.) 16; Islamization 14, 15, 20–21, 23, 34, 37n45; Khyber Pakhtunkhawa Province (KP), tribal areas in 9, 12n17, 14, 27, 120n10, 161–2, 163, 167–8, 189, 212; law enforcement agencies, role of 20–21; *Maula Jat* (Yunus Malik, 1979) 32; multiple documentary functions 19; Muslim sexuality, territorial nature of 27; Muslim world, literature on films made in 37n43; 'national' question, religious identity and 23; parallels with other activist film currents 15, 28–32, 34; political corruption 21; political dimensions of feminist documentary film 23–4; post-Third-Worldist approach 7, 15, 23, 28, 30–31, 34, 36n26–7, 38n57–8, 185n112, 186, 199, 203n55; power of filmmakers 25; reality and 'realism,' representation of 25–6; religious fundamentalism, opposition to 17–18, 28; representations of history, need for re-evaluation of 16; *Sharia*

222 *Index*

laws 18, 20, 22, 26–7, 28, 31, 35n20; spatial boundaries, women filmmakers and 14, 26–8; subversion, cinema of 28–9; Talibanization 2, 4, 6, 8, 20, 23; talking heads, visual dullness of 24, 25, 36n35, 172; theoretical framework or pre-existing study, absence of 14; Third Cinema 7, 15, 28–31, 34, 36n27, 37n44, 38n47–8, 38n52, 118, 186, 198, 199; The Roots of Third Cinema: New Cinema of Latin America (Chanan, M.) 30; tribal traditions and customs 6, 20, 35n20, 152; women and documentary activism 21–2; YouTube 30
Afkhami, Mahnaz 129, 172n1
Afzal-Khan, Fawzia 72–3n4, 201n18
Agha, Saira 176n35
AGHS Burns Unit and Monitoring Cell 138–9
AGHS Legal Aid Cell: *Burnt Victims: Scars on the Society* (2002) 9, 136–9, 140, 169, 174n18, 192; injustices on film, activist documentaries and legacy on Islamization 41, 74n19; vicious 'honour-killing' system, women as victims of 136–9
Ahmad, Nazir 76n34
Ahmed, Dr Iftikhar 143, 178n49
Ahmed, Ishtiaq 125n51
Ahmed, Khalid 212n5
Ahmed, Shoaib 39n68
Ahsan, Hafiz 101–2
Akhtar, Naseem 156–7
Al Qaida 4, 8, 84, 85, 86, 90, 98, 99, 101, 102, 103, 112, 113, 116, 118, 120n8, 123n40, 124n45
Alam, Ayesha 94
Alam, Gulzar 91, 93, 94, 168
Ali, Hazrat 112
Ali, Imtiaz 121–2n25
Ali, Mubarak 11n5
Ali, Muneeb 76n34
Ali, Rabia 215, 216n10
Ali, Shaheen Sardar 79n58
Ali, Wajahat 39n71
Ali Institute of Education (AIE) 196
Ali Khan, Begum Raa'na Liaquat 49, 72n3
All Pakistan Women's Association (APWA) 49, 72n3
alliances and collaborations in Pakistan, repression and 2–3
Amanpour, Christiane 158
Amnesty International (AI) 75n27, 79n64, 80–81n72, 80n68, 83n96, 142, 157, 168, 176n40, 177n47, 182n82, 215n8, 216n11
Ansler, Eve 94, 122n27
Anti-Acid Campaign (Project SAAVE) 141, 176n36, 189, 200n5
Anwar, Muhammad Nadeem 76n34
Armes, Roy 37n43
Asghar, Ali 127n62
Asia Foundation 194
Asian-American Network Against Abuse of human rights (ANAA) 157
Asian Human Rights Commission (AHRC) 197
Asian Legal Resource Centre (ALRC) 197
ASR (Impact-Applied Socio-economic Research Foundation and Resource Centre) 41
Attiq-ur-Rehman, Shaheen 154
Aurat Foundation (Woman Foundation) 41, 60, 73n5, 73n10
authoritarian suppression, opposition to 17–18
auto-ethnography in film 18
autobiographical representations, relevance of 25–6
Awami National Party (ANP) 93
Awan, Zia 61, 145–6, 147, 149–50
Azhar, Nasreen 48
Aziz, Dr Zafar 133
Aziz, K.K. 37–8n46
Aziz, Razia 93
Aziz, Shaukat 157

Baba Khel, Muhammad Ali 182n85, 182n86
Babar, Dr Abdul 133–4
Bajoria, Jayshree 124n43
Bakhtiar, Nilofer 158
Baloch, Sharjil 143, 178n49
Bano, Iqbal 178n54
Bari, Farzana 73n5, 172n4
Barnouw, Erik 19, 34, 35n15, 120n9
Basant (Spring) festival in Lahore 95, 100
Bashir, Mahtab 178n51
Batool, Narjees 149
BBC (British Broadcasting Corporation) 123n34, 125–6n52, 126n55, 159–60, 180n66, 180n67; Urdu Service Online *Shehar Kahani* (City Stories) series 195
Beaconhouse National University (BNU): film and television production studies at 193; films about violence against women shown at 198
Beattie, Keith 18, 34, 35n12, 74n20

Befare 161, 183n93
Beg, General Mizra Aslam 96, 97
beheadings 111, 125n48
Bennion, Jackie 124n46
Bhabha, Homi K. 71–2, 83n103
Bhattacharya, Sanchita 213n7
Bhatti, Arif Iqbal Husain 80n71
Bhatti, Shahbaz 69
Bhutto, Asad Ullah 146, 147, 149
Bhutto, Benazir 126n58, 160; injustices on film 54, 58, 76n39, 81n74
Bhutto, Haleema 178n51
Bhutto, Nusrat 176n37
Bhutto, Zulfikar Ali 77–8n51
Bibi, Asia 68–70, 83n92
Bibi, Nasreen 106
Bibi, Safia 48
Bilal, Malik 164
Bin Laden, Osama 90, 98, 100, 102, 103, 105, 118
Blasphemy Laws 8, 12n14, 40, 64–5, 66, 68, 69, 70, 71, 80n68–70, 81n74, 82n78, 82n81, 208–10
Boal, Augusto 194
Bokhari, Shahnaz 138, 175n25
Bokra, Aftab 39n67
Bolitho, Hector 76n34
Boone, Jon 39n70
British High Commission 194, 197
Brown, Allison 37n43
Bruno, Greg 124n43
Burki, S.J. and Baxter, C. 12n13
Burnt Victims: Scars on the Society (AGHS Legal Aid Cell, 2002) 9, 136–9, 140, 169, 174n18, 192
Buttar, Dr Amna 157
Buzdar, Dr Saeed 148, 149
Buzdar, Sardar Ashiq Khan 145

Canadian International Development Agency (CIDA) 195
CBC (Canadian Broadcasting Corporation) 46, 128n71
censorship and socio-political constraints 10, 14, 18, 29, 32, 34, 37n45, 68, 75n26, 191, 192
Chamieh. Jebran 11n6
Chanan, Michael 29–30, 34, 38n52, 38n54, 203n47, 203n49
chastity of women, males as guardians of 142
Chaudhry, Chief Justice Iftikhar Muhammad 138, 183n91
Chaudhry, Group Captain Cecil 66, 67

Chaudhry, Imran 82n90
Chaudhuri, Shohini 37n43
Choonara, Samina 82n79
cinema in Pakistan under Islamization 32–3
Cinema Novo 7, 15, 28, 29, 30, 31, 34, 118, 186; arrival of 199
cinéma vérité 24
Clark, Grace 212n2
Clinton, Hillary 158
Cockburn, Patrick 127n65
Cohen, Deborah 37n43
Cold Comfort (Sharmeen Obaid-Chinoy, 2006) 8, 105–9, 116, 124n44, 124n46
Colin-Dönmez, Gönül 37n43
collective revolution, facilitatation of 16–17
colonial institutions, inheritance of 1
committed documentary, concept of 19
communication technologies, advances in 198
consciousness-raising 2, 3, 5, 9, 10, 186, 188, 189, 191, 192–3, 197, 199–200, 201n24; activist film practices, accountability and perspectives on 17, 19, 20, 21, 23, 24, 26, 29, 31, 33, 37n43; injustices on film, activist documentaries and legacy on Islamization 40, 59, 64, 71; vicious 'honour-killing' system, women as victims of 136, 139, 141, 145, 161, 168, 169, 171, 172
Constable, Pamela 126n54
contextual and historical approach to documentary filmmaking, perspectives on 14, 15–18, 34
Council of Islamic Ideology (CII): injustices on film, activist documentaries and legacy on Islamization 60; vicious 'honour-killing' system, women as victims of 138
Coverdale, Linda 180n65
Cowasjee, Ardeshir 172n3
Criminal Law Amendment Act (2004) 148–9
cross-cultural predicament of Muslim women 129
Cuny, Marie-Thérèse 154, 180n65
Curzon of Kedleston, Lord George Nathaniel 122n29

Dabashi, Hamid 37n43
Darra Adam Khel 92, 94, 122n26, 164
Darul-Uloom-Haqqania madrasa 92
Darul-Uloom-Nomania madrasa 103

Dawn Media Newsgroup TV 194
Dawn News TV 196
Dawood, Shimaila Matri 78n57
democratization of art, advocacy for 16
Deputy Superintendent Police (DSPs) 134
Devi, Kalpana 143, 146
Directorate General of Films and Publications (DFP) 1, 10n1
discussion, documentaries and facilitation of 19
documentary film practices 6, 8, 9, 11–12n9, 12n12, 40, 64, 72n2, 169, 190–92; critical perspectives on 14–39; documentary techniques, implications of 24; emerging directions for 192–200; foreign collaborations and funding 191–2; middle-class urban backgrounds of documentarists, issue of 192; multiple documentary functions 19; parallels with other activist film currents 15, 28–32, 34; personal and professional in film making, balance between 191–2; reality and 'realism,' representation of 25–6; representations of history, need for re-evaluation of 16; talking heads, visual dullness of 24, 25, 36n35, 172; women and documentary activism 21–2
domestic television media outlets, growth of 192
Domestic Violence (Prevention and Protection) Act (2009) 138
Don't Ask Why (Sabiha Sumar, 1999) 7, 50–54, 59, 70–71, 74–5n23–4, 77n40, 77n42, 83n96
D'Silva, Rensil 203n53

Ebrahim, Zofeen T. 183n88
Edge, Dan 124–5n47
Edge, Rebecca 79n65
Electronic Media Regulatory Authority Ordinance (PEMRA) 193–4
Ellis, Jack C. 18, 34, 35n13, 203n48
environmental issues 21, 194
Espinosa, Julio Garcia 16–18, 31, 34, 35n7, 83n104, 200n2
ethnomedia, development and 160–61, 170–71
exhibition sites, expansion of 198–200

Fair, C. Christine 120n7
Faiz, Faiz Ahmad 150, 178n54
Fareed, Ghulam 152–3, 156
fatwa (religious edict) 66
Fazl-e-Haq, Maulvi 80n71

Federal Investigation Agency of Pakistan (FIA) 167
Federal *Shariat* Court (FSC): injustices on film, activist documentaries and legacy on Islamization 48, 68; vicious 'honour-killing' system, women as victims of 165
feminist theory: feminist frameworks, theoretical application of 21, 35n20, 171–2; feminist realism 24; film theory 22–3; perspectives on documentary film and activism 14, 20–26, 34
film festivals and screening sites 195–8
film studies institutes 5, 6, 10, 193
film video work 15–16
filmmaking institutes, expanding number of 198–9, 200n9
'Focus on Pakistan: Filmmaking for Social Change' 196
For a Place Under the Heavens (Sabiha Sumar, 2003) 7, 54–9, 70–71, 74–5n24, 77n49, 83n96, 90
foreign collaborations and funding 191–2
Forman Christian College University (FCC) 196
Friday Times 94, 96–7, 122n28
Fuller, Michael 124n44

Ganguly, Sumit 78n54
Gazdar, Mushtaq 12n12, 32, 34, 38n60
gender-specificity in: abuse and marginalization 129; honour and shame 176n38; Islamic society 18, 28, 35n20, 130, 186–7; justice 172; oppressions 20, 27; patriarchal morality 172; punishments 130; ruthless forms of violence committed against women, visual testimony to 171; spatial boundaries 7, 27, 34; state-sponsored discrimination 129; tribal customs 15, 23, 31, 186; violence against women 129–30, 160, 192
Geo Newsgroup TV 194
Getino, Octavio 28, 29, 31, 34, 37n44, 38n47, 38n51, 128n69
Gibb, H.A.R. 11n7
Gilani, Iqtidar 174n16
A Girl in the River: The Price of Forgiveness (Sharmeen Obaid-Chinoy, 2015) 85, 120n6
Global Opportunity Fund (British FCO) 144
Gohar, Ali 177n48
Gohar, Bushra 93

Gohar, Madeeha 64, 79n64
Goodenough, Patrick 76n36
Goraya, Naheed S. 122n29
Griffin, Michael 119n1
Gul, Lieutenant-General Hameed 96, 98

Haider, Syed Afzal 60
Haq, Maulana Abdul 121–2n25
Haq, Maulana Nawaz Jhangvi 123n40
Haq, Riazul 12–13n19
Haroon, Anis 60
Harrow, Kenneth W. 37n43
Hartsock, Nancy C. M. 21, 34, 36n23, 173n11
Hashmi, Tufail 60
Hassan, S. Raza 120n13
Hassan, Yasmeen 177n43, 215n5
Hayat, A.A. 173n14, 176n38, 177n41, 177n45, 215–16n9, 215n2
Hazard, Patrick 202n39, 202n40
Heinrich Böll Stiftung Foundation 11n2, 161, 183n96–7, 200n8
Hilal-e-Imtiaz 141
Hillauer, Rebecca 37n43
historical facts, state-enforced manipulation of 37–8n46
HIV/AIDS 161, 167, 181n79, 183n95
'honour,' perspectives on 141–3
honour-killings *see karo kari*
Hoodbhoy, Pervez 120n14
Horn, Graham 79n65
Hudood Ordinance 1979: Divine Law, or Law of One Man? (NCSW, 2005) 7, 59–64, 71, 79n60
Hudood Ordinances 7, 40, 46, 59–64, 71, 74n16, 75n30, 79n60, 204–5, 206–7n4; *see also Zina Hudood* Ordinance
Hum TV 194
Human Rights Commission of Pakistan (HRCP) 194; injustices on film, activist documentaries and legacy on Islamization 42; Report (2008) 172–3n5; Report (2010) 173n7; Report (2014) 173n6, 184–5n111; terror, cinema on 93; vicious 'honour-killing' system, women as victims of 148, 168
human rights violations 4, 15, 20, 32, 112, 129–30, 172, 197
Hussain, Khalid 120–21n16
Hussain, Neelam 73n9, 82n79
Hussain, Rizwan 124n42
Hussain, Zahid 78n56, 211–12, 212n1, 212n4

imperfect cinema 16–17, 72, 187
For an Imperfect Cinema (Espinosa, J.G.) 16, 35n7, 83n104, 200n2
Imran, Myra 175n24
Imran, Rahat 12n12, 36n22, 74n23, 75n29
Indian Held Kashmir (IHK) 99
Indus Valley School of Art and Architecture (IVSAA), digital film and video production studies at 193
injustices on film, activist documentaries and legacy on Islamization 7–8, 40–83, 187; activism-oriented women's movement 42; AGHS Legal Aid Cell 41, 74n19; All Pakistan Women's Association (APWA) 49, 72n3; ASR (Impact-Applied Socio-economic Research Foundation and Resource Centre) 41; *Aurat* Foundation (Woman Foundation) 41, 60, 73n5, 73n10; Canadian Broadcasting Corporation (CBC) 46; consciousness-raising 40, 59, 64, 71; Council of Islamic Ideology (CII) 60; *Don't Ask Why* (Sabiha Sumar, 1999) 7, 50–54, 59, 70–71, 74–5n23–4, 77n40, 77n42, 83n96; *fatwa* (religious edict) 66; Federal *Shariat* Court (FSC) 48, 68; *Hudood Ordinance 1979: Divine Law, or Law of One Man?* (NCSW, 2005) 7, 59–64, 71, 79n60; Human Rights Commission of Pakistan (HRCP) 42; imperfect cinema 72; Interactive Resource Centre (IRC) 42; *Jaloos* (Procession, Simorgh Productions, 1988) 7, 42–5, 64, 70, 71, 73n8, 74n18–19; *Jamaat-e-Islami* 53; Lawyers for Human Rights and Legal Aid (LHRLA) 41, 61; *Muttahida Majlis-e-Amal* (MMA, United Action Front) 63; National Assembly 60; National Commission for Justice and Peace (NCJP) 64–70, 71; National Commission on the Status of Women (NCSW) 42, 59–64, 71; non-governmental organizations (NGOs) 41, 42; Pakistan Muslim League (PML) 60; Pakistan Penal Code (PPC) 69; Pakistan People's Party Patriots (PPPP) 60; Pakistan Women Lawyers Association (PAWLA) 41; *For a Place Under the Heavens* (Sabiha Sumar, 2003) 7, 54–9, 70–71, 74–5n24, 77n49, 83n96, 90; Progressive Women's Association (PWA) 41; Punjab Women Lawyers Association (PWLA) 43; re-*membered*, re-*membering* and 71–2;

226 Index

Sharia laws 40, 41, 43, 46, 48, 49, 64, 70, 72, 75n27, 79n59; *Shirkat Gah* (Participation Forum) 41, 73n14; *Simorgh* Women's Resource and Publication Centre and Collective 41, 42–5, 73n9–10; *A Sun Sets In* (NCJP, 2000) 7, 64–70, 71, 79n65; *Tehreek-e-Taliban Pakistan* (TTP) 69; *Who Will Cast the First Stone?* (Sabiha Sumar, 1988) 7, 45–50, 59, 70–71, 74–5n23–4; Women's Action Forum (WAF) 43, 48; women's resistance movement and organizations 41–2; ZDF/Arte in Germany 46

Institute of Labour Education and Research 197

Inter-Services Intelligence (ISI) 98

Inter-Services Public Relations (ISPR) 103–4

Interactive Resource Centre (IRC) 194–5, 201n24, 202n25–6; injustices on film, activist documentaries and legacy on Islamization 42

Internally Displaced People (IDPs) 85, 112, 167

International Children's Film Festival (LICFF) 196–7, 202n31–6

International Labour Organization (ILO) 161

International Women's Day 197

International Women's Rights Action Watch 73n5, 172n4

International Women's Rights Forum 155

Intesarur-ur-Rashid, Dr. (Mayo Hospital, Lahore) 136–7

investigative-journalistic approach 86

Iqbal, Justice Nasira Javed 61–2, 63

Iqbal, Nasir 82n82

Iqbal, Shoaib 72–3n4, 202n34

IRC-*Umeed Jawan* (Fresh Hope) collaborative series 195

Islamic State of Iraq and Syria (ISIS) movement 118

Islamization 1–2, 3, 4, 6, 7–8, 11n3, 11n8, 186–7, 190, 191, 201n22, 207n5; activist film practices, perspective on 14, 15, 20–21, 23, 34, 37n45; cinema in Pakistan under 32–3; legacy of, activist documentaries against 40–46, 48, 50, 52, 58–60, 63–4, 68, 70, 71–2, 72n1, 72n4, 73n14, 77n43–4, 78n55, 79n59, 79n66; *Qisas* and *Diyat*, laws of 43, 146, 163, 164, 183n91, 214–16, 216n11; radicalization of *madrasas* 8, 53, 78n56, 84–5, 87–9, 92, 103, 108–9, 110, 112–15, 116–17, 119n2, 188, 211–13; terror, cinema on 84, 85, 90, 116, 119n1; vicious 'honour-killing' system, women as victims of 129; *see also* religion in Pakistan, politicization of

Jabbar, Mehreen 195
Jacob, Peter 81n75
Jadeed Refugee Camp 86, 88–9, 112
Jahangir, Asma 48, 67–8, 74n16, 74n19, 75n30, 76n36, 205n1
Jalbani, Abbas 129, 172n2, 179n61
Jaloos (Procession, *Simorgh* Productions, 1988) 7, 42–5, 64, 70, 71, 73n8, 74n18–19
Jamaat-e-Islami: injustices on film, activist documentaries and legacy on Islamization 53; terror, cinema on 104–5; vicious 'honour-killing' system, women as victims of 146–7
Jamaat-ud-Dawa militant religious group 106–9
Jamaat-ul-Ahrar 118
Jamia Islamia madrasa 88
Jamiat-e-Ulema Islam (JUI) 92
Jan, Roshan 46–7
Jatoi, Sarfraz Khan 148
Jawad, Dr Mohammad 139, 140
Jehangir, Munizae 119n4
Jesus Christ 81–2n77
jihad (struggle) 57, 58, 70, 74n23, 78n55–6, 211, 212n1, 212n4, 218; terror, cinema on 84, 88, 95, 106, 116, 117, 118, 123n33, 124n45, 125n48; vicious 'honour-killing' system, women as victims of 150
jihadist militancy, socio-political consequences of 85–6
jihadist organizations (and ideologies) 85, 86, 88, 89, 99–100, 101, 105, 108–9, 110, 115, 116, 118, 119n2, 125n48, 188
Jillani, Hina 60, 63, 74n16, 74n19, 75n30, 134, 135, 205n1
Jinnah, Muhammad Ali 49, 76n34
jirga (tribal juries) 130, 141, 142–3, 147–8, 149–50, 160, 162, 164, 166, 168, 176n39, 177n48, 178n51, 182n84
Jokhio, Ikhlaq 145
Joseph, Dr Bishop John 64–8, 71, 80–81n72, 81n74
Journal of International Women's Studies (JIWS) 74n23, 75n29

Joyce, Nancy 37n43
Junge, Daniel 120n6, 176n31

Kahuta Research Laboratories 97
Kalma Tayyabah 110, 125n50
Kapoor, Kareena 90
Karachi International Children's Film Festival (KICFF) 196
Karachi University (KU), film and television production studies at 193
KaraFilm Festival 12n18, 178n49, 195, 202n27
karo kari (honour-killings) 9, 130, 142, 143–50, 169–70, 173n7, 177n46, 178–9n55, 178n49, 178n51, 188
Keuper, Jay 120n11
Khalil, Noor Akbar 177n42
Khalil, Shaimaa 120n6
Khan, A. Mukhtar 126n53
Khan, Dr Abdul Qadeer 97, 98, 123n35
Khan, Justice Dr Fida Mohammad 165
Khan, Kabir 203n52
Khan, Major General Tariq 113
Khan, Sairah Irshad 75n28, 76n37, 200n7
Khan, Shah Rukh 77n42, 77n47
Khan, Shahnaz 206–7n4
Khan, Sumera 175n24
Khan, Yaqoob 154–5
Khator, Neha 126n57
Khattab, Raja Omar 114
Khattak, Afrasiab 93
Khel, Darra Adam 122n26
Khokhar, Nisar 146, 148
Khomeini, Ayatollah Ruhollah 66
Khoso, Imtiaz 102
Khyber Pakhtunkhawa Province (KP): terror, cinema on 86, 120n10, 127n64; tribal areas in 9, 12n17, 14, 27, 120n10, 161–2, 163, 167–8, 189, 212
Kids for Kids International Film Festival 196
Kleinhans, Chuck 15–16, 34, 35n3, 83n98, 117, 127n61, 173n12, 184n109
Koch, Andrew 123n34
Koinange, Jeff 75n27
Kristoff, Nicholas D. 156–7, 181n72
Kumara, Sarath 122n31
Kumharo, Sardar Himat 148

Lahore College for Women University (LCWU) 198
Lahore University of Management Sciences (LUMS) 198
Lari, Maliha Zia 215n3

law enforcement agencies, role of 20–21
Law of Evidence 8, 12n14, 20, 40, 43, 48, 49, 61–2, 70, 71, 74n17, 75n29, 204, 206–7
Lawal, Amina 75n27
Lawyers for Human Rights and Legal Aid (LHRLA): injustices on film, activist documentaries and legacy on Islamization 41, 61; vicious 'honour-killing' system, women as victims of 145
Leaman, Oliver 37n43
legacy of Islamization, activist documentaries against 40–46, 48, 50, 52, 58–60, 63–4, 68, 70, 71–2, 72n1, 72n4, 73n14, 77n43–4, 78n55, 79n59, 79n66
Lesage, Julia 23–4, 25, 34, 36n30, 181n80, 182n83
Little Big Shots International Film Festival for Kids 196
Lok Rehas Theatre Group 194
London International Documentary Festival (LIDF) 197
Los Angeles International Children Film Festival 196

Maati TV 194
McLane, Betsy A. 18, 34, 35n13, 203n48
madrasas, radicalization of 8, 53, 78n56, 188, 211–13; terror, cinema on 84–5, 87–9, 92, 103, 108–9, 110, 112–15, 116–17, 119n2
Mai, Mukhtaran 151–2, 153–4, 155–60, 170, 179n60, 179n61, 180–81n71, 180n64, 180n65, 180n69; Glamour 'Bravest Woman of the Year Award (2005)' 158
Malik, Yunus 38n61
Malkmus, Lizbeth 37n43
Mansoor, Shoaib 203n51
Manzur, Shazia 67
Marquand, Robert 11n4
Marsden, Peter 119n3
Martineau, Barbara Halpern 24–5, 34, 36n35, 185n113
Masih, Ayub 66, 80–81n72, 80n71
Masih, Manzur 65, 80n71
Masih, Rahmat 80n71
Masood, Dr Khalid 60
Mastoi, Salma 156
Mastoi, Taj 156
Mastois (and family power of) 152–3, 154–5, 156, 159

228 Index

Mateela Film Festival 195–6
Maula Jat (Yunus Malik, 1979) 32
Mayo Hospital 133, 134, 135, 136
Mazhar, Muhammad Saleem 122n29
Meerwala 151–2, 153, 154, 156, 160, 170, 179n60–61, 180n64
Mehdi, Rubya 173n10
Mehsud, Baitullah 125n51, 126n58
Mehsud, Hakimullah 114, 126n58
Mernissi, Fatima 7, 27, 34, 37n41, 128n68
Minallah, Samar 9, 20, 119n4, 186–7, 188–9; 'honour-killing' system, women as victims of 160–68, 170–71, 181n79, 182n82, 182n84, 183n87, 183n91–84n99, 184n106–7
Ministry of Women Development (MoWD) 138
Mohammad, Jani 148
Mohammad, Khal 87–8, 89
Mohsin, Jugnu 94, 96–7
Mokhtar, Shehram 201n16
Morgan, Adrian 80n71
Mossad (Israeli Intelligence Agency) 99
Mukherjee, Rani 77n47
Mukhtar Mai Women's Welfare Organization (MMWWO) 158–9
Mumtaz, Khawar 73n12, 73n14–15, 75n32, 77–8n51, 77n43, 79n59, 206n1, 206n3
Mumtaz, Samiya 82n79
Musharraf, General Pervaiz (and regime of) 3, 8, 39n69, 188; injustices on film 42, 54, 59, 76n36, 77n48; radicalization of *madrasas* and 212, 213n7; terror, cinema on 84, 85, 90, 95, 96–7, 98–9, 100, 101, 102, 103, 105, 116, 122–3n32, 123n35, 123n36, 124n43; vicious 'honour-killing' system, women as victims of 148, 156, 158, 159, 180–81n71, 180n67
Muslim sexuality, territorial nature of 27
Muslim *ummah* (Muslim brotherhood) 146
Muslim women, cross-cultural predicament of 129
Muslim world, literature on films made in 37n43
Muttahida Majlis-e-Amal (MMA, United Action Front) 90–91, 92–3, 94, 121n22; injustices on film, activist documentaries and legacy on Islamization 63

Nadeem, Shahid 11n8, 64–8, 71, 79n64–5, 82n79
Naficy, Hamid 37n42, 37n43

Naghma (Afghan woman singer) 168
Naheed, Kishwar 160, 181n76
Naqvi, Mohammad Ali 120n11, 151–60, 170, 179n57, 179n58; *Shame* (2006) 151–60, 170, 179n58
The Nation 128n67
National Assembly: injustices on film, activist documentaries and legacy on Islamization 60; vicious 'honour-killing' system, women as victims of 138
National College of Arts (NCA), film and television production studies at 193
National Commission for Justice and Peace (NCJP) 64–70, 71; *A Sun Sets In* (2000) 7, 64–70, 71, 79n65
National Commission on the Status of Women (NCSW) 42, 59–64, 71; *Hudood Ordinance 1979: Divine Law, or Law of One Man?* (2005) 7, 59–64, 71, 79n60
'national' question, religious identity and 23
Naviwala, Nadia 73n6
Nayyar, A.H. 37–8n46, 78n55, 212n3
Nelson, Kristina 127n59
New York Times 39n69, 85, 180n70, 181n72; New York Times Television (NYTT) 29, 122; vicious 'honour-killing' system, women as victims of 156, 158
Newsline Publications 194
Niazi, Amanullah 101
Niazi, Zamir 37n45
Nichols, Bill 18, 19, 34, 35n10, 35n18, 122n30, 200n3; injustices on film 68, 76n38, 77n41, 82n84, 83n101; vicious 'honour-killing' system, women as victims of 167, 174n17, 175n22, 179n56, 183n89, 184n102, 184n105
Nizam-e-Adl (System of Justice) Ordinance 112, 126n53
Nizamuddin, Mufti 57
non-governmental organizations (NGOs) 3, 11–12n9, 11n2, 12n11, 195, 200n8; injustices on film, activist documentaries and legacy on Islamization 41, 42, 73n6, 73n9–10; vicious 'honour-killing' system, women as victims of 138, 150, 161, 177n42, 181n75
North West Frontier Province (NWFP) 12, 86, 90, 92, 93, 98, 102, 105, 110, 112, 118, 120n10, 121n22, 126n53, 127n60

Index 229

Obaid-Chinoy, Sharmeen 8, 20, 211; *Cold Comfort* (2006) 8, 105–9, 116, 124n44, 124n46; *A Girl in the River: The Price of Forgiveness* (2015) 85, 120n6; Oscar-winning documentaries, enthusiasm for 191–2; *Pakistan: On A Razor's Edge* (2004) 8, 95–100, 105, 116, 122n29, 126n57; *Pakistan's Double Game* (2005) 8, 100–105, 116, 123n39; *Pakistan's Taliban Generation* (2009) 8, 109–15, 116, 124–5n47; Project SAAVE (Stand Against Acid Violence), initiation of 189; *Reinventing the Taliban?* (2003) 8, 90–95, 116; *Saving Face* (2011) 9, 85, 119n5, 120n6, 139–41, 169, 176n31, 176n33, 189, 191; spatial boundaries, concept of (and working around) 186–7; terror, cinema on 84–5, 85–115, 115–19, 119n5, 120n6, 120n11, 121n18, 122n29, 123n39, 124–5n46–7, 124n44, 127n62, 187–8; *Terror's Children* (2003) 8, 85, 86–9, 109, 112, 116, 120n11; vicious 'honour-killing' system, women as victims of 139–41, 169–70, 176n31, 176n32, 176n36, 184n103
Okin, Susan Moller 21, 34, 36n25, 184n101
Omar, Mullah Mohammad 119n1, 121–2n25
Onal, Ayse 176–7n40
Oxfam 11n2, 195, 200n8

Pakistan: access to exhibition, difficulties for 199–200; accountability in, cinema of 3–4, 6–7, 31, 199, 200; ActionAid 194, 195; activist documentary film and video practices, emergence and significance of 3–4; Ali Institute of Education (AIE) 196; alliances and collaborations in, repression and 2–3; Asia Foundation 194; Asian Human Rights Commission (AHRC) 197; Asian Legal Resource Centre (ALRC) 197; BBC Urdu Service Online *Shehar Kahani* (City Stories) series 195; Beaconhouse National University (BNU): film and television production studies at 193; films about violence against women shown at 198; Blasphemy Laws 8, 12n14, 40, 64–5, 66, 68, 69, 70, 71, 80n68–70, 81n74, 82n78, 82n81, 208–10; British High Commission 194, 197; Canadian International Development Agency (CIDA) 195; Cinema Novo, arrival of 199; colonial institutions, inheritance of 1; communication technologies, advances in 198; *Dawn* Media Newsgroup TV 194; *Dawn* News TV 196; Directorate General of Films and Publications (DFP) 1; documentary film practices in 190–92; domestic television media outlets, growth of 192; Electronic Media Regulatory Authority Ordinance (PEMRA) 193–4; emerging directions for documentary cinema in 192–200; exhibition sites, expansion of 198–200; film festivals and screening sites 195–8; film studies institutes 193; filmmaking institutes, expanding number of 198–9, 200n9; 'Focus on Pakistan: Filmmaking for Social Change' 196; foreign collaborations and funding 191–2; Forman Christian College University (FCC) 196; *Geo* Newsgroup TV 194; Hudood Ordinances 7, 40, 46, 59–64, 71, 74n16, 75n30, 79n60, 204–5, 206–7n4; *Hum* TV 194; Human Rights Commission of (HRCP) 194; Indus Valley School of Art and Architecture (IVSAA), digital film and video production studies at 193; Institute of Labour Education and Research 197; Interactive Resource Centre (IRC) 194–5, 201n24, 202n25–6; International Children's Film Festival (LICFF) 196–7, 202n31–6; International Women's Day 197; IRC-*Umeed Jawan* (Fresh Hope) collaborative series 195; Karachi International Children's Film Festival (KICFF) 196; Karachi University (KU), film and television production studies at 193; *KaraFilm* Festival 12n18, 178n49, 195, 202n27; Lahore College for Women University (LCWU) 198; Lahore University of Management Sciences (LUMS) 198; Law of Evidence 8, 12n14, 20, 40, 43, 48, 49, 61–2, 70, 71, 74n17, 75n29, 204, 206–7; *Lok Rehas* Theatre Group 194; *Maati* TV 194; *Mateela* Film Festival 195–6; middle-class urban backgrounds of documentarists, issue of 192; National College of Arts (NCA), film and television production studies at 193; *Newsline* Publications 194; Oxfam 195; personal and professional in film making, balance between 191–2; Punjab

University (PU), films about violence against women shown at 198; *Qisas* and *Diyat,* Laws of 43, 146, 163, 164, 183n91, 214–16, 216n11; radicalization of *madrasas* in 8, 53, 78n56, 84–5, 87–9, 92, 103, 108–9, 110, 112–15, 116–17, 119n2, 188, 211–13; religion in, politicization of 1–2, 3, 5–6, 8, 9, 11n5, 11n8, 15, 20, 31, 40, 42, 54, 64–5, 68, 70, 85, 186, 187; Shaheed Zulfikar Ali Bhutto Institute of Science and Technology (SZABIST), film and television production studies at 193; *Shirkat Gah* (Participation Forum) 41, 73n14; *Shirkat Gah* Women's Resource Centre, Lahore 197–8; WLUML-*Shirkat Gah* initiative 197–8; society in, analysis of filmic reflections on 4–5; spatial boundaries in, concept of 7, 14, 26–8, 34, 37n41, 118, 128n68, 186–7; state of, formation of 1; television and media organizations 193–5; Television Corporation (PTV) 1, 79n64, 182n82, 190, 194; Third Cinema aesthetics of activism 199; training, film production, and screening opportunities, limits on 191; United States Institute of Peace 195; *Vasakh* Documentary Film Festival 195–6; Violence Against Women (VAW), awareness about 197; 'Violence Is Not Our Culture' 198; Women Living Under Muslim Laws (WLUML) 197; Women Reclaiming and Redefining Culture (WRRC) programme 197; Women's International Shared Experience project (WISE) 197, 203n42, 203n44; YouTube 194, 197; ZAB Media Festival 193; *see also* activist film practices; injustices on film; Islamization; Sharia laws; terror, cinema on; vicious 'honour-killing' system, women as victims of

Pakistan: On A Razor's Edge (Sharmeen Obaid-Chinoy, 2004) 8, 95–100, 105, 116, 122n29, 126n57

Pakistan Muslim League (PML) 60

Pakistan Penal Code (PPC): injustices on film, activist documentaries and legacy on Islamization 69; vicious 'honour-killing' system, women as victims of 134, 167

Pakistan People's Party Patriots (PPPP) 60

Pakistan Women Lawyers Association (PAWLA) 41

Pakistan's Double Game (Sharmeen Obaid-Chinoy, 2005) 8, 100–105, 116, 123n39

Pakistan's Taliban Generation (Sharmeen Obaid-Chinoy, 2009) 8, 109–15, 116, 124–5n47

Palejo, Sassi 147

panchayat (tribal councils) 130, 141, 142–3, 151, 152, 158, 160

Paracha, Nadeem F. 33, 38n61, 38n66

Parveen, Sakina and Martha 134–5

Parveen, Shahida 46, 47, 75n31

Pashtunwali, tribal codes of 102

Patai, Raphael 177n45

Patel, Justice Rashida 177n46, 214, 215n1, 215n6

Patel, Supreme Court Justice Dorab 48–9, 76n33

patriarchy 9, 14, 18, 19, 21, 22, 23, 24, 25, 27, 28, 34; injustices on film and 46, 48, 49, 53, 58; patriarchal tribal customs 7, 31, 130, 171, 181n79; terror, cinema on 86; vicious 'honour-killing' system, women as victims of 129, 141, 142, 143, 145, 149, 156, 160, 161, 169, 172

Patrick, Huma 173n10, 174n16

Paul, Bishop Bonaventure 67

Pearl, Daniel 86, 120n12, 123n40

Pickthall, Muhammad Marmaduke 121n24

political corruption 21

political dimensions of feminist documentary film 23–4

politics and religion, militant mix of 84

post-Third-Worldist approach 7, 15, 23, 28, 30–31, 34, 36n26–7, 38n57–8, 185n112, 186, 199, 203n55

power of filmmakers 25

Prevention of Anti-Women Practices (Criminal Law Amendment) Bill (2008) 140

Prix Jeunesse Festival, Munich 196

Progressive Women's Association (PWA): injustices on film, activist documentaries and legacy on Islamization 41; vicious 'honour-killing' system, women as victims of 138

Prophet Muhammad 11n4, 11n7, 80n68, 80n71, 125n50, 127n59; Asia Bibi and remarks about 69; Blasphemy Laws and 209–10; honour, brotherhood and 146

Provincially Administered Tribal Areas (PATA) 112

Pukhtunwali, tribal codes of 163–4

Punjab University (PU), films about violence against women shown at 198
Punjab Women Lawyers Association (PWLA) 43

Qadri, Malik Mumtaz Hussain 69, 83n91
Qanun-e-Shahadat see Law of Evidence
Qasim, Muhammad 174n16
Qazi, Samiya Raheel 63
Qisas and *Diyat,* Laws of 43, 146, 163, 164, 183n91, 214–16, 216n11
Quran 11n4, 11n7, 146, 151, 153, 164, 200n4, 204; injustices on film 52–3, 58, 60, 62–3, 70, 77–8n51, 81n76; terror, cinema on 87, 89, 114, 115, 121n17, 121n24, 127n59

Rabinowitz, Paula 18, 34, 35n11, 74n22, 200n6
radicalization of *madrasas* 8, 53, 78n56, 188, 211–13; terror, cinema on 84–5, 87–9, 92, 103, 108–9, 110, 112–15, 116–17, 119n2
Rafi, Mehnaz 43, 60
Rafi, Yumna 175n30
Randeep, Ramesh 122–3n32
Rashid, Ahmed 96–7, 120n8, 123n33
RAW (Indian Intelligence Agency) 99
Rehman, Ahmar 174n18
Rehman, Sherry 60
Rehman, Waseefullah and Abdur 113
Reinventing the Taliban? (Sharmeen Obaid-Chinoy, 2003) 8, 90–95, 116
religion in Pakistan, politicization of 1–2, 3, 5–6, 8, 9, 11n5, 11n8, 15, 20, 31, 40, 42, 54, 64–5, 68, 70, 85, 186, 187
religious fundamentalism, opposition to 17–18, 28
re-membered, re-*membering* and 71–2
Renov, Michael 19, 20, 34, 35n16, 68, 74n21, 83n83, 83n99, 184n110
restrictive boundaries, crossing of 86
Riaz-ul-Hassan 201n18
Rizvi, High Court Judge Majida 42, 59, 60–61
Robbins, Ed 121n18, 122n29
Rocha, Glauber 29, 31, 34, 38n50, 128n70, 203n54
Rushdie, Salman 66, 80–81n72

Sabir, Arman 120n13
Saeed, Nadeem 154, 156, 180n64
Saeed, Tariq 81n76
Sajjad, Jam 38n65

Sakina, Ghulam 46, 47–8, 49, 76n36
Saleem, Samia 203n44
Salim, Ahmad 37–8n46, 212n3
Sami-ul-Haq, Maulana 92, 96, 98, 121–2n25
Samuel, Patras 66
Sangtani Women Rural Development Organization in Rajanpur 149
Sardar Ali, Shaheen 58
Sarwar, Mohammad 75n31
Sattar, Abdul 125n48
Saving Face (Sharmeen Obaid-Chinoy, 2011) 9, 85, 119n5, 120n6; vicious 'honour-killing' system, women as victims of 139–41, 169, 176n31, 176n33, 189, 191
sectarian clashes between *Shias* and *Sunnis* 102
Seshadri-Crooks, Kalpana 72–3n4
Shabab-e-Milli (MMA Youth Wing) 93
Shafik, Viola 15, 34, 34n2, 83n97
Shah, Bina 39n69
Shah, Nadia 173n13
Shah, Saeed 82n88
Shah, Senator Yasmin 177n42
Shah, Syed Ali 83n91
Shaheed, Farida 73n12, 73n14, 74n15, 75n32, 77–8n51, 77n43, 206n1, 206n3
Shaheed Zulfikar Ali Bhutto Institute of Science and Technology (SZABIST), film and television production studies at 193
Shahid, Shamim 127n66
Shahzad, Faisal 127n64
Shakir, Naeem 207n5
Shame: A Tale of Karo Kari (*Dastak* Society for Communication, 2005) 9, 143–50, 169, 178n49, 192
'shame,' perspectives on 141–3
Shame (Mohammad Ali Naqvi, 2006) 151–60, 170, 179n58
Shaqoor (brother of Mukhtaran Mai) 152–3, 154–5, 156
Sharia laws 1–2, 4, 5, 6, 7–8, 10, 11n7, 186, 187, 191–2; activist film practices, perspective on 18, 20, 22, 26–7, 28, 31, 35n20; injustices on film 40, 41, 43, 46, 48, 49, 64, 70, 72, 75n27, 79n59; legacy of Islamization, activist documentaries against 40–46, 48, 50, 52, 58–60, 63–4, 68, 70, 71–2, 72n1, 72n4, 73n14, 77n43–4, 78n55, 79n59, 79n66; terror, cinema on 90, 91, 107, 111–12, 114, 119n1, 121n22, 125n51; vicious

'honour-killing' system, women as victims of 163, 164–5; *Zina Hudood* Ordinance and 8, 12n14, 20, 41, 42, 43, 46–7, 48–9, 59, 61, 62–3, 70, 73n14, 75n29, 76n35, 204–5, 206, 207n5
Sharif, Mian Nawaz 81n74
Sharif, Nawaz 79n66, 170
Shea, Nina 80–81n72, 82n81
Sheikh, Justice Munir A. 134
Sheikh, Saleem 179n62
Sher, Ferida 73n8
Shields, Brooke 158
Shirkat Gah (Participation Forum) 41, 73n14
Shirkat Gah-WLUML initiative 197–8
Shirkat Gah Women's Resource Centre, Lahore 197–8
Shohat, Ella 22–3, 30–31, 34, 36n26, 36n27, 38n57, 185n112, 203n55
Sikand, Yoginder 78n54
Simorgh Women's Resource and Publication Centre and Collective 41, 42–5, 73n9–10; *Jaloos* (Procession, 1988) 7, 42–5, 64, 70, 71, 73n8, 74n18–19; *Stove Burning: Neither Coal Nor Ashes* (1993) 9, 130, 131–6, 138, 140, 169, 173n13, 174n16, 192
Sindhu, Amar 147
Smaje, Chris 179n59
socio-political conditions and events in films, importance of connections between 15
Solanas, Fernando 1, 28, 29, 31, 34, 37n44, 38n47, 38n51, 128n69
spatial boundaries: in Pakistan, concept of 7, 14, 26–8, 34, 37n41, 118, 128n68, 186–7; women filmmakers and 14, 26–8
Stefano, Berti 181–2n81
stoning to death 46, 63, 73n14, 75n27, 125n51, 204
stove-burning 130, 134, 136, 138, 141, 142
Stove Burning: Neither Coal Nor Ashes (*Simorgh* Productions, 1993) 9, 130, 131–6, 138, 140, 169, 173n13, 174n16, 192
Streefland, Pieter 81–2n77
study, parameters of: contextual-reading approach 4, 186; films in study, access to 4; inter-disciplinary approach 5–6, 186; methodology 5–6; objectives for analysis 4–5; secondary sources 6; society in, analysis of filmic reflections on 4–5

subversion, cinema of 28–9
Sultan, Major-General Shaukat 103–4
Sumar, Sabiha 20, 90, 119n4; *Don't Ask Why* (1999) 7, 50–54, 59, 70–71, 74–5n23–4, 77n40, 77n42, 83n96; injustices on film 45–59, 64, 70–71, 74–5n23–4, 76n37, 76n39, 77n40, 77n42, 77n46, 77n49, 77n50, 83n94, 83n96; *For a Place Under the Heavens* (2003) 7, 54–9, 70–71, 74–5n24, 77n49, 83n96, 90; vicious 'honour-killing' system, women as victims of 186–7, 191, 200n7; *Who Will Cast the First Stone?* (1988) 7, 45–50, 59, 70–71, 74–5n23–4
A Sun Sets In (NCJP, 2000) 7, 64–70, 71, 79n65
Sunnah 11n7, 60, 146, 204
Swara: A Bridge Over Troubled Waters (Samar Minallah, 2003) 9, 161–8, 170–71, 181n79, 182n82, 188–9
Swara (compensatory giving away of minor girls in forced marriages) 9, 12n16, 20, 130, 161–8, 170–71, 182n84–5, 183n87, 183n91, 184n107, 188, 200n4
Swat Valley: terror, cinema on 111–12, 125n51, 126n53, 168; vicious 'honour-killing' system, women as victims of 168
Symington, Annabel 39n69

Talibanization: activist film practices, accountability and perspectives on 2, 4, 6, 8, 20, 23; terror, cinema on 84–5, 86, 90, 92, 94, 95, 105, 109, 111, 115, 116, 117
talking heads, visual dullness of 24, 25, 36n35, 172
Tapper, Richard 37n43
Taseer, Salman 69, 82n87, 83n91, 176n37
Taseer, Shahbaz 69, 82n90
Tehreek-e-Taliban Pakistan (TTP): injustices on film, activist documentaries and legacy on Islamization 69; terror, cinema on 114
television and media organizations 193–5
Television Corporation of Pakistan (PTV) 1, 79n64, 182n82, 190, 194
terror, cinema on 8, 84–128, 187–8, 199; *Al Qaida* 4, 8, 84, 85, 86, 90, 98, 99, 101, 102, 103, 112, 113, 116, 118, 120n8, 123n40, 124n45; *Awami*

Index   233

National Party (ANP) 93; *Basant* (Spring) festival in Lahore 95, 100; beheadings 111, 125n48; *Cold Comfort* (Sharmeen Obaid-Chinoy, 2006) 8, 105–9, 116, 124n44, 124n46; Darra Adam Khel 92, 94, 122n26, 164; *Darul-Uloom-Haqqania madrasa* 92; *Darul-Uloom-Nomania madrasa* 103; *Friday Times* 94, 96–7; *A Girl in the River: The Price of Forgiveness* (Sharmeen Obaid-Chinoy, 2015) 85, 120n6; Human Rights Commission of Pakistan (HRCP) 93; Indian Held Kashmir (IHK) 99; Inter-Services Intelligence (ISI) 98; Inter-Services Public Relations (ISPR) 103–4; Internally Displaced People (IDPs) 112; investigative-journalistic approach 86; Islamic State of Iraq and Syria (ISIS) movement 118; Islamization 84, 85, 90, 116, 119n1; *Jadeed* Refugee Camp 86, 88–9, 112; *Jamaat-e-Islami* 104–5; *Jamaat-ud-Dawa* militant religious group 106–9; *Jamaat-ul-Ahrar* 118; *Jamia Islamia madrasa* 88; *Jamiat-e-Ulema Islam* (JUI) 92; *jihadist* militancy, socio-political consequences of 85–6; *jihadist* organizations (and ideologies) 85, 86, 88, 89, 99–100, 101, 105, 108–9, 110, 115, 116, 118, 119n2, 125n48, 188; Kahuta Research Laboratories 97; *Kalma Tayyabah* 110, 125n50; Khyber Pakhtunkhwa Province (KP) 86, 120n10, 127n64; Mossad (Israeli Intelligence Agency) 99; *Muttahida Majlis-e-Amal* (MMA, United Action Front) 90–91, 92–3, 94, 121n22; *Nizam-e-Adl* (System of Justice) Ordinance 112, 126n53; North West Frontier Province (NWFP) 12, 86, 90, 92, 93, 98, 102, 105, 110, 112, 118, 120n10, 121n22, 126n53, 127n60; *Pakistan: On A Razor's Edge* (Sharmeen Obaid-Chinoy, 2004) 8, 95–100, 105, 116, 122n29, 126n57; *Pakistan's Double Game* (Sharmeen Obaid-Chinoy, 2005) 8, 100–105, 116, 123n39; *Pakistan's Taliban Generation* (Sharmeen Obaid-Chinoy, 2009) 8, 109–15, 116, 124–5n47; *Pashtunwali,* tribal codes of 102; politics and religion, militant mix of 84; Provincially Administered Tribal Areas (PATA) 112; radicalization of *madrasas* 84–5, 87–9, 92, 103, 108–9, 110, 112–15, 116–17, 119n2; RAW (Indian Intelligence Agency) 99; *Reinventing the Taliban?* (Sharmeen Obaid-Chinoy, 2003) 8, 90–95, 116; restrictive boundaries, crossing of 86; *Saving Face* (Sharmeen Obaid-Chinoy, 2011) 9, 85, 119n5, 120n6; sectarian clashes between *Shias* and *Sunnis* 102; *Shabab-e-Milli* (MMA Youth Wing) 93; *Sharia* laws 90, 91, 107, 111–12, 114, 119n1, 121n22, 125n51; Swat Valley 111–12, 125n51, 126n53, 168; Talibanization 84–5, 86, 90, 92, 94, 95, 105, 109, 111, 115, 116, 117; *Tehreek-e-Taliban Pakistan* (TTP) 114; *Terror's Children* (Sharmeen Obaid-Chinoy, 2003) 8, 85, 86–9, 109, 112, 116, 120n11; United Nations High Commissioner for Refugees (UNHCR) 89, 121n16; *Vagina Monologues* (Eve Ansler) 94

Terror's Children (Sharmeen Obaid-Chinoy, 2003) 8, 85, 86–9, 109, 112, 116, 120n11
Teshome, Gabriel H. 29, 34, 38n48
Third Cinema 7, 15, 28–31, 34, 36n27, 37n44, 38n47–8, 38n52, 118, 186, 198; aesthetics of activism 199
The Roots of Third Cinema: New Cinema of Latin America (Chanan, M.) 30
Thomas, Dorothy Q. 76n35
Toronto International Children's Film Festival 196
training, film production, and screening opportunities, limits on 191
tribal traditions and customs 6, 20, 35n20, 152
Trinh T. Minh-ha 16, 18, 34, 35n5, 127n63, 184n108

Ullah, Raza 76n34
United Nations: Convention on the Elimination of all Forms of Discrimination Against Women (CEDAW) 130; Convention on the Rights of the Child 181–2n81; High Commissioner for Refugees (UNHCR) 89, 121n16
United States Institute of Peace 195
Usman, Nadia 174–5n21
Usmani, Justice Shaiq 60, 63

Vagina Monologues (Eve Ansler) 94
Vajpayee, Atal Behari 95, 99, 122–3n32
Vasakh Documentary Film Festival 195–6

Index

vicious 'honour-killing' system, women as victims of 8–9, 129–85, 188–9; *AASRA* (Support) 138; acid-attacks 85, 94, 119n5, 129, 130, 136, 138, 139–40, 141–2, 169, 174n19–20, 175n25, 175n30, 188, 189, 191, 198; Acid Control and Acid Crime Prevention Bill (2010) 140; Acid Control and Burn Crime Prevention Act (2010) 138; Acid Survivors Foundation (ASF) of Pakistan 138, 139; Acid Survivors Trust International (ASTI) 138; AGHS Burns Unit and Monitoring Cell 138–9; AGHS Legal Aid Cell 136–9; Amnesty International (AI) 157; Anti-Acid Campaign (Project SAAVE) 141; Asian-American Network Against Abuse of human rights (ANAA) 157; Befare 161, 183n93; *Burnt Victims: Scars on the Society* (AGHS Legal Aid Cell, 2002) 9, 136–9, 140, 169, 174n18, 192; chastity of women, males as guardians of 142; consciousness-raising 136, 139, 141, 145, 161, 168, 169, 171, 172; Council of Islamic Ideology (CII) 138; Criminal Law Amendment Act (2004) 148–9; cross-cultural predicament of Muslim women 129; Deputy Superintendent Police (DSPs) 134; Domestic Violence (Prevention and Protection) Act (2009) 138; ethnomedia, development and 160–61, 170–71; Federal Investigation Agency of Pakistan (FIA) 167; Federal *Shariat* Court (FSC) 165; gender-specific abuse in name of culture 129; gender-specific violence against women 129–30; Global Opportunity Fund (British FCO) 144; Heinrich Böll Stiftung Foundation 161; *Hilal-e-Imtiaz* 141; HIV/AIDS 161, 167, 181n79, 183n95; 'honour,' perspectives on 141–3; Human Rights Commission of Pakistan (HRCP) 148, 168; human rights violations 129–30; International Labour Organization (ILO) 161; Islamization 129; *Jamaat-e-Islami* 146–7; *jirga* (tribal juries) 130, 141, 142–3, 147–8, 149–50, 160, 162, 164, 166, 168, 176n39, 177n48, 178n51, 182n84; *karo kari* (honour-killings) 9, 130, 142, 143–50, 169–70, 173n7, 177n46, 178–9n55, 178n49, 178n51, 188; Lawyers for Human Rights and Legal Aid (LHRLA) 145; marginalization in name of culture 129; *Mastois* (and family power of) 152–3, 154–5, 156, 159; Mayo Hospital 133, 134, 135, 136; Meerwala 151–2, 153, 154, 156, 160, 170, 179n60–61, 180n64; Ministry of Women Development (MoWD) 138; Mukhtar Mai Women's Welfare Organization (MMWWO) 158–9; Muslim *ummah* (Muslim brotherhood) 146; National Assembly 138; New York Times 156, 158; Pakistan Penal Code (PPC) 134, 167; *panchayat* (tribal councils) 130, 141, 142–3, 151, 152, 158, 160; patriarchal tribal customs 130; Prevention of Anti-Women Practices (Criminal Law Amendment) Bill (2008) 140; Progressive Women's Association (PWA) 138; *Pukhtunwali,* tribal codes of 163–4; ruthless forms of violence committed against women, visual testimony to 171; *Sangtani* Women Rural Development Organization in Rajanpur 149; *Saving Face* (Sharmeen Obaid-Chinoy, 2011) 139–41, 169, 176n31, 176n33, 189, 191; *Shame: A Tale of Karo Kari* (*Dastak* Society for Communication, 2005) 9, 143–50, 169, 178n49, 192; 'shame,' perspectives on 141–3; *Shame* (Mohammad Ali Naqvi, 2006) 151–60, 170, 179n58; *Sharia* laws 163, 164–5; state-sponsored gender-discrimination 129; stove-burning 130, 134, 136, 138, 141, 142; *Stove Burning: Neither Coal Nor Ashes* (*Simorgh* Productions, 1993) 9, 130, 131–6, 138, 140, 169, 173n13, 174n16, 192; *Swara: A Bridge Over Troubled Waters* (Samar Minallah, 2003) 9, 161–8, 170–71, 181n79, 182n82, 188–9; *Swara* (compensatory giving away of minor girls in forced marriages) 9, 12n16, 20, 130, 161–8, 170–71, 182n84–5, 183n87, 183n91, 184n107, 188, 200n4; Swat Valley 168; UN Convention on the Elimination of all Forms of Discrimination Against Women (CEDAW) 130; violence and discrimination, widespread forms of 130; Women's Rights Forum (US) 157
Violence Against Women (VAW), awareness about 197
'Violence Is Not Our Culture' 198
Von Planta, Claudio 123n39

Wahab, Shaista 121n21
al-Wahhab, Muhammad ibn Abd 11n4
Walbridge, Linda S. 81–2n77, 81n73
Waldman, Diane 25–6, 34, 36n36, 184n114
Wali, Asfandyar 93
Walker, Janet 25–6, 34, 36n36, 185n114
Walsh, Declan 82n89, 83n95, 126n58
Wardak, Ali 177n48
Warrick, Joby 127n60
Waseem, Mohammad 194
Washington Post 123n38
Waugh, Thomas 19, 34, 35n14, 70–71, 83n98, 127n61, 184n104, 185n113, 200n1
Weiss, Anita M. 212n2
Who Will Cast the First Stone? (Sabiha Sumar, 1988) 7, 45–50, 59, 70–71, 74–5n23–4
Willemen, Paul 38n47
Witte, Griff 127n60
women and documentary activism 21–2
Women Living Under Muslim Laws (WLUML) 197
Women Reclaiming and Redefining Culture (WRRC) programme 197
Women's Action Forum (WAF) 43, 48
Women's International Shared Experience project (WISE) 197, 203n42, 203n44
women's resistance movement and organizations 41–2
Women's Rights Forum (US) 157

Yaqub, Father 66
Youngerman, Barry 121n21
Yousufzai, Hassan M. 177n48

YouTube: activist film practices, accountability and perspectives on 30; Pakistan 194, 197
Yusufzai, Rahimullah 176n39

ZAB Media Festival 193
Zahid, Chief Justice Nasir Aslam 61, 62–3, 147–8
Zahoor-ul-Haq, FSC Justice 48
Zaidi, Hasan 195
Zaidi, Mazhar 39n69
Zardari, Asif Ali 100, 112, 126n53, 141, 189
Zargam, Abu 107–8
ZDF/Arte in Germany 46
Zehri, Senator Israrullah 177n42
Zeta-Jones, Catherine 158
Zia, Maheen 20, 21, 119n4, 195
Zia, Shahla 73n5, 172n4
Zia-ul-Haq, General (and regime of): activist film practices, perspectives on 14, 15, 32–3, 37n45; injustices on film 40–44, 46, 49–50, 54–5, 58–9, 64–5, 68, 70, 73n11, 76n36, 77n44, 78n52, 79n66, 80n68, 81n74; Islamization and 1–2, 3–4, 6, 7, 8, 11n3, 11n5, 11n8, 186–7, 201n22, 206, 207n5; martial law, implementation of 1–2, 3–4, 6, 7, 8, 11n3, 11n5, 11n8, 12n13; radicalization of *madrasas* and 211, 212n2; terror, cinema on 84, 85, 90, 116, 119n1; vicious 'honour-killing' system, women as victims of 129, 178n54
Zina Hudood Ordinance 8, 12n14, 20, 41, 42, 43, 46–7, 48–9, 59, 61, 62–3, 70, 73n14, 75n29, 76n35, 204–5, 206, 207n5
Zuberi, Danish 148–9, 150

eBooks
from Taylor & Francis
Helping you to choose the right eBooks for your Library

Add to your library's digital collection today with Taylor & Francis eBooks. We have over 50,000 eBooks in the Humanities, Social Sciences, Behavioural Sciences, Built Environment and Law, from leading imprints, including Routledge, Focal Press and Psychology Press.

Choose from a range of subject packages or create your own!

Benefits for you
- Free MARC records
- COUNTER-compliant usage statistics
- Flexible purchase and pricing options
- 70% approx of our eBooks are now DRM-free.

Benefits for your user
- Off-site, anytime access via Athens or referring URL
- Print or copy pages or chapters
- Full content search
- Bookmark, highlight and annotate text
- Access to thousands of pages of quality research at the click of a button.

Free Trials Available

We offer free trials to qualifying academic, corporate and government customers.

eCollections
Choose from 20 different subject eCollections, including:

- Asian Studies
- Economics
- Health Studies
- Law
- Middle East Studies

eFocus
We have 16 cutting-edge interdisciplinary collections, including:

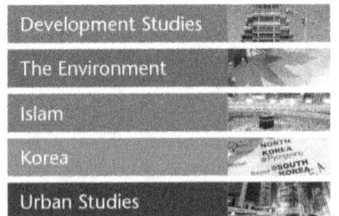

- Development Studies
- The Environment
- Islam
- Korea
- Urban Studies

For more information, pricing enquiries or to order a free trial, please contact your local sales team:

UK/Rest of World: **online.sales@tandf.co.uk**
USA/Canada/Latin America: **e-reference@taylorandfrancis.com**
East/Southeast Asia: **martin.jack@tandf.com.sg**
India: **journalsales@tandfindia.com**

www.tandfebooks.com

For Product Safety Concerns and Information please contact our EU
representative GPSR@taylorandfrancis.com
Taylor & Francis Verlag GmbH, Kaufingerstraße 24, 80331 München, Germany

www.ingramcontent.com/pod-product-compliance
Lightning Source LLC
Chambersburg PA
CBHW062131300426
44115CB00012BA/1887